London 2010

A SELECTION OF RESTAURANTS & HOTELS

Commitments

"This volume was created at the turn of the century and will last at least as long."

This foreword to the very first edition of the MICHELIN Guide, written in 1900, has become famous over the years and the Guide has lived up to the prediction. It is read across the world and the key to its popularity is the consistency of its commitment to its readers, which is based on the following promises.

→ Anonymous inspections

Our inspectors make regular and anonymous visits to hotels and restaurants to gauge the quality of products and services offered to an ordinary customer. They settle their own bill and may then introduce themselves and ask for more information about the establishment. Our readers' comments are also a valuable source of information, which we can then follow up with another visit of our own.

→ Independence

Our choice of establishments is a completely independent one, made for the benefit of our readers alone. The decisions to be taken are discussed around the table by the inspectors and the editor. The most important awards are decided at a European level. Inclusion in the Guide is completely free of charge.

→ Selection & choice

The Guide offers a selection of the best hotels and restaurants in every category of comfort and price. This is only possible because all the inspectors rigorously apply the same methods.

→ Annual updates

All the practical information, the classifications and awards are revised and updated every single year to give the most reliable information possible.

Consistency: The criteria for the classifications are the same in every country covered by the Michelin Guide.

→ And our aim...

...to do everything possible to make travel, holidays and eating out a pleasure, as part of Michelin's ongoing commitment to improving travel and mobility.

Dear reader

We are delighted to introduce the fourth edition of the Michelin Guide for London.

We make this guide for you and value your opinions, so let us know what you think about this guide and about the restaurants we have recommended.

All the restaurants within this guide have been chosen first and foremost for the quality of their cooking. You'll find comprehensive information on over 450 dining establishments within these pages and they range from gastropubs and neighbourhood brasseries to internationally renowned restaurants. The diverse and varied selection also bears testament to the rich and buoyant dining scene in London, with the city now enjoying a worldwide reputation for the quality and range of its restaurants.

You'll see that Michelin Stars are not our only awards – look out also for the Bib Gourmands. These are restaurants where the cooking is still carefully prepared but in a simpler style and, priced at under £28 for three courses, they represent excellent value for money.

As well as the restaurants, our team of independent inspectors has also chosen 50 hotels. These carefully selected hotels represent the best that London has to offer, from the luxurious and international to the small and intimate. All have been chosen for their individuality and personality.

Consult the Michelin Guide at www.viamichelin.com
and write to us at themichelinguide-gbirl@uk.michelin.com

Contents

Commitments 2
Dear reader 3
How to use this guide 6
A culinary history of London 8

Where to **eat**

Alphabetical list of restaurants 409
Starred restaurants 12
Bib Gourmand 14
Restaurants by cuisine type 15
Restaurants with outside dining 21
Open late 22
Open on Sunday 24

CENTRAL LONDON 29

- Mayfair • Soho • St James's 30
- Strand • Covent Garden 90
- Belgravia • Victoria 100
- Regent's Park • Marylebone 122
- Bloomsbury • Hatton Garden • Holborn 140
- Bayswater • Maida Vale 156
- City of London • Clerkenwell • Finsbury • Southwark 168
- Chelsea • Earl's Court • Hyde Park • Knightsbridge • South Kensington 210
- Kensington • North Kensington • Notting Hill 240

K. Blackwell / MICHELIN

GREATER LONDON 255

O. Chapuis/MICHELIN

▶ North-West 258

Archway • Belsize Park • Camden Town • Crouch End • Dartmouth Park • Euston • Fortis Green • Hampstead • Highgate • Kensal Green • Kilburn • Primrose Hill • Queen's Park • Swiss Cottage • Tufnell Park • West Hampstead • Willesden Green

▶ North-East 278

Barnsbury • Bow • Canonbury • Hackney • Hoxton • Islington • Mile End • Shoreditch • Stoke Newington • • Tottenham

▶ South-East 296

Blackheath • Canary Wharf • Elephant & Castle • Forest Hill • Greenwich • Kennington • Limehouse • Spitalfields • Wapping • West Dulwich • Whitechapel

▶ South-West 310

Acton Green • Balham • Barnes • Battersea • Brixton • Chiswick • Clapham • Ealing • East Sheen • Fulham • Hammersmith • Kew • Putney • Richmond • Teddington • Tooting • Twickenham • Wandsworth • Wimbledon

Where to **stay**

A selection of hotels 357

Maps **& plans**

Index of maps 406

Map of London Underground 413

How to use this guide

Restaurant classified according to comfort
(particularly pleasant if in red)

- X Quite comfortable
- XX Comfortable
- XXX Very comfortable
- XXXX Top class comfort
- XXXXX Luxury in the traditional style

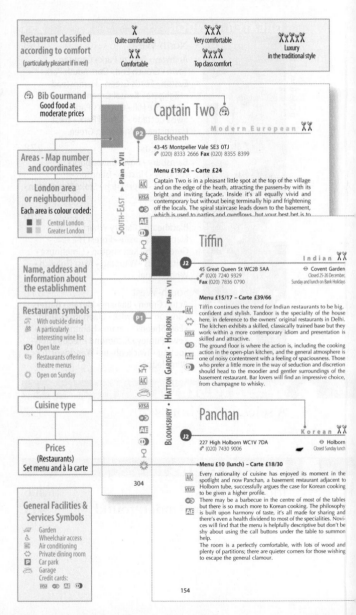

Bib Gourmand
Good food at moderate prices

Areas - Map number and coordinates

London area or neighbourhood
Each area is colour coded:
- Central London
- Greater London

Name, address and information about the establishment

Restaurant symbols
- With outside dining
- A particularly interesting wine list
- Open late
- Restaurants offering theatre menus
- Open on Sunday

Cuisine type

Prices
(Restaurants)
Set menu and à la carte

General Facilities & Services Symbols
- Garden
- Wheelchair access
- Air conditioning
- Private dining room
- Car park
- Garage
- Credit cards:

SOUTH-EAST ▶ Plan XVII

Captain Two

Modern European XX

P2

Blackheath

43-45 Montpelier Vale SE3 0TJ
(020) 8333 2666 **Fax** (020) 8355 8399

Menu £19/24 – Carte £24

Captain Two is in a pleasant little spot at the top of the village and on the edge of the heath, attracting the passers-by with its bright and inviting façade. Inside it's all equally vivid and contemporary but without being terminally hip and frightening off the locals. The spiral staircase leads down to the basement, which is used to parties and overflows, but your best bet is to

304

BLOOMSBURY · HATTON GARDEN · HOLBORN ▶ Plan VI

Tiffin

Indian XX

J2

45 Great Queen St WC2B 5AA
(020) 7240 9329
Fax (020) 7836 0790

⊖ Covent Garden
Closed 25-26 December, Sunday and lunch on Bank Holidays

Menu £15/17 – Carte £39/66

P1

Tiffin continues the trend for Indian restaurants to be big, confident and stylish. Tandoor is the speciality of the house here, in deference to the owners' original restaurants in Delhi. The kitchen exhibits a skilled, classically trained base but they work within a more contemporary idiom and presentation is skilled and attractive.

The ground floor is where the action is, including the cooking action in the open-plan kitchen, and the general atmosphere is one of noisy contentment with a feeling of spaciousness. Those who prefer a little more in the way of seduction and discretion should head to the moodier and gentler surroundings of the basement restaurant. Bar lovers will find an impressive choice, from champagne to whisky.

Panchan

Korean XX

J2

227 High Holborn WC1V 7DA
(020) 7430 9006

⊖ Holborn
Closed Sunday lunch

Menu £10 (lunch) – Carte £18/30

Every nationality of cuisine has enjoyed its moment in the spotlight and now Panchan, a basement restaurant adjacent to Holborn tube, successfully argues the case for Korean cooking to be given a higher profile.

There may be a barbecue in the centre of most of the tables but there is so much more to Korean cooking. The philosophy is built upon harmony of taste, it's all made for sharing and there's even a health dividend to most of the specialities. Novices will find that the menu is helpfully descriptive but don't be shy about using the call buttons under the table to summon help.

The room is a perfectly comfortable, with lots of wood and plenty of partitions; there are quieter corners for those wishing to escape the general clamour.

154

Hotel classification according to comfort
(particularly pleasant if in red)

- Quite comfortable
- Comfortable
- Very comfortable
- Top class comfort
- Luxury in the traditional style

Hotel symbols

- **39 rm** Number of rooms
- Breakfast included (or not)
- Prices for a single/double room
- Quiet hotel
- With restaurant
- Swimming pool
- Spa
- Sauna
- Tennis
- Exercise room
- Lift
- Broadband connection
- Wireless
- Satellite TV
- Equipped conference room

Map coordinates

⊖ Underground station

Agatha's

I2

15 Charlotte St W1T 1RJ ⊖ Goodge Street
(020) 7806 2000 **Fax** (020) 7806 2002

44 rm – ♦£247/282 ♦♦£347, ☕ £19 – 8 suites
Hercule *(See restaurant listing)*

Charlotte Street

...ion, within strolling distance of Soho, or ... own private screening room that attract ...n industry sorts and arty souls who have ... own, but the stimulating way in which it ...and the prevailing vibe.
... warehouse has been deftly transformed ...l and proves that comfort and design can ... and that something good has come from ...ıg a combination of abstract art, sculpture ...rtists of the neighbouring Bloomsbury set, ...be also quite English in tone. The drawing ...ress-free areas, in contrast to the bustle of ...restaurant.
...bedrooms are one-off pieces of furniture ...rawer fabrics and fittings, all supported by ...amme of virtually constant refurbishment. ... enthusiastic and confident. The loft and ...l stir emotions of envy and desire or, if

WESTMINSTER ▸ Plan V

373

Le Petit François ✿✿

G3 French XXXX

43 Upper Brook St W1K 7QR ⊖ Marble Arch
(020) 7408 0881
Fax (020) 7491 4387
Closed Christmas-New Year, Sunday, Saturday lunch and Bank Holidays – booking essential

Menu £48 – Carte £60/130

Le Gavroche

In today's rush for the new and the novel, we sometimes forget about the jewels we already have. Le Petit Fran ois is guaranteed its own chapter when the history of British gastronomy is written and today, over forty years after it first opened in Chelsea, it's still maintaining its own high standards and respect for tradition. The service is unerringly professional: this is where any budding restaurateur should come if they want to learn how things are done 'properly' and one can observe the hierarchical structure from one's chair. The room retains a clubby and masculine feel but it also offers a palpable sense of history; those new to the restaurant are guided gently through its customs and politely reminded of its traditions.

The menu represents classic French cuisine and not just an English idea of French cuisine; a style of food which is becoming rarer by the day. A Soufflé Suissesse is rich enough to live on for days and the use of luxury items, from lobster to foie gras, would make Epicurus blanch. Those who prefer a lighter style, however, are not ignored.

MAYFAIR • SOHO • ST JAMES'S ▸ Plan II

First Course
- Hot foie gras and crispy duck pancake flavoured with cinnamon.
- Lobster mousse with caviar and champagne butter sauce.

Main Course
- Roast saddle of rabbit with crispy potatoes and parmesan.
- Whole roast John Dory with artichokes, olive oil mashed potato.

Dessert
- Bitter chocolate and praline 'indulgence'.
- Iced amaretto nougat with cherries cooked in red wine syrup.

41

Area - Map number

Stars for good cooking ✿ to ✿✿✿

✿ **Starred restaurant symbol**

Sample menu for starred restaurant

A culinary history of London

London, influenced by worldwide produce arriving via the Thames, has always enjoyed a close association with its food, though most of the time the vast majority of its people have looked much closer to home for their sustenance.

Even as far back as the 2nd century AD, meat was on the menu: the profusion of wildlife in the woods and forests around London turned it into a carnivore's paradise, thereby setting the tone and the template. Large stoves were employed to cook everything from pork and beef to goose and deer. The Saxons added the likes of garlic, leeks, radishes and turnips to the pot, while eels became a popular staple in later years.

WHAT A LARK!

By the 13th century, the taste for fish had evolved to the more exotic porpoise, lamprey and sturgeon, with saffron and spices perking up the common-or-garden meat dish. Not that medieval tastes would have been considered mundane to the average 21st century diner: Londoners of the time would think nothing about devouring roasted thrush or lark from the cook's stalls dotted around the city streets. And you'd have been unlikely to hear the cry "Eat your greens!" In the 15th century the vegetable diet, such as it was, seemed to run mainly to herbs such as rosemary, fennel, borage and thyme.

As commercial and maritime success burgeoned in the age of the Tudors, so tables began to groan under the weight of London's penchant for feasting. No excess was spared, as oxen, sheep, boars and pigs were put to the griddle; these would have been accompanied by newly arrived yams and sweet potatoes from America and 'washed down' with rhubarb from Asia. People on the streets could 'feast-lite': by the 17th century hawkers were offering all sorts of goodies on the hoof.

FULL OF BEANS

All of this eating was of course accompanied by a lot of drinking. Though much of it took place in the alehouses and taverns - which ran into the thousands - by the 18th century coffee houses had become extraordinarily popular. These were places to do business as well as being convenient 'for passing evenings socially at a very small charge'.

Perhaps the biggest revolution in eating habits came midway through the 19th century when the first cavernous dining halls and restaurants appeared. These 'freed' diners from the communal benches of the cook-house and gave them, for the first time, the chance for a bit of seclusion at separate tables. This private dining experience was an egalitarian movement: plutocrats may have had their posh hotels, but the less well-off were buttering teacakes and scones served by 'nippies' at the local Lyons Corner House.

Influenced by post-World War II flavours brought in by immigrants from Asia, the Caribbean and Africa, Londoners can now enjoy an unparalleled cuisine alive with global flavours, while the worlds of food and drink have fused remarkably well in recent years with the growing excellence of the gastropub, which had its roots in the creative maelstrom of the capital.

C.Labonne / MICHELIN

Stéphanie Guillaume/Fotolia.com

Where to **eat**

Starred restaurants

Within this selection, we have highlighted a number of restaurants for their particularly good cooking. When awarding one, two or three Michelin Stars there are a number of factors we consider: the quality and compatibility of the ingredients, the technical skill and flair that goes into their preparation, the clarity and combination of flavours, the value for money and, above all, the taste. Equally important is the ability to produce excellent cooking not once but time and time again. Our inspectors make as many visits as necessary, so that you can be sure of the quality and consistency.

A two or three star restaurant has to offer something very special in its cuisine; a real element of creativity, originality or personality that sets it apart from the rest. Three stars – our highest award – are given to the very best.

Cuisines in any style and of any nationality are eligible for a star. The decoration, service and comfort have no bearing on the award.

Let us know what you think, not just about the stars but about all the restaurants in this guide.

The awarding of a star is based solely on the quality of the cuisine.

N : highlights those establishments newly promoted to one, two or three stars.

✿✿✿

Exceptional cuisine, worth a special journey.

One always eats here extremely well, sometimes superbly. Distinctive dishes are precisely executed, using superlative ingredients.

Alain Ducasse at The Dorchester **N**	XXXXX	34
Gordon Ramsay	XXXX	229

✿✿

Excellent cooking, worth a detour.

Skillfully and carefully crafted dishes of outstanding quality.

L'Atelier de Joël Robuchon	X	94
Le Gavroche	XXXX	56
Hibiscus	XXX	60
The Ledbury **N**	XXX	248
Marcus Wareing at The Berkeley	XXXX	110
Pied à Terre	XXX	152
The Square	XXXX	80

✿

A very good restaurant in its category.

A place offering cuisine prepared to a consistently high standard.

Amaya	XXX	104
Apsleys (at The Lanesborough Hotel) **N**	XXXX	105
Arbutus	X	36
L'Autre Pied	XX	126
Benares	XXX	42
Bingham Restaurant (at Bingham Hotel) **N**	XX	344
Chez Bruce	XX	351
Club Gascon	XX	184
Galvin at Windows (at London Hilton Hotel) **N**	XXXX	55
The Glasshouse	XX	339
The Greenhouse	XXX	58
Hakkasan	XX	148
The Harwood Arms **N**	🍺	331
Hélène Darroze (at The Connaught)	XXXX	59
Kai	XXX	63
Locanda Locatelli	XXX	131
Maze	XXX	65
Murano	XXX	68
Nahm (at The Halkin Hotel)	XX	111
Nobu (at The Metropolitan Hotel)	XX	69
Nobu Berkeley St	XX	70
Quilon	XXX	115
Rasoi	XX	237
Rhodes Twenty Four	XXX	199
Rhodes W1 (Restaurant)	XXXX	135
River Café	XX	338
Roussillon	XXX	117
St John	X	201
Semplice	XX	78
Sketch (The Lecture Room and Library)	XXXX	79
Tamarind **N**	XXX	83
Texture **N**	XX	136
Tom Aikens	XXX	238
La Trompette	XXX	324
Umu	XXX	85
Wild Honey	XX	88
Yauatcha	XX	89
Zafferano	XXX	120

Bib Gourmand

Restaurants offering good quality cooking for less than £28 (price of a 3 course meal excluding drinks)

Al Duca	X	35
The Anchor and Hope	(pub)	176
Bar Trattoria Semplice **N**	X	40
Benja	XX	43
Bocca di Lupo **N**	X	45
Bradley's	XX	274
The Brown Dog	(pub)	317
Brula	X	349
Cafe Spice Namaste	XX	308
Chapters	XX	300
Comptoir Gascon	X	185
Dehesa	X	52
The Drapers Arms **N**	(pub)	289
500 **N**	X	262
Foxtrot Oscar	X	228
Galvin Bistrot de Luxe	XX	129
Giaconda Dining Room	X	147
Great Queen Street	X	147
The Havelock Tavern	(pub)	337
Hereford Road	X	162
Ma Cuisine (Kew)	X	340
Ma Cuisine (Twickenham)	X	350
Malabar	X	249
Mango and Silk	X	329
Market	X	264
Medcalf	X	192
Metrogusto	XX	290
The Modern Pantry	X	193
Le Provence **N**	X	317
Salt Yard	X	154
Sushi-Hiro **N**	X	328
Terroirs **N**	X	99
Upstairs	XX	321
Via Condotti	XX	87

Restaurants by Cuisine Type

American

Automat	X	37

Asian

Champor-Champor	X	181
Cicada	X	182
Cocoon	XX	51
Crazy Bear	XX	146
E & O	XX	245
Eight over Eight	XX	226
Goldfish	X	268
Great Eastern Dining Room	XX	286
Kiasu	X	163
Singapore Garden	XX	275
Taman Gang	XX	82
XO	XX	263

Beef specialities

Goodman	XX	54
The Grill Room	X	349
Hawksmoor	X	305
Kew Grill	XX	340
Maze Grill	XX	64

British

The Anchor and Hope	🍺 ☺	176
Axis	XXX	93
Bedford and Strand	X	95
Bentley's (Grill)	XXX	43
Bluebird	XX	219
Bumpkin (North Kensington)	X	244
Bumpkin (South Kensington)	X	221
Butlers Wharf Chop House	X	180
Cat and Mutton	🍺	284
Corrigan's Mayfair	XXX	51
The Dartmouth Arms	🍺	303
The Drapers Arms	🍺 ☺	289
The Fat Badger	🍺	246
Great Queen Street	X ☺	147
The Harwood Arms	🍺 ✿	331
Hereford Road	X ☺	162
Hix Oyster and Chop House	X	188
Inn the Park	X	62
Magdalen	X	191
Market	X ☺	264
Medcalf	X ☺	192
The National Dining Rooms	X	67
Paternoster Chop House	X	196
Quality Chop House	X	198
Quo Vadis	XXX	74
Rex Whistler at Tate Britain	XX	116
Rhodes Twenty Four	XXX ✿	199
Rivington Grill (Greenwich)	X	303
Rivington Grill (Shoreditch)	X	294
Roast	XX	200
Rules	XX	99
St John	X ✿	201
St John Bread and Wine	X	306
Shepherd's	XXX	118
Tate Modern (Restaurant)	X	203

Chinese

Baozi Inn	X	39
Bar Shu	X	40
Ba Shan	X	41
China Tang	XXXX	49
Dragon Castle	XX	302
Good Earth	XX	228
Hakkasan	XX ✿	148
Haozhan	XX	57
Kai	XXX ✿	63
Ken Lo's Memories of China	XX	109

Mao Tai	XX	332
Maxim	XX	328
Memories of China	XX	250
Min Jiang	XXX	250
Mr Chow	XX	232
Pearl Liang	XX	164
Phoenix Palace	XX	133
Plum Valley	XX	72
Snazz Sichuan	XX	267
Yauatcha	XX✿	89

Eastern European

Baltic	XX	177

French

L'Absinthe	X	271
Admiralty	XX	93
Alain Ducasse at The Dorchester	XXXXX✿✿✿	34
Almeida	XX	288
Angelus	XX	160
L'Atelier de Joël Robuchon	X✿✿	94
Aubaine	X	216
L'Auberge	XX	341
L'Aventure	XX	127
Bellamy's	XX	41
Belvedere	XXX	243
Bibendum	XXX	218
Bistro Aix	X	265
Bleeding Heart	XX	145
Le Boudin Blanc	XX	45
Boundary	XXX	292
Brasserie Roux	XX	46
Brasserie St Jacques	XX	46
Brula	X☺	349
Cafe Boheme	X	47
Le Cercle	XX	223
Chelsea Brasserie	XX	224
Chez Bruce	XX✿	351
Chez Kristof	XX	336
The Clerkenwell Dining Room	XX	183
Clos Maggiore	XX	96
Club Gascon	XX✿	184
Le Colombier	XX	225
Comptoir Gascon	X☺	185
Coq d'Argent	XXX	186
Galvin at Windows (at London Hilton Hotel)	XXXX✿	55
Galvin Bistrot de Luxe	XX☺	129
Le Gavroche	XXXX✿✿	56
Gordon Ramsay	XXXX✿✿✿	229
Hélène Darroze at The Connaught	XXXX✿	59
Incognico	XX	149
The Ledbury	XXX✿✿	248
Lobster Pot	X	304
Luc's Brasserie	XX	190
Ma Cuisine (Kew)	X☺	340
Ma Cuisine (Twickenham)	X☺	350
Marcus Wareing at The Berkeley	XXXX✿✿	110
Mon Plaisir	XX	150
Morgan M	XX	282
1901	XXX	194
Notting Hill Brasserie	XX	251
Papillon	XX	233
Pearl	XXX	151
La Petite Maison	XX	72
Poissonnerie de l'Avenue	XX	235
Le Pont de la Tour	XXX	197
La Poule au Pot	X	114
Racine	XX	236
The Restaurant at The Petersham	XXX	346
Rhodes W1 (Restaurant)	XXXX✿	135
Roussillon	XXX✿	117
Sauterelle	XX	200
Sketch (The Lecture Room and Library)	XXXX✿	79
Spread Eagle	XX	304
The Square	XXXX✿✿	80
Terroirs	X☺	99
Tom's Kitchen	X	236
Les Trois Garçons	XX	306
La Trouvaille	XX	84
Le Vacherin	XX	325
Villandry	XX	138
Villandry Kitchen	X	155
The Wallace	X	139

Greek

Real Greek Mezedopolio	X	287

Indian

Amaya	XXX ✿	104
Benares	XXX ✿	42
Bengal Clipper	XX	177
Bombay Brasserie	XXXX	219
Café Lazeez	XX	48
Cafe Spice Namaste	XX ☺	308
Chor Bizarre	XX	50
Chutney Mary	XXX	225
The Cinnamon Club	XXX	107
Cinnamon Kitchen	XX	183
Dockmaster's House	XXX	300
Eriki	XX	274
Imli	X	61
Indian Zing	XX	337
Kastoori	X	348
Malabar	X ☺	249
Mango and Silk	X ☺	329
Memories of India on the River	XXX	332
Mint Leaf	XX	66
Mint Leaf Lounge	XX	193
Moti Mahal	XX	151
Painted Heron	XX	233
La Porte des Indes	XX	133
Quilon	XXX ✿	115
Rasa	X	294
Rasa Samudra	XX	153
Rasa Travancore	X	295
Rasoi	XX ✿	237
Red Fort	XXX	74
Swagat	X	346
Tamarind	XXX ✿	83
Tangawizi	X	350
Trishna	X	137
Urban Turban	X	166
Veeraswamy	XX	86
Zaika	XX	253
Zayna	XX	139

Innovative

Archipelago	XX	144
Eastside Inn	XXX	187
L'Etranger	XX	227
The Greenhouse	XXX ✿	58
Hibiscus	XXX ✿✿	60
Maze	XXX ✿	65
Pied à Terre	XXX ✿✿	152
The Providores	XX	134
Texture	XX ✿	136
Tom Aikens	XXX ✿	238
Trinity	XX	326

International

Cantina Vinopolis	X	181
The Ivy	XXX	97
Light House	X	352
Michael Moore	X	132
The Modern Pantry	X ☺	193
1 Lombard Street	XXX	195
Sketch (The Gallery)	XX	77
Union Café	X	137

Italian

Al Duca	X ☺	35
A Cena	XX	348
Alloro	XX	35
L'Anima	XXX	292
Apsleys (at The Lanesborough Hotel)	XXXX ✿	105
Arturo	X	160
Assaggi	X	161
Avista	XXX	38
Il Baretto	X	127
Bar Trattoria Semplice	X ☺	40
Bocca di Lupo	X ☺	45
Caffé Caldesi	X	128
Cantina Del Ponte	X	180
Caraffini	XX	222
Carpaccio	XX	223
Cecconi's	XXX	49
Cibo	X	244
Il Convivio	XX	108
Daphne's	XX	226
Dolada	XX	52
Edera	XX	246
Enoteca Turi	XX	342
Fifteen London	X	286
500	X ☺	262
Franco's	XX	54

Latium	XXX	130
Locanda Locatelli	XXX ✿	131
Manicomio (Chelsea)	X	231
Manicomio (City of London)	XX	191
Metrogusto	XX ☺	290
Olivo	X	112
Osteria Dell' Angolo	XX	113
Osteria Emilia	X	263
Quadrato	XXX	302
Quirinale	XX	116
Riva	X	318
River Café	XX ✿	338
Santini	XXX	118
Sardo	XX	154
Sardo Canale	XX	273
Sartoria	XXX	76
Semplice	XX ✿	78
Terranostra	X	204
Theo Randall	XXX	82
Timo	XX	251
Toto's	XXX	239
Trenta	XX	165
Vasco and Piero's Pavilion	XX	86
Via Condotti	XX ☺	87
Vineria	XX	138
Zafferano	XXX ✿	120

Italian influences

The Coach and Horses	🍺	185
Murano	XXX ✿	68
Petersham Nurseries Café	X	345
The Phoenix (Putney)	X	342
Water House	XX	288

Japanese

Abeno	X	143
Atami	XX	106
Chisou	X	50
Dinings	X	129
Kiku	XX	62
Kiraku	X	327
Matsuba	X	345
Matsuri - High Holborn	XX	150
Matsuri - St James's	XX	64
Nobu (at The Metropolitan Hotel)	XX ✿	69
Nobu Berkeley St	XX ✿	70
Roka	XX	153
Sake No Hana	XXX	76
Sumosan	XX	81
Sushi-Hiro	X ☺	328
Sushi-Say	X	277
Tsunami (Bloomsbury)	X	155
Tsunami (Clapham)	X	326
Umu	XXX ✿	85
Zuma	XX	239

Korean

Asadal	XX	144

Latin American

Floridita	XX	53

Lebanese

Fakhreldine	XX	53
Kenza	XX	189
Levant	XX	130
Noura Brasserie	XX	112

Malaysian

Awana	XXX	217

Mediterranean

Le Café du Jardin	X	95
Dehesa	X ☺	52
Harrison's	X	316
Moro	X	194
Ottolenghi	X	291
Portal	XX	198
Le Provence	X ☺	317
St Alban	XXX	75
Salt Yard	X ☺	154
Sam's Brasserie	X	323
Whitechapel Gallery Dining Room	X	308

Modern European

Acorn House	X	143
The Ambassador	X	176
Arbutus	X ✿	36

Aurora X 37
L'Autre Pied XX✿ 126
Avenue XX 38
Babylon XX 243
Bank XX 106
Bingham Restaurant (at Bingham Hotel) XX✿ 344
Blueprint Café X 178
Bob Bob Ricard XX 44
Bonds XXX 179
The Botanist XX 220
Bradley's XX☺ 274
Brasserie James X 315
Le Café Anglais XX 161
The Cafe at Sotheby's X 47
Le Caprice XX 48
The Chancery XX 182
Chapters XX☺ 300
Charlotte's Place X 327
Clarke's XX 245
Le Deuxième XX 96
Devonshire Terrace XX 186
Fifth Floor XXX 227
Fig X 282
The Forge XX 97
Four O Nine XX 325
Giaconda Dining Room X☺ 147
The Glasshouse XX✿ 339
Gordon Ramsay at Claridge's XXXX 57
High Timber XX 188
Hoxton Apprentice X 287
Hush XX 61
Island XX 162
Kensington Place X 247
The Larder XX 189
Launceston Place XXX 247
The Lock XX 295
Lutyens XXX 190
The Mercer XX 192
Mews of Mayfair XX 66
Odette's XX 272
Patterson's XX 71
Plateau XX 301
Portrait X 73
Quaglino's XX 73
Ransome's Dock X 320
Rhodes W1 Brasserie XX 134
Skylon XXX 202
Smiths of Smithfield XX 202
Sonny's XX 318
Stanza XX 81
La Trompette XXX✿ 324
Upstairs XX☺ 321
Village East X 205
Vinoteca X 205
Wapping Food X 307
The White Swan XX 207
Whits XX 252
Wild Honey XX✿ 88
The Wolseley XXX 87
York and Albany XX 265

Moroccan

Momo XX 67
Pasha XX 234

North African

Azou X 335

Polish

Wódka X 252

Scottish

Boisdale XX 107
Boisdale of Bishopsgate XX 178

Seafood

Bentley's (Oyster Bar) X 44
Bibendum Oyster Bar X 218
Fish Hook X 322
J. Sheekey XX 98
J. Sheekey Oyster Bar X 98
Olivomare X 113
One-O-One XXX 232
Scott's XXX 77
Wright Brothers X 208

Spanish

Barrafina X 39
Cambio de Tercio XX 222
Cigala X 145
El Pirata De Tapas X 164
Fino XX 146

L Restaurant and Bar	XX	249
Tapas Brindisa	X	203
Tierra Brindisa	X	84

Thai

Bangkok	X	217
Benja	XX ☺	43
Blue Elephant	XX	330
Chada	XX	320
Chada Chada	X	128
Mango Tree	XX	109
Nahm at The Halkin Hotel	XX ✿	111
Nipa	XX	163
Saran Rom	XXX	334
Simply Thai	X	347

Traditional

Brew Wharf	X	179
The Butcher and Grill	X	319
Foxtrot Oscar	X ☺	228
High Road Brasserie	XX	323
Konstam at the Prince Albert	X	149
Lamberts	X	316
Langan's Coq d'Or	XX	230
Marco	XX	231
The Ritz Restaurant	XXXXX	75
A Taste of McClements	XX	341
Tom Ilić	X	321
Vivat Bacchus	XX	206
Vivat Bacchus London Bridge	XX	206
Walnut	X	276

Turkish

Ozer	XX	132

Vegetarian

Vanilla Black	XX	204

Vietnamese

Au Lac	X	285

Restaurants with outside dining

Restaurant		Page
The Admiral Codrington	🍺	216
Anglesea Arms	🍺	334
Aurora	X	37
The Avalon	🍺	315
L'Aventure	XX	127
Babylon	XX	243
Bank	XX	106
The Barnsbury	🍺	289
Bar Trattoria Semplice	X ☺	40
Belvedere	XXX	243
Bingham Restaurant at Bingham Hotel	XX ✿	344
Bleeding Heart	XX	145
Boisdale	XX	107
The Bolingbroke	🍺	319
The Bollo	🍺	314
Le Boudin Blanc	X	45
Brasserie James	X	315
Brew Wharf	X	179
The Brown Dog	🍺 ☺	317
The Bull	🍺	270
Bull and Last	🍺	266
The Butcher and Grill	X	319
Butlers Wharf Chop House	X	180
Cantina Del Ponte	X	180
Caraffini	XX	222
Carpenter's Arms	🍺	335
Chapters	XX ☺	300
Chez Kristof	XX	336
Cigala	X	145
Cinnamon Kitchen	XX	183
Clissold Arms	🍺	267
The Coach and Horses	🍺	185
Coq d'Argent	XXX	186
The Dartmouth Arms	🍺	303
The Dartmouth Castle	🍺	336
Dehesa	X ☺	52
Devonshire Terrace	XX	186
The Devonshire	🍺	322
The Drapers Arms	🍺 ☺	289
Duke of Sussex	🍺	314
The Empress of India	🍺	284
The Engineer	🍺	272
Fig	X	282
Great Queen Street	X ☺	147
The Gun	🍺	301
The Havelock Tavern	🍺 ☺	337
High Road Brasserie	XX	323
High Timber	XX	188
Hix Oyster and Chop House	X	188
The House	🍺	283
Hoxton Apprentice	X	287
Hush	XX	61
Indian Zing	XX	337
Inn the Park	X	62
Junction Tavern	🍺	275
Langan's Coq d'Or	XX	230
The Ledbury	XXX ✿✿	248
The Lock	XX	295
Ma Cuisine (Kew)	X ☺	340
The Magdala	🍺	268
Manicomio (Chelsea)	X	231
Medcalf	X ☺	192
Memories of India on the River	XXX	332
The Modern Pantry	X ☺	193
Momo	XX	67
The Morgan Arms	🍺	283
The Narrow	🍺	305
The Northgate	🍺	290
Odette's	XX	272
Olivomare	X	113
The Only Running Footman	🍺	71
Oxo Tower	XXX	195
Oxo Tower Brasserie	X	196
Painted Heron	XX	233
Paternoster Chop House	X	196
Petersham Nurseries Café	X	345
The Phoenix (Chelsea)	🍺	234
The Phoenix (Putney)	X	342
Plateau	XX	301
Le Pont de la Tour	XXX	197
La Poule au Pot	X	114
Prince Albert	🍺	264
Princess Victoria	🍺	347
Quadrato	XXX	302

The Queens Pub and Dining Room 🍺 266
Ransome's Dock X 320
Rex Whistler at Tate Britain XX 116
The Ritz Restaurant XXXXX 75
River Café XX ✿ 338
Rose and Crown XX 269
The Rosendale 🍺 307
Sands End 🍺 333
Santini XXX 118
Saran Rom XXX 334
Sardo Canale XX 273
Smiths of Smithfield XX 202
Toto's XXX 239
La Trompette XXX ✿ 324
The Victoria 🍺 329
Villandry Kitchen X 155
Vineria XX 138
Wapping Food X 307
Water House XX 288
The Waterway 🍺 167
The Well 🍺 207
The Wells 🍺 269
York and Albany XX 265

Open late

Al Duca X ☺ 35
Amaya XXX ✿ 104
Angelus XX 160
Arbutus X ✿ 36
Assaggi XX 161
Automat X 37
L'Aventure XX 127
Baltic XX 177
Barrafina X 39
Ba Shan X 41
Bengal Clipper XX 177
Bentley's (Grill) XXX 43
Bentley's (Oyster Bar) X 44
Bibendum XXX 218
Bistro Aix XX 265
Blue Elephant XX 330
Bob Bob Ricard XX 44
Bocca di Lupo X ☺ 45
Boisdale XX 107
Bombay Brasserie XXXX 219
Le Boudin Blanc X 45
Bradley's XX ☺ 274
Brasserie St Jacques XX 46
The Butcher and Grill X 319
Butlers Wharf Chop House X 180
Le Café Anglais XX 161
Cafe Boheme X 47
Le Café du Jardin X 95
Café Lazeez XX 48
Caffé Caldesi X 128
Cambio de Tercio XX 222
Le Caprice XX 48
Cecconi's XXX 49
Chada XX 320
Chada Chada X 128
Chapters XX ☺ 300
Chez Kristof XX 336
China Tang XXXX 49
Chor Bizarre XX 50
Cibo X 244
Cinnamon Kitchen XX 183
The Clerkenwell Dining Room XX 183
Clos Maggiore XX 96
Cocoon XX 51
Corrigan's Mayfair XXX 51
Le Deuxième XX 96
Devonshire Terrace XX 186
Dragon Castle XX 302
Eastside Inn XXX 187
Eight over Eight XX 226
Fakhreldine XX 53
Floridita XX 53
The Forge XX 97
Franco's XX 54
Galvin at Windows (at London Hilton Hotel) XXXX ✿ 55
Le Gavroche XXXX ✿✿ 56

Good Earth	XX	228
Gordon Ramsay	XXXX ✿✿✿	229
Gordon Ramsay at Claridge's	XXXX	57
Great Eastern Dining Room	XX	286
The Greenhouse	XXX ✿	58
Hakkasan	XX ✿	148
Haozhan	XX	57
High Road Brasserie	XX	323
Hush	XX	61
Imli	X	61
Incognico	XX	149
The Ivy	XXX	97
J. Sheekey	XX	98
J. Sheekey Oyster Bar	X	98
Levant	XX	130
Locanda Locatelli	XXX ✿	131
Malabar	X ☺	249
Mao Tai	XX	332
Marco	XX	231
Maxim	XX	328
Maze Grill	XX	64
Memories of India on the River	XXX	332
Mews of Mayfair	XX	66
Michael Moore	X	132
Mint Leaf	XX	66
Mint Leaf Lounge	XX	193
The Modern Pantry	X ☺	193
Momo	XX	67
Mon Plaisir	XX	150
Moti Mahal	XX	151
Mr Chow	XX	232
Nahm at The Halkin Hotel	XX ✿	111
The Narrow	🍺	305
Nobu (at The Metropolitan Hotel)	XX ✿	69
Nobu Berkeley St	XX ✿	70
Notting Hill Brasserie	XX	251
Noura Brasserie	XX	112
Olivo	X	112
Olivomare	X	113
Oxo Tower	XXX	195
Oxo Tower Brasserie	X	196
Ozer	XX	132
Papillon	XX	233
Pasha	XX	234
Patterson's	XX	71
Pearl Liang	XX	164
The Phoenix (Putney)	X	342
Phoenix Palace	XX	133
Pied à Terre	XXX ✿✿	152
Plateau	XX	301
Plum Valley	XX	72
Poissonnerie de l'Avenue	XX	235
Le Pont de la Tour	XXX	197
La Porte des Indes	XX	133
La Poule au Pot	X	114
Quaglino's	XX	73
Quality Chop House	X	198
Ransome's Dock	X	320
Red Fort	XXX	74
Roka	XX	153
Rose and Crown	XX	269
Roussillon	XXX ✿	117
Rules	XX	99
St Alban	XXX	75
Sake No Hana	XXX	76
Salt Yard	X ☺	154
Shepherd's	XXX	118
Sketch (The Gallery)	XX	77
Snazz Sichuan	XX	267
Sonny's	XX	318
Sumosan	XX	81
Swagat	X	346
Taman Gang	XX	82
Tamarind	XXX ✿	83
Tapas Brindisa	X	203
Terroirs	X ☺	99
Texture	XX ✿	136
Theo Randall	XXX	82
Timo	XX	251
Toto's	XXX	239
Les Trois Garcons	XX	306
La Trouvaille	XX	84
Tsunami (Bloomsbury)	X	155
Union Café	X	137
Via Condotti	XX ☺	87
Wild Honey	XX ✿	88
The Wolseley	XXX	87
Yauatcha	XX ✿	89
York and Albany	XX	265
Zuma	XX	239

Open on Sunday

Abeno 143
L'Absinthe 271
The Admiral Codrington 216
Amaya 104
The Ambassador 176
The Anchor and Hope 176
Angelus 160
Anglesea Arms 334
Arbutus 36
L'Atelier de Joël Robuchon 94
Aubaine 216
Au Lac 285
Aurora 37
Automat 37
L'Autre Pied 126
The Avalon 315
Awana 217
Azou 335
Baltic 177
The Barnsbury 289
Barrafina 39
Bar Shu 40
Ba Shan 41
Benares 42
Bengal Clipper 177
Bentley's (Oyster Bar) 44
Bibendum 218
Bibendum Oyster Bar 218
Bluebird 219
Blue Elephant 330
Bob Bob Ricard 44
The Bolingbroke 319
The Bollo 314
Bombay Brasserie 219
The Botanist 220
Le Boudin Blanc 45
Brasserie Roux 46
Brasserie St Jacques 46
The Brown Dog 317
Builders Arms 220
The Bull 270
Bumpkin (North Kensington) 244
Butlers Wharf Chop House 180
The Cadogan Arms 221
Le Café Anglais 161
Cafe Boheme 47
Le Café du Jardin 95
Cambio de Tercio 222
Cantina Del Ponte 180
Le Caprice 48
Carpenter's Arms 335
Cat and Mutton 284
Cecconi's 49
Chapters 300
Chelsea Brasserie 224
Chelsea Ram 224
Chez Bruce 351
Chez Kristof 336
China Tang 49
Chutney Mary 225
Cigala 145
Clarke's 245
Clissold Arms 267
Clos Maggiore 96
The Coach and Horses 185
Le Colombier 225
Coq d'Argent 186
Corrigan's Mayfair 51
Crazy Bear 146
Daphne's 226
The Dartmouth Arms 303
The Dartmouth Castle 336
Le Deuxième 96
Dragon Castle 302
The Drapers Arms 289
Duke of Sussex 314
E & O 245
The Ebury 108
Edera 246
El Pirata De Tapas 164
The Empress of India 284
The Engineer 272
Eriki 274
L'Etranger 227
Fakhreldine 53
The Farm 330
The Fat Badger 246
Fifteen London 286
Fish Hook 322
The Forge 97
Four O Nine 325
The Fox 293
Foxtrot Oscar 228
Galvin at Windows (at London Hilton Hotel) 55
Galvin Bistrot de Luxe 129
The Garrison 187
The Glasshouse 339
Goldfish 268
Good Earth 228
Gordon Ramsay at Claridge's 57
The Gun 301
Hakkasan 148
Haozhan 57
The Havelock Tavern 337
Hereford Road 162
High Road Brasserie 323
High Timber 188
Hix Oyster and Chop House 188
The House 283
Hoxton Apprentice 287
Imli 61
Indian Zing 337
Inn the Park 62

Island	XX	162
The Ivy	XXX	97
J. Sheekey	XX	98
J. Sheekey Oyster Bar	X	98
Junction Tavern	🍺	275
Kai	XXX ✿	63
Kastoori	X	348
Kensington Place	X	247
Kew Grill	XX	340
Kiasu	X	163
Langan's Coq d'Or	XX	230
Launceston Place	XXX	247
The Ledbury	XXX ✿✿	248
Levant	XX	130
Locanda Locatelli	XXX ✿	131
Lots Road Pub and Dining Room	🍺	230
L Restaurant and Bar	XX	249
Ma Cuisine (Kew)	X ☺	340
The Magdala	🍺	268
Malabar	X ☺	249
Mango Tree	XX	109
Manicomio (Chelsea)	X	231
Mao Tai	XX	332
Matsuri - St James's	XX	64
Maze	XXX ✿	65
Maze Grill	XX	64
Memories of India on the River	XXX	332
Metrogusto	XX ☺	290
The Morgan Arms	🍺	283
Moro	X	194
Mr Chow	XX	232
The Narrow	🍺	305
Nobu (at The Metropolitan Hotel)	XX ✿	69
The Northgate	🍺	290
North London Tavern	🍺	271
Noura Brasserie	XX	112
L'Oasis	🍺	291
Odette's	XX	272
Olivomare	X	113
One-O-One	XXX	232
The Only Running Footman	🍺	71
Oxo Tower	XXX	195
Oxo Tower Brasserie	X	196
Ozer	XX	132
Painted Heron	XX	233
The Pantechnicon Rooms	🍺	114
Pasha	XX	234
Pearl Liang	XX	164
The Peasant	🍺	197
La Petite Maison	XX	72
The Phoenix (Chelsea)	🍺	234
Phoenix Palace	XX	133
The Pig's Ear	🍺	235
Plum Valley	XX	72
Poissonnerie de l'Avenue	XX	235
Le Pont de la Tour	XXX	197
La Porte des Indes	XX	133
La Poule au Pot	X	114
Prince Albert	🍺	264
Prince Alfred and Formosa Dining Room	🍺	165
Prince Arthur	🍺	285
Prince of Wales	🍺	343
The Princess of Shoreditch	🍺	293
Princess Victoria	🍺	347
Le Provence	X ☺	317
The Providores	XX	134
Quadrato	XXX	302
Quaglino's	XX	73
Quality Chop House	X	198
The Queensbury	🍺	276
The Queens Pub and Dining Room	🍺	266
Quilon	XXX ✿	115
Racine	XX	236
The Restaurant at The Petersham	XXX	346
Rex Whistler at Tate Britain	XX	116
Rhodes W1 Brasserie	XX	134
The Ritz Restaurant	XXXXX	75
Rivington Grill (Shoreditch)	X	294
Roka	XX	153
The Rosendale	🍺	307
Rules	XX	99
St Alban	XXX	75
St John's Tavern	🍺	262
St John Bread and Wine	X	306
Salisbury	🍺	333
The Salusbury	🍺	273
Sam's Brasserie	X	323
Sands End	🍺	333
Saran Rom	XXX	334
Sardo Canale	XX	273
Scott's	XXX	77
Singapore Garden	XX	275
Skylon	XXX	202
Smiths of Smithfield	XX	202
Snazz Sichuan	XX	267
The Spencer Arms	🍺	343
Spread Eagle	XX	304
Tamarind	XXX ✿	83
Tapas Brindisa	X	203
A Taste of McClements	XX	341
The Thomas Cubitt	🍺	119
Tom's Kitchen	X	236
Toto's	XXX	239
Trishna	X	137
La Trompette	XXX ✿	324
Tsunami (Clapham)	X	326
Urban Turban	X	166
Le Vacherin	XX	325
Veeraswamy	XX	86
The Victoria	🍺	329
Village East	X	205
Villandry Kitchen	X	155
Walnut	X	276
The Warrington	🍺	166
The Waterway	🍺	167
The Well	🍺	207
The Wells	🍺	269
Wild Honey	XX ✿	88
The Wolseley	XXX	87
XO	XX	263
Yauatcha	XX ✿	89
York and Albany	XX	265
Zafferano	XXX ✿	120
Zaika	XX	253
Zayna	XX	139
Zuma	XX	239

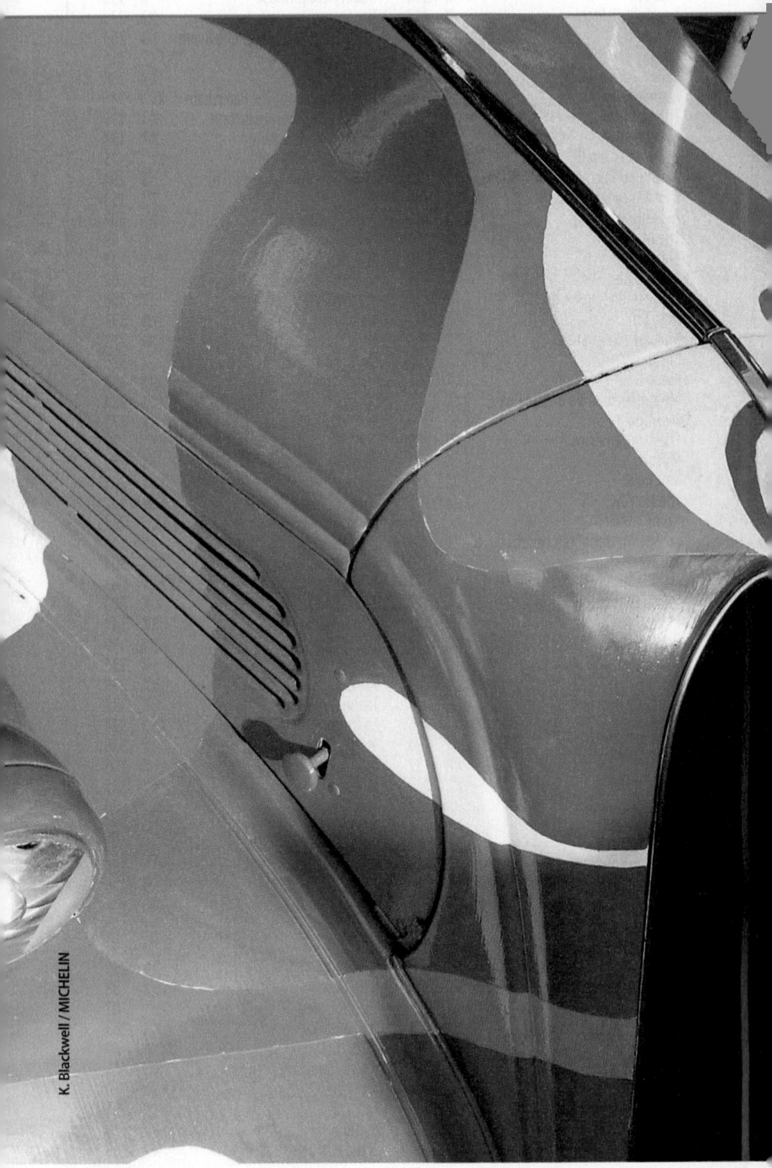

K. Blackwell / MICHELIN

Central London

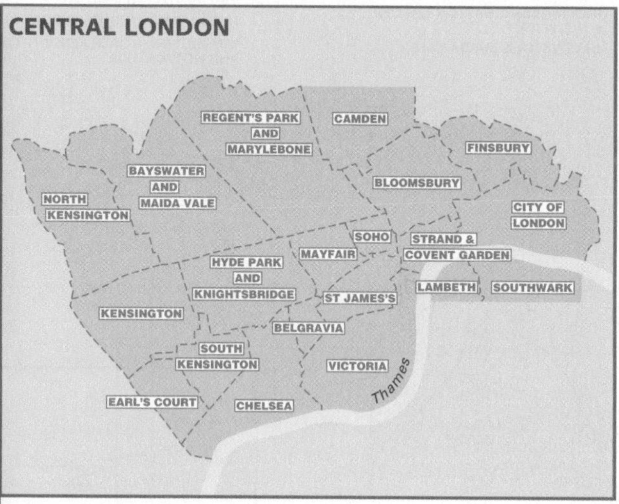

▶ Mayfair • Soho • St James's 30

▶ Strand • Covent Garden 90

▶ Belgravia • Victoria 100

▶ Regent's Park • Marylebone 122

▶ Bloomsbury • Hatton Garden • Holborn 140

▶ Bayswater • Maida Vale 156

▶ City of London • Clerkenwell • Finsbury • Southwark 168

▶ Chelsea • Earl's Court • Hyde Park • Knightsbridge • South Kensington 210

▶ Kensington • North Kensington • Notting Hill 240

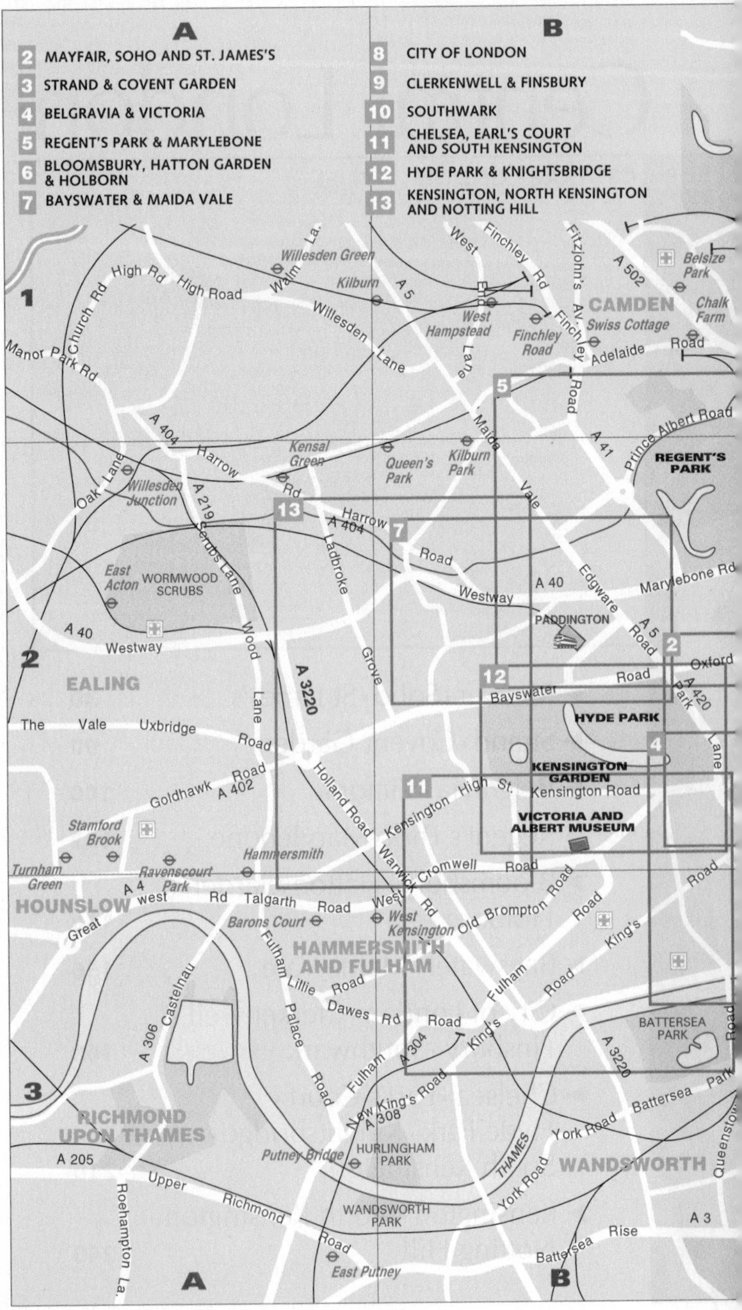
A
B
2 MAYFAIR, SOHO AND ST. JAMES'S
3 STRAND & COVENT GARDEN
4 BELGRAVIA & VICTORIA
5 REGENT'S PARK & MARYLEBONE
6 BLOOMSBURY, HATTON GARDEN & HOLBORN
7 BAYSWATER & MAIDA VALE
8 CITY OF LONDON
9 CLERKENWELL & FINSBURY
10 SOUTHWARK
11 CHELSEA, EARL'S COURT AND SOUTH KENSINGTON
12 HYDE PARK & KNIGHTSBRIDGE
13 KENSINGTON, NORTH KENSINGTON AND NOTTING HILL
1
2
3
Willesden Green
Kilburn
West Hampstead
Finchley Road
Swiss Cottage
Belsize Park
Chalk Farm
CAMDEN
Adelaide Road
High Rd
High Road
Church Rd
Manor Park Rd
Walm La.
Willesden Lane
West End Lane
Finchley Rd
Fitzjohn's Av.
A 502
A 5
Finchley Road
A 404
Harrow Rd
Kensal Green
Queen's Park
Kilburn Park
Maida Vale
A 41
Prince Albert Road
REGENT'S PARK
Oak Lane
Willesden Junction
A 219
Scrubs Lane
Harrow Road
A 404
Ladbroke Grove
Westway
A 40
PADDINGTON
Edgware Road
A 5
Marylebone Rd
East Acton
WORMWOOD SCRUBS
A 40
Westway
Wood Lane
A 3220
EALING
The Vale
Uxbridge Road
Bayswater Road
Oxford
A 420
Park Lane
HYDE PARK
KENSINGTON GARDEN
Kensington Road
VICTORIA AND ALBERT MUSEUM
Goldhawk Road
A 402
Holland Road
Kensington High St.
Stamford Brook
Hammersmith
Turnham Green
Ravenscourt Park
Cromwell Road
Warwick Rd
HOUNSLOW
A 4
Great West Rd
Talgarth Road
Barons Court
West Kensington
West
Old Brompton Road
Road
King's Road
HAMMERSMITH AND FULHAM
Fulham Road
Lillie Road
Dawes Rd
Road
Fulham Palace Road
A 306
Castelnau
A 304
Fulham
King's
A 3220
BATTERSEA PARK
Road
Park
New King's Road
A 308
RICHMOND UPON THAMES
A 205
Putney Bridge
HURLINGHAM PARK
THAMES
York Road
Battersea
WANDSWORTH
Queenstown
Upper Richmond Road
Roehampton La.
WANDSWORTH PARK
York Road
A 3
Battersea Rise
East Putney
A
B

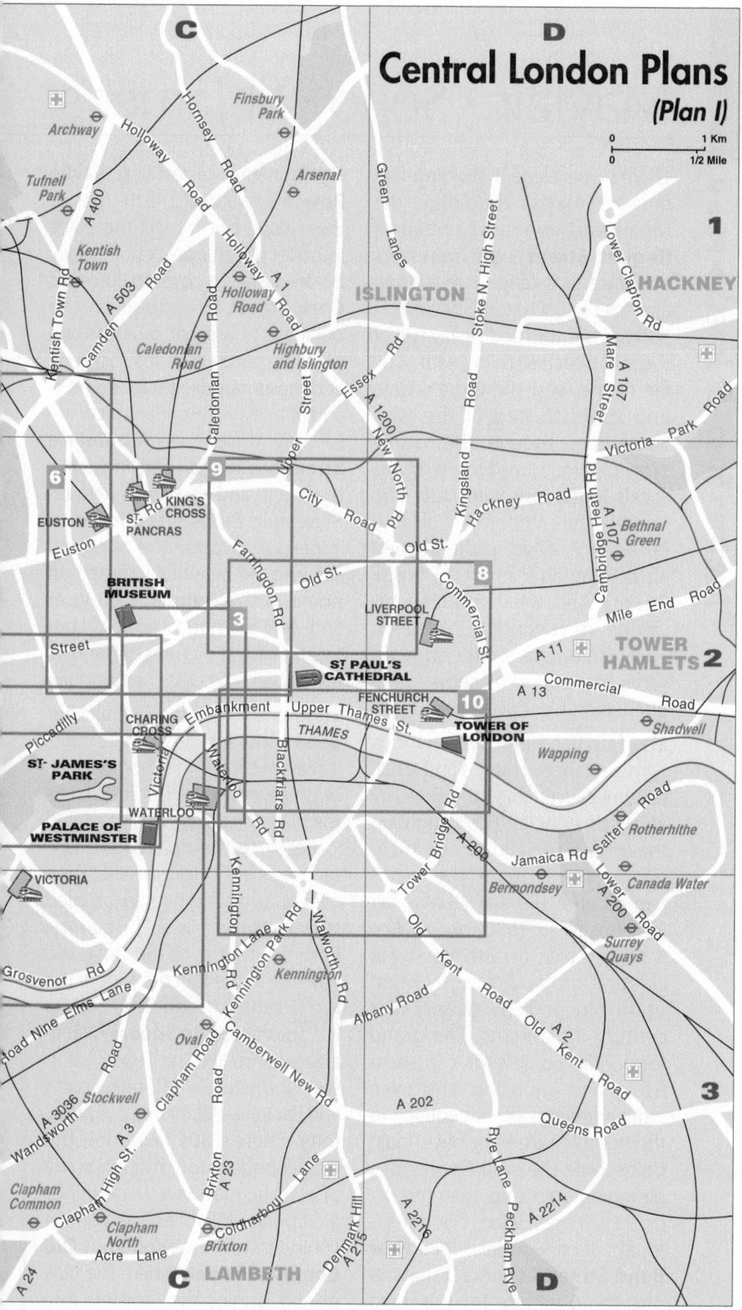
Central London Plans
(Plan I)
0 1 Km
0 1/2 Mile
C
D
1
2
3
Archway
Holloway
Hornsey
Road
Finsbury
Park
Arsenal
Tufnell
Park
A 400
Kentish
Town
Kentish Town Rd
Camden
A 503
Road
Holloway
A 1
Road
Holloway
Road
Caledonian
Road
Caledonian
Highbury
and Islington
Green
Lanes
ISLINGTON
Stoke N. High Street
Road
Lower Clapton
Rd
HACKNEY
Mare
Street
A 107
Victoria
Park
Road
Essex
Rd
A 1200
New
North
Rd
Upper
Street
Kingsland
Hackney
Road
City
Road
Cambridge Heath Rd
A 107
Bethnal
Green
EUSTON
Euston
ST. PANCRAS
KING'S CROSS
Rd
Old St.
Farringdon Rd
Old St.
Commercial St.
Mile
End
Road
BRITISH
MUSEUM
LIVERPOOL
STREET
TOWER
HAMLETS
A 11
Street
ST. PAUL'S
CATHEDRAL
A 13
Commercial
Road
Piccadilly
CHARING
CROSS
Embankment
Upper
Thames
St.
FENCHURCH
STREET
TOWER OF
LONDON
Shadwell
THAMES
ST. JAMES'S
PARK
Victoria
Waterloo
Blackfriars
Rd
Wapping
WATERLOO
PALACE OF
WESTMINSTER
Rd
Tower Bridge
Rd
A 200
Salter
Road
Rotherhithe
Jamaica Rd
Bermondsey
Lower
A 200
Road
Canada Water
VICTORIA
Kennington
Surrey
Quays
Grosvenor
Rd
Lane
Nine Elms
Kennington
Lane
Kennington Park Rd
Kennington
Walworth
Rd
Old
Kent
Road
Albany Road
Road
Oval
Camberwell New
Rd
Old
A 2
Kent
Road
Clapham Road
Road
Wandsworth
A 3036
Stockwell
A 202
A 3
Queens Road
Clapham High St.
Brixton
A 23
Lane
Rye Lane
Clapham
Common
Clapham
Clapham
North
Coldharbour
Brixton
Denmark Hill
A 215
A 2216
Peckham Rye
A 2214
Acre
Lane
A 24
LAMBETH
Mile End
Road

Mayfair · Soho · St James's

There's one elegant dividing line between Mayfair and Soho - the broad and imposing sweep of **Regent Street** - but mindsets and price tags keep them a world apart. It's usual to think of easterly Soho as the wild and sleazy half of these ill-matched twins, with Mayfair to the west the more sedate and sophisticated of the two. Sometimes, though, the natural order of things runs awry: why was rock's legendary wild man Jimi Hendrix, the embodiment of Soho decadence, living in the rarefied air of Mayfair's smart 23 Brook Street? And what induced Vivienne Westwood, punk queen and fashionista to the edgy, to settle her sewing machine in the uber-smart Conduit Street?

Mayfair has been synonymous with elegance for three and a half centuries, ever since the Berkeley and Grosvenor families bought up the local fields and turned them into posh real estate. The area is named after the annual May fair introduced in 1686, but suffice it to say that a raucous street celebration would be frowned upon big time by twenty-first century inhabitants. The grand residential boulevards can seem frosty and imposing, and even induce feelings of inadequacy to the humble passer-by but should he become the proud owner of a glistening gold card, then hey ho, doors will open wide. Claridge's is an art deco wonder, while **New Bond Street** is London's number one thoroughfare for the most chi-chi names in retailing. **Savile Row** may sound a little 'passé' these days, but it's still the place to go for the sharpest cut in town, before sashaying over to compact **Cork Street** to indulge in the purchase of a piece of art at one of its superb galleries. Science and music can also be found here, and at a relatively cheap price: the Faraday Museum in **Albemarle Street** has had a sparkling refurbishment, and the Handel House Museum in Brook Street boasts an impressive two-for-one offer: you can visit the beautifully presented home of the German composer and view his musical scores… before looking at pictures of Hendrix, his 'future' next door neighbour.

Soho challenges the City as London's most famous square mile. It may not have the money of its brash easterly rival, but it sure has the buzz. It's always been fast and loose, since the days when hunters charged through with their cries of 'So-ho!' Its narrow jumbled streets throng with humanity, from the tourist to the tipsy, the libertine to the louche. A lot of the fun is centred round the streets just south of **Soho Square,** where area legends like The Coach & Horses ('Norman's Bar'), Ronnie Scott's and Bar Italia cluster in close proximity. There's 80s favourite, the Groucho Club, too, though some of its lustre may have waned since a corporate takeover. The tightest t-shirts in town are found in **Old Compton Street,** where the pink pound jangles the registers in a swathe of gay-friendly bars and restaurants. To get a feel of the 'real' Soho, where old engraved signs enliven the shop fronts and the market stall cries echo back to the 1700s, a jaunt along **Berwick Street** is always in vogue, taking in a pint at the eternally popular Blue Posts, an unchanging street corner stalwart that still announces 'Watney's Ales' on its stencilled windows.

Not a lot of Watney's ale was ever drunk in **St James's;** not a lot of ale of any kind for that matter. Champagne and port is more the style here, in the hushed and reverential gentlemen's clubs where discretion is the key, and change is measured in centuries rather than years. The sheer class of the area is typified by **Pall Mall's** Reform Club, where Phileas Fogg wagered that he could zip round the world in eighty days, and the adjacent **St James's Square,** which was the most fashionable address in London in the late seventeenth century, when dukes and earls aplenty got their satin shoes under the silver bedecked tables.

C. Barrely / MICHELIN

Mayfair, Soho and St James's
(Plan II)

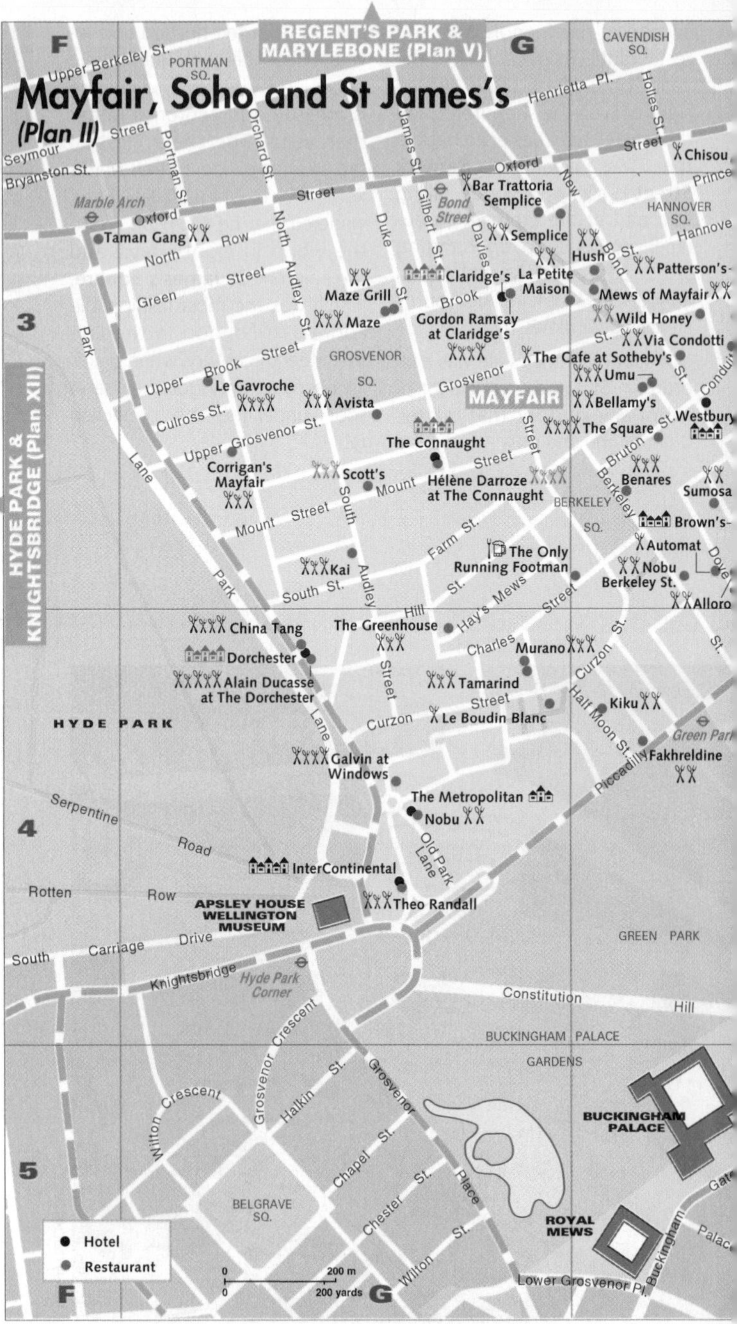

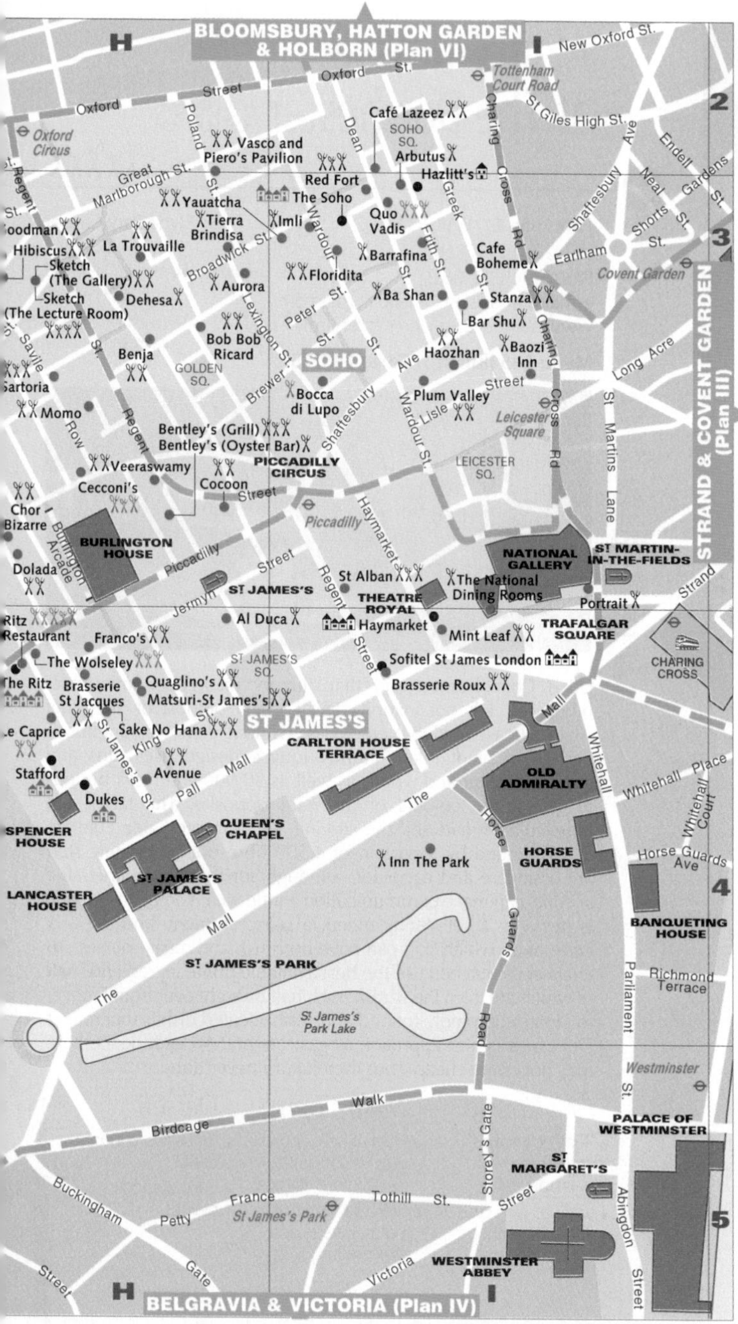

BLOOMSBURY, HATTON GARDEN & HOLBORN (Plan VI)
H
I
2
3
4
5
New Oxford St.
Oxford St.
Oxford Street
Oxford Circus
Tottenham Court Road
St Giles High St.
Café Lazeez
SOHO SQ.
Arbutus
Hazlitt's
Vasco and Piero's Pavilion
Red Fort
The Soho
Yauatcha
Tierra Brindisa
Imli
Quo Vadis
Barrafina
Floridita
Ba Shan
Cafe Boheme
Stanza
Bar Shu
Baozi Inn
Haozhan
Plum Valley
Bocca di Lupo
Great Marlborough St.
Goodman
Hibiscus
La Trouvaille
Sketch (The Gallery)
Sketch (The Lecture Room)
Dehesa
Aurora
Bob Bob Ricard
Benja
GOLDEN SQ.
SOHO
Sartoria
Momo
Bentley's (Grill)
Bentley's (Oyster Bar)
Veeraswamy
Cocoon
PICCADILLY CIRCUS
Cecconi's
Chor Bizarre
BURLINGTON HOUSE
Burlington Arcade
Dolada
Piccadilly
Jermyn Street
ST JAMES'S
St Alban
THEATRE ROYAL Haymarket
The National Dining Rooms
NATIONAL GALLERY
ST MARTIN-IN-THE-FIELDS
Portrait
TRAFALGAR SQUARE
Mint Leaf
Al Duca
Ritz Restaurant
Franco's
The Wolseley
The Ritz
Brasserie St Jacques
Quaglino's
Matsuri-St James's
ST JAMES'S SQ.
Sofitel St James London
Brasserie Roux
CHARING CROSS
Le Caprice
Sake No Hana
ST JAMES'S
CARLTON HOUSE TERRACE
Stafford
Dukes
Avenue
King St.
St James's St.
Pall Mall
OLD ADMIRALTY
Whitehall
Whitehall Place
Whitehall Court
SPENCER HOUSE
QUEEN'S CHAPEL
Inn The Park
HORSE GUARDS
Horse Guards Ave
Horse Guards Road
ST JAMES'S PALACE
LANCASTER HOUSE
BANQUETING HOUSE
The Mall
ST JAMES'S PARK
St James's Park Lake
Richmond Terrace
Parliament St.
Westminster
Birdcage Walk
Storey's Gate
PALACE OF WESTMINSTER
ST MARGARET'S
Buckingham Gate
Petty France
Tothill St.
Street
St James's Park
Abingdon Street
WESTMINSTER ABBEY
Victoria Street
Charing Cross Rd
Leicester Square
LEICESTER SQ.
St Martins Lane
Long Acre
Covent Garden
Shaftesbury Ave
Neal St.
Endell St.
Earlham St.
Shorts Gardens
Wardour St.
Dean St.
Frith St.
Greek St.
Lexington St.
Broadwick St.
Brewer St.
Peter St.
Lisle Street
Haymarket
Regent St.
Savile Row
Poland St.
STRAND & COVENT GARDEN (Plan III)
Strand
BELGRAVIA & VICTORIA (Plan IV)

Alain Ducasse at The Dorchester ✿✿✿

French XXXXX

G4

Park Lane ✉ W1K 1QA
✆ (020) 7629 8866
Fax (020) 7629 8686
e-mail alainducasse@thedorchester.com
www.alainducasse-dorchester.com

Menu £45 (lunch) – Carte £45/75

⊖ Hyde Park Corner
Closed 1-23 August, dinner 25 December, 26-30 and lunch 31 December, 1-4 January, Saturday lunch, Sunday and Monday

Alain Ducasse

VISA MC AE

Coco Chanel once said that "luxury must be comfortable, otherwise it is not luxury". The London outpost of über-chef Alain Ducasse's global empire is, without doubt, a sumptuous and extravagant affair. Patrick Jouin's design uses tans and creams, leather and wood, as well as 30,000 green silk buttons to reflect the colours of the park opposite. The tables are immaculately laid and the striking, semi-private Table Lumière is surrounded by a curtain of 4,500 fibre optics. Waiting staff are a sincere and eager lot, although sometimes impenetrable accents can make communication a little wearisome. The choice is between a set tasting menu, a seasonal menu and the à la carte, with which you can have both fish and meat courses. 16 chefs in the kitchen use the best available prime ingredients, half of which are from the British Isles, half brought over from France, to create supremely refined and sophisticated dishes that reflect Ducasse's lighter approach to gastronomy. An experience here may not come cheap - but then luxury never does.

First Course

- Roasted chicken and lobster with sweetbreads.
- Scallops with ceps and potato gnocchi.

Main Course

- Fillet of beef and foie gras Rosinni with 'sacristain' potatoes.
- Sea bass with razor clams, parsley and shellfish jus.

Dessert

- "Baba like in Monto-Carlo".
- Coco-caramel delight.

Al Duca

H4 **Italian**

4-5 Duke of York St SW1Y 6LA
(020) 7839 3090
Fax (020) 7839 4050
e-mail alduca@btconnect.com
www.alduca_restaurant.co.uk

Piccadilly Circus
Closed one week Christmas, Sunday and Bank Holidays

Menu £28

A/C VISA AE

Fresh and invigorating Italian cooking is the draw at Al Duca, nestling among the galleries, outfitters and historic pubs of St James's. The set menus offer an appealing mix of dishes which boast a nicely balanced simplicity while still delivering on flavour. There's a daily-changing pasta and risotto and the kitchen demonstrates a light and confident touch, as well as an obvious appreciation of the ingredients. Furthermore, it represents very good value, especially when you consider the location. Service makes up in efficiency what is lacks in personality. The crisp terracotta interior of tiles and stone means that noise has a tendency to bounce around the place a little when busy, which it nearly always is - and deservedly so.

Alloro

H3 **Italian**

19-20 Dover St W1S 4LU
(020) 7495 4768
Fax (020) 7629 5348
e-mail alloro@londonfinediningroup.com
www.alloro-restaurant.co.uk

Green Park
Closed 25 December, Saturday lunch and Sunday

Menu £32/35

A/C VISA AE

Alloro celebrates its 10th anniversary in 2010 and this comparative longevity owes much to its sensible prices, confident service and easy-to-eat Italian food. The current chef has been here for nearly half the restaurant's life; he comes from Piedmont and manages to sneak in a few specialties from his home region. The menu offers an appealing choice and nicely balanced selection, from a crisp chicory salad with bottarga to slow-cooked lamb shoulder, with all breads and pastas being made in-house. It's priced per number of courses taken; having all four represents the best value. Noise drifts in from the adjacent, boisterous baretto and so ensures that the atmosphere in the comfortable and urbane restaurant is always lively.

Arbutus

Modern European

13

63-64 Frith St ✉ W1D 3JW
(020) 7734 4545
Fax (020) 7287 8624
e-mail info@arbutusrestaurant.co.uk
www.arbutusrestaurant.co.uk

⊖ Tottenham Court Road
Closed 25-26 December and 1 January

Menu £16 (lunch) – Carte £28/38

A/C VISA MC AE

Arbutus

The recession has meant that chefs across the land have been forced to earn their keep. This means thinking about value and being creative: using their kitchen skills so that less fashionable cuts of meat can be made just as enticing as luxury ingredients. A trip to Arbutus would show them what's possible because here you'll find food that's at the smart end of bistro-style cooking, done in an intelligent and affordable way. The fact that the regulars quickly snap up the pieds et paquets and ox heart tells you everything: there is a lot of preparation behind the scenes and no easy short-cuts to this sort of food – it's all down to very good cooking, in-depth understanding of produce and an aversion to frippery. Neither is there anything phoney about the service which is confident and comfortably paced rather than the rush you might expect in such a busy restaurant. The lunch and pre-theatre menus are a positive steal; the selection of wines by the carafe work wonderfully well and the atmosphere is always fun.

First Course

- Squid and mackerel burger with parsley and razor clams.
- Carpaccio of lamb with ricotta and pine nuts.

Main Course

- Saddle of rabbit, cottage pie and broad beans.
- Roast cod with chicken wings and potato purée.

Dessert

- White peach with thyme and strawberry sorbet.
- Baked egg custard with Seville orange marmalade.

Aurora

H3 **Modern European**

49 Lexington St ✉ W1F 9AP
✆ (020) 7494 0514
e-mail sohoaurora@gmail.com
www.aurorasoho.co.uk

⊖ Piccadilly Circus
Closed 25-26 December and Bank Holidays – booking essential

Carte approx. £26

VISA MC AE

This is one of those no-nonsense restaurants where most of the customers are regulars who just get on with it. It all happens in a cramped 18th century house, with a rough and ready feel enlivened with more than a hint of gothic. Tables are tightly packed and the ground floor is a buzzy place; go downstairs if you're after some intimacy. The menu changes every month and the cooking is satisfying, rustic and relatively straightforward; the best dishes are those that have roots closer to home. Those regulars ensure the steak is never removed and there's always a pasta and a salad dish. The jewel is the delightful walled garden – unique in Soho. It all works at Aurora, which is why it is now virtually an institution.

Automat

H3 **American**

33 Dover St ✉ W1S 4NF
✆ (020) 7499 3033
Fax (020) 7499 2682
e-mail info@automat-london.com
www.automat-london.com

⊖ Green Park
Closed 25-26 December and 1 January

Carte £39/52

A/C VISA MC AE

Automat, an American-style brasserie, comes divided into three: the first section by the entrance is the least enticing as those waiting for tables will stand around near yours; the mid-section comes decked out in the style of a railway carriage and the third is undoubtedly where the action is. The open kitchen and noise bouncing of the white tiles creates quite a buzzy vibe. The menu could have come direct from NYC. You'll find chowder, cakes of the crab and cheese variety, burgers and steaks, although in portions more European than Stateside. Brunch here is the genuine article. Where the authenticity falls down is in the service which lacks that energetic confidence and relentless efficiency one usually finds across the 'pond'.

Avenue

H4

Modern European XX

7-9 St James's St ✉ SW1A 1EE
✆ (020) 7321 2111
Fax (020) 7321 2500
e-mail avenuereservations@danddlondon.com
www.theavenue-restaurant.co.uk

⊖ Green Park
Closed Sunday

Menu £23 – Carte dinner £24/36

A/C VISA MC AE

Judging by the number of suited business types standing around the long bar this is clearly a good place to close deals. Its brash and boisterous atmosphere puts it in sharp contrast to the Gentlemen's Clubs that still populate St James's and the unsullied sheer whiteness of the place keeps everyone alert. The number of larger tables also makes it less suited to those hoping for a little intimacy. The cooking is crisp and fresh, from an all-encompassing menu that keeps its influences within Europe but also has a growing British element. There's everything from smoked salmon, fishcakes and blade of beef to burgers, bream and – to celebrate the deal – oysters and caviar. Service comes with an urgency which isn't always called for.

Avista

G3

Italian XXX

Millennium Mayfair H,
39 Grosvenor Sq ✉ W1K 2HP
✆ (020) 7596 3399
Fax (020) 7596 3443
e-mail reservations@avistarestaurant.com
www.avistarestaurant.com

⊖ Bond Street
Closed 25 December, Saturday lunch, Sunday and Bank Holidays

Menu £20 (lunch) – Carte £30/49

A/C VISA MC AE

Avista occupies the generous space within the Millennium Hotel that was previously farmed out to Brian Turner. Not only did they soften the room but they also added a separate street entrance which helps in establishing the restaurant's identity, despite the best efforts of the intrusively anodyne music. Veneto born Chef Michele Granziera, a Zafferano alumnus, has created a menu that traverses Italy and marries the rustic with the more refined. There are dishes designed for sharing as well as pre-starter 'snacks' if you really can't wait. The homemade pastas are a particular highlight, while the kitchen's creativity is given full rein on the 'Surprise' seven course menu which is available at dinner.

Baozi Inn

13 **Chinese**

25 Newport Court WC2H 7JS — Leicester Square
(020) 7287 6877 — Closed 24-25 December

Carte £19/25

Further proof that Chinatown is shaking off its tired, touristy image comes in the shape of Baozi Inn. Granted, there's nothing particularly noteworthy about the predictable surroundings of red lanterns and chunky tables but the friendly staff are welcoming and eager to please and the food is generously sized. It's also hard to blow your budget, which is especially significant as they only take cash. The eponymous baozi, or steamed filled buns, are a good way to start, although one is certainly enough; dishes have a fiery Sichuan slant and you'll feel the force in the noodle soup. The peanut and rolled tofu skin salad makes a perfect, calming side dish. Only Chinese beer is served but that's the ideal accompaniment anyway.

Barrafina

13 **Spanish**

54 Frith St W1D 3SL — Tottenham Court Rd
(020) 7813 8016
Fax (020) 7734 7593
e-mail info@barrafina.co.uk
www.barrafina.co.uk

Carte £22/35 s

VISA MC AE

London has been a bit iffy about restaurants that don't take reservations but Barrafina is the likely candidate to buck that trend. This is the newest sibling to the Hart brothers' Fino restaurant and its success is down to its mix of satisfyingly unfussy and authentic tapas and a buzzy atmosphere. Seafood is a speciality and the fish displays an exhilarating freshness; the Jabugo ham is also well worth trying. Four dishes per person is about par and the choice varies from razor clams a la plancha and tuna tartar to grilled chorizo and lamb sweetbreads with capers. It all centres around a counter, with seating for 20, so be prepared to talk to your neighbour - another thing that's never caught on in the capital. Be sure to try one of the sherries.

Bar Shu

I3 **Chinese**

28 Frith St ✉ W1D 5LF ⊖ Leicester Square
✆ (020) 7287 8822 Closed 25 December – booking advisable
Fax (020) 7287 8858
e-mail headoffice@bar-shu.co.uk

Carte £28/38

The fiery flavours of China's Sichuan Province are featured at the perennially busy Bar Shu and those who like their food hot will not be disappointed. Liberal amounts of peppers and chillies are used by the Sichuanese to combat the effects of a humid, wet climate while the region's reputation as a land of plenty are reflected in the variety of ingredients and the large number of specialities. The waiting team may appear reluctant to engage with their customers but the menu helpfully has pictures of the various dishes to help the novice. Sichuan cooking is also well-known for the strange names it gives its more famous dishes and most are featured, so look out for 'pock marked old woman's bean curd' or 'husband and wife meat slices.'

A/C VISA MC AE

Bar Trattoria Semplice

G3 **Italian**

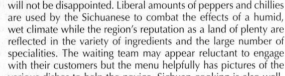

22 Woodstock St ✉ W1C 2AR ⊖ Bond Street
✆ (020) 7491 8638
www.bartrattoriasemplice.com

Menu £16 (lunch) – Carte £24/29

Bar Trattoria Semplice was opened in late 2008 by the same expert team behind Semplice which is just yards away. This is a simpler, more accessible but by no means inferior little sister. The tone is set by the old Berkel meat slicer by the entrance and the cheeses and cured meats above the bar. Oak-topped tables, creams and burgundies and a photo of a Tuscan dawn create a relaxed but bubbly room. The kitchen goes back to basics, with its emphasis on flavour and value. There's a giveaway set lunch menu and each month specialities from a different region of Italy, such as Piedmont or Lazio, feature. Desserts come from the trolley just like trattorie of old; wines are available in 500ml carafes and the bar has an easy, all day menu.

A/C VISA MC AE

Ba Shan

I3 **Chinese** X

24 Romilly St ✉ W1D 5AH
✆ (020) 7287 3266
Fax (020) 7494 4228
e-mail headoffice@bar-shan.co.uk

⊖ Leicester Square
Closed Christmas – booking advisable

Carte £18/28 s

A/C VISA MC AE

Ba Shan is the third enterprise from the team who brought you Bar Shu and Baozi Inn. While this cosy place still has some Sichuan leanings, it mainly focuses on traditional styles from Northern areas and Henan province. Somewhat confusingly, there are two menus: one 'snack', the other 'home-style' - but just pick from both. Dry-wok dishes are plentiful and the guotie dumplings are their own take on a classic. Shaanxi flatbread 'sandwiches' or pork Chaoshou are a good way to start; noodles and vegetables come dressed with a provocative amount of chilli. Decoratively, it treads a fine line between cute and kitsch. There are three or four tables in each of the five rooms and service copes well with the constant influx of customers.

Bellamy's

H3 **French** XX

18 Bruton Pl ✉ W1J 6LY
✆ (020) 7491 2727
Fax (020) 7491 9990
e-mail info@bellamysrestaurant.co.uk
www.bellamysrestaurant.co.uk

⊖ Bond Street
Closed Saturday lunch, Sunday and Bank Holidays

Menu £29 – Carte £35/58

A/C VISA MC AE

If Audrey Tautou ever opened a shop it would probably look a little like Bellamy's: it's sweet, petite and pretty. The counter doubles as the oyster bar but turn left and you'll find yourself in a roomy, ersatz French brasserie, complete with assorted Gallic posters and accented waiters. The menu covers all bases, from foie gras and caviar to duck rillettes and entrecôtes and the kitchen keeps to the classic techniques and combinations. The good value little set menu offers some financial sanctuary from the more robust prices on the à la carte, although the cover charge is an unwelcome anachronism. The lunchtime crowd are mostly male, suited and serious but dinner is more relaxed, while the mews location adds to the feeling of exclusivity.

Benares ✿

Indian XXX

H3

12a Berkeley Square House ✉ W1J 6BS ⊖ Green Park
✆ (020) 7629 8886
Fax (020) 7499 2430
e-mail reservations@benaresrestaurant.co.uk
www.benaresrestaurant.com

Menu £25 (lunch) – Carte £45/122

A/C
VISA
AE

Benares

Named after the Holy City on the Ganges, Benares is a very smart Indian restaurant, sitting pretty in Berkeley Square. You'll be escorted up to the first floor by a charming member of staff who sets the tone for the whole experience; all members of staff come across very well, even when they're rushed off their feet. The restaurant is a smart and very convivial affair, with the best tables being the corner ones, numbers 17 and 24. It is surrounded by discreet private dining areas, which always seem to be busy but without affecting the quality of service in the main room. Chef Atul Kochhar may have become quite a regular on our TV screens but he also keeps a firm grip on his restaurant. The culinary influences come from across all parts of India but many of the dishes are given an innovative little twist or tweak. However, flavours remain authentic and that's largely due to the deft spicing. Lamb dishes are particularly succulent, but it is in the fish dishes where the skill and care of the kitchen is most evident.

First Course

- Soft shell crab with squid salad.
- Lamb, chicken tikka and king prawn kebab platter.

Main Course

- Grilled roe deer fillet with yellow pumpkin risotto.
- Fried John Dory with peas and tomato chutney.

Dessert

- Rose panna cotta with raspberry mousse.
- Chocolate mousse with praline ice cream.

Benja

H3 — Thai XX

17 Beak St ✉ W1F 9RW
✆ (020) 7287 0555
Fax (020) 7287 0056
e-mail info@krua.co.uk
www.benjarestaurant.com

⊖ Oxford Circus
Closed 25 December, 1 January, lunch Sunday and Bank Holidays – booking essential at dinner

Menu £30 (dinner) – Carte £25/39

A/C VISA MC AE

Have a cocktail in the intimate basement Na Ga bar before venturing upstairs in this sleek and colourful converted townhouse. Either stop at the ground floor with its moody styling or head further upwards to the bigger and brighter first floor room; wherever you sit you'll get very charming service. The Thai food is carefully prepared and packed with punchy flavours – the chef is not afraid of using authentic spicing although you can stipulate how spicy you want your salad. Two of the signature dishes are chargrilled sirloin with holy basil, chilli and garlic sauce and steamed sea bass with a delicate lime sauce. Lunch is a speedier affair, when you choose the main ingredient and the desired accompaniments.

Bentley's (Grill)

H3 — British XXX

11-15 Swallow St ✉ W1B 4DG
✆ (020) 7734 4756
Fax (020) 7758 4140
e-mail reservations@bentleys.org
www.bentleys.org

⊖ Piccadilly Circus
Closed 25 December and 1 January

Menu £20 (lunch) – Carte £33/45

A/C VISA MC AE

The beloved institution called Bentley's continues to enjoy its new lease of life. The green neon sign is still outside but these days the upstairs dining room has a contemporary feel with leather chairs, fabric covered walls and paintings of boats and fish for those who haven't twigged what's on the menu. One thing that will probably never change is the clubby feel and the preponderance of suited male customers. Seafood also remains the draw, with fish on the bone dissected at the table something of a house speciality. Much of the produce comes from St Ives and Looe in Cornwall and the freshness is palpable. Dover and Lemon soles feature strongly, as do oysters and soups whilst the breads and beef remind you that owner Richard Corrigan is Irish.

Bentley's (Oyster Bar)

H3 **Seafood** X

11-15 Swallow St ✉ W1B 4DG ⊖ Piccadilly Circus
✆ (020) 7734 4756
Fax (020) 7758 4140
e-mail reservations@bentleys.org
www.bentleys.org

Menu £20 (lunch) – Carte £33/45

A/C There's something about Swallow Street that always seems to get the taste buds going. Bentley's small reception area acts for both the upstairs restaurant and the ground floor Oyster bar so be patient; dining on the ground floor means you'll be ushered through the curtain into a dimly lit bar, with marbled-topped tables, banquette seating and places laid up at the counter. Oysters are naturally one of the main features, and the fish pie is a popular choice, but there are usually lots of daily specials and these often represent the most appealing option. The restaurant's illustrious past is almost tangible and the atmosphere is chummy and clubby, helped along with noise from the bar on the other side and the evening pianist.

VISA MC AE

Bob Bob Ricard

H3 **Modern European** XX

1 Upper James St ✉ W1F 9DF ⊖ Oxford Circus
✆ (020) 3145 1000
Fax (020) 7851 9308
e-mail reservations@bobbobricard.com
www.bobbobricard.com

Carte £26/49

A/C "Taste is the enemy of creativeness" said Pablo Picasso. The creatively decorated Bob Bob Ricard was set up to compete with the traditional grand cafés and diners by serving anything to anyone at anytime. Your table could be getting stuck into beef Wellington while your neighbours are spooning an evening bowl of cornflakes – and no one raises an eyebrow. If your doctor has prescribed a diet of caviar and jelly then this place is ideal. Each table even has a button to press if you want more champagne. Don't get palmed off with a table by the entrance: to get the full, flamboyant effect of all the smoked glass and marble you need to be in the body of the restaurant. But spare a thought for the waiters in those bubblegum-pink waistcoats.

VISA MC AE

Bocca di Lupo

I3 **Italian**

12 Archer St ✉ WID 7BB
✆ (020) 7734 2223
www.boccadilupo.com

⊖ Piccadilly Circus
Closed Sunday – booking essential

Carte £23/31

Deservedly busy from the day it opened, Bocca di Lupo is one of the best things to have arrived in Soho since the espresso bar. But be sure to sit at the marble counter in front of the chefs rather than at one of the faux-distressed tables at the back – not only is the atmosphere here more fun but the food is often better as it hasn't hung around the waiters' station waiting to be delivered. Each item has its region of origin within Italy noted on the menu and is available in a large or smaller size. The flavours don't hang back and over-ordering in all the excitement is very hard to resist. Highlights include the veal and pork agnolotti, the poussin in bread, the suckling pig and tripe; but leave room for dessert too.

Le Boudin Blanc

G4 **French**

5 Trebeck St ✉ W1J 7LT
✆ (020) 7499 3292
Fax (020) 7495 6973
e-mail reservations@boudinblanc.co.uk
www.boudinblanc.co.uk

⊖ Green Park
Closed 24-26 December

Menu £15 (lunch) – Carte £27/47

Shepherd Market is the true heart of Mayfair, as it was here that the original May fair was held before the area was developed in the 18C into the village-like quarter it is now. The atmosphere may be a little less licentious these days but there's still a certain breeziness in the air and Le Boudin Blanc brings along some Gallic joie de vivre. The place is always busy and there's seating for about 150 but the first floor is marginally less frantic. The crowds are attracted by authentic and satisfying French classics, from snails and fish soup to confit of duck or beef tartare. Side orders can push up the final bill but there's a good value lunch and early evening menu. If you want more responsive service, try practising your French.

Brasserie Roux

I4 French XX

8 Pall Mall ✉ SW1Y 5NG ⊖ Piccadilly Circus
✆ (020) 7968 2900
Fax (020) 7747 2251
e-mail info@brasserieroux.com
www.brasserieroux.com

Menu £20/21 – Carte £32/49

The term 'brasserie' does not really prepare you for the grandeur of a room that once formed part of a banking hall. Those giant lamps are needed to counter such an enormous ceiling and the leather armchairs and large tables up the ante on the comfort front. It is a surprise, therefore, to discover there's a weekly changing set menu that's not only keenly priced but also includes two glasses of wine. The 'brasserie' label certainly makes more sense when talking about the food; expect comforting classics like blanquette de veau or baba au rhum alongside terrines and plenty of grilled meats and fish. Add to this some pasta dishes, a few salads and a children's menu and you'll find that there's something for everyone.

Brasserie St Jacques

H4 French XX

33 St James's Street ✉ SW1A 1HD ⊖ Green Park
✆ (020) 7839 1007
Closed Christmas, New Year and Saturday lunch
Fax (020) 7839 3204
e-mail info@brasseriestjacques.co.uk
www.brasseriestjacques.co.uk

Carte £30/50

33 St James's Street has been home to a number of restaurants: most recently Fiore and, most notably, Pétrus. Its current incumbent is Brasserie St Jacques which represented owner Claudio Pulze's 51st restaurant opening. The layout of the room has never done any of the restaurants any great favours and this time is no exception: the bar may have been moved and some big Gallic posters and smoky mirrors hung but the place does lack that buzz one would expect from a brasserie. But where that name does apply more aptly is in the menu: it offers all the usual favourites from escargots to coq au vin, terrines to entrecôtes; the occasional Gascony accent comes courtesy of Pierre Koffman who was the consultant chef.

The Cafe at Sotheby's

F1 — **Modern European**

34-35 New Bond St ✉ W1A 2AA
(020) 7293 5077
Fax (020) 7293 6993
e-mail ken.hall@sothebys.com
www.sothebys.com

⊖ Bond Street
Closed 24 December-4 January, Saturday and Sunday – booking essential – lunch only

Carte £25/33 s

'Café' is something of a misnomer as this is a thoroughly civilised, comfortable and urbane little spot for morning coffee, lunch or afternoon tea, located within the world famous auction house. It spills into the lobby but the best tables are those against the wall, with the banquette seating. Mirrors and Cecil Beaton photographs lighten the space and the waitresses are a charming and efficient group. The lunch menu is a short but well-balanced affair, mixing the light with the more substantial and dishes are fresh and invigorating, including the popular lobster sandwich; a permanent feature. The wine list is also diminutive but the dozen or so wines are varied and well chosen. Bookings are essential, especially on sale days.

Cafe Boheme

I3 — **French**

13 Old Compton St ✉ W1D 5JQ
(020) 7734 0623
Fax (020) 7434 3775
e-mail info@cafeboheme.co.uk
www.cafeboheme.co.uk

⊖ Leicester Square
Closed 25 December

Carte £24/36

Cafe Boheme became an ersatz Parisian brasserie (but without the accents), following its most recent makeover a couple of years back. It comes complete with zinc topped bar surrounded by an animated crowd of wine drinkers, globe lights and brown banquettes; only a consumptive Mimi is missing. However, its main selling point is its accessibility: things kick off at 7.30am with breakfast and the place doesn't shut again until 2.45am the following morning. Straightforward Gallic comfort food is the draw and with eggs Benedict, snails, duck confit, assorted salads and bavette steak on the menu there's something for everyone, at any time. The pace is frenetic, the location ideal for theatregoers and the staff do a sterling job in keeping up.

Café Lazeez

Indian ✗✗

I2

21 Dean St ✉ W1D 3TN
☎ (020) 7434 9393
Fax (020) 7434 0022
e-mail reservations@lazeezsoho.com
www.lazeez.sohocom

⊖ **Tottenham Court Road**
Closed 25 December, 1 January and Sunday

Carte £27/35

A/C
i⊘i
🎭
VISA
MC
AE
⓪

The ground floor bar, attached to the Soho Theatre next door, is a useful place to know because, if you time it right, you can find yourself in relatively composed surroundings compared to many of Soho's more excitable bars. What's more, you just need to head downstairs for something to eat. Sketches of former Indian prime ministers adorn the brightly coloured walls, service is conscientious and the best tables are the booths by the staircase. The open-plan kitchen exhibits a certain ambition, encouraged by the restaurant's owners.   Several dishes come appealingly presented in earthenware dishes; there's clarity to the flavours and vigour in their construction. The wine list is also not your normal drab affair.

Le Caprice

Modern European ✗✗

H4

Arlington House,
Arlington St ✉ SW1A 1RJ
☎ (020) 7629 2239
Fax (020) 7493 9040
e-mail reservation@le-caprice.co.uk
www.le-caprice.co.uk

⊖ **Green Park**
Closed 24-26 December and 1 January

Menu £20 – Carte £33/53

A/C
i⊘i
🎭
☀
VISA
MC
AE
⓪

When a restaurant is described as an "institution" one thinks of somewhere stuffy, old and probably a little smelly. For more than 25 years Le Caprice has proved that a clubby, senior restaurant can actually be warm, fun and feverishly fashionable and the only anachronism here is the cover charge. The pianist and the long bar add a hint of old New York while the black and white décor and David Bailey photographs give it a certain timelessness. The position and size of your table will depend on the extent of your celebrity or patronage but the service is commendably democratic. Easy-eating is the order of the day and the appealing menu has everything from eggs Benedict to rump of veal. The Caesar salad and salmon fishcakes are permanent fixtures.

Cecconi's

H3 — Italian XXX

5a Burlington Gdns ✉ W1S 3EP — ⊖ Green Park
✆ (020) 7434 1500 — Closed 25 December – booking essential
Fax (020) 7434 2020
e-mail giacomo@cecconis.co.uk
www.cecconis.com

Carte £22/45

Clubs have had VIP areas for years so it was inevitable that certain restaurants that pride themselves on their celestial clientele would create a semi-private area for those who can't bear the thought of mere mortals watching them eat. That being said, the bar at Cecconi's is an appealing spot and more of a destination than most; their Bellinis are legendary. Those more interested in the food will find that carpaccios and tartares are the house specialities but this type of Italian comfort eating has something for everyone. Lobster spaghetti and veal Milanese are the top sellers and Super Tuscans have a page to themselves on the wine list. Breakfast is as busy as dinner and weekend brunches are languid affairs.

China Tang

G4 — Chinese XXXX

Park Lane ✉ W1A 2HJ — ⊖ Hyde Park Corner
✆ (020) 7629 9988 — Closed 25 December
Fax (020) 7629 9595
e-mail chinatang@dorchesterhotel.com
www.thedorchester.com

Menu £15 (lunch) – Carte £40/70

Those familiar with the boutiques of Sir David Tang will recognise that seductive scent sprayed in the entrance of his shimmering restaurant within The Dorchester Hotel. The main room is a buzz of activity, with the noise spilling out from the large tables in the centre; regulars head for the library side, from where one can take in the whole room. In contrast to these sleek and decorative surroundings, the kitchen is a model of conservatism and rightly sticks to what it does best, namely classic Cantonese cooking. Peking duck and roasted meats are the highlights, but check out the chef's recommendations at the back of the menu, such as abalone and 'Buddha jumps over the wall'. Service is well meaning but sometimes lacks a personality of its own.

Chisou

H2 — **Japanese**

4 Princes St ✉ W1B 2LE — ⊖ Oxford Circus
Closed 24-31 December, Sunday and Bank Holidays except Easter

☎ (020) 7629 3931
Fax (020) 7629 5255
e-mail chisoujpr@aol.com
www.chisou.co.uk

Menu £17 (lunch) – Carte £28/46

Chisou proves that size should be no obstacle to providing good service so you'll find plenty of staff are on hand to guide you through the Japanese food. While it may be intimate, they are generous with the table size and spacing. The kitchen is headed up by a Japanese speaking Sri Lankan; he's often seen manning the sushi counter and has the owner's permission to source ingredients entirely on quality rather than cost restrictions. Specialities, from a menu that covers all points, include Tuna yukke, Gyu tataki (seared beef) and Hourensou (spinach) salad. There are some good value set lunch menus and next door is the useful 'Go Chisou,' where the growing local Japanese community go to get their Bento boxes.

A/C VISA AE

Chor Bizarre

H3 — **Indian**

16 Albemarle St ✉ W1S 4HW — ⊖ Green Park
Closed Sunday lunch

☎ (020) 7629 9802
Fax (020) 7493 7756
e-mail chorbizarrelondon@oldworldhospitality.com
www.chorbizarre.com

Menu £18 (lunch) – Carte £30/45

No two tables are the same shape and the restaurant is decked out with an eccentric but strangely uplifting mix of old doors, curios, mismatched chairs and trinkets, which is all very appropriate as the name translates as "thieves' market". The menu is a long and chatty tome; each page is filled with dishes, explanations, drawings and anecdotes so it can take quite a while to work your way through it. The cooking is competent and consistent; Northern Indian dishes are the speciality but there is much to be said for ordering a thali and sharing the bounty on your silver platter. If only the staff could add more warmth and personality to proceedings instead of concentrating so much on speedy delivery from the kitchen.

A/C VISA AE

Cocoon

H3 **Asian** XX

65 Regent St ✉ W1B 4EA
✆ (020) 7494 7600
Fax (020) 7494 7607
e-mail reservations@cocoon-restaurants.com
www.cocoon-restaurants.com

⊖ Piccadilly Circus
Closed Saturday lunch and Sunday

Menu £25/50 – Carte £28/45

A/C VISA MC AE

A quick glance at the menu would suggest a Japanese restaurant: sushi, sashimi, Bento boxes and tempura all feature prominently and you may find yourself transfixed by the master craftsman behind one of the counters doing his thing with a very large knife. However, on closer investigation, you'll find dishes whose influences owe more to Korea, China and Thailand, while others are shaped more from the culinary zeitgeist. The common theme, though, is sharing, so ordering should be a group activity, and staff give good advice. The place seats 170 but is cleverly divided and the styling and décor are decidedly space-age. Lunches are relatively calm affairs with shoppers in for salads and Bento boxes. It all hots up big-time in the evenings.

Corrigan's Mayfair

G3 **British** XXX

28 Upper Grosvenor Street
✉ W1K 7EH
✆ (020) 7499 9943
Fax (020) 7499 9321
e-mail reservations@corrigansmayfair.com
www.corrigansmayfair.com

⊖ Marble Arch
Closed 24 to 27 December, 1 January and Saturday lunch

Menu £27 (lunch) – Carte £30/48

A/C VISA MC AE

Richard Corrigan's flagship restaurant may have opened at the end of 2008 but feels as though it has been around for years. It's comfortable, clubby yet quite glamorous and Martin Brudnizki's design includes some playful features, such as the feather-covered lamps that give a nod to the restaurant's forte, which is game. The menu is lengthy and the food largely a celebration of British and Irish cooking. It is also fiercely seasonal, which makes having the day's special always a worthwhile choice. This relatively straightforward style of cooking still requires care and precise timing but sometimes the kitchen takes its eye off the ball. Service is smooth and well organised but the anachronistic cover charge is an unwelcome sight.

Dehesa

H3 **Mediterranean**

25 Ganton St ✉ W1F 9BP
✆ (020) 7494 4170
Fax (020) 7494 4175
e-mail info@dehesa.co.uk
www.dehesa.co.uk

⊖ Oxford Circus
Closed 1 week Christmas and Sunday dinner

Carte £20/30

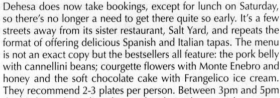

Dehesa does now take bookings, except for lunch on Saturday, so there's no longer a need to get there quite so early. It's a few streets away from its sister restaurant, Salt Yard, and repeats the format of offering delicious Spanish and Italian tapas. The menu is not an exact copy but the bestsellers all feature: the pork belly with cannellini beans; courgette flowers with Monte Enebro and honey and the soft chocolate cake with Frangelico ice cream. They recommend 2-3 plates per person. Between 3pm and 5pm the kitchen takes a breather so the choice becomes ham on or off the bone, charcuterie and cheese. The drinks list is worthy of a visit in itself. Dehesa is a wooden area of Spain and home to Ibérico pigs who produce such great ham.

A/C VISA MC AE

Dolada

H3 **Italian**

13 Albemarle St ✉ W1S 4HJ
✆ (020) 7409 1011
Fax (020) 7493 0081
e-mail manager@dolada.co.uk
www.dolada.co.uk

⊖ Green Park
Closed Christmas and New Year, Saturday lunch and Sunday

Menu £21/26 – Carte £30/42

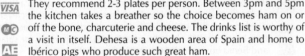

The owner bought the restaurant after falling in love with the receptionist; now that's amore. He's since changed the name from Mosiaco to Dolada, in honour of his chef's family restaurant in Pieve d'Alpago. It's still a somewhat corporate-looking basement restaurant, with lots of marble, but the effusive welcome and confident service create a sociable spirit. The chef, liberated from serving local Venetian specialities back home, is clearly taken with the idea of cooking dishes from across Italy and introduces his own touches: his spaghetti carbonara is a deconstructed affair, where the egg, pasta, pancetta and pecorino sit separately in the bowl, waiting to be mixed. Dishes in his tasting menu display even greater originality.

A/C VISA MC AE

Fakhreldine

H4 **Lebanese** XX

85 Piccadilly W1J 7NB — Green Park
(020) 7493 3424
Fax (020) 7495 1977
e-mail info@fakhreldine.co.uk
www.fakhreldine.co.uk

Menu £14/25 – Carte £25/40

This first-floor Lebanese restaurant, with views over Green Park, may be approaching its 30th birthday but, thanks to fairly frequent and dramatic redesigns, it keeps itself fresh and relevant. A striking copper-topped bar is the first thing one notices and this, along with the adjacent lounge, attracts a fairly youthful weekend crowd. Beech panelling, mirrors and glass combine to create an elegant restaurant where nattily-dressed waiters provide competent service. The menu keeps things classical, from falafel to baba ghanoush, kibbe to makanek. The day's specials are pinned to the front of the menu and are usually a good bet, although the four set menus at the back will provide a nicely balanced meal.

Floridita

I3 **Latin American** XX

100 Wardour St W1F 0TN — Tottenham Court Road
(020) 7314 4000
Fax (020) 7314 4040
www.floriditalondon.com

Closed 25-26 December, 1 January, Sunday, Monday and Bank Holidays – dinner only

Menu £39 – Carte £27/63

It's Salsa all the way, from the spicy food to the live music and dancing. If you think the ground floor with its Mediterranean tapas is busy, try downstairs for size. Here you'll find yourself in a huge nightclub-style space boasting an impressive cocktail list and a variety of Latin American dishes, from Cuban classics like ropa vieja to a whole-roast suckling pig and a large selection of assorted cuts of Argentinean beef aged for 28 days. It's not cheap but then again everything is done very well and everyone is here for a Big Night Out. The bands are flown in from Cuba, the music starts at 7.30pm and the party atmosphere never lets up. Those whose pace is more Cohiba than Mojito can nip next door to La Casa del Habano.

Franco's

H4 **Italian** XX

61 Jermyn St ✉ SW1Y 6LX
✆ (020) 7499 2211
Fax (020) 7495 1375
e-mail admin@francoslondon.com
www.francoslondon.com

⊖ Green Park
Closed Sunday and Bank Holidays – booking essential

Menu £25 (lunch) – Carte £35/51

A/C VISA MC AE

Franco's first opened in the 1940s and, understandably, was beginning to show its age until gracefully withdrawing from the scene for a while, before bursting back in 2005 with a fresh new image. It then managed the difficult trick of both attracting new admirers and hanging onto the loyalty of existing fans. The dining room is spread over two floors, with the ground floor the most popular, and the decoration pays homage to the era of its original opening. The sartorially immaculate regulars continue to gather at their favoured hours so arriving with reservations is recommended, especially at lunch. The seasonally-informed Italian menu is constantly evolving and the cooking is both bold and generous but refined where it should be.

Goodman

H3 **Beef specialities** XX

26 Maddox Street ✉ W1S 1QH
✆ (020) 7499 3776
e-mail david@goodmanrestaurants.com
www.goodmanrestaurants.com

⊖ Oxford Circus
Closed Easter, 25 December, 1 January and Sunday – booking essential

Menu £15 (lunch) – Carte £28/47

A/C VISA MC AE

Goodman is a Russian-owned New York steakhouse in Mayfair – which sounds like a sketch from the UN's Christmas party. Wood and leather give it an authentic feel and it has captured that macho swagger that often seems to accompany the eating of red meat. Tables are usually full of guffawing men, with their jackets thrown over the back of their chairs and their sleeves rolled up. The American and Irish beef is mostly grain fed and either dry or wet aged in-house – Australian beef is an option at lunch. It is cooked in a Josper oven using a blend of three types of charcoal and offered with a choice of four sauces. The steaks are certainly worth coming for, especially the rib-eye, although side dishes are more variable in quality.

Galvin at Windows ✿

French XXXX

G4

London
Hilton Hotel, 22 Park Lane ✉ W1K 1BE
✆ (020) 7208 4021
Fax (020) 7208 4144
e-mail reservations@galvinatwindows.com
www.galvinatwindows.com

⊖ Hyde Park Corner
Closed Saturday lunch and Sunday dinner

Menu £25/58

A/C
VISA
MC
AE

Galvin at Windows

Some restaurants hit the ground running, others take longer to find their feet. There have never been any doubts about the magnificence of the views from this restaurant on the 28th floor of the Hilton Hotel, nor about the capabilities of the well-drilled serving brigade who are attentive without being over-solicitous; but now the quality of the cooking has climbed to similarly lofty heights. André Garrett and his team appear to have greater confidence in their own abilities so now avoid the inclination towards over-elaboration and instead let the ingredients speak for themselves, whether that's a tender fillet of Scottish beef with foie gras or a braised fillet of halibut with crab and lemon oil. Flavours are adeptly balanced and complementary, while presentation, notwithstanding some crowd-pleasing use of gold leaf, is measured and appetising. The best tables for lunch are those on the near side looking down over Buckingham Palace; the far side gazing north over twinkling city lights is the better option for dinner.

First Course

- Foie gras with pain d'épices and hazelnuts.
- Scallops with crispy peanuts and cauliflower purée.

Main Course

- Fillet and peppered short rib of beef with Swiss chard and shallots.
- Sea bass with pumpkin gnocchi and ginger.

Dessert

- Strawberry vacherin with basil and champagne.
- Dark chocolate palet d'or, cookie crumbs and malted milk ice cream.

Le Gavroche ✿✿

French XXXX

G3

43 Upper Brook St ✉ W1K 7QR
✆ (020) 7408 0881
Fax (020) 7491 4387
e-mail bookings@le-gavroche.com
www.le-gavroche.co.uk

⊖ Marble Arch
Closed Christmas and New Year, Saturday lunch, Sunday and Bank Holidays – booking essential

Menu £48 (lunch) – Carte £59/137

A/C
VISA
MC
AE

Le Gavroche

Just reading the menu will harden your arteries. You couldn't eat here every day, although there are possibly some who have tried, but that is what makes Le Gavroche so special – this is a restaurant all about indulgence. Michel Roux and his head chef Rachel Humphrey run a team of over 20 chefs – there's a similar number in the service team – and their focus is on preparing unapologetically classic and extravagant French dishes. They also appreciate that many come here for specific dishes, such as the foie gras, grouse in season, the Soufflé Suissesse or the Omelette Rothschild, and that the art of creating specialities is in ensuring they are prepared to a consistently high standard. The room still has that masculine, clubby feel but is big enough to accommodate larger parties without intimidating the tables of two. Service is structured and formal; the Austrian twins are the most memorable and efficient members of the team, which is now run by Emmanuel who spent a decade working his way up to the top spot. Things change slowly here and that's part of its appeal.

First Course
- Hot duck foie gras and crispy pancake flavoured with cinnamon.
- Scallops baked in the shell with ginger.

Main Course
- Roast saddle of rabbit with crispy potatoes and Parmesan.
- Halibut and lobster with peas and grilled confit potatoes.

Dessert
- Bitter chocolate and praline 'indulgence'.
- Omelette Rothschild.

Gordon Ramsay at Claridge's

G3

Modern European XXXX

Brook St ✉ W1K 4HR
✆ (020) 7499 0099
Fax (020) 7499 3099
e-mail reservations@gordonramsay.com
www.gordonramsay.com

⊖ Bond St
booking essential

Menu £30/70

The managers still invite diners for a post-prandial tour of the kitchen and, as his name is above the door, some of those diners inevitably believe they're about to meet a big Scottish bloke. As befits a restaurant within the stately surroundings of Claridge's hotel, the room is elegant and grandiose and the service ceremonial and structured. The chance to see someone "off the telly" also means that its popularity remains undiminished and this is often the favoured destination for those in a celebratory mood. The menu is faithful to the Gordon Ramsay formula of largely classical cooking but sadly some of the lustre and general care has gone missing from the preparation and this can make the final bill seem somewhat unmerited.

Haozhan

I3

Chinese XX

8 Gerrard St ✉ W1D 5PJ
✆ (0207) 4343 838
Fax (0207) 4349 991
e-mail info@haozhan.co.uk
www.haozhan.co.uk

⊖ Leicester Square
Closed 24-25 December

Menu £10 (lunch) – Carte £21/41

The hardest thing to find in Chinatown has always been a decent Chinese restaurant but in amongst the sea of mediocrity came Haozhan which translates, appropriately enough, as "good place to eat." The majority of the menu is Cantonese with the odd Sichuan punch and some Taiwanese and Malaysian specialities. Eschew the usual perennials in favour of more modern dishes such as Assam prawns or Sanpei chicken; the homemade tofu is a particular strength. Presentation is strong; ingredients are very fresh; flavours are clear and well-judged and it's even worth staying for dessert. Greens and blacks add to the contemporary feel of the place, which is spread over two floors. Service also bucks the local trend, being knowledgeable and helpful.

The Greenhouse ✿

Innovative XXX

G4

27a Hay's Mews ✉ W1J 5NY
✆ (020) 7499 3331
Fax (020) 7499 5368
e-mail reservations@greenhouserestaurant.co.uk
www.greenhouserestaurant.co.uk

⊖ Hyde Park Corner
Closed 24 December-5 January, Saturday lunch, Sunday and Bank Holidays

Menu £29/65

A/C
VISA
AE

The Greenhouse

The chef, Antonin Bonnet, trained under celebrated French chef Michel Bras and spent time as personal chef to Marlon Abela, whose restaurant this is. He is the kind of chef who is always looking at new techniques and approaches to cooking and his style leans towards artfully constructed dishes, where the main ingredient is subtly enhanced with contrasting textures and creative combinations. France provides the main influence but he is not afraid of using, for example, the occasional Moroccan spice or Asian twist. The restaurant has clear ambitions and this goes a long way in accounting for the number of loyal and supportive guests, although the kitchen can sometimes overreach itself in trying to be original. The wine list is one of the most comprehensive you'll come across. Service is formal and structured but sometimes staff go missing in action. The restaurant itself remains fresh and contemporary, thanks to regular reinvestment – and its terrific mews location adds to the somewhat clubby and exclusive feel.

First Course

- Foie gras with cherries, tonka bean cream and kirsch.
- Asparagus with Parmesan and truffles.

Main Course

- Pigeon with sesame seeds, baby spinach and pommes soufflé.
- Pithiviers of calves sweetbreads.

Dessert

- "Snix" - chocolate, salted caramel and peanuts.
- Coconut sorbet with mango and passion fruit jelly.

Hélène Darroze at The Connaught ✿

G3

French XXXX

Carlos Place ✉ W1K 2AL
✆ (020) 3147 7200
Fax (020) 7314 3537
e-mail dining@the-connaught.co.uk
www.the-connaught.co.uk

⊖ Bond St
Closed 1 week January, 1 week August, Sunday dinner and Monday – booking essential

Menu £35/75

VISA
MC
AE

The Connaught

Hélène Darroze has rather taken to London and finds that she now spends 60% of her time here, rather than at her other place in Paris. London has also taken to her and she has been particularly surprised by our less rigid approach to what constitutes dinner time than our French counterparts. India Mahdavi's design has created a very attractive room by softening all that mahogany wall panelling. Service has also found its feet and comes across as professional, courteous and refreshingly free from the sort of arrogance that can blight certain establishments of this nature. Hélène's native region of Landes informs her cooking but she has also discovered the wealth of quality ingredients available in the UK. Add to this her use of interesting flavours from sunnier climates and you end up with dishes such as Scottish langoustine with tandoori spices, saddle of Welsh lamb in a crust of pimientos del piquillo and an apricot dessert with Sichuan peppercorn ice cream. Sometimes presentation is a little overworked but there is no denying the boldness of the cooking.

First Course

- Gillardeau oyster tartare with Aquitaine caviar jelly.
- Summer vegetables with corn tart, Iberico Lomo and lemon.

Main Course

- Pigeon 'flambé au capucin' with green pea mousseline.
- Lobster with tandoori spices, carrot and spring onion.

Dessert

- Carupano chocolate cream with lavender praline.
- Pistache de Sicile with yoghurt sorbet.

Hibiscus ✿✿

Innovative XXX

H3

29 Maddox St ✉ W1S 2PA
✆ (020) 7629 2999
Fax (020) 7514 9552
e-mail enquiries@hibiscusrestaurant.co.uk
www.hibiscusrestaurant.co.uk

⊖ Oxford Circus
Closed 10 days Christmas-New Year, Sunday, Monday and Saturday lunch except 15 November-23 December

Menu £25/85

A/C
VISA
AE

Hibiscus

Following the maxim 'he who stops being better stops being good', chef-owner Claude Bosi took himself off to Kyoto for what the French call a 'stage' and what we refer to more prosaically as 'work experience', and returned with a greater appreciation of precision cooking, general knife skills and the importance of maintaining exacting standards. He has since dispensed with a lot of those foams and jellies and concentrates more on natural flavours and relatively simpler presentation which reflects a greater confidence in his own abilities. Claude is a 'chef's chef' so you'll often see a table of boys in ill-fitting suits sampling as much of the menu as they can manage and making mental notes. The kitchen team here are a well-drilled outfit; they may use the occasional Asian note to bring out the flavour of, say, the Goosnargh duck, but they also have a very solid classical base. Desserts remain a real strength: the chocolate tart is hard to beat, although the soufflés come a pretty close second.

First Course

- Sweetbreads with oak smoked goat's cheese and onion fondue.
- Tartar of mackerel with wasabi and honey dressing.

Main Course

- Chicken stuffed with crayfish, girolles and green mango.
- Black bream with morels, black olives and coffee sauce.

Dessert

- Tart of sweet peas, mint and sheep's whey with coconut ice cream.
- Toasted rice soufflé with white peach.

Hush

H3 **Modern European** XX

8 Lancashire Court,
Brook St ✉ W1S 1EY
✆ (020) 7659 1500
Fax (020) 7659 1501
e-mail info@hush.co.uk
www.hush.co.uk

⊖ Bond Street
Closed 25-27 December, 1 January and Sunday – booking essential

Carte £28/41

Hush has done what all restaurants should do and listened to its customers, who liked the smart upstairs dining room but preferred the more accessible, brasserie-style menu from the busy ground floor room. The result is that this menu is now served throughout and one can see the appeal: it offers a range of straightforward, mostly European classics, from burgers to risotto and salads to sausages as well as dishes like eggs Benedict for late-risers. Upstairs also has the stylish destination bar but that can't compete with the large and delightful courtyard terrace. Popular private dining rooms mean the receptionist is more air-traffic controller than hostess and staff do spend a little too much of their time rushing hither and thither.

Imli

I3 **Indian** X

167-169 Wardour St ✉ W1F 8WR
✆ (020) 7287 4243
Fax (020) 7287 4245
e-mail info@imli.co.uk
www.imli.co.uk

⊖ Tottenham Court Road

Menu £10/12 – Carte £18/24

'Relatively timely food' may not sound quite as snappy as 'fast food' but Imli proves that, if you don't want to linger long over a meal, there are alternatives to multinationals. It may be an Indian restaurant but 'tapas' is the shorthand for dishes that are diminutive and involve sharing. The menu is short, well-priced and to the point; three dishes per person should suffice, although the hungry should go for the 'Taste of Imli'. The cooking is a combination of street food and some regional, particularly Northern Indian, influences; vegetarians will find themselves with plenty of choice. Where Imli has borrowed from the 'experts' is in its use of bright lighting and vivid colours to encourage a rapid turnover.

Inn the Park

British

I4

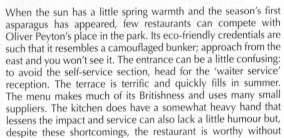

St James's Park ✉ SW1A 2BJ
✆ (020) 7451 9999
Fax (020) 7451 9998
e-mail info@innthepark.com
www.innthepark.com

⊖ Charing Cross
Closed 25 December

Menu £15 (dinner) – Carte £30/36

VISA MC

When the sun has a little spring warmth and the season's first asparagus has appeared, few restaurants can compete with Oliver Peyton's place in the park. Its eco-friendly credentials are such that it resembles a camouflaged bunker; approach from the east and you won't see it. The entrance can be a little confusing: to avoid the self-service section, head for the 'waiter service' reception. The terrace is terrific and quickly fills in summer. The menu makes much of its Britishness and uses many small suppliers. The kitchen does have a somewhat heavy hand that lessens the impact and service can also lack a little humour but, despite these shortcomings, the restaurant is worthy without being pious and the setting is glorious.

Kiku

Japanese

H4

17 Half Moon St ✉ W1J 7BE
✆ (020) 7499 4208
Fax (020) 7409 3259
www.kikurestaurant.co.uk

⊖ Green Park
Closed 25 December, 1 January, lunch Sunday and Bank Holidays

Menu £18/46 – Carte £33/55

A/C VISA MC AE

Kiku is a traditional Japanese restaurant, which makes it something of a rarity these days. The menus are numerous and varied, offering sushi to assorted kaiseki, a selection of soba noodle dishes, salads and casseroles; the lunch time menus are very popular locally. Apart from the kaiseki set menus, the prices are not unreasonable when one considers the Mayfair location, the crisp and understated décor and the endearingly charming staff who can swiftly soothe the most cantankerous of diner. They are also on hand to offer sensible advice. The best place to sit is in the raised section at the back with its own sushi counter; here it's never quite so busy and you get to really appreciate the skills of the chefs.

Kai ✿

G3 **Chinese** XXX

65 South Audley St ✉ W1K 2QU
⊖ Hyde Park Corner
✆ (020) 7493 8988
Fax (020) 7493 1456
e-mail kai@kaimayfair.co.uk
www.kaimayfair.co.uk
Closed 25-26 December and 1 January – booking essential

Menu £22 (lunch) – Carte £38/91

A/C · VISA · MC · AE

Kai

Kai is very much a Mayfair restaurant: one or two of your fellow diners will resemble arms dealers and some of the prices on the menu will make your bank manager weep. But the star of the show is Alex Chow's highly skilled and creative kitchen. His menu comes with little anecdotes and stories which are too long to read in company but they do highlight the restaurant's general enthusiasm. The cooking is confident and dishes come packed with clean flavours, with equal care going into preparing the classics as goes into the more innovative choices. The sweet-natured serving team are a mix of Malaysian and Chinese and they know who their regulars are, of which there are plenty. As a result, certain dishes can never be removed from the menu such as the wasabi prawns, the Peking duck and the excellent pumpkin cream dessert. Prices do vary quite wildly, from the very costly Imperial Delicacies to the reasonably priced selection of poultry dishes. The restaurant is spread over two floors, with the lower level being a little more intimate.

First Course

- Wasabi prawns with mango and basil seeds.
- Scallop and tiger prawns with glass noodles.

Main Course

- Lamb with Sichuan peppercorns, mushroom and bamboo shoots.
- Yin-Yang Dover sole.

Dessert

- Peranakan mango cake with coconut sugar milkshake.
- Almond jelly with exotic fruits and syrup.

Matsuri - St James's

H4 **Japanese** XX

15 Bury St ✉ SW1Y 6AL ⊖ Green Park
✆ (020) 7839 1101 Closed 25 December
Fax (020) 7930 7010
e-mail dine@matsuri-restaurant.com
www.matsuri-restaurant.com

Carte £29/69

Matsuri is now as much of a St James's stalwart as some of the galleries and gentlemen's outfitters that surround it. This original branch is more traditional in feel than its sleeker Holborn sibling and its longevity can be put down to its reliable food and sweet-natured service. You're escorted downstairs to one of the teppan-yaki tables, or alternatively you can sit at the sushi counter, where you'll find yourself presented with a plethora of menus. The food is largely traditional, which makes a nice change from the current fad of 'reinterpreting' Japanese cuisine, and the Scottish beef is the star of the theatrical teppan-yaki. Dinner doesn't come cheap but, thanks to the assorted set menus, lunch represents decent value.

Maze Grill

G3 **Beef specialities** XX

10-13 Grosvenor Sq ✉ W1K 6JP ⊖ Bond Street
✆ (020) 7495 2211
Fax (020) 7592 1603
e-mail mazegrill@gordonramsay.com
www.gordonramsay.com

Menu £18 (lunch) – Carte £34/61

If Maze is the smooth sophisticate then Maze Grill is its red-blooded American cousin, for this place is all about beef. It also feels more like a part of the Marriott Hotel to which it is attached. The assorted cuts, from Casterbridge grain-fed and Hereford grass-fed through to Creekstone prime USDA corn-fed and Wagyu, are brought to your table and individually described. Your preferred steak is then given a blast in the super-hot broiler before being served on a wooden board. There are plenty of sides and sauces to accompany your meat and these, along with the starters or small plates, can beef up your bill, although the wine prices are kept relatively reasonable. There are other fish and meat choices available if you don't fancy a steak.

Maze ✿

Innovative XXX

G3

10-13 Grosvenor Sq ✉ W1K 6JP ⊖ Bond Street
✆ (020) 7107 0000
Fax (020) 7592 1603
e-mail maze@gordonramsay.com
www.gordonramsay.com

Menu £23 (lunch) – Carte £49/69

Gordon Ramsay Holdings

A/C

VISA

AE

Now that the reception area is no longer in the room, the slightly more spacious bar has become more popular for pre and post prandial drinks. The other main change has been in the menus - there are now just two options at dinner: the seven course Chef's menu and the main menu, from which you choose about four dishes from the three pages titled 'cold and warm', 'fish and meat' and 'vegetarian'. Jason Atherton and his kitchen produce diminutive but imaginative constructions that pack a punch but are also balanced and satisfying. While there's a high degree of originality and boldness, there is also a fundamental understanding of what goes with what and the importance of textural contrast. The deconstructed 'BLT' is a favourite, thanks largely to the power of television, and the peanut butter and cherry jam 'sandwich' is another constant on the menu. Maze remains the most original of the restaurants in the Gordon Ramsay repertoire, where the atmosphere is always buoyant, thanks largely to the service and style of the room.

First Course

- Crab salad with pickled mooli, apple jelly and Bloody Mary sorbet.
- Pea velouté with lobster and Parmesan parfait.

Main Course

- Pigeon with ganache, blueberries and red wine.
- Red mullet with cuttlefish, garlic and rabbit bolognese.

Dessert

- Chocolate delice with honey, Banyuls and olive oil ice cream.
- Peanut butter and cherry jam sandwich.

Mews of Mayfair

H3 **Modern European** XX

10-11 Lancashire Court, Brook St (first floor) ✉ W1S 1EY
✆ (020) 7518 9388
Fax (020) 7518 9389
e-mail info@mewsofmayfair.com
www.mewsofmayfair.com

⊖ Bond Street
Closed 25-26 December and Sunday

Menu £19 (lunch) – Carte £29/36

Mews manages that trick of being cool and bright in summer and warm and inviting in winter. The relative serenity of the pretty restaurant is in sharp contrast to the crowds in the narrow lane and busy cocktail bar below, while the private dining room on the next floor up is a very pleasant space. The menu is very appealing and sufficiently sensitive to the changing seasons, so expect venison in winter, spring lamb and summer fruit. Simpler dishes are also pepped up, so burgers come with an optional foie gras topping and fish and chips arrive with a wasabi tartare. Flavours are sometimes compromised by an over-eagerness to make dishes look pretty but prices are generally sensible and the atmosphere thoroughly civilised.

VISA MC AE

Mint Leaf

I4 **Indian** XX

Suffolk Pl ✉ SW1Y 4HX
✆ (020) 7930 9020
Fax (020) 7930 6205
e-mail reservations@mintleafrestaurant.com
www.mintleafrestaurant.com

⊖ Piccadilly Circus
Closed 25-26 December, 1 January, lunch Saturday and Sunday

Menu £17 (lunch) – Carte £31/55

A/C

Indian restaurants come in a variety of guises these days: Mint Leaf is from the contemporary, slick and designery school. This vast subterranean space with its moody lighting can seat over 250 but it comes divided into seven different areas so you're never rattling around. There is also an enormous bar running the length of the room for those wanting to make a night of it. The menu is also quite a lengthy affair, with many choices available in small or larger sizes. The best bet is to share a few dishes such as the soft shell crab or jumbo prawns, and then have your own curry – the kitchen's strength. The serving team are a mixed bunch: some will explain dishes enthusiastically; others seem keener upselling drinks.

VISA MC AE

Momo

H3

Moroccan XX

25 Heddon St ✉ W1B 4BH
✆ (020) 7434 4040
Fax (020) 7287 0404
e-mail info@momoresto.com
www.momoresto.com

⊖ Oxford Circus
Closed 25 December, 1 January and Sunday lunch

Menu £19/45 – Carte £20/43

A/C VISA MC AE

Lanterns, rugs, trinkets and music all contribute to the authentic Moroccan atmosphere that makes Momo such a fun night out. That being said, it's even more fun if you come with friends as tables of two can get somewhat overawed. The menu is divided into three: a somewhat expensive set menu, traditional dishes and Momo specialities. The traditional section is the best as here you'll find the classics from pastilla to tagines; the Momo specialities are more contemporary in their make-up. Whatever you order, you'll end up with a pile of couscous and enough good food to last the week. The wine list lacks affordable bottles but there's a great bar downstairs. If it weren't for the absence of cigarette smoke, you could be in Marrakech.

The National Dining Rooms

I3-4

British X

Sainsbury Wing, The National Gallery,
Trafalgar Sq ✉ WC2N 5DN
✆ (020) 7747 2525
e-mail enquiries@thenationaldiningrooms.co.uk
www.thenationaldiningrooms.co.uk

⊖ Charing Cross
Closed 25-26 December and 1 January – lunch only

Menu £24 – Carte approx. £32

A/C VISA MC AE

There's usually a queue but don't panic – it's either those wanting the bakery section or others realising they should have booked. Oliver Peyton's restaurant on the first floor of the National Gallery's Sainsbury Wing is a bright, open affair, enriched by Paula Rego's complex mural 'Crivelli's Garden.' Ask for a table by the window, not just for the views of Trafalgar Square but also because the other half of the room is darker and under the eaves of the early Renaissance on the floor above. The menu champions British cooking and produce; fish and cheeses are the highlight – pies and puds will write-off the afternoon. The set menu represents decent value and is popular with the customers, who resemble a bridge club up from Winchester for the day.

Murano ✿

Italian influences XXX

G4

20 Queen St ✉ W1J 5PR
✆ (020) 7592 1222
Fax (020) 7592 1213
e-mail murano@gordonramsay.com
www.angelahartnett.com

⊖ Green Park
Closed Sunday

Menu £25/55

A/C
VISA
MC
AE
①

Gordon Ramsay Holdings

The Murano style is most evident in the glassware and the swirls on the wall and, less obviously, in the ceiling light 'sculpture'. The room is a long and narrow one – ask for a table by the front window as they're slightly more packed in towards the back – while the creams and greens combine to create a luminous feel that becomes quite intimate when they lower the lights in the evening. Angela Hartnett has established her reputation through a fairly unique style of cooking that combines classical techniques with Italian influences. Stars of the show include the dried meats and the expertly rendered risottos and pasta dishes which predominantly feature as starters. Many ingredients come from within the British Isles and from wherever they are best, such as Cornish lamb or Scottish beef. Combinations are well-judged and flavours clear. Lunch represents very decent value and there's also a very appealing vegetarian menu. The Italian sommelier is knowledgeable, enthusiastic and offers sensible advice.

First Course

- Scallops with gnocchi, apple and cucumber chutney.
- Cavatelli with braised rabbit, tomato and olives.

Main Course

- Côte de veau with asparagus, mushrooms and hazelnut velouté.
- Sea bass with pepper stew, chicory and a clam and chorizo vinaigrette.

Dessert

- Caramelia chocolate mousse, Sacher sponge and chocolate ice cream.
- Pistachio soufflé with chocolate sauce and macaroons.

Nobu ✿

G4 **Japanese** XX

19 Old Park Lane ✉ W1Y 1LB
✆ (020) 7447 4747
Fax (020) 7447 4749
e-mail london@noburestaurants.com
www.noburestaurants.com

⊖ Hyde Park Corner
Closed 25 December and 1 January – booking essential

Menu £50/90 – Carte £70/90

Nobu

Consistency has long been the hallmark of this Nobu, which opened in 1997 as the first European branch of this international chain of stylish restaurants, having closely followed Manhattan's original. They now number over twenty and are spread around the world, but the two London branches can be considered the pick of the bunch and much of the credit is down to the long-standing executive chef, Mark Edwards. He has also been responsible for introducing the Osusume menu which is exclusive to London and is aimed at offering neophytes the opportunity of discovering what makes the food – Japanese with South American influences – quite so interesting. The flavours are unique, the combinations wholly complementary, the ingredients top-notch and desserts have been reinvigorated. It's little wonder its dishes have been plagiarised across the city. The restaurant is perhaps now less glitzy than its younger sibling but it still appeals to a fashionable crowd. If you really can't live without your Nobu, they'll now even come to your home and do your dinner party for you.

First Course

- Yellowtail sashimi with jalapeno and yuzu soy dressing.
- Crispy pork belly with spicy miso and ginger salsa.

Main Course

- Black cod with miso.
- Wagyu and foie gras with ponzu.

Dessert

- Chocolate bento box with green tea ice cream.
- Lychee granite with orange soup with hazelnut ice cream.

Nobu Berkeley St ✿

Japanese XX

H3

15 Berkeley St ✉ W1J 8DY
✆ (020) 7290 9222
Fax (020) 7290 9223
e-mail berkeleyst@noburestaurants.com
www.noburestaurants.com/berkeley

⊖ Green Park
Closed 25 December, and lunch Saturday and Sunday

Carte £44/65

A/C
VISA
MC
AE

Nobu

If you see photos of assorted celebrities arriving at, or heading off from a Nobu restaurant then, chances are, it is this one. Despite the constant presence of paparazzi outside and its glitzy reputation, this is a restaurant that still does things properly. There are 45 chefs in the kitchen, 60% of whom are Japanese, and considerable care is evident in the food. Nobu tacos are a great way of getting things started and staff are sincere and well informed if you need help. Greatest hits like yellowtail sashimi, black cod with miso and shrimp tempura remain on the menu but each Nobu has some unique element and at Nobu Berkeley St it is the wood oven. The cabbage steak with truffles is a top seller and the crispy pork belly with spicy miso is also well worth trying. Anyone whose fame does not extend beyond their own home needs to book well in advance to get a sensible time for their table; otherwise try pitching up at 7pm and you may just get lucky. Alternatively, try lunch and a bento box with some organic juice.

First Course

- Yellowtail sashimi with jalapeno.
- Tuni sashimi salad.

Main Course

- Black cod with miso.
- Wagyu rump tataki.

Dessert

- Chocolate bento box with green tea ice cream.
- Lemon grass panna cotta with pineapple.

The Only Running Footman

Gastropub

H3

5 Charles St ✉ W1J 5DF ⊖ Green Park.

✆ (020) 7499 2988

Fax (020) 7629 8061

e-mail info@therunningfootman.biz

www.therunningfootman.biz

Menu £15 – Carte £26/35

The Union flag flying outside tells you everything about this pub's attitude, for here our own culinary heritage is celebrated. The ground floor is small, atmospheric and always packed – it's first-come-first-served. The menu hits the bullseye: who can resist an omelette Arnold Bennett for breakfast, potted shrimps for lunch or some haddock for dinner? You can even order a sausage sarnie to take away. Upstairs you can book, it's all rather plush and the menu is more ambitious. You do get to order the rib of beef for two; otherwise you may just wish you were downstairs with a pork pie and piccalilli. This charming, characterful and centrally located pub is the perfect antidote to all those pubs still serving Thai curry.

VISA

AE

Patterson's

Modern European

H3

4 Mill St ✉ W1S 2AX ⊖ Oxford Street

✆ (020) 7499 1308 Closed 25-26 December

Fax (020) 7491 2122

e-mail info@pattersonsrestaurant.co.uk

www.pattersonsrestaurant.com

Menu £23 (lunch) – Carte £23/45

A family moving from a small fishing village in the Scottish borders to the middle of Mayfair may sound like one of those dependable fish-out-of-water comedies, but that is exactly what the Pattersons did back in 2003, and theirs remains one of the few family-run restaurants in this part of town. Father and son in the kitchen still get much of the seafood from their erstwhile home and even supply a number of other restaurants. Their fairly extensive menus feature a lot of Scottish produce in general but it's the seafood that's generally best and the cooking influences come largely from within Europe. It's a deceptively large place, fresh and uncluttered in its decoration, but can still provide a fairly intimate setting.

A/C

VISA

AE

La Petite Maison

GH3 **French** XX

54 Brooks Mews ✉ W1K 4EG
✆ (020) 7495 4774
e-mail info@lpmlondon.co.uk
www.lpmlondon.co.uk

⊖ Bond Street
Closed 25-26 December

Carte £32/98 s

Packed from the moment it opened in 2007, La Petite Maison brings a little piece of Nice to Mayfair. The appeal is sunny French Mediterranean cooking and its healthy bounty of artichokes, lemons, olives, peppers and tomatoes. 'Food is served to help yourself' it proclaims, which translates as 'you may want to share,' but you don't have to, as the dishes are of normal size. However, with over 20 starters including pissaladière, sardines and squid, it may be worth ordering a few. The whole roast black-leg chicken with foie gras has proved a hit, as have the fish main courses. As one would expect, there's plenty of rosé on the wine list. Their slogan is 'Tous célèbres ici', which means lots of all-year tans and good tailoring.

Plum Valley

I3 **Chinese** XX

20 Gerrard St ✉ W1D 6JQ
✆ (020) 7494 4366
Fax (020) 7494 4367
e-mail sooannliew@yahoo.co.uk

⊖ Leicester Square
Closed 25 December

Carte £21/44

Is Chinatown finally casting off its tourist-trap reputation? Plum Valley is the latest venture with genuine aspirations to open in Gerrard Street and its contemporary styling gives the street a much-needed boost. The striking black façade makes it easy to notice, while flattering lighting and layered walls give the interior a dash of sophistication. The chef is from Chiu Chow, a region near Guangdong, and his menu is largely based on Cantonese cooking, with occasional forays into Vietnam and Thailand as well as the odd nod towards contemporary presentation. Dim sum is his kitchen's main strength which fits nicely with the all-day opening of the restaurant. If only those doing the service could muster the same levels of enthusiasm.

Portrait

I3 **Modern European**

National Portrait Gallery, 3rd Floor,
St Martin's Pl ✉ WC2H 0HE
✆ (020) 7312 2490
e-mail portrait.reservation@searcys.co.uk
www.searcys.co.uk

⊖ Charing Cross
Closed 24-26 December
– booking essential
– lunch only

Menu £23 – Carte £31/40

Portrait is on the third floor of the Ondaatje wing of the National Portrait Gallery and is run by the Searcy's catering company. You needn't ask for a window seat because the views, of recognisable rooftops and Nelson standing proudly in Trafalgar Square, are just as good from any of the tables. Although open for breakfast and tea, this is principally a lunchtime operation, with dinner limited to Thursdays and Fridays - the nights of the gallery's extended opening hours. The à la carte menu keeps things relatively light and the influences mostly from Europe; there is a good value set menu at weekends. This is a useful spot, not only for gallery visitors but also for those attending matinee performances at the numerous theatres nearby.

A/C VISA MC AE

Quaglino's

H4 **Modern European**

16 Bury St ✉ SW1Y 6AL
✆ (020) 7930 6767
Fax (020) 7930 2732
e-mail quaglinos@danddlondon.com
www.quaglinos.co.uk

⊖ Green Park
Closed 25 December, Sunday and Bank Holidays – booking essential

Menu £20 – Carte £33/46

Quaglino's has been around long enough for us to forget what an impact its re-opening had, back in the early 1990s. The large bar, the sweeping staircase, the cigarette girls and the bustle of a vast, glamorous restaurant really set London's collective pulse racing at the time. Today, the 'scene' may have moved elsewhere but Quaglino's still offers a good night out. The menu is an appealing mix of brasserie style favourites, with traditional French dishes marked out in red. Grilled meats are done well but the shellfish and seafood are the stars of the show and the kitchen understands the importance of freshness and simplicity. Lunch and early evening set menus are well-priced. The bar, with live music, is a great spot for pre or post prandial drinks.

A/C VISA MC AE

Quo Vadis

13

British XXX

26-29 Dean St ✉ W1D 3LL
✆ (020) 7437 9585
Fax (020) 7734 7593
e-mail info@quovadissoho.co.uk
www.quovadis.co.uk

⊖ Tottenham Court Road
Closed 24-25 December and Bank Holidays

Menu £20 (lunch) – Carte £33/47

A/C VISA MC AE

Quo Vadis has been a Soho landmark since the 1920s and its renewal by the Hart brothers in 2008 ensured that it will be around for many years to come. The menu is of the instantly appealing variety and successfully evokes the classic British grill restaurant. Start with whitebait, razor clams or perhaps some pasta; follow with Hereford beef from the grill or roast turbot and finish with ginger cake or treacle tart. Or just come in for an omelette. Prices are fair, especially with the lunch and pre-theatre menus; and at least that cover charge includes an unlimited water supply. The frosted glass façade adds a dash of intrigue and the art deco elegance combined with a crisp, fresh feel provides suitably comfortable surroundings.

Red Fort

13

Indian XXX

77 Dean St ✉ W1D 3SH
✆ (020) 7437 2525
Fax (020) 7434 0721
e-mail info@redfort.co.uk
www.redfort.co.uk

⊖ Tottenham Court Road
Closed 25 December and lunch Saturday, Sunday and Bank Holidays – booking advisable at dinner

Menu £20/35 – Carte £35/42

A/C VISA MC AE

Dumpukht biryani (using Welsh lamb); monkfish tikka; tandoori jhinga (mildly spiced prawns) and baby aubergines with chilli are the signature dishes of this long-standing Indian restaurant, where the ingredients are top-notch and the rich sauces all made from scratch. The mango kulfi and the various homemade chutneys will also impress, while the menu gets subtly tweaked on a daily basis. The interior provides a sleek and understated homage to Lal Quila, the Red Fort in Delhi; the stone, imported from Rajasthan, combines with the waterfall to create quite a feature. The presence of plenty of managers ensures that service moves along nicely and the doorman is now back on watch. Akbar is the basement bar, with resident DJ.

The Ritz Restaurant

Traditional XXXXX

H4

150 Piccadilly ✉ W1J 9BR ⊖ Green Park
✆ (020) 7493 8181
Fax (020) 7493 2687
e-mail enquire@theritzlondon.com
www.theritzlondon.com

Menu £37/46 – Carte £48/98 s

Not only is dinner at The Ritz Restaurant a grand old occasion but it also acts as a history lesson to any students of hospitality on how things were meant to be done. The room is certainly unmatched in the sheer lavishness of its Louis XVI decoration; the table settings positively gleam thanks to all that polishing and there are probably more ranks to the serving team than in a ship's company. Little wonder they insist on jackets and ties. The Ritz Classics could be a saddle of Kentish lamb or a roast sirloin; Ritz Traditions could be smoked salmon carved at your table or Dover Sole filleted in front of you. If you want the full experience, have the Sonata Menu - six courses paired with wine - and go at the weekend for a dinner dance.

A/C VISA AE

St Alban

Mediterranean XXX

I3

4-12 Regent St ✉ SW1Y 4PE ⊖ Piccadilly Circus
✆ (020) 7499 8558
Fax (020) 7499 6888
e-mail info@stalban.net
www.stalban.net

Closed 25-26 December, 1 January, Sunday dinner and August Bank Holiday

Carte £25/57

A/C VISA AE

It may not garner the same number of mentions in the shiny rags as its sibling The Wolseley, but St Alban's star is undimmed. The seating is great: the tops of the chairs are the same height as the tables and this encourages the community feel and general buzz. The touches of decorative psychedelia are offset by slate and the loos must be the smartest in London. For the cooking, think sunshine: the kitchen looks to the colours and freshness of Spain, Portugal, Italy and France for inspiration. Dishes like Sardinian fish stew or roasted double veal chop with ratatouille are packed with flavour and are eminently satisfying, while the wood-fired oven and charcoal grill add a terrific smokiness to others. Service is polished and fleet of foot.

Sake No Hana

H4 **Japanese** XXX

23 St James's St ✉ SW1A 1HA
✆ (020) 7925 8988
Fax (020) 7925 8999
e-mail reservations@sakenohana.com
www.sakenohana.com

⊖ Green Park
Closed 24-25 December and Sunday lunch

Carte £20/60

A/C VISA MC AE

As with most restaurants, things look a little different in the second year than they did when the place opened. At Sake No Hana the idea of not offering wine along with the shochu and sake lasted about six months. The menu is also now considerably shorter. It is dominated by sashimi and sushi, after which one is expected to order a grilled dish and perhaps one of their 'special plates'- which could be fried tofu with bonito flakes – then end with some miso soup. Service can be hit and miss and whilst all that cedar wood goes some way towards hiding the ugliness of this '60s building, one does get the impression that this isn't yet the finished article as the overall experience can be a little lacklustre and quite expensive.

Sartoria

H3 **Italian** XXX

20 Savile Row ✉ W1S 3PR
✆ (020) 7534 7000
Fax (020) 7534 7070
e-mail sartoriareservations@danddlondon.com
www.danddlondon.com

⊖ Green Park
Closed 25 December, Sunday, Saturday lunch and Bank Holidays

Menu £24 – Carte £29/39

A/C VISA MC AE

If you're going to have any restaurant occupying a prime site in Savile Row then it might as well be Italian as they know one or two things about tailoring themselves. Sartoria is an elegant, smartly dressed restaurant that always seems to exude a certain poise and self-assurance, along with a little charm. There are subtle allusions to tailoring in the decoration and the sofa-style seating in the middle of the room is very appealing. The à la carte menu is an extensive number and prices can quickly add up, but the cooking, which covers all parts of the country, is undertaken with care and it's apparent that the ingredients are top-notch. Service is also not lacking in confidence and is overseen by assorted suited managers.

Scott's

G3

Seafood XXX

20 Mount St ✉ W1K 2HE
(020) 7495 7309
Fax (020) 7647 6326
www.scotts-restaurant.com

Bond St
Closed 25-26 December and 1 January

Carte £41/69

Scott's is one of those rare restaurants which is both fashionable and also has a palpable sense of history. As soon as you're through the door, you'll find the aroma and the bustle an enticing draw. Purportedly Ian Fleming's favourite restaurant, it still appeals to those whose faces we recognise and everyone looks as though they've dressed up for the occasion. The wood panelling is juxtaposed with modern art and the bar forms a striking centrepiece. The menu offers an enticing and varied choice, from caviar to razor clams, oysters to spider crabs and sea bass and turbot. The fish is cooked with skill and innate understanding. If only the taciturn staff could crack the occasional smile and add some personality to their efficiency.

A/C · VISA · MC · AE

Sketch (The Gallery)

H3

International XX

9 Conduit St ✉ W1S 2XG
(020) 7659 4500
Fax (020) 7629 1683
e-mail info@sketch.uk.com
www.sketch.uk.com

Oxford Street
Closed 25-26 December, Sunday, Monday lunch and Bank Holidays – booking essential – dinner only

Carte £32/52

Art and food have been linked since bison first appeared in Palaeolithic cave drawings; The Gallery at Sketch just connects the two in more of a 21st century sort of way. During the day it's an art gallery, with regularly changing exhibitions featuring mostly video art thanks to the projectors and the huge white space. In the evening it transforms itself into a lively brasserie, with the videos still dancing around the walls. France provides the starting point for the cooking but along the way it picks up influences from Italy to Japan which seems to suit the international crowd. It doesn't come cheap but that's the price for exclusivity. For a less frenzied but even more expensive affair, head upstairs to The Lecture Room & Library.

A/C · VISA · MC · AE

Semplice ✿

Italian XX

G3

9-10 Blenheim St ✉ W1S 1LJ
✆ (020) 7495 1509
Fax (020) 7493 7074
e-mail info@ristorantesemplice.com
www.ristorantesemplice.com

⊖ Bond Street
Closed 2 weeks Christmas, 4 days Easter, Saturday lunch and Sunday – booking essential at dinner

Menu £19 (lunch) – Carte £33/38

A/C
VISA
MC
AE

Semplice

Semplice may now have an excitable baby sister just yards away but that doesn't mean the owners have taken their eye off the ball here; the two kitchen brigades are kept separate and only the bread and ice creams are shared. If anything, creating a diffusion line has allowed them to focus here more on providing their regular guests – of whom there are many – with a first rate culinary experience without being forced into being all things to all people. Using small, specialist suppliers has been the key to their success and the kitchen remains loyal to its north Italian roots. The main ingredient of each dish is allowed to shine, whether that's the scallops with picked ginger, the veal wrapped in Parma ham or the pan-fried rabbit with artichoke sauce. The Fassone carpaccio and the Milanese risotto with bone marrow are two of the dishes that keep those regulars particularly content. The set lunch menu represents exceptional value and includes a glass of wine and coffee. The gold waves and lacquered ebony panels add a hint of luxury to a room that always appears warm and welcoming.

First Course

- Fassone beef carpaccio.
- Ravioli with pheasant and thyme sauce.

Main Course

- Milk-fed veal wrapped in Parma ham with mushrooms, courgettes and tomato.
- Sea bass with spinach and chickpea purée.

Dessert

- Domori chocolate fondant.
- Grappa Poli panna cotta with pear and ginger sauce.

Sketch (The Lecture Room & Library) ✿

French XXXXX

H3

9 Conduit St, First Floor ✉ W1S 2XG
✆ (020) 7659 4500
Fax (020) 7629 1683
e-mail info@sketch.uk.com
www.sketch.uk.com

⊖ Oxford Street
Closed 25-30 December, 17-30 August, Saturday lunch, Sunday, Monday and Bank Holidays – booking essential

Menu £35/95 – Carte £64/100

A/C, VISA, MC, AE

Sketch

A new head chef, originally from Brittany, has arrived and with him has come a subtly lighter style of cooking. This works well as here, in the sumptuous surrounding of Sketch's Lecture Room and Library, as with all of Pierre Gagnaire's restaurants around the world, each dish comes sub-divided into their various components which all arrive in assorted vessels. In the past, they haven't always equated to the sum of their parts but now greater clarity means you leave feeling sated rather than physically assaulted. The menus are also less confusing: there are two tasting menus in the evening, one of which is vegetarian, and an à la carte, although the prices can still baffle as a starter may sometimes be more expensive than a main course. The service is now more organised and confident; the result of firmer management and clearer objectives. The room within this 18C townhouse remains one of London's most vivid and ornate but one that boasts a healthy lack of pomposity or unnecessary formality.

First Course

- Langoustine 'addressed in five ways'.
- 'Perfume of the earth'.

Main Course

- Fillet of Bavarian Simmental beef.
- Sea bass, mackerel, whelks and smoked duck.

Dessert

- Pierre Gagnaire's 'Grand Dessert'.
- Gâteau au chocolat.

The Square ✿✿

H3 **French** XXXX

6-10 Bruton St ✉ W1J 6PU
✆ (020) 7495 7100
Fax (020) 7495 7150
e-mail reception@squarerestaurant.com
www.squarerestaurant.com

⊖ Green Park
Closed 25 December, 1 January and lunch Saturday, Sunday and Bank Holidays

Menu £35/75

A/C
VISA
MC
AE

The Square

The Square has always engendered loyalty from its large customer base which in turn allowed it to escape the worst of the 2009 downturn. Philip Howard, one of the capital's most personable chefs, has always been a constant presence in the kitchen and it is his careful navigation that has kept the restaurant away from choppy waters. He has also clearly been a major influence on many of those talented chefs who have passed through his kitchen and who are now making names for themselves. They would have learnt the importance of clarity of flavour, of menu balance and sound technique, as well as the fundamentals of having a healthy respect and understanding of prime ingredients. Service at The Square these days displays a greater degree of warmth and personality and the front of house team are no longer exclusively French. There is also a renewed vitality to all the extra little courses and freebies that all add to the overall experience and make the final bill, however high, feel like good value.

First Course

- Langoustine with Parmesan gnocchi and truffle.
- Aubergine caviar with stuffed courgette flower.

Main Course

- Beef with red wine ravioli and smoked black pepper.
- Sea bass with squid ink macaroni, sardine and tomato.

Dessert

- Brillat-Savarin cheesecake with passion fruit and mango.
- Peach Melba soufflé.

Stanza

I3 **Modern European** XX

97-107 Shaftesbury Ave ✉ W1D 5DY ⊖ Leicester Square
✆ (020) 7494 3020
Closed Sundays and Bank Holidays
Fax (020) 7494 3050
e-mail reception@stanzalondon.com
www.stanzalondon.com

Carte £21/38

It's a tad confusing as Stanza was once called Teatro which is now the name of the private members bar. But just take the stairs up to the first floor, which is much nicer than first impressions lead you to believe, and ask for a window table facing Chinatown. The seasonal menu offers gutsy and confident modern cooking with full-on flavours, matched with friendly service. The pre/post theatre menus are the draw so don't be afraid to ask for them, although those sneaky extras can push your final bill up further that you anticipated. Time your meal right, and you could find yourself popping across to the adjoining bar for some post-prandial salsa or speed-dating – just some of the events they organise there.

Sumosan

H3 **Japanese** XX

26 Albemarle St ✉ W1S 4HY ⊖ Green Park
✆ (020) 7495 5999
Closed 25-26 and 31 December, lunch Saturday, Sunday and Bank Holidays
Fax (020) 7355 1247
e-mail info@sumosan.com
www.sumosan.com

Menu £23 (lunch) – Carte £32/59

As an unwelcome hangover from a time when all London restaurants were packed every night, you're still told more than once what time you're expected to leave before you've actually ordered anything and, for some of the staff, smiling is clearly considered far too uncool. This is a shame because Sumosan gets a lot of things right. Granted, some of the customers spend more time choosing their cocktail than their food but the kitchen does produce some interesting innovations and modern interpretations of Japanese flavours; the sushi and sashimi are particularly good and there is wide-ranging choice, from the rich duck with lingonberries to the subtle soft shell crab. If only the place could be a little less self-absorbed.

Taman Gang

Asian XX

F3

141 Park Lane ✉ W1K 7AA
✆ (020) 7518 3160
Fax (020) 7518 3161
e-mail info@tamangang.com
www.tamangang.com

⊖ Marble Arch
Closed Sunday, Monday and Bank Holidays – dinner only

Carte £25/73

As they take your coat and lead you downstairs, the number of fresh orchids you pass should alert you to the fact that they're not exactly giving it away here. You'll be led to a table in the central 'horseshoe' shape or on one of the sides; the latter are better for the romantically inclined. 'Pan-Asian' is the catch-all description of the menu. The ubiquitous black cod with miso is there – perhaps it's a legal requirement - as is 'modern' sushi, but the chefs, who are mostly Chinese and Malaysian, know their Asian flavours and ingredients are good. However, that final bill can creep up if you start ordering a number of the tempting sounding 'small plates', especially with the 15% service charge added on top.

Theo Randall

Italian XXX

G4

1 Hamilton Place, Park Lane ✉ W1J 7QY
✆ (020) 7409 3131
Fax (020) 7493 3476
e-mail london@ihg.com
www.london.intercontinental.com

⊖ Hyde Park Corner
Closed Saturday lunch, Sunday and Bank Holidays

Menu £27 (lunch and early/late dinner) – Carte £45/55

Theo Randall's profile is increasing thanks to greater media exposure and his eponymous restaurant has also bedded in well. The philosophy of the River Café, where he was head chef previously, has been drilled into his team: excellent ingredients and clear flavours. The menu is printed before each service depending on what's in season and top condition, although the scallops, veal chop and pasta cappelletti have all become regular features, as has the flourless chocolate cake. The wood oven is a preferred method of cooking. The restaurant may be in a hotel but there's always someone poised to greet you and the atmosphere in the large, contemporary room is refreshingly unceremonial; you can even just pop in for some pasta at the bar.

Tamarind ✿

G4

Indian XXX

20 Queen St ✉ W1J 5PR
✆ (020) 7629 3561
Fax (020) 7499 5034
e-mail manager@tamarindrestaurant.com
www.tamarindrestaurant.com

⊖ Green Park
Closed 25 December, 1 January and Saturday lunch

Menu £19/52 – Carte £38/63

A/C · VISA · MC · AE

Tamarind

2009 saw Tamarind reclaim its position as one of London's premier Indian restaurants. This return to form was due to the earnest and enthusiastic Alfred Prasad and his reinvigorated kitchen. Gone is the complacency that marred the previous year; now the kitchen team are focused on carefully and consistently producing high quality food. The menu is appealing and not overlong – one's principal decision is between ordering a kebab or curry as a main course. Spicing is subtle and brings out the natural flavours of the ingredients, whether that's the ground lamb in the Tulsi Seekh kebab or the simmered chicken in the Adraki Murgh. Vegetable dishes are prepared with equal care and provide interesting counterpoints to the main dishes. Tamarind has always made the best of its basement location, albeit one that's in the heart of Mayfair. The smoked mirrors, gilded columns and copper-coloured chargers give the room a sophisticated veneer, although there are times when some of that polish wouldn't go amiss with the serving team.

First Course
- Scallops with star anise and smoked peppers.
- Lamb cutlets with smoked tomato and chutney.

Main Course
- Lamb shank with spices, yoghurt and chillies.
- Monkfish, lime and green chilli kebab.

Dessert
- Grilled pineapple with rose petal ice cream.
- Chocolate mousse with cinnamon and orange zest.

Tierra Brindisa

Spanish X

H3

46 Broadwick St ✉ W1F 7AF ⊖ Tottenham Court Rd
✆ (020) 7534 1690
Fax (020) 7534 1699
e-mail office@tierrabrindisa.com
www.brindisatapaskitchens.com

Closed Sunday – booking essential at dinner

Menu £30 – Carte £21/28

VISA MC AE

For over twenty years Brindisa have been suppliers of the best Spanish produce so it was a logical decision to open a tapas bar, which they did in Borough Market back in 2004. The success of Tapas Brindisa led to this second venture, this time in the middle of Soho media-land. Tierra Brindisa is a slightly more structured affair, albeit one that is equally busy and bustling – but at least they take reservations. Again, this is all about the product which, thanks to the quality, doesn't need much doing to it – dishes are never overcrowded and flavours natural. There's a daily cazuela to satisfy the hungry and, owing to popular demand, suckling pig and shoulder of lamb come in larger sizes. Be sure to end with a Turrón mousse.

La Trouvaille

French XX

H3

12A Newburgh St ✉ W1F 7RR ⊖ Oxford Circus
✆ (020) 7287 8488
Fax (020) 7434 4170
e-mail contact@latrouvaille.co.uk
www.latrouvaille.co.uk

Closed 25 December, Saturday lunch, Sunday, Monday dinner and Bank Holidays

Menu £20/35

VISA MC AE

Newburgh Street is a charming cobbled street and La Trouville is the perfect little restaurant to find on it, but don't try the obvious corner door - the entrance is down the alley. The ground floor is a great spot for wine and charcuterie but head upstairs for 'Le Dining Room.' Decoratively it's bright and appealing, if somewhat offbeat: those clear plastic chairs catch your eye but numb your bum. The place is owned and passionately run by a couple of proud northern Frenchmen and their set menus offer French classics with the occasional modern twist: their frog's legs can come with a curry sauce; their banana bavarois with guava and tamarillo. The wines are mostly organic and curiously all come from the south.

Umu ✿

H3 **Japanese** XXX

14-16 Bruton Pl ✉ W1J 6LX
✆ (020) 7499 8881
Fax (020) 7016 5120
e-mail reception@umurestaurant.com
www.umurestaurant.com

⊖ Bond Street
Closed 24 December-7 January, Saturday lunch, Sunday and Bank Holidays

Menu £21 (lunch) – Carte £33/76

A/C · VISA · MC · AE

Umu

Whether it's the seductive lighting, the discreet location or the delicate nature of the food, Umu has always seemingly appealed to couples in the early throws of romantic entanglement, although the fact that this is also the restaurant of choice of many a corporate bigwig means there will also be equal numbers of suits in. The hostess greets arrivals with enough enthusiasm to compensate for the somewhat po-faced persona of the waiting staff, from whom guidance or advice has to sometimes be coaxed. The menu consists of three pages of parchment: the first is the do-it-yourself à la carte; page two is for 'classic' and 'modern' sushi which comes from the large counter in the centre of the room and page three describes the six seasonally-changing, multi-course kaiseki menus. Most go for the kaiseki experience, where dishes arrive in the traditional order for greater appreciation of the harmony of textures, temperatures and flavours. Around 60% of ingredients come directly from Japan, along with an impressive selection of over 160 different varieties and styles of sake.

First Course

- Sweet shrimp with sake jelly and caviar.
- Matsutake mushrooms with chicken and eel.

Main Course

- Grilled skill fish teriyaki, citrus flavoured radish and wasabi.
- Tiger prawn tempura, pepper and lotus root.

Dessert

- Chocolate fondant with white miso ice cream.
- Kyoto sundae.

Vasco and Piero's Pavilion

Italian XX

H2–3

15 Poland St ✉ W1F 8QE
(020) 7437 8774
Fax (020) 7437 0467
e-mail eat@vascosfood.com
www.vascosfood.com

⊖ Tottenham Court Road
Closed Saturday lunch, Sunday and Bank Holidays – booking essential at lunch

Menu £32 (dinner) – Carte lunch £27/38

A/C VISA MC AE

Those who think that Soho is changing too quickly and is beginning to lose its personality can take heart with the continuing presence of Vasco and Piero's Pavilion, which has been in Poland Street since 1989, having first opened in Oxford Street in the 1970s. The menu still changes twice a day and much of the meat, cheese, vegetables and truffles come from small, family producers back in Umbria. Specialities from the region also include guinea fowl and cured pork, while the home-made pastas are an obvious strength. Dishes come with an appetising simplicity that has been perfected over the years and, for this, the restaurant is rewarded with a very loyal clientele, many of whom don't even need to look at a menu.

Veeraswamy

Indian XX

H3

Victory House, 99 Regent St
(entrance on Swallow St) ✉ W1B 4RS
(020) 7734 1401
Fax (020) 7439 8434
e-mail veeraswamy@realindianfood.com
www.realindianfood.com

⊖ Piccadilly Circus
Closed dinner 25 December

A/C

Menu £21 (lunch) – Carte £32/44

VISA MC AE

The manager here knows not to come between a regular and their favourite table: some were first brought here by their grandparents and are now, in turn, introducing their own grandchildren to London's oldest surviving Indian restaurant, which dates from 1926. You'd be excused for thinking it might be a tad old-fashioned but Veeraswamy is anything but: it is awash with vibrant colours and always full of bustle. The Hyderabad lamb biryani may have been on the original menu but there are plenty of other dishes with a more contemporary edge. The meaty Madagascar prawns are a good way of kicking things off; slow-cooked lamb dishes are also done very well. There's a tasting menu available and desserts, prepared with a flourish, shouldn't be ignored.

Via Condotti

H3 — **Italian**

23 Conduit St ✉ W1S 2XS
(020) 7493 7050
Fax (020) 7409 7985
e-mail info@viacondotti.co.uk
www.viacondotti.co.uk

⊖ Oxford Circus
Closed Christmas, New Year, Sunday and Bank Holidays

Menu £28 – Carte £25/39

Claudio Pulze is one of London's most successful restaurateurs and if anyone wonders why, then a trip to Via Condotti will go some way to explaining. For starters, the kitchen knows what's seasonal and at its best throughout the year so the menu changes often; prices are also pragmatic and represent good value considering the quality of cooking. It also manages to feel like a neighbourhood restaurant – no mean feat when you consider that Conduit Street, just like its eponymous namesake in Rome, has enough exclusive boutiques to satisfy both the haves and the have-yachts. Pasta dishes are a real strength of the kitchen and the kitchen has a nice light touch. The best spot to sit is at the back, next to the Arlecchino pictures.

The Wolseley

H4 — **Modern European**

160 Piccadilly ✉ W1J 9EB
(020) 7499 6996
Fax (020) 7499 6888
e-mail reservations@thewolseley.com
www.thewolseley.com

⊖ Green Park
Closed 25 December, 1 January, August Bank Holiday and dinner 24 and 31 December – booking essential

Carte £21/47

Opened back in 2003, The Wolseley did not take long to earn iconic status, thanks to its stylish décor, celebrity following and smooth service. Its owners, Chris Corbin and Jeremy King, created a restaurant in the style of a grand European café, all pillars, arches and marble. Open from breakfast until late, the flexible menu offers everything from Austrian and French classics to British staples, so the daily special could be coq au vin or Lancashire hot pot. Pastries come from the Viennoiserie and lunch merges into Afternoon tea. So, one table could be tucking into Beluga caviar or a dozen oysters while their neighbours enjoy a salt beef sandwich or eggs Benedict. The large clock reminds you that there are probably others waiting for your table.

Wild Honey ✿

Modern European XX

H3

12 St George St ✉ W1S 2FB
⊖ Oxford Circus
✆ (020) 7758 9160
Closed 25-26 December and 1 January
Fax (020) 7493 4549
e-mail info@wildhoneyrestaurant.co.uk
www.wildhoneyrestaurant.co.uk

Menu £19 (lunch) – Carte £29/39 s

Michelin

A wood-panelled, former private members club in Mayfair's heartland suggests perhaps somewhere on the crusty side, with school food and high prices but, in the case of Wild Honey, that couldn't be further from the truth. This is all about relaxed but comfortable dining, where the highly skilled cooking is a model of resourcefulness and the prices – when one considers the postcode and the quality of the food – are laudable. The kitchen also proves that good food means good ingredients, but not necessarily expensive ones. The menus are hugely appealing and those seasonal ingredients are used at their peak; plates are never overcrowded and each component serves a purpose - there is nothing ostentatious here. Like watching a talented sportsman, a lot of hard work and experience goes into making it seem so easy. The bouillabaisse and the wild honey ice cream are constants and the wine list is equally magnanimous in its prices, with all bottles also available by the carafe. To cap it all, service is personable and unobtrusive.

First Course

- Rabbit and foie gras boudin blanc with peas.
- Smoked eel with chicken wings and sweetcorn.

Main Course

- Cod with potato gnocchi and sea purslane.
- Belly pork with girolles and broad beans.

Dessert

- Cherry clafoutis with almond sorbet.
- Vanilla cheesecake with raspberries.

Yauatcha ✿

13 **Chinese** XX

15 Broadwick St ✉ W1F 0DL
✆ (020) 7494 8888
Fax (020) 7287 6959
e-mail mail@yauatcha.com
www.yauatcha.com

⊖ Tottenham Court Road
Closed 24-25 December

Carte £21/67

A/C · VISA · MC · AE

Yauatcha

China and Britain: two countries inexorably linked through tea. If you want to see what this looks like in practice, then go along one afternoon to Yauatcha and witness a British institution given an Asian twist. The cakes, tarts and pastries are good too, although for that we have to thank a French pastry chef - and that's a whole different story. There is nowhere quite like Yauatcha: a dim sum restaurant that's so successful, where the food is so good and the surroundings so slick and stylish, that customers find it hard to be in and out in the allocated 1hr 45minutes. The trick is to spend time eating and chatting, rather than ordering so crack on with that bit. Around three dim sum per person followed by some sharing of noodles or a stir-fry should do the trick and, while you wait for it to arrive, have one of their terrific cocktails. Stand-out dishes are the Scallop Shumai, the Prawn Cheung Fun, the baked Venison Puff and the Kung Po Chicken; but don't ignore dessert, especially the roasted pineapple with praline parfait.

First Course

- King crab dumpling.
- Baked venison puff.

Main Course

- Crispy duck with Thai spring onion and cucumber.
- Chilli soft shell crab with almond.

Dessert

- Roasted pineapple with praline parfait and ice cream.
- Pear millefeuille with smoked cream.

Strand · Covent Garden

It's fitting that Manet's world famous painting 'Bar at the Folies Bergère' should hang in the **Strand** within a champagne cork's throw of theatreland and Covent Garden. This is the area perhaps more than any other which draws in the ticket-buying tourist, eager to grab a good deal on one of the many shows on offer, or eat and drink at fabled shrines like J.Sheekey or Rules. It's here the names already up in lights shine down on their potential usurpers: celeb wannabes heading for The Ivy, West Street's perennially fashionable restaurant. It's here, too, that Nell Gwyn set up home under the patronage of Charles II, while Oscar Wilde revelled in his success by taking rooms at the Savoy.

The hub of the whole area is the piazza at **Covent Garden,** created by Inigo Jones four hundred years ago. It was given a brash new lease of life in the 1980s after its famed fruit and veg market was pulled up by the roots and re-sown in Battersea. Council bigwigs realised then that 'what we have we hold', and any further redevelopment of the area is banned. Where everyone heads is the impressive covered market, within which a colourful jumble of arts and crafts shops gels with al fresco cafés and classical performers proffering Paganini with your cappuccino. Outside, under the portico of St Paul's church, every type of street performer does a turn for the tourist trade. The best shops in Covent Garden, though, are a few streets north of the market melee, emanating out like bicycle spokes from Seven Dials.

For those after a more highbrow experience, one of London's best attractions is a hop, skip and *grand jeté* from the market. Around the corner in **Bow Street** is the city's famed home for opera and ballet, where fire – as well as show-stopping performances – has been known to bring the house down. The **Royal Opera House** is now in its third incarnation, and it gets more impressive with each rebuild. The handsome, glass-roofed Floral Hall is a must-see, while an interval drink at the Amphitheatre Café Bar, overlooking the piazza, is de rigeur for show goers. At the other end of the Strand the **London Coliseum** offers more opera, this time all performed in English. Down by Waterloo Bridge, art lovers are strongly advised to stop at **Somerset House** and take in one of London's most sublime collections of art at the Courtauld Gallery. This is where you can get up close and personal to Manet's barmaid, as well as an astonishing array of Impressionist masters and twentieth century greats. The icing on the cake is the compact and accessible eighteenth century building that houses the collection: real icing on a real cake can be found in a super little hidden-away café downstairs.

Of a different order altogether is the huge **National Gallery** at

Trafalgar Square which houses more than two thousand Western European pieces (it started off with 38). A visit to the modern Sainsbury Wing is rewarded with some unmissable works from the Renaissance. It can get just as crowded in the capital's largest Gallery as in the square outside, so a good idea is to wander down **Villiers Street** next to Charing Cross station and breathe the Thames air along the Victoria Embankment. Behind you is the grand Savoy Hotel, which reopens in 2009 after major refurbishment; for a better view of it, you can head even further away from the crowds on a boat trip from the **Embankment,** complete with on-board entertainment. And if the glory of travel in the capital, albeit on the water, has whetted your appetite for more, then pop into the impressively renovated Transport Museum in Covent Garden piazza, where gloriously preserved tubes, buses and trains from the past put you in a positive frame of mind for the real live working version you'll very probably be tackling later in the day.

AGE / PHOTONONSTOP

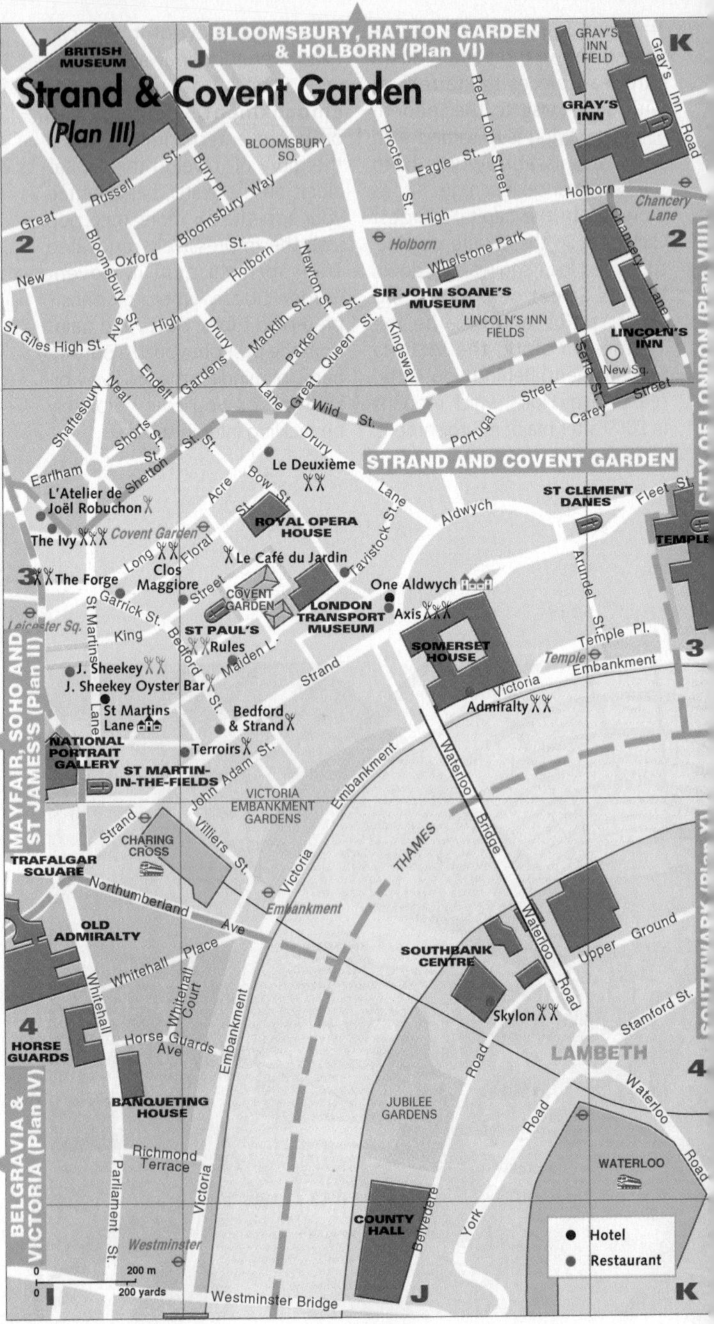
Strand & Covent Garden
(Plan III)
BLOOMSBURY, HATTON GARDEN & HOLBORN (Plan VI)
STRAND AND COVENT GARDEN
MAYFAIR, SOHO AND ST JAMES'S (Plan II)
BELGRAVIA & VICTORIA (Plan IV)
BRITISH MUSEUM
BLOOMSBURY SQ.
GRAY'S INN FIELD
GRAY'S INN
SIR JOHN SOANE'S MUSEUM
LINCOLN'S INN FIELDS
LINCOLN'S INN
Le Deuxième
L'Atelier de Joël Robuchon
The Ivy
Clos Maggiore
The Forge
ROYAL OPERA HOUSE
Le Café du Jardin
COVENT GARDEN
LONDON TRANSPORT MUSEUM
ST PAUL'S
Rules
One Aldwych
Axis
SOMERSET HOUSE
ST CLEMENT DANES
TEMPLE
J. Sheekey
J. Sheekey Oyster Bar
St Martins Lane
Bedford & Strand
Terroirs
Admiralty
NATIONAL PORTRAIT GALLERY
ST MARTIN-IN-THE-FIELDS
VICTORIA EMBANKMENT GARDENS
CHARING CROSS
TRAFALGAR SQUARE
OLD ADMIRALTY
HORSE GUARDS
BANQUETING HOUSE
SOUTHBANK CENTRE
Skylon
LAMBETH
JUBILEE GARDENS
WATERLOO
COUNTY HALL
THAMES
Hotel
Restaurant
200 m
200 yards

Admiralty

J3 **French** XX

Somerset House,
The Strand ✉ WC2R 1LA
✆ (020) 7845 4646
Fax (020) 7845 4658
e-mail info@theadmiraltyrestaurant.com
www.theadmiraltyrestaurant.com

⊖ Temple
Closed Sunday – booking essential

Carte £23/33

VISA MC AE

Skate through to the south building of the magnificent 18C Somerset House and enter through the door marked 'Navy Office' to find The Admiralty restaurant – but book first because this isn't such a well-kept secret anymore and it often plays host to corporate dos. Shipshape chandeliers and aquamarine colours add to the nautical theme, although it's a pity the riverside terrace is a separate operation. The kitchen focuses on France but adds a contemporary edge; there are nods towards the Mediterranean and vegetarians are thoughtfully considered. Lunch combines the à la carte with a no-choice 3 courser; dinner sees a good value set menu and a mood that's a little gentler because "at the Admiralty…love levels all ranks".

Axis

J3 **British** XXX

1 Aldwych ✉ WC2B 4RH
✆ (020) 7300 0300
Fax (020) 7300 0301
e-mail axis@onealdwych.com
www.onealdwych.com

⊖ Temple
Closed Easter weekend, Christmas, Saturday lunch, Sunday and Bank Holidays

Menu £20 (lunch) – Carte £30/39

A/C VISA MC AE

Larger parties don't dominate the room as they once did as the restaurant now has slightly fewer tables and the last makeover, when they added some soft green fabrics on the walls and a bamboo-effect façade to the enormous futuristic mural, has lightened the mood a little. Anticipation is still heightened by the spiral marble staircase leading down to the restaurant, which must have one of the highest ceilings in London. The menu is more British than ever and greater emphasis is placed on provenance: you may find Lincolnshire rabbit, Herdwick lamb or Loch Duart salmon on the menu. The Grill section remains and there are also dishes for two, such as Rump of veal or Tarte Tatin. It's part of One Aldwych Hotel, although you wouldn't know it.

L'Atelier de Joël Robuchon ✿✿

French

13

13-15 West St ✉ WC2H 9NE
⊖ Leicester Square
✆ (020) 7010 8600
Fax (020) 7010 8601
e-mail info@joelrobuchon.co.uk
www.joel-robuchon.com

Menu £25 – Carte £34/81

A/C
VISA
AE

L'Atelier de Joel Robuchon

London's L'Atelier de Joël Robuchon differs from his other 'branches' dotted around the world's culinary hotspots by being two restaurants under one roof: on the ground floor is L'Atelier itself, with an open kitchen and large counter; upstairs is the monochrome La Cuisine, a slightly more structured, sleek and more brightly-lit affair with table seating. Apart from a few wood-fired dishes upstairs, the menus are largely similar. The cooking is artistic, creative and occasionally playful; it is technically very accomplished and highly labour intensive – there are over thirty chefs in the building – but it is never overworked and each dish is perfectly balanced, its flavours true and its taste exquisite. French is the predominant influence, supported by other Mediterranean flavours, and ordering a number of smaller dishes is the best way to fully appreciate Robuchon's craft and vision, although your final bill can be pretty lofty. Service is expertly timed and confident and sitting at the counter will give you some insight into this most polished of operations.

First Course

- Langoustine fritter with basil sauce.
- Poached foie gras, red wine jelly and beetroot tartare.

Main Course

- Quail stuffed with foie gras, truffle mash.
- John Dory with artichokes and onions.

Dessert

- Araguani chocolate with white chocolate ice cream.
- White peach with lemon grass and meringue.

Bedford & Strand

J3 **British**

1a Bedford St ✉ WC2E 9HH
✆ (020) 7836 3033
e-mail hello@bedford-strand.com
www.bedford-strand.com

⊖ Charing Cross
Closed 25 December-1 January, Saturday lunch, Sunday and Bank Holidays – booking essential

Carte £22/32

VISA MC AE

They call themselves a 'wine room and bistro' which neatly sums up both the philosophy and the style of the place - interesting wines, reassuringly familiar food and relaxed surroundings. It's named, American-style, after the cross streets so it's easy to find and the basement location shouldn't be off-putting. The after-work crowd have largely dispersed by 8ish in the evening but it all remains fairly energetic, helped along by a bright and sprightly team. British and Mediterranean comfort food is the mainstay of the menu, with a choice ranging from fish soup and risotto to cottage pie, with classic deli food served at the bar. The wine list has been thoughtfully put together and comes accompanied by some sensible pricing.

Le Café du Jardin

J3 **Mediterranean**

28 Wellington St ✉ WC2E 7BD
✆ (020) 7836 8769
Fax (020) 7836 4123
e-mail info@lecafedujardin.com
www.lecafedujardin.com

⊖ Covent Garden
Closed 25-26 December

A/C

Menu £17 (lunch) – Carte £27/33

VISA MC AE

The advantage of a theatre-land restaurant is that you'll be offered a good value set price menu and be guaranteed to be in your seat in time for curtain-up. Le Café du Jardin fulfils these duties admirably, with a weekly changing set menu with plenty of choice and staff whose commitment cannot be faulted, especially considering last orders are taken up to midnight. The downside is that the service can take time to change gear and those in for a more leisurely meal later in the evening could find themselves nursing their coffees sooner than they expect. Cooking is sunny and Mediterranean in influence, with plenty of pastas and grilled meats and fish. The ground floor is where the bustle is; downstairs is calmer and cooler in summer.

Clos Maggiore

IJ3 **French** XX

33 King St ✉ WC2E 8JD ⊖ Leicester Square
✆ (020) 7379 9696
Fax (020) 7379 6767
e-mail enquiries@closmaggiore.com
www.closmaggiore.com

Menu £20 (lunch) – Carte £30/43

Exceptional value lunch and pre-theatre (up to 6.30pm) menus ensure that Clos Maggiore is never anything other than very busy. Despite its touristy location, this is not a restaurant merely pandering to a transient trade but one with a surprisingly neighbourly feel and plenty of regulars. The cooking shows flair and ambition, with its roots firmly within France; the set menus show off the kitchen's shrewd purchasing and imagination. Meanwhile, the extensive à la carte allows the chef free rein and his dishes are creative, neat and balanced; the wine list is also a serious volume. The best seats are at the back in the conservatory; the roof opens in summer. Service is structured and quite formal but also comes with personality.

Le Deuxième

J3 **Modern European** XX

65a Long Acre ✉ WC2E 9JH ⊖ Covent Garden
✆ (020) 7379 0033 Closed 25-26 December
Fax (020) 7379 0066
e-mail info@ledeuxieme.com
www.ledeuxieme.com

Menu £17 (lunch) – Carte £30/32

Depending on which direction you've come from, this is either the first, or the last, restaurant in Covent Garden. Either way, it's a world away from the plethora of tourist joints which cover the surrounding streets. For a start, the service is enthusiastic, while the room has a warmth and an unthreatening neutrality. The cooking is also above this neighbourhood's norm. Lunch and pre-theatre menus are a steal and come with sufficient choice while the à la carte offers a balanced and comprehensive choice. Whilst there may be the occasional Asian note, the thrust remains within Europe, with a Franco-Italian emphasis so expect risotto, gnocchi, foie gras and lemon tart. It shares the same owners as Le Café du Jardin.

The Forge

13 **Modern European** XX

14 Garrick Street ✉ WC2E 9BJ ⊖ Leicester Square
✆ (020) 7379 1432 Closed 24 to 26 December
Fax (020) 7379 1530
e-mail info@theforgerestaurant.co.uk
www.theforgerestaurant.co.uk

Menu £17 (lunch) – Carte £29/38

A/C

The owners appear to have Covent Garden sewn up as this is their third venture in the neighbourhood, after Le Café du Jardin and Le Deuxième. However, restaurant genealogists will recognise the place as Inigo Jones, whose star sparkled in the late '70s. The Forge has clearly looked more towards local stalwarts like The Ivy for inspiration: the menu is a long A3 affair, offering everything from eggs Benedict and plates of pasta to foie gras or Dover sole. The lunch and pre/post theatre menus are competitively priced. Apart from the odd Asian flavour, most influences are kept within the Med but there's also an eagerness to use seasonal British produce. It's a large, open room with a downstairs bar and last orders are taken at midnight.

VISA MC AE

The Ivy

13 **International** XXX

1-5 West St ✉ WC2H 9NQ ⊖ Leicester Square
✆ (020) 7836 4751 Closed 24-26 December and 1 January
www.the-ivy.co.uk

A/C

Carte £32/51

The members-only Ivy Club may have siphoned off the top tier of regulars but The Ivy restaurant continues to attract new blood. It's still the sort of restaurant where everyone looks up from their food to see who's just arrived but nowadays that's just as likely to be a reality TV contestant as a theatrical knight. Getting a table remains a challenge; try calling on the day – if they offer the bar, accept, because you may get bumped up into the restaurant. But the great thing about The Ivy is that it's impossible not to find the menu appealing: perfectly gratinated shepherd's pie, plump fishcakes, eggs Benedict, nursery puddings – they're all here and all done well. Staff earn their crust by frequently but discreetly re-laying the tables.

VISA MC AE

J. Sheekey

13 **Seafood** XX

28-32 St Martin's Court ✉ WC2 4AL
(020) 7240 2565
Fax (020) 7497 0891
e-mail reservations@j-sheekey.co.uk
www.j-sheekey.co.uk

⊖ Leicester Square
Closed 25-26 December and 1 January – booking essential

Menu £26 (weekend lunch) – Carte £30/55

When one thinks of fashionable restaurants one usually thinks of the glossy and the new but J. Sheekey has been doing its thing since 1896 and its sense of Englishness and links to the theatre still draw a crowd. It helps that they also do fish and seafood rather well, by keeping it all simple. The reassuring sight of potted shrimps, fruits de mer, fishcakes, fish pies and Dover Sole all feature and can be followed by uncomplicated fruit tarts or chocolate puddings so you leave feeling immeasurably satisfied, although a little lighter in the wallet. There are five sections and if you're a regular or your name's been up in lights, then you'll be given a choice of table. Those tables are quite compact but that just adds to the bonhomie.

J. Sheekey Oyster Bar

13 **Seafood** X

28-32 St Martin's Court ✉ WC2 4AL
(020) 7240 2565
Fax (020) 7497 0891
e-mail reservation@j-sheeky.co.uk
www.j-sheeky.co.uk

⊖ Leicester Square
Closed 25-26 December and 1 January

Carte £26/32

The frustrating thing about many restaurants is that their perennial popularity scuppers the chances of a spontaneous visit resulting in a table. The good people at J.Sheekey have sought to remedy this by thoughtfully knocking through into what was Tom's Bookshop next door and creating this accessible little addendum. You'll find the same classic recipes and appetisingly fresh seafood as the main restaurant - they've just shaved off a little of the portion size and, in turn, lopped off a few quid. The fish pie remains the crowd pleaser but it's hard to ignore the fruits de mer if there are two of you. It's open all day and decorated with Alison Jackson photos; sit at the bar and wonder how they managed to make it feel as though it's been here for ever.

Rules

J3 — British XX

35 Maiden Lane ✉ WC2E 7LB — ⊖ Leicester Square

✆ (020) 7836 5314

Fax (020) 7497 1081

e-mail info@rules.co.uk

www.rules.co.uk

Closed 4 days Christmas – booking essential

A/C **Carte £30/47**

Some restaurants don't even last 1798 days; Rules opened in 1798, at a time when the French were still revolting, and has been a bastion of Britishness ever since. Virtually every inch of wall is covered with a cartoon or painting and everyone from Charles Dickens to Buster Keaton has passed through its doors. The first floor is now a bar; time it right and you'll spot some modern-day theatrical luminaries who use it as a Green Room. The hardest decision is whether to choose the game, which comes from their own estate in the Pennines, or one of their celebrated homemade pies. Be sure to leave room for their proper puddings, which come with lashings of custard - no wonder John Bull was such a stout fellow. It makes you proud.

VISA MC AE

Terroirs

J3 — French X

5 William IV St ✉ WC2N 4DW — ⊖ Charing Cross

✆ (020) 7036 0660

e-mail enquiries@terroirswinebar.com

www.terroirswinebar.com

Carte £22/28

There can be a lack of cohesion in the service and if you haven't booked you may have to queue, but when food this good is priced so well and it's all done in such a fun atmosphere, then who's complaining? The style is somewhere between a wine bar and bistro and the look is 'flea market chic'. The chef is a Francophile foodie and he had the Parisian bistros in mind when creating this, but he also adds Italian or Spanish flavours. You can come in for just a one-plate meal but then you'll have to fight temptation: Boquerones will get the tastebuds going; sweet, aromatic charcuterie comes on boards, succulent bavette arrives in a hot pan and the crêpes with salted caramel provide a great finish. Equal thought has gone into the wine list and its prices.

VISA MC AE

Belgravia · Victoria

The well-worn cliché 'an area of contrasts' certainly applies to these ill-matched neighbours. To the west, Belgravia equates to fashionable status and elegant, residential calm; to the east, Victoria is a chaotic jumble of backpackers, milling commuters and cheap-and-not-always-so-cheerful hotels. At first sight, you might think there's little to no common ground, but the umbilical cord that unites them is, strange to say, diplomacy and politics. Belgravia's embassies are dotted all around the environs of **Belgrave Square,** while at the furthest end of bustling Victoria Street stands **Parliament Square.**

Belgravia – named after 'beautiful grove' in French - was developed during the nineteenth century by Richard Grosvenor, the second Marquess of Westminster, who employed top architect Thomas Cubitt to come up with something rather fetching for the upper echelons of society. The grandeur of the classical designs has survived for the best part of two centuries, evident in the broad streets and elegant squares, where the rich rub shoulders with the uber-rich beneath the stylish balconies of a consulate or outside a high-end antiques emporium. You can still sample an atmosphere of the village it once was, as long as your idea of a village includes exclusive designer boutiques and even more exclusive mews cottages.

By any stretch of the imagination you'd have trouble thinking of **Victoria** as a village. Its local railway station is one of London's major hubs and its bus station brings in visitors from not only all corners of Britain, but Europe too. Its main 'church', concealed behind office blocks, could hardly be described as humble, either: **Westminster Cathedral** is a grand concoction based on Istanbul's Hagia Sophia, with a view from the top of the bell tower which is breathtaking. From there you can pick out other hidden charms of the area: the dramatic headquarters of Channel 4 TV, the revolving sign famously leading into New Scotland Yard, and the neat little Christchurch Gardens, burial site of Colonel Blood, last man to try and steal the Crown Jewels. Slightly easier for the eye to locate are the grand designs of **Westminster Abbey,** crowning glory and resting place of most of England's kings and queens, and the neo-gothic pile of the **Houses of Parliament.** Victoria may be an eclectic mix of people and architectural styles, but its handy position as a kind of epicentre of the Westminster Village makes it a great place for political chit-chat. And the place to go for that is The Speaker, a pub in Great Peter Street, named after the Commons' centuries-old peacekeeper and 'referee'. It's a backstreet gem, where it's not unknown for a big cheese from the House to be filmed over a pint.

Winston Churchill is someone who would have been quite at home holding forth at The Speaker, and half a mile away in King Charles Street, based within the **Cabinet War Rooms** – the secret underground HQ of the war effort - is the Churchill Museum, stuffed full of all things Churchillian. However, if your passion is more the easel and the brush, then head down to the river where another great institution of the area, **Tate Britain,** gazes out over the Thames. Standing where the grizzly Millbank Penitentiary once festered, it offers, after the National Gallery, the best collection of historical art in London. There's loads of space for the likes of Turner and Constable, while Hogarth, Gainsborough and Blake are well represented, too. Artists from the modern era are also here, with Freud and Hockney on show, and there are regular installations showcasing upwardly mobile British talent. All of which may give you the taste for a trip east along the river to Tate Modern. This can be done every twenty minutes courtesy of the Tate-to-Tate boat service, which handily stops en-route at the London Eye, and, even more handily, sports eye-catching Damien Hirst décor and a cool, shiny bar.

visitlondon.com / MICHELIN

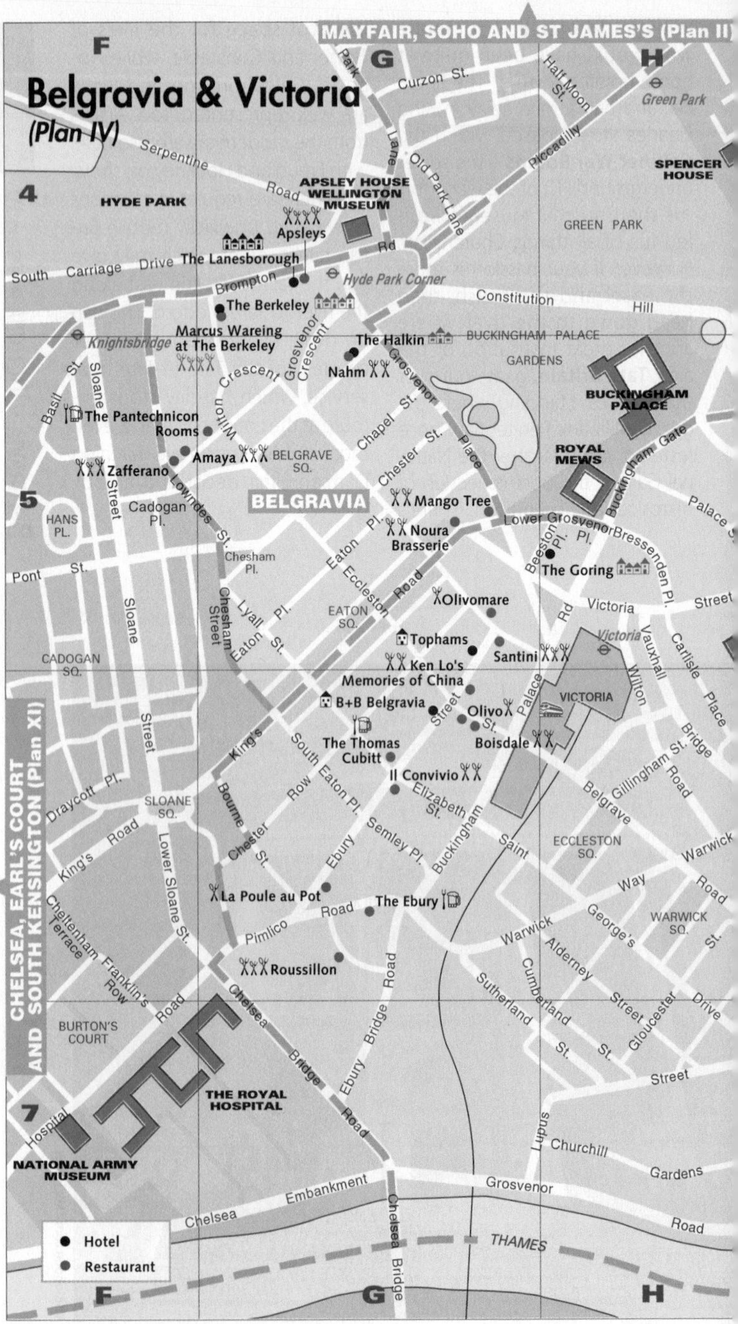
Belgravia & Victoria
(Plan IV)
MAYFAIR, SOHO AND ST JAMES'S (Plan II)
CHELSEA, EARL'S COURT AND SOUTH KENSINGTON (Plan XI)
HYDE PARK
APSLEY HOUSE WELLINGTON MUSEUM
Apsleys
The Lanesborough
The Berkeley
Marcus Wareing at The Berkeley
The Halkin
Nahm
The Pantechnicon Rooms
Amaya
Zafferano
BELGRAVE SQ.
BELGRAVIA
Mango Tree
Noura Brasserie
The Goring
Olivomare
Tophams
Santini
Ken Lo's Memories of China
B+B Belgravia
Olivo
The Thomas Cubitt
Boisdale
Il Convivio
La Poule au Pot
The Ebury
Roussillon
GREEN PARK
SPENCER HOUSE
Green Park
Hyde Park Corner
Knightsbridge
BUCKINGHAM PALACE GARDENS
BUCKINGHAM PALACE
ROYAL MEWS
VICTORIA
Victoria
HANS PL.
CADOGAN SQ.
Cadogan Pl.
Chesham Pl.
EATON SQ.
SLOANE SQ.
ECCLESTON SQ.
WARWICK SQ.
BURTON'S COURT
THE ROYAL HOSPITAL
NATIONAL ARMY MUSEUM
THAMES
Curzon St.
Half Moon St.
Piccadilly
Park Lane
Old Park Lane
Serpentine Road
South Carriage Drive
Brompton Rd
Constitution Hill
Grosvenor Crescent
Grosvenor Place
Wilton Crescent
Chapel St.
Chester St.
Basil St.
Sloane Street
Lowndes St.
Pont St.
Eaton Pl.
Eccleston St.
Lower Grosvenor Pl.
Beeston Pl.
Bressenden Pl.
Buckingham Gate
Palace St.
Victoria Street
Vauxhall Bridge Road
Carlisle Place
Wilton Rd
Buckingham Palace Rd
Lyall St.
Eaton Pl.
Chesham Street
King's Road
South Eaton Pl.
Ebury Street
Elizabeth St.
Semley Pl.
Buckingham Palace Rd
Gillingham St.
Belgrave Road
Warwick Way
Saint George's Drive
Draycott Pl.
Bourne St.
Chester Row
Lower Sloane St.
Pimlico Road
Cheltenham Terrace
Franklin's Row
Chelsea Bridge Road
Ebury Bridge Road
Warwick Sq.
Alderney Street
Cumberland St.
Sutherland St.
Gloucester St.
Lupus St.
Churchill Gardens
Hospital Road
Chelsea Embankment
Grosvenor Road
Chelsea Bridge
Hotel
Restaurant
F
G
H
4
5
7

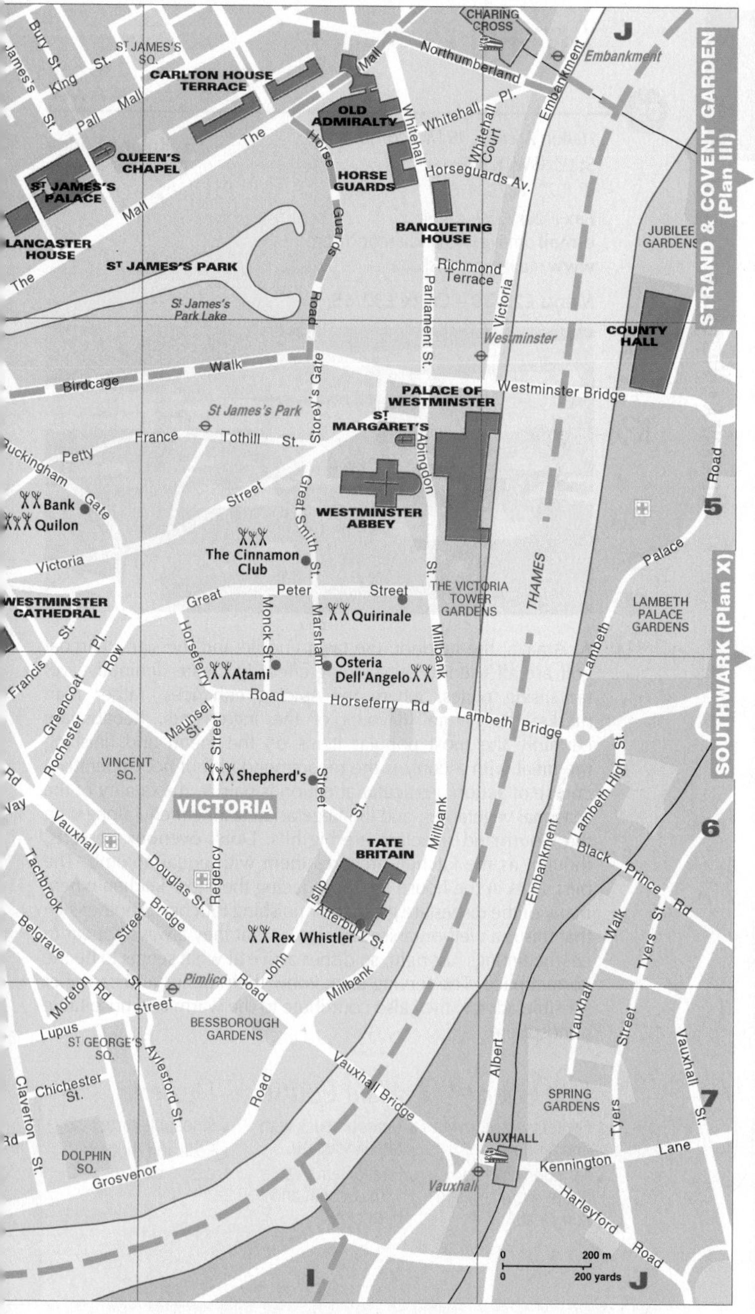
CHARING CROSS
Embankment
STRAND & COVENT GARDEN (Plan III)
ST JAMES'S SQ.
CARLTON HOUSE TERRACE
OLD ADMIRALTY
QUEEN'S CHAPEL
ST JAMES'S PALACE
HORSE GUARDS
BANQUETING HOUSE
LANCASTER HOUSE
ST JAMES'S PARK
St James's Park Lake
JUBILEE GARDENS
COUNTY HALL
Westminster
PALACE OF WESTMINSTER
St James's Park
ST MARGARET'S
WESTMINSTER ABBEY
Bank
Quilon
The Cinnamon Club
WESTMINSTER CATHEDRAL
THE VICTORIA TOWER GARDENS
THAMES
Quirinale
LAMBETH PALACE GARDENS
SOUTHWARK (Plan X)
Atami
Osteria Dell'Angelo
Shepherd's
VINCENT SQ.
VICTORIA
TATE BRITAIN
Rex Whistler
Pimlico
BESSBOROUGH GARDENS
ST GEORGE'S SQ.
DOLPHIN SQ.
SPRING GARDENS
VAUXHALL
Vauxhall
Bury St
King St.
Pall Mall
The Mall
Horse Guards Road
Northumberland
Whitehall Pl.
Whitehall
Whitehall Court
Horseguards Av.
Richmond Terrace
Parliament St.
Victoria Embankment
Birdcage Walk
Storey's Gate
Westminster Bridge
Tothill St.
Petty France
Buckingham Gate
Great Smith St.
Abingdon St.
Victoria Street
Great Peter Street
Marsham Street
Monck St.
Horseferry Road
Millbank
Lambeth Bridge
Lambeth Palace Road
Lambeth High St.
Francis St.
Greencoat Pl.
Rochester Row
Maunsel St.
Regency Street
Vauxhall Bridge Road
Douglas St.
Tachbrook Street
Belgrave Road
Bridge St.
John Islip St.
Atterbury St.
Black Prince Rd
Albert Embankment
Vauxhall Walk
Tyers St.
Vauxhall Street
Moreton St.
Lupus Street
Aylesford St.
Chichester St.
Claverton St.
Grosvenor Road
Vauxhall Bridge
Kennington Lane
Harleyford Road
I
J
5
6
7
0
200 m
200 yards

Amaya ✿

F5 **Indian** XXX

Halkin Arcade, 19 Motcomb St ✉ SW1X 8JT
✆ (020) 7823 1166
Fax (020) 7259 6464
e-mail amaya@realindianfood.com
www.realindianfood.com

⊖ Knightsbridge
Closed 25 December

Menu £25/39 – Carte £32/65

A/C VISA MC AE

At Amaya, the tandoor, the tawa griddle and the sigri charcoal grill are all used to outstanding effect to create diminutive yet tantalising plates, where the spicing enhances, rather than masks, the natural flavours of the ingredients. Kebabs are certainly the most popular items on the menu and finishing the meal with a curry is the recommended (but not imperative) course of action. Particular attention is paid to the quality of the seasonal vegetables, and the Vegetarian tasting menu along with the Gourmand selection are big hits. Don't overlook desserts, though, as the kitchen prepares them with equal aplomb. The best seats in the house are those facing the show kitchen where many of the dishes are given their finishing touches. Another sign that this is a well-organised kitchen is that they always appear to get the timings just right, so dishes arrive at what seems to be the correct pace. The serving team know their menus and can offer sensible advice; they also contribute to the warm and hospitable atmosphere.

First Course

- Oysters with coconut and ginger.
- Tandoori chicken chops with chilli and curry leaf.

Main Course

- Tandoori duck with tamarind glaze.
- Fillet of lemon sole with coconut and herb crust.

Dessert

- Pineapple tarte tatin.
- Rose and rhubarb crème brûlée.

Apsleys ✿

G4 Italian XXXX

Hyde Park Corner ✉ SW1X 7TA ⊖ Hyde Park Corner
✆ (020) 7259 5599
Fax (020) 7333 7255
e-mail apsley@lanesborough.com
www.apsleys.co.uk

Menu £26 (lunch) – Carte £47/74

A/C · VISA · MC · AE

The Lanesborough

If at first you don't succeed…In 2008 a £2million refit and new look courtesy of New York based designer Adam Tihany created a striking setting that the food, at the time, failed to match. The hotel then went to Heinz Beck for help and, as a result, Apsleys has found the perfect marriage of elegant surroundings and ambitious cuisine. Beck is a German-born chef responsible for some pretty fine Italian cooking in his restaurant La Pergola in Rome and it is one of his acolytes who has taken over the kitchens here. Those who think Italian can only be of the rustic, thrown-together variety might be disappointed because here each dish is carefully executed and artfully presented. The majority of the produce is directly imported from Italy and those dishes marked out as being Heinz Beck's signature dishes, such as the roasted pigeon or the carbonara fagottelli, are certainly the stars of the show. The serving team are a smooth and well-versed bunch and, although the room is grand and quite formal in style, the atmosphere is largely spirited.

First Course
- Sea bass with cannolo, celery and melon.
- Carbonara fagotelli.

Main Course
- Roast pigeon with pearl onions and a mustard seed sauce.
- Olive-crusted turbot with vegetable caponata.

Dessert
- Crunchy chocolate dome with salted pine nut ice cream.
- Pear cake with amaretto and cinnamon ice cream.

Atami

Japanese XX

I6

37 Monck St (entrance on Great Peter St) ✉ SW1P 2BL
✆ (020) 7222 2218
Fax (020) 7222 2788
e-mail mail@atami-restaurant.com
www.atami-restaurant.com

⊖ Pimlico
Closed Saturday lunch and Sunday

Menu £23/45 – Carte approx. £22

A/C VISA MC AE

Named after one of Japan's best known hot spring resorts, Atami is the latest in a line of stylishly decorated Japanese restaurants that have proved very popular over the last few years by mixing the traditional with the decidedly contemporary. The difference is that here prices are a little more down to earth. The serving team offer the novice expert guidance around the menu and, alongside the sushi and sashimi, expect to find ingredients of a more European provenance paired in some unexpected yet delicate combinations. Bamboo, leather, mirrors, glass and natural woods combine to create a sensual and striking space, illuminated by four large ceiling orbs. The bar is tucked away discreetly but is equally appealing and strangely calming.

Bank

Modern European XX

H5

45 Buckingham Gate
✉ SW1E 6BS
✆ (020) 7630 6644
Fax (020) 7630 5663
e-mail alison.berry@bankrestaurants.com
www.bankrestaurants.com

⊖ St James's Park
Closed Saturday lunch, Sunday and Bank Holidays – booking essential at lunch

Carte £34/49

A/C VISA MC AE

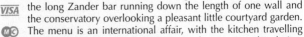

Unlike certain financial institutions, this bank seems to know what it's doing. It occupies a generous space within the Crowne Plaza Hotel but, as it has its own street entrance, feels very much like a stand-alone restaurant. It's bright and breezy inside, with the long Zander bar running down the length of one wall and the conservatory overlooking a pleasant little courtyard garden. The menu is an international affair, with the kitchen travelling to all parts, but it's clearly laid out. Steaks are a popular choice; there are plenty of pasta dishes and whether you like your fish in a pie or cooked with Thai herbs, there's something for you. The biggest surprise is the thoroughly cheerful and unexpectedly enthusiastic service.

Boisdale

Scottish XX

G6

15 Eccleston St ✉ SW1W 9LX
✆ (020) 7730 6922
Fax (020) 7730 0548
e-mail info@boisdale.co.uk
www.boisdale.co.uk

⊖ Victoria
Closed 1 week Christmas, Saturday lunch and Sunday

Carte £26/89

Acres of tartan, whiskies galore, haggis, mash and neeps - Boisdale couldn't be more Scottish if it sang Scots Wha Hae and did the Highland Fling. Owner Ranald Macdonald bought various parts of the building at different times, hence the charmingly higgledy-piggledy layout. The original Auld restaurant is the more characterful; the Macdonald Bar has more buzz and nightly live jazz and a large cigar selection add to the masculine feel. The menu features plenty of Scottish produce, from Orkney herring to Shetland scallops, but the stand-outs are the four varieties of smoked salmon, followed by the 28-day aged Aberdeenshire cuts of beef. Ignore the lacklustre tomato and watercress garnish and just savour the quality of the meat.

The Cinnamon Club

Indian XXX

I5

30-32 Great Smith St
✉ SW1P 3BU
✆ (020) 7222 2555
Fax (020) 7222 1333
e-mail info@cinnamonclub.com
www.cinnamonclub.com

⊖ St James's Park
Closed 26 December, Sunday and Bank Holidays

Menu £19 – Carte £30/53

The Grade II listed former Westminster library may seem an unlikely setting for an Indian restaurant but it works surprisingly well. The shelves of books are still there on the mezzanine level of the large main room where the action is, although the smaller front room has better air-conditioning. There are two bars: the one downstairs is the livelier. A variety of menus are on offer and prices can get quite steep but the cooking clearly displays ambition and innovation. Many of the ingredients may be more European, like Herdwick lamb or Anjou pigeon, but the cooking techniques, colours and spices are resolutely Indian. Staff are on the ball, as you'd expect from somewhere serving over 200 people twice a day.

Il Convivio

G6 **Italian** XX

143 Ebury St ✉ SW1W 9QN
✆ (020) 7730 4099
Fax (020) 7730 4103
e-mail comments@etruscarestaurants.com
www.etruscarestaurants.com

⊖ Sloane Square
Closed 26 December-4 January, Sunday and Bank Holidays

Carte £33/47

A/C VISA MC AE

You know you're in a serious Italian restaurant when the autumnal truffle season produces specialities on the menu featuring the white truffle - tartufo bianco, the king of truffles. Indeed, there's no denying the quality of the produce here, whether it's the milk-fed lamb, Angus beef or wild sea bass. Pasta is also something of a house speciality and any of the half-dozen choices can be taken as a starter, middle or main course. Found within an attractive Georgian house, the poet Dante is celebrated in the name and the decoration of the restaurant and lines of his poetry are embossed on the wall. The best place to sit is either at the front, overlooking the street, or right at the back under the retractable roof.

The Ebury

G6 **Gastropub**

11 Pimlico Rd ✉ SW1W 8NA
✆ (020) 7730 6784
Fax (020) 7730 6149
e-mail info@theebury.co.uk
www.theebury.co.uk

⊖ Sloane Square.
Closed 25-26 December

Menu £17 (lunch) – Carte £30/45

A/C VISA MC AE

Grab a passing waiter to get yourself seated otherwise they'll assume you've just come for a drink at the bar and will ignore you. Once you've got your feet under one of the low-slung tables, however, you'll find everything moves up a gear. This is a rather smart affair and provides an object lesson in how to draw in punters. That means a varied menu, from burger to black bream, assorted salads that show some thought, three vegetarian dishes and main courses that display a degree of originality. Add to that a conscientious kitchen, a wine list that offers plenty by the glass and carafe, and weekend brunch that goes on until 4pm and it's little wonder the place is always so busy. The waiters come with French accents and self-confidence.

Ken Lo's Memories of China

G6 **Chinese** XX

65-69 Ebury St ✉ SW1W 0NZ
✆ (020) 7730 7734
Fax (020) 7730 2992
e-mail moc@londonfinedininggroup.com
www.londonfinedininggroup.com

⊖ Victoria
Closed Christmas-New Year, Sunday lunch and Bank Holidays

Menu £20/32 s – Carte £24/60 s

A/C VISA MC AE

The restaurant may have changed hands over the years but the late Ken Lo was responsible for putting the place on the map all those years ago and so it's appropriate to find his name still in the title. The restaurant belies its age in its looks. It is bright, modern and quite minimalist in its design but also manages to be warm and welcoming. Chinese script, lattice panels and well-dressed tables ensure a sense of comfort and style. The length of the menu can appear a little bewildering, as can the seemingly eccentric numbering system, but the dishes come carefully prepared. The set menus are often the easier option and take you on a gastronomic tour of China. Service is positive, well marshalled and clued-up.

Mango Tree

G5 **Thai** XX

46 Grosvenor Pl ✉ SW1X 7EQ
✆ (020) 7823 1888
Fax (020) 7838 9275
e-mail info@mangotree.org.uk
www.mangotree.org.uk

⊖ Victoria
Closed 25 December and 1 January

Menu £20 (lunch) – Carte £30/36

A/C VISA MC AE

There are other Mango Trees in Bangkok and Dubai which tells you that this branch is not going to be some humble little local – we're talking loud, polished and none too cheap. That being said, it still equates to a good night out, thanks to the large bar and the well-versed team who all have the latest ordering gizmos at their disposal. The menu covers all bases and is logically laid out; there are plenty of milder stir-fries, hotter curries and appealing starters and dishes are prepared with almost unexpected care and respect. With some judicious ordering and sharing, that final bill can be kept to moderate levels. Anyone not sated can order the Dessert Selection: a taster of all the desserts. The loos are virtually a taxi ride away.

Marcus Wareing at The Berkeley ✿✿

French XXXX

G4

Wilton Pl ✉ SW1X 7RL
✆ (020) 7235 1200
Fax (020) 7235 1266
e-mail marcuswareing@the-berkeley.co.uk
www.marcus-wareing.com

⊖ Knightsbridge
Closed Saturday lunch and Sunday

Menu £35/75

A/C

VISA

AE

Getting divorced from Gordon Ramsay was never going to be easy and, sure enough, Marcus Wareing has been going through the various stages; of anger, bitterness and public recriminations. Now it looks as though both parties are finally moving toward the final phases of resolution and acceptance. This means that here in his restaurant he can get his head down and concentrate on producing confident and expertly constructed dishes, instilled with some of his own personality. His influences and techniques are still largely French but the ingredients are seasonal and mostly British, so you can expect the likes of Dorset turbot with frog's legs and a snail beignet or Scottish scallops with a matelote sauce. There is a boldness to the conception of certain dishes – rather than pointless experimentation – and flavours have real clarity. The initial upheaval was felt a little in the service, which wobbled slightly as newer members bedded in but is now more confident; the restaurant manager has also brought a less haughty approach. The Chef's Table is one of the best in town.

First Course

- Foie gras with apricot compote and amaretti crumble.
- Scallops and cod with cauliflower and shallot dressing.

Main Course

- Sea bass with langoustines, smoked eel and asparagus.
- Suckling pig with braised chicory and pomme mousseline.

Dessert

- Iced lime mousse with pineapple carpaccio.
- Wild honey and milk chocolate gâteau.

Nahm ✿

G5 — **Thai** XX

5 Halkin St ✉ SW1X 7DJ — ⊖ Hyde Park Corner
✆ (020) 7333 1234 — booking advisable
Fax (020) 7333 1100
e-mail res@nahm.como.bz
www.halkin.como.bz

Menu £30 (lunch)/55 – Carte £39/46

The blend of copper tones, wood and candlelight, along with an understated hint of Asian design, means the restaurant fits in well within the slick and stylish surroundings of the boutique Halkin hotel. David Thompson's signature dishes, which are based on Royal Thai traditions, are prepared with a sure hand by his head chef, Matthew Albert and the fieriness and vitality of the food contrasts with these serene surroundings. The menu is varied and regularly changing, with proteins ordered according to the UK seasons and vegetables chosen on the Thai calendar. The fresh and vibrant salads are a great way to start things off and provide contrast to the rich curries which not only have real intensity and depth but also display those most important elements of Thai cuisine: balance and harmony. You should opt for the nahm arharn set menu to get the complete experience and if you ask the staff for advice don't expect a brief answer – they know what they're talking about and have all spent time in the kitchen. Rice and noodles form the basis of a great lunch deal.

First Course

- Salted chicken wafers, longans, Thai basil.
- Coconut curry with minced monkfish.

Main Course

- Pork belly, braised with peanuts.
- Scallop salad with coconut and lemongrass.

Dessert

- Coconut cake with rambutans and perfumed syrup.
- Palm nuts with mango, Chinese dates and coconut.

Noura Brasserie

G5 **Lebanese** XX

16 Hobart Pl ✉ SW1W 0HH ⊖ Victoria
✆ (020) 7235 9444
Fax (020) 7235 9244
e-mail noura@noura.co.uk
www.noura.co.uk

Menu £20/30 – Carte £24/39

The Belgravia branch was the first of the Lebanese Noura restaurants to appear on these shores and such is its appeal that it's an all-day operation. You're greeted by the enticing sight of sweet, sticky pastries and it's here at the bar where you can grab a quick bite. The majority go through to the large, lustrous restaurant where there's seating for over about 100; the vast kitchen occupies the whole of the basement. Everything is prepared from scratch so the food is fresh and zingy and hummus comes with authentic oomph. Platters and mezzes are the way to go but be sure to finish with the pastries or the homemade ice creams, the flavours of which could include rosewater or clotted cream. Staff have a certain seen-it-all insouciance.

Olivo

G6 **Italian** X

21 Eccleston St ✉ SW1W 9LX ⊖ Victoria
✆ (020) 7730 2505 Closed Bank Holidays and lunch Saturday and Sunday
Fax (020) 7823 5377
e-mail maurosanna@oliveto.fsnet.co.uk
www.olivorestaurant.com

Menu £23 (lunch) – Carte dinner £32/36

Olivo is one of those places that, despite the constant banging of the front door, the somewhat monosyllabic waitress and the permanently aloof manager, are always bursting with bonhomie. The restaurant is simply kitted out in blues and yellows and its infectious atmosphere is most evident at lunch. It celebrates all things Sardinian so start with a glass of Vernaccia and carta di musica bread and finish with a glass of Mirto after you've had the sebada cheese fritters for dessert. Lunch is set priced and dinner à la carte; both are nicely balanced and appealing affairs, with the 'spaghetti alla bottarga' being an unquestionable highlight. The wine list is concise but decent value and bottles can be bought at nearby Olivino.

Olivomare

G5

Seafood X

10 Lower Belgrave St ✉ SW1W 0LJ
✆ (020) 7730 9022
Fax (020) 7823 5377
e-mail maurosanna@oliveto.fsnet.co.uk
www.olivorestaurants.com

⊖ Victoria
Closed Bank Holidays

Carte £34/42

Olivomare is one of those restaurants that make you want to live by the sea and, looking at the produce in their shop next door, that sea would be the Tyrrhenian. The room's piscatorial decoration – a sort of Philippe Starck gone fishin' – works well, especially when it's so cleverly lit. The menu changes every fortnight and has a Sardinian base to it. The kitchen buys the freshest fish, treats it with respect and uses traditional recipes. The fritto misto is excellent; razor clams and octopus have quite a following and the spaghetti with bottarga or half a lobster are favourites too. Be sure to end with gelato, which is also available in the shop, Olivino. Service would be better if they took their blinkers off and looked around more.

A/C VISA MC AE

Osteria Dell' Angolo

I6

Italian XX

47 Marsham St. ✉ SW1P 3DR
✆ (020) 3268 1077
Fax (020) 3268 1073
e-mail osteriadell-angolo@btconnect.com
www.osteriadellangolo.co.uk

⊖ St. James's Park
Closed 25 December, Saturday lunch, Sunday and Bank Holidays

Menu £20 (lunch) – Carte £29/49

In over 30 years in London, Claudio Pulze has opened more that 50 restaurants so you could say he knows what he's going. One of his most recent ventures is this Italian restaurant opposite the Home Office which is altogether smarter than the name suggests. It's bright and sunny inside, with a front bar; larger groups should ask for tables 14 or 15. The enthusiastic team is run by an effusive manager who recognises all his regulars. There is a subtle Tuscan element to the cooking but the kitchen is also prone to adding a little playfulness or doing a little reinterpreting of the classics. Pastas and breads, made downstairs, are very good. The wine list is well-priced and includes a decent choice by the glass.

A/C VISA MC AE

The Pantechnicon Rooms

G5 **Gastropub**

10 Motcomb St ✉ SW1X 8LA ⊖ Knightsbridge.
✆ (020) 7730 6074 Closed 25 December to 1 January
Fax (020) 7730 6055
e-mail reservations@thepantechnicon.com
www.thepantechnicon.com

Carte £28/40

It took the owners over a year to transform the distinctly unprepossessing Turks Head and turn it into this smart new pub that matches their other place nearby, The Thomas Cubitt. It's named after the art and antique repository that stood on Motcomb Street until it was destroyed by fire in 1874; a painting of which graces the smart upstairs restaurant. The menu is a sophisticated number, with oysters, caviar and shellfish having their own sections along with cocktails and champagne. Downstairs the menu gets tweaked slightly so that the starters become 'small plates' but otherwise there is little difference; influences are kept within Europe, the seafood is well worth exploring and dishes come daintily presented.

La Poule au Pot

G6 **French**

231 Ebury St ✉ SW1W 8UT ⊖ Sloane Square
✆ (020) 7730 7763 Closed 25-26 December and 1 January
Fax (020) 7259 9651

Menu £23 (lunch) – Carte £32/45

Trends may come, styles may go, but the one constant will always be La Poule au Pot. As Gallic as a Gauloise and as French as a frog's leg, this long-standing favourite, with its exuberant decoration of hanging baskets of dried flowers and assorted horticultural knick-knacks, has been entertaining everyone from the romantically entwined to groups of friends out for fun for many years. Somehow all the disparate elements just seem to gel wonderfully well and it's reassuring to know that not everything is fashion led. It's not just the atmosphere: the classic country cooking is also responsible for drawing the crowds. Expect a selection of rustic favourites from coq au vin to crème brûlée, supplemented by daily specials.

Quilon ✿

H5 **Indian** XXX

41 Buckingham Gate ✉ SW1 6AF
✆ (020) 7821 1899
Fax (020) 7233 9597
e-mail info@quilonrestaurant.co.uk
www.quilon.co.uk

⊖ St James's Park
Closed Saturday lunch

Menu £22/37 – Carte dinner £37/47

A/C VISA

Quilon is one of the capital's Indian restaurants that's setting the benchmark for others. Its success lies firmly with chef Sriram Aylur and his brigade who are committed to constantly improving and developing their dishes but who also understand the importance of consistency. Sriram describes his cooking as "Westernised versions of authentic southwest Indian dishes but with better ingredients". Much produce comes from within the UK and the spices, which are imported from India, are ground in the kitchen. The menu changes seasonally; fish is naturally a strength, whether in a broth, a curry or roasted in a plantain leaf and, as in Kerala, there are plenty of vegetarian dishes; be sure to order paratha. The large mural is a bold attempt to infuse a large dining room (which is actually part of a hotel, although you wouldn't really know it) with a sense of India; try to sit in a section off to one side rather than in the body of the room. Staff know their menu well and offer sound guidance.

First Course
- Spiced oysters and lentils with onion relish.
- Cauliflower with yoghurt and green chilli.

Main Course
- Koondapur halibut curry and tamarind gravy.
- Malabar lamb biryani.

Dessert
- Spiced dark chocolate and hazelnut mousse.
- Mango and rice pudding with cardamom.

Quirinale

Italian XX

15

North Court, 1 Great Peter St ✉ SW1P 3LL
(020) 7222 7080
e-mail info@quirinale.co.uk
www.quirinale.co.uk

⊖ Westminster
Closed August, 1 week Christmas - New Year, Saturday lunch and Sunday

Menu £23 (lunch) – Carte £32/45

VISA MC AE

Named after one of the Seven Hills of Rome where the Italian head of state resides, Quirinale lies in the shadow of Parliament. It's easy to miss as the discreet entrance is tucked inside a mansion block entrance. Descend the wide tiled staircase and you'll find yourself in a surprisingly bright and contemporary styled restaurant, where the service is scrupulously slick and the atmosphere discreet. The chef hails from Brescia but his seasonally-changing menu is all-encompassing, with a few more Sicilian and Neapolitan touches. Pastas are home-made, cooking shows a light touch and the wine list covers all parts. There's a large selection of cheeses that are worth exploring, all sourced from small, artisan suppliers.

Rex Whistler

British XX

16

Tate Britain, Millbank ✉ SW1P 4RG
(020) 7887 8825
Fax (020) 7887 8892
e-mail britain.restaurant@tate.org.uk
www.tate.org.uk/britain/eatanddrink

⊖ Pimlico
Closed 24-26 December – booking essential – lunch only

Menu £20 – Carte £31/38

A/C VISA MC AE

Galleries everywhere are finally seeing the value of having a decent restaurant but the one here at Tate Britain has been going since 1972. It's a spacious, masculine room, offering the diner the added appeal of being surrounded by the striking Rex Whistler mural 'In Pursuit of Rare Meats', painted in 1927. Just as the gallery celebrates British art, so the menu does its bit for Blighty: there's a daily catch from the Newlyn day boats and the chips are even cooked in dripping. Meanwhile, the fruity puddings illustrate why this part of the meal is our culinary crowning glory. The wine list is truly excellent: it is intelligently laid out, full of gems and has over 80 half bottles, many of which are from wines rarely seen in halves.

Roussillon ✿

G6 **French** XXX

16 St Barnabas St ✉ SW1W 8PE
✆ (020) 7730 5550
Fax (020) 7824 8617
e-mail alexis@roussillon.co.uk
www.roussillon.co.uk

⊖ Sloane Square
Closed Christmas to New Year, Saturday lunch and Sunday

Menu £35/55

A/C VISA MC AE

Of all the restaurants in London with Michelin stars, Roussillon is probably the least well known. This is probably one of its great strengths as the only people it panders to are the innumerable locals, who in turn like to keep their favourite restaurant a secret. The great strength of Alexis Gauthier and his kitchen is their ability to remind us all of what things can really taste of - especially vegetables - and he spends a great deal of time hunting for those of the best possible quality and then uses them at the optimum time. He even offers an 8 course 'Menu Légume' so if you know anyone who doesn't eat their greens then bring them here and they'll soon realise what they are missing out on. The cooking is classically French in its influences and techniques and the flavours are subtle and nuanced. The other attraction is the wine list which contains plenty of underappreciated gems from Roussillon, the Languedoc and the South West of France. The room is comfortable yet discreet and the atmosphere generally convivial.

First Course

- Black truffle risotto with Parmesan tuiles.
- Ballotine of quail with foie gras and ceps.

Main Course

- Sea bass with artichokes and confit tomatoes.
- Veal shoulder with carrot and pomme gaufrettes.

Dessert

- Louis XV crunchy praline and chocolate.
- Strawberry vacherin with vanilla ice cream.

Santini

Italian XXX

G5

29 Ebury St ✉ SW1W 0NZ
✆ (020) 7730 4094
Fax (020) 7730 0544
e-mail info@santini-restaurant.com
www.santini-restaurant.com

⊖ Victoria
Closed 23-27 December, 1 January , Easter, lunch Saturday and Sunday

Menu £25 (dinner) – Carte £29/54

Like many of its bronzed customers, Santini really comes into its own in the summer: the white walls and marble flooring are crisp and cooling and the terrace must be one of the largest around. Family-owned since 1984, it has never been the cheapest Italian around but then this was never the sort of place that pretended to be accessible to all and the service is decidedly old-school; the type that intimidated you when you were young. But the food, with its mild Venetian accent, is very good. Homemade pastas are excellent and the zabaglione is a gloriously rich concoction. Further evidence of the restaurant's self-belief is in the number of times its name appears in dishes, so you can follow insalata Santini with branzino Santini.

Shepherd's

British XXX

I6

Marsham Court, Marsham St ✉ SW1P 4LA
✆ (020) 7834 9552
Fax (020) 7233 6047
e-mail admin@langansrestaurants.co.uk
www.langansrestaurants.co.uk

⊖ Pimlico
Closed 25 December, Saturday, Sunday and Bank Holidays – booking essential

Menu £35

Looking at the number of shiny pates and pin-striped suits that pile into Shepherd's for lunch you'd be forgiven for thinking that 'Blair's Babes' never left much of a legacy. This is a classic, old-school blokey institution that could show some of those new restaurants a thing or two. For starters, it runs on wheels and gives the punters what they want. The atmosphere is animated throughout, but the booths are the best places to sit. The menu is a combination of classic dishes and brasserie favourites but your best bet is to head for those bits of the menu that read like a UKIP manifesto – the fiercely British specialities, like the daily roast or the Dover Sole, followed by an indulgent dessert like a sponge pudding.

The Thomas Cubitt

G6 **Gastropub**

44 Elizabeth Street ✉ SW1W 9PA ⊖ Sloane Square.
✆ (020) 7730 6060
Fax (020) 7730 6055
e-mail reservations@thethomascubitt.co.uk
www.thethomascubitt.co.uk

Closed 24 December to 1 January – booking essential

Menu £25 (lunch) – Carte £28/40

VISA MC AE

The Thomas Cubitt is a pub of two halves: on the ground floor it's perennially busy and you can't book which means that if you haven't arrived by 7pm then you're too late to get a table. However, you can reserve a table upstairs, in a dining room that's a model of civility and tranquillity. Here, service comes courtesy of a young team where the girls are chatty and the men unafraid of corduroy. Downstairs you get fish and chips; here you get pan-fried fillet of brill with oyster beignet and truffled chips. The cooking is certainly skilled, quite elaborate in its construction and prettily presented. So, take your pick: upstairs can get a little pricey but is ideal for entertaining the in-laws; if out with friends then crowd in downstairs.

Zafferano ✿

Italian XXX

F5

15 Lowndes St ✉ SW1X 9EY
✆ (020) 7235 5800
Fax (020) 7235 1971
e-mail info@zafferanorestaurant.com
www.zafferanorestaurant.com

⊖ Knightsbridge
Closed Christmas-New Year – booking essential

Menu £45 (dinner) – Carte lunch £45/60

A/C VISA AE

Such is the enduring nature of Zafferano's popularity that it is always busy, almost from the moment they unlock the front door each day. We all like a bit of bustle and bonhomie in a restaurant and this place doesn't disappoint, although the waiters do have a propensity to charge around as though their pants are on fire. If you favour less frenzy then ask to sit in the smaller end room. The deli may not have worked but the bar has proved a big success - regulars sometimes just pop in there for a plate of pasta. In fact, a plate of pasta should be ordered wherever you're sitting as it is a real strength of the kitchen, which operates under the expert guidance of Andy Needham who proves that Yorkshire doesn't just produce great cricketers. His menus provide an object lesson in how to satisfy your customers: they are reassuringly recognisable yet also seasonal and are supplemented with a few daily specials. The assured cooking ensures that natural flavours are to the fore. The wine list also continues to grow, with the recent addition of more choice from southern parts.

First Course
- Roasted onion with cheese fondue and white truffle.
- Langoustine fricassee with baby artichoke.

Main Course
- Flat spaghetti with tomato and lobster.
- Roast Gressingham duck with honey and balsamic.

Dessert
- Chocolate fondant with gianduia chocolate ice cream.
- Cherry and almond tart with iced milk.

Regent's Park · Marylebone

The neighbourhood north of chaotic Oxford Street is actually a rather refined place where shoppers like to venture for the smart boutiques, and where idlers like to saunter for the graceful parkland acres full of rose gardens and quiet corners. In fact, Marylebone and Regent's Park go rather well together, a moneyed village with a wonderful park for its back garden.

Marylebone may now exude a fashionable status, but its history tells a very different tale. Thousands used to come here to watch executions at Tyburn gallows, a six hundred year spectacle that stopped in the late eighteenth century. Tyburn stream was covered over, and the area's modern name came into being as a contraction of St Mary by the Bourne, the parish church. Nowadays the people who flock here come to gaze at less ghoulish sights, though some of the inhabitants of the eternally popular Madame Tussauds deserved no better fate than the gallows. South across the busy Marylebone Road, the preponderance of swish restaurants and snazzy specialist shops announces your arrival at **Marylebone High Street.** There are patisseries, chocolatiers, cheese shops and butchers at every turn, nestling alongside smart places to eat and drink. At St Marylebone Church, each Saturday heralds a posh market called Cabbages & Frocks, where artisan food meets designer clothing in a charming garden. Further down, the century old Daunt Books has been described as London's most beautiful bookshop: it has long oak galleries beneath graceful conservatory skylights. Close by, the quaintly winding Marylebone Lane boasts some truly unique shops like tiny emporium The Button Queen, which sells original Art Deco, Victorian and Edwardian buttons. In complete contrast, just down the road from here is the mighty **Wigmore Hall,** an art nouveau gem with great acoustics and an unerringly top-notch classical agenda that can be appreciated at rock-bottom prices. Meanwhile, art lovers can indulge an eclectic fix at the **Wallace Collection** in **Manchester Square,** where paintings by the likes of Titian and Velazquez rub shoulders with Sevres porcelain and grand Louis XIV furniture.

Regent's Park – an idyllic Georgian oasis stretching off into London's northern suburbs - celebrates its two hundredth birthday in 2011. Before architect John Nash and his sponsor The Prince Regent gave it its much-loved geometric makeover, it had been farming land, and prior to that, one of Henry VIII's hunting grounds. His spirit lives on, in the sense that various activities are catered for, from tennis courts to a running track. And there are animals too, albeit not roaming free, at **London Zoo,** in the park's northerly section. Most people, though, come here to while away an hour or two around the boating lake or amble the Inner Circle which contains **Queen Mary's Gardens** and their enchanting bowers of fragrant roses. Others come for a summer sojourn to the Open Air Theatre where taking in a performance of 'A Midsummer Night's Dream' is very much ***de rigueur***. The Regent's Canal provides another fascinating element to the park. You can follow its peaceful waters along a splendid walk from the **Little Venice** houseboats in the west, past the golden dome of the **London Central Mosque,** and on into the north-west confines of Regent's Park as it snakes through London Zoo, before it heads off towards Camden Lock. On the other side of Prince Albert Road, across from the zoo, the scenic glory takes on another dimension with a climb up Primrose Hill. Named after the grassy promontory that sets it apart from its surrounds, to visitors this is a hill with one of the best panoramas in the whole of London; to locals (ie, actors, pop stars, media darlings and the city set) it's an ultra fashionable place to live with pretty Victorian terraces and accordingly sky-high prices. Either way you look at it (or from it), it's a great place to be on a sunny day with the breeze in your hair.

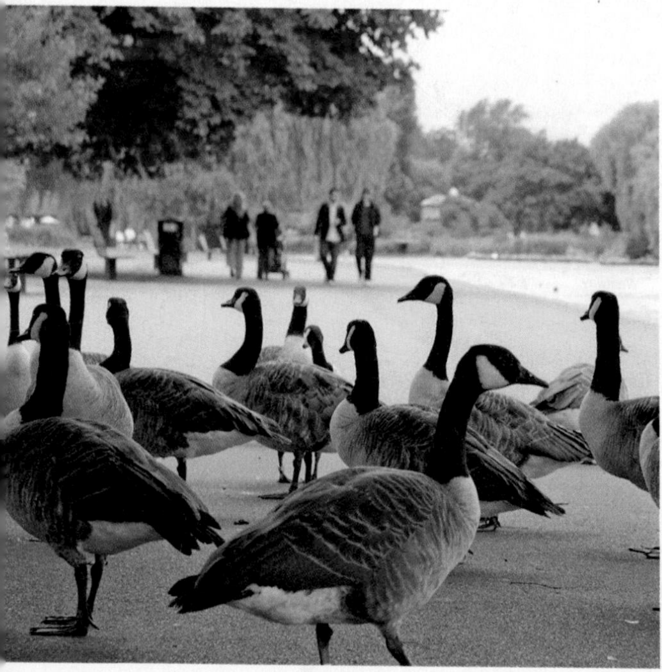

C. Eymenier / MICHELIN

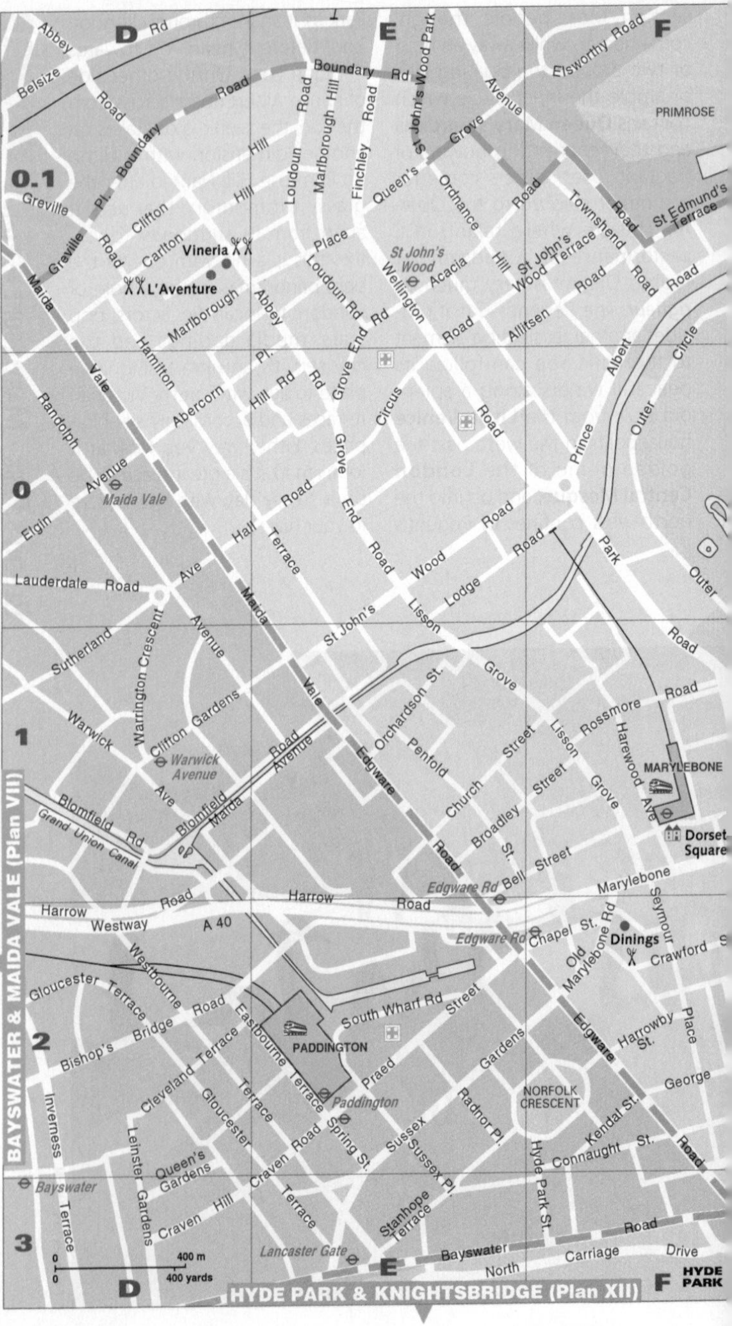
D
E
F
0.1
0
1
2
3
PRIMROSE
Vineria
L'Aventure
St John's Wood
Maida Vale
Warwick Avenue
MARYLEBONE
Dorset Square
Edgware Rd
Dinings
PADDINGTON
Paddington
NORFOLK CRESCENT
Bayswater
Lancaster Gate
HYDE PARK
Abbey Rd
Belsize Road
Boundary Road
Boundary Rd
Greville Pl.
Greville Rd
Clifton Hill
Carlton Hill
Loudoun Road
Marlborough Hill
Finchley Road
St John's Wood Park
Queen's Grove
Elsworthy Road
Avenue Road
Ordnance Hill
Townshend Road
St Edmund's Terrace
St John's Wood Terrace
Acacia Road
Wellington Road
Allitsen Road
Prince Albert Road
Outer Circle
Hamilton Terrace
Marlborough Place
Loudoun Rd
Grove End Rd
Abbey Rd
Hill Rd
Circus Road
Abercorn Pl.
Randolph Avenue
Elgin Avenue
Lauderdale Road
Hall Road
Maida Vale
Park Road
Lodge Road
St John's Wood Road
Lisson Grove
Sutherland Avenue
Warrington Crescent
Clifton Gardens
Warwick Ave
Blomfield Rd
Blomfield Road
Maida Avenue
Grand Union Canal
Orchardson St.
Penfold St.
Church Street
Broadley St.
Bell Street
Rossmore Road
Harewood Ave
Edgware Road
Harrow Road
Westway
A 40
Marylebone Road
Chapel St.
Old Marylebone Rd
Seymour Place
Crawford St.
Westbourne Terrace
Gloucester Terrace
Bishop's Bridge Road
Eastbourne Terrace
South Wharf Rd
Praed Street
Sussex Gardens
Harrowby St.
George St.
Kendal St.
Connaught St.
Radnor Pl.
Cleveland Terrace
Inverness Terrace
Leinster Gardens
Queen's Gardens
Craven Hill
Craven Road
Craven Terrace
Spring St.
Sussex Pl.
Stanhope Terrace
Hyde Park St.
Bayswater Road
North Carriage Drive
400 m
400 yards
BAYSWATER & MAIDA VALE (Plan VIII)
HYDE PARK & KNIGHTSBRIDGE (Plan XII)

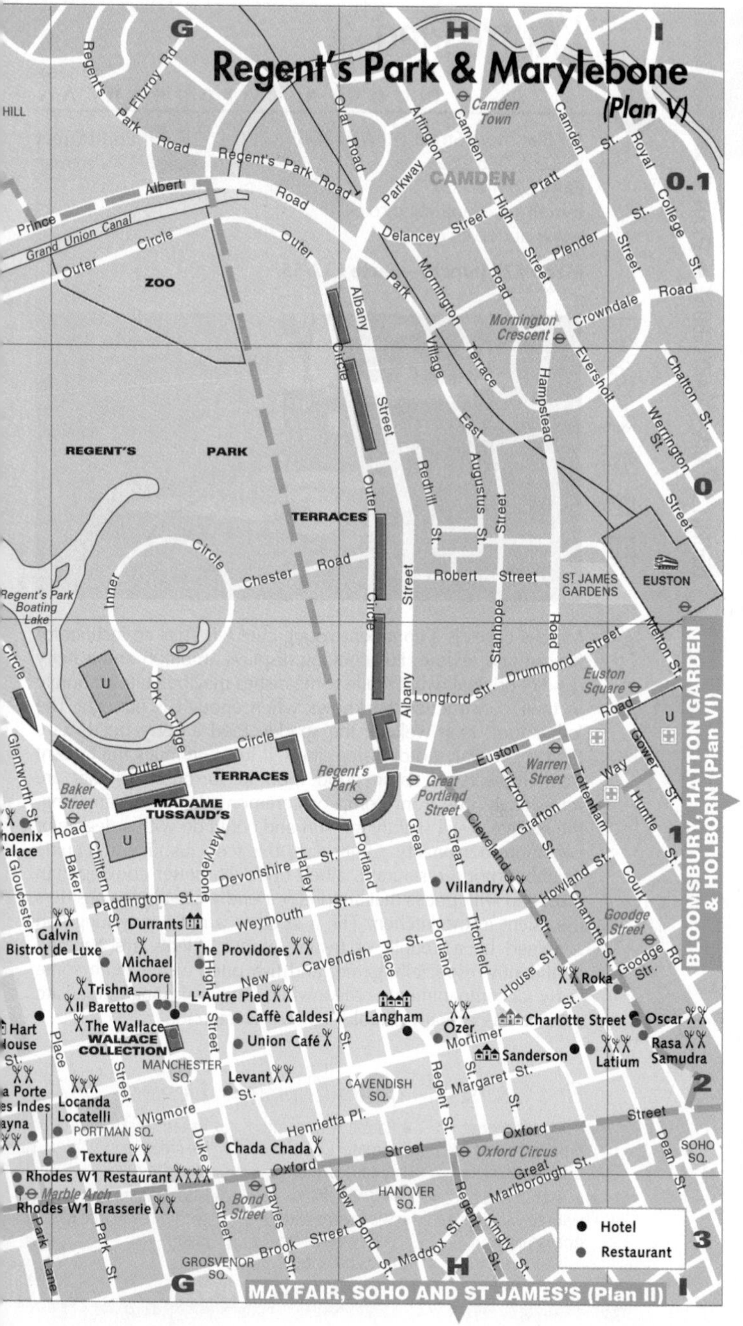

Regent's Park & Marylebone
(Plan V)
G
H
I
0.1
0
1
2
3
HILL
Regent's Park Road
Fitzroy Rd
Regent's Park Road
Oval Road
Arlington
Camden Town
Camden
CAMDEN
Camden St.
Royal College St.
Prince Albert Road
Grand Union Canal
Outer Circle
ZOO
Parkway
Delancey Street
High Street
Pratt
Plender
St.
Street
Road
Outer Park
Mornington Road
Mornington Crescent
Crowndale
Albany Circle
Village
Terrace
Eversholt
Chalton St.
Werrington St.
Street
Hampstead
East
Redhill St.
Augustus St.
Street
Albany Street
REGENT'S
PARK
TERRACES
Outer Circle
Inner Circle
Chester Road
Robert Street
ST JAMES GARDENS
EUSTON
Regent's Park Boating Lake
Circle
Stanhope
Road
Melton St.
U
York Bridge
Longford St.
Drummond Street
Euston Square
Road
Outer Circle
TERRACES
Regent's Park
Euston
Warren Street
Gower St.
Way
Fitzroy
Tottenham
Great Portland Street
Huntley St.
Baker Street
MADAME TUSSAUD'S
Cleveland
Grafton
Glentworth St.
Phoenix Palace
Road
U
Marylebone
Portland
Great
Great
Howland St.
Court
Gloucester
Baker
Chiltern
Devonshire St.
Harley
Villandry
Charlotte
Paddington St.
St.
Weymouth
Str.
Goodge Street
Galvin Bistrot de Luxe
Durrants
Michael Moore
The Providores
High
Cavendish
Place
St.
Portland
Titchfield
House St.
Goodge Str.
Rd
Roka
Trishna
New
L'Autre Pied
St.
Il Baretto
Caffè Caldesi
Langham
Ozer
Charlotte Street
Oscar
Hart House
The Wallace
WALLACE COLLECTION
Union Café
St.
Mortimer
Sanderson
Latium
Rasa Samudra
St.
Place
Street
MANCHESTER SQ.
Levant
St.
CAVENDISH SQ.
Margaret St.
La Porte des Indes
Locanda Locatelli
Wigmore
Regent St.
Henrietta Pl.
St.
Street
Royna
PORTMAN SQ.
Duke
Chada Chada
Oxford
Dean St.
SOHO SQ.
Texture
Street
Oxford Circus
Rhodes W1 Restaurant
Oxford
HANOVER SQ.
Great Marlborough St.
Marble Arch
Bond Street
Davies
New Bond
Regent
Rhodes W1 Brasserie
Street
Kingly
Park Lane
Park St.
Brook Street
St.
Maddox St.
St.
GROSVENOR SQ.
Hotel
Restaurant
BLOOMSBURY, HATTON GARDEN & HOLBORN (Plan VI)
MAYFAIR, SOHO AND ST JAMES'S (Plan II)

L'Autre Pied ✿

Modern European XX

G2

REGENT'S PARK • MARYLEBONE ▶ PLAN V

5-7 Blandford Street ✉ W1U 3DB
(020) 7486 9696
Fax (020) 7486 5067
e-mail info@lautrepied.co.uk
www.lautrepied.co.uk

⊖ Bond Street
Closed 23-29 December

Menu £21 (lunch) – Carte £37/55

A/C VISA MC AE

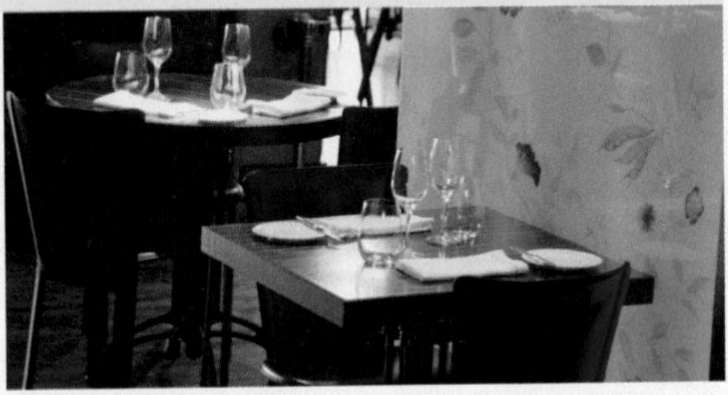

L'Autre Pied

Marcus Eaves is a confident young chef who has an instinct for flavour and texture. His cooking displays ambition and a hefty dose of originality but while some dishes may be quite elaborate in their construction he knows when enough is enough. The 'other foot' may well be the sparkly Pied à Terre but L'Autre Pied is certainly no diffusion line – it just continues the current trend for serving damn good food in surroundings that are refreshingly free from pomp or ceremony. In fact, if anything, the service is still slightly too stiff and could do with a degree or two more personality. Otherwise, this feels just like a genuine neighbourhood restaurant, albeit one with better cooking than most and with prices that are pretty friendly when one considers the talent in the kitchen. The à la carte is not overly long and is joined by a couple of tasting menus. Meats are handled confidently, especially game, and fish often arrives with some burly accompaniments. Meanwhile, the Valrhona chocolate mousse has virtually established its own fan club.

First Course

- Seared foie gras, artichokes and pineapple sorbet.
- Chestnut and bacon velouté with smoked goats milk.

Main Course

- Rabbit with confit tomato, Dauphine potatoes and smoked eel.
- Sea bream with celery, watercress and choucroute.

Dessert

- Baked Alaska, basil ice cream and strawberries.
- Chocolate mousse with passion fruit ice cream.

L'Aventure

DO-1 **French** XX

3 Blenheim Terrace ✉ NW8 0EH ⊖ St John's Wood
✆ (020) 7624 6232
Fax (020) 7625 5548

Closed 15-31 August, first week January, Saturday lunch, Sunday and Bank Holidays

Menu £20/38

VISA MC AE

Tailor-made for anyone with a sound grasp of French wishing to impress a date - the menu is written entirely in French so politely decline the waiter's offer of a quick translation and wait for the admiring looks. What's more, if it's a warm day, you'll be sitting in the enchanting front terrace where the shrubs are covered in twinkly lights. This is a charming neighbourhood restaurant with a cosy and warm interior, owned and run by the delightful Catherine who'll make you feel you're being unfaithful if you don't return. The set menu is good value at lunch but pricier at dinner when the well-heeled locals come out. Expect the French bourgeois classics, from artichoke salad to rack of lamb and an ile flottante to finish.

Il Baretto

G2 **Italian** X

43 Blandford St ✉ W1U 7HF ⊖ Baker Street
✆ (020) 7486 7340
e-mail ilbaretto@hotmail.co.uk
www.ilbaretto.co.uk

Closed 25 December-1 January and Sunday

Carte £20/45

A/C VISA MC AE

Arjun Waney, the man behind Roka, Zuma and La Petite Maison, now gives Italy a go. The site had been Italian for a while and came complete with the wood-fired oven which is undoubtedly the star of the show. The ground floor wine bar doubles as a reception/holding area for the main basement room which comes with reclaimed brick walls and terracotta tiled flooring; the open kitchens somehow compensate for the lack of windows. Look for dishes marked in red on the extensive menu, such as the succulent lamb cutlets or the whole sea bass as they are cooked in the wood-fired oven or on the robata grill. Unless you're sticking to pizza, the final bill can be more than expected. Staff are in black and display varying degrees of commitment.

Caffé Caldesi

Italian

G2

1st Floor, 118 Marylebone Lane
W1U 2QF
(020) 7487 0754
Fax (020) 7935 8832
e-mail caffe@caldesi.com
www.caldesi.com

Bond Street
Closed 25-26 December, 1 January and Sunday lunch

Carte £24/41

A/C VISA MC AE

Simpler is often better but that doesn't always mean cheaper. Caffé Caldesi began as the informal relation to the now closed Caldesi further down the road by offering a more relaxed environment. The ground floor of this converted corner pub is the all-day café-bar part of the operation with the main restaurant upstairs. Here you'll find a bright and colourful room with a very genial atmosphere. The cheeses may be Tuscan but otherwise there's no single dominant Italian region on the menu. Instead it offers a selection of satisfying and earthy dishes, with the home-made pastas particularly good. Plates arrive with appetisingly simple presentation and flavours are bold and balanced, but you may find that the final bill is a little more than you were expecting.

Chada Chada

Thai

G2

16-17 Picton Pl W1U 1BP
(020) 7935 8212
Fax (020) 7924 2791
e-mail enquiry@chadathai.com
www.chadathai.com

Bond Street
Closed Sunday and Bank Holidays

Menu £14/21 – Carte £23/32

A/C VISA MC AE

The welcome may occasionally be a little timid, the decoration relatively featureless and the tables don't have space for too many dishes but Chada Chada retains a sense of authenticity that eludes the plethora of chain restaurants which surround James Street. The menu has been spruced up a little and offers a comprehensive tour around all parts of Thailand. The main course involves choosing your main ingredient, such as prawn or duck, and then deciding on the best accompaniments. The kitchen does the familiar well, which makes sense as it has a regular following who know what they like. It also doesn't hang around in sending forth the dishes which not only come in generous proportions but are also competitively priced.

Dinings

F2 — **Japanese** X

22 Harcourt St. ✉ W1H 4HH
✆ (020) 7723 0666
Fax (020) 7723 3222
e-mail dinings@hotmail.com
www.dinings.co.uk

⊖ Marylebone
Closed lunch Saturday, Sunday and Bank Holidays – booking essential

Carte £29/40

VISA MC AE

The smiling chefs greet you from behind the sushi counter which acts as a prompt to the girls in the basement to rush upstairs and escort you back down below. The idea behind Dinings is to resemble an after-work Japanese izakaya, or pub, and this they achieve. Staff outnumber guests and their service is endearingly sweet, while comfort levels are modest – chairs are built for purpose rather than comfort. The atmosphere is chummy and music loud. The young owner has come from Nobu-land and the food calls itself 'Japanese tapas'; shorthand for small plates of diligently prepared dishes, similar in style to his alma mater in its mix of traditional and modern but without the lofty price tag. Puddings are more your classic French variety.

Galvin Bistrot de Luxe

G2 — **French** XX

66 Baker St ✉ W1U 7DJ
✆ (020) 7935 4007
Fax (020) 7486 1735
e-mail info@galvinrestaurants.com
www.galvinrestaurants.com

⊖ Baker Street
Closed 25-26 December and 1 January

Menu £16 – Carte £23/35

A/C VISA MC AE

Chris and Jeff Galvin are two of the nicest chefs around and their eponymous 'bistrot de luxe' in Baker Street is testament to their integrity and dedication. It has swiftly and deservedly become a classic, thanks to a combination of immensely satisfying French cooking and a devoted following; some regulars have even asked if they could put in a shift in the kitchen. The menu would warm the heart of Escoffier and features the classics, from steak tartare to daube of beef, soupe de poissons to tarte au citron; all are executed with care and understanding and narrowing down your choice won't be easy. Prices are also commendable given the central location and the smart, panelled surroundings; the balanced wine list too focuses on affordability.

Latium

Italian XXX

H2

21 Berners St, Fitzrovia ✉ W1T 3LP ⊖ Oxford Circus
✆ (020) 7323 9123
Fax (020) 7323 3205
e-mail info@latiumrestaurant.com
www.latiumrestaurant.com

Closed 25-26 December, 1 January, Saturday lunch and Sunday

Menu £20/30

A/C VISA MC AE

The last revamp made it brighter and more contemporary but such is the loyalty of its followers that a simple lick of paint would have been enough. There's now a window into the kitchen for those who like to know where their food comes from, and a chef's table for those who want to watch them at it. Tables by the entrance are given away first but it's worth asking to be seated further in; you'll almost certainly be accommodated as staff are a friendly and considerate bunch. The chef-owner is from Lazio, hence the name, so expect cooking that is free from over-elaboration. Recipes from across Italy also feature and many use British ingredients. The good value lunch menu changes weekly and homemade ravioli is the speciality.

Levant

Lebanese XX

G2

Jason Court, 76 Wigmore St ✉ W1U 2SJ ⊖ Bond Street
✆ (020) 7224 1111
Fax (020) 7486 1216
e-mail reservations@levant.co.uk
www.levant.co.uk

Menu £28 (dinner) – Carte £30/40

A/C VISA MC AE

The enticing scent of joss sticks and hookah pipes, belly dancing and pumping Arabic beats mean that Levant is guaranteed to provide a more exotic dining experience than most restaurants. Its basement location, lanterns and low-slung bar add further to the mystique and, as with anywhere offering a hint of spice, diners adopt the principle of safety in numbers and come in larger groups. With all these elements, it is almost a surprise to discover that equal care and enthusiasm has gone into the food. The kitchen uses good ingredients to create satisfying Lebanese dishes ideal for sharing. Avoid the more expensive set menus and head for the à la carte, with its appealing selection of falafel, pastries, char-grills and slow-roasted specialities.

Locanda Locatelli ✿

Italian XXX

G2

8 Seymour St ✉ W1H 7JZ
✆ (020) 7935 9088
Fax (020) 7935 1149
e-mail info@locandalocatelli.com
www.locandalocatelli.com

⊖ Marble Arch
Closed Bank Holidays

Carte £39/57

A/C · VISA · MC · AE

Locanda Locatelli

When your clientele is made up of lots of buffed and shiny people then it is important that you're looking pretty good yourself. So every year the cherry wood is given a fresh coat of varnish and the tan leather seating gets a good clean and this keeps the room looking dapper and slick. Despite the vicissitudes of fashion, Locanda Locatelli has remained an ever popular choice for the cognoscenti, thanks largely to the excellence of the cooking. The large serving team in their black shirts and white ties may look like they've just come from a Sicilian wedding, but they get the job done with alacrity and efficiency. The menu offers around ten dishes per section so there is enough choice for everyone, even those with food allergies. Pasta is a perennial highlight, especially the risotto and gnocchi, and desserts, which always include the toothsome tiramisu and tart of the day, are expertly rendered with flair and care. Thinly sliced calf's head makes an interesting start, while unfussy presentation allows the quality of the fish to really shine.

First Course

- Pheasant ravioli.
- Scallops with celeriac purée and saffron vinaigrette.

Main Course

- Rabbit with Parma ham, radicchio and polenta.
- Sea bream with fennel and bagna cauda sauce.

Dessert

- Tasting of Amedei chocolate.
- Amaretto parfait with chocolate sauce.

Michael Moore

G2

International

19 Blandford St ✉ W1U 3DH
⊖ Baker Street
✆ (020) 7224 1898
Closed Christmas-New Year, Saturday lunch, Sunday and Bank Holidays
Fax (020) 7224 0970
e-mail info@michaelmoorerestaurant.com
www.michaelmoorerestaurant.com

Menu £18 (lunch) – Carte £33/49

Michael Moore is a classically trained chef who has created a welcoming little restaurant. He describes his cooking as 'global cuisine' but that really just means the occasional Asian note to what are fairly conventional combinations and constructions. There may be a slight tendency towards over-elaboration but there's no doubting the quality of the produce and the attractive presentation. The menu changes every six weeks, although the regulars insist that certain favourite dishes remain. The room is cosy and compact, with small tables and seating for just thirty-two. By contrast, the service is surprisingly formal and somewhat ceremonial which occasionally leads to a bottleneck in the middle of the room.

VISA MC AE

Ozer

H2

Turkish

5 Langham Pl, Regent St ✉ W1B 3DG
⊖ Oxford Circus
✆ (020) 7323 0505
Fax (020) 7323 0111
e-mail info@sofra.co.uk
www.ozer.co.uk

Menu £11/15 – Carte £26/41 s

A/C

Huseyin Ozer may have built the successful Sofra chain but Ozer is clearly where his heart lies. His passion and pride in Turkish and Ottoman cuisine is clear for all to see – anyone who prints on their menu an offer to replace any dish not enjoyed must feel confident about his kitchen. The hot and cold meze is the main attraction here, especially the platters which represent good value. The crusty bread and hummus is almost a meal in itself and the borek, kofte and the skewered and chargrilled meats are all done well. There's an occasional modern twist and any overeating can be justified by considering just how healthy this cuisine is. The large front bar gets as packed as ever and the restaurant itself has just as many devotees.

VISA MC AE

Phoenix Palace

F1 — **Chinese** XX

5 Glentworth St ✉ NW1 5PG
✆ (020) 7486 3515
Fax (020) 7486 3401
e-mail info@phoenixpalace.co.uk
www.phoenixpalace.co.uk

⊖ Baker Street
Closed 25 December

Carte £22/37

A/C · VISA · MC · AE

The habit of displaying photos of visiting celebs is usually limited to places once patronised by Telly Savalas or a finalist from Opportunity Knocks but at Phoenix Palace there's a genuinely impressive wall of fame. Like everyone else, they come for the carefully prepared food and infectious atmosphere. The menu is an undeniably lengthy tome but it's sensibly divided; look out for fish dishes like steamed sea bass which is ideal for sharing, and the chef's specials at the back, with the dim sum the best lunch option. The twenty chefs, who are mostly from Hong Kong, exhibit a lightness of touch which is evident in all the dishes. The room is vast but the service is capable and well-organised; orders are taken up to 11.30pm.

La Porte des Indes

F2 — **Indian** XX

32 Bryanston St ✉ W1H 7EG
✆ (020) 7224 0055
Fax (020) 7224 1144
e-mail london.reservation@laportedesindes.com
www.laportedesindes.com

⊖ Marble Arch
Closed 25-26 December and 1 January

Menu £15/28 – Carte £22/42

A/C · VISA · MC · AE

The façade gives little away but step in and you'll be instantly transported to what looks like the set from the latest Bollywood movie. Spread over two floors, La Porte des Indes really is vast and it's decorated in a spectacularly unrestrained display of palms trees, murals and waterfalls. The equally exuberant Jungle Bar is a popular place to kick off the evening. The menu offers something for everyone, including specialities from Pondicherry and others influenced by French India. Vegetarians are particularly well catered for and cookery demonstrations are held regularly for those wishing to learn more about Indian food. For those after a memento of their meal here, there is a little shop in the entrance lobby.

The Providores

Innovative XX

G2

109 Marylebone High St ✉ W1U 4RX ⊖ Bond Street
✆ (020) 7935 6175 Closed 25 to 29 December and 1-2 January
Fax (020) 7935 6877
e-mail anyone@theprovidores.co.uk
www.theprovidores.co.uk

Menu £42 (dinner) – Carte (lunch) £35/50

A/C VISA MC AE

New Zealander Peter Gordon showcases his unique style of fusion cooking upstairs at The Providores. It uses flavours, spices and ingredients from around the world, including many from Australasia, in complex but texturally estimable dishes. The most recent development is that all dishes for dinner now come in starter-size. This more labour-intensive menu means a greater choice – three dishes plus a dessert should suffice for most – although it doesn't come cheap. It's still a bunfight in the ground floor Tapa Room, with its global tapas, but fight your way through it and up the stairs and you'll be greeted by charming and helpful staff, a simply furnished room and a lively atmosphere. The wines are almost exclusively from New Zealand.

Rhodes W1 Brasserie

Modern European XX

F3

Great Cumberland Pl ✉ W1H ⊖ Marble Arch
✆ (020) 7616 5930
Fax (020) 7479 3888
e-mail brasserie@rhodesw1.com
www.rhodesw1.com

Menu £17 (lunch) – Carte £26/38

A/C VISA MC AE

They've got their work cut out filling a space as big as this, because it does need to be close to capacity to get the atmosphere going. That said, the serving team do keep themselves busy and genuinely look after their customers. It's actually better to approach it from the lobby of the hotel than its separate street entrance which leads you through the equally large bar. The menu content differs little between lunch and dinner except for the Express lunch for those on the run: you get starter, main course and dessert all on one plate. Gary Rhodes signature dishes like salmon fishcakes are all in evidence, but so are other more European influences so expect risotto, Greek salads, osso bucco, crab bisque and the like.

Rhodes W1 (Restaurant) ✿

F3 — **French** XXXX

Great Cumberland Place ✉ W1H 7DL — ⊖ Marble Arch
✆ (020) 7616 5930
Fax (020) 7479 3888
e-mail restaurant@rhodesw1.com
www.rhodesw1.com

Closed Christmas, 1 week August, Sunday-Tuesday and Bank Holidays – booking advisable

Menu £24/50

VISA · MC · AE

Rhodes W1

Gary Rhodes' serious minded restaurant not only provides respite from the masses that gather around Marble Arch but also provides a contrasting environment to the equally excitable Cumberland Hotel within which it is located. But if you enter directly from the street through the heavy black door, you won't be aware of the hotel connection at all. There are just twelve tables in the restaurant and when you book one it's yours for however long you want it – this isn't the sort of place where they try to re-lay your table while you're having coffee. Kelly Hoppen's design is about texture and warmth, with crystal chandeliers hanging seductively over each table. Gary Rhodes may be best known as a champion of British traditions and recipes but here the influences come more from across the Channel. Whether the cooking techniques are French or the ingredients from southerly parts, what does remain steadfastly Rhodesesque is the appealingly uncluttered presentation, the complementary combinations of flavours and the ease of eating.

First Course

- Salad of artichokes with wild mushrooms, truffle and duck egg.
- Foie gras with gingerbread and pineapple.

Main Course

- Salmon with parsley gnocchi, snails and roast garlic.
- Best-end of lamb with bacon, broad beans and feta cheese.

Dessert

- Apricot soufflé with white chocolate ice cream and apricot sauce.
- Apple parfait with sorbet and doughnuts.

Texture ✿

Innovative XX

G2

34 Portman Square
W1H 7BY
(020) 7224 0028
e-mail info@texture-restaurant.co.uk
www.texture-restaurant.co.uk

Marble Arch
Closed 1 week Christmas, first 2 weeks August, Sunday and Monday

Menu £22 (lunch) – Carte £38/55

Michelin

Chef-owner Agnar Sverrisson and his business partner Xavier Rousset, who trained as a sommelier, have steadily gone about creating an exceedingly good restaurant. The Champagne bar at the front has become a destination in itself and is separated from the restaurant by a large cabinet so you never feel too detached from it. The high ceilings add a little grandeur and the service is very pleasant, with staff all ready with a smile. Agnar's cooking is a little less showy than when Texture first opened in 2007 and is all the better for that; you feel he's now cooking the food he wants to cook rather than the food he thought he should be cooking. Iceland is his country of birth so it is no surprise to find lamb, cod (whose crisp skin is served with drinks), langoustine and skyr, the dairy product that nourished the Vikings. There's considerable technical skill and depth to the cooking but dishes still appear light and refreshing and, since the use of cream and butter is largely restricted to the desserts, you even feel they're doing you good.

First Course

- Pigeon with sweetcorn, bacon popcorn and red wine.
- Langoustine with coco beans, barley and herbs.

Main Course

- Icelandic cod with chorizo, squid and artichokes.
- Duck with spring roll, plum, mango and soy.

Dessert

- Strawberries with granola and milk ice cream.
- Valrhona white chocolate soup with sugar snap peas and ginger.

Trishna

G2 **Indian**

15-17 Blandford St ✉ W1U 3DG ⊖ Baker Street
✆ (020) 7935 5624
Fax (020) 7935 9259
e-mail info@trishnalondon.com
www.trishnalondon.com

Menu £17 (lunch) – Carte £27/43

A/C VISA MC AE

The service can wobble at times and the acoustics in the two simply decorated rooms aren't great but Trishna, a franchise of the rightly celebrated Mumbai restaurant, is a great addition to Marylebone's foodie quarter. The alluring array of dishes, with the emphasis firmly on fish and seafood, come with both wine and beer pairing suggestions. They have substituted the Indian species for domestic varieties and dishes are for sharing – this is the sort of food where you want to roll up your sleeves and get stuck in. Stand-outs include the gloriously rich Cornish brown crab with butter and garlic and the crisp Isle of Wight plaice with pea and mint. Avoid going à la carte and head for the far more reasonably priced 8 course tasting menu.

Union Café

G2 **International**

96 Marylebone Lane ✉ W1U 2QA ⊖ Bond Street
✆ (020) 7486 4860
Fax (020) 7935 1537
www.brinkleys.com

Closed Sunday dinner and Bank Holidays

Carte £31/38

A/C VISA MC AE

The egalitarianism suggested by the name is entirely matched by its quasi-industrial looks; the exposed ducts, open kitchen and bustling atmosphere tell you straight away that this is no place for standing on ceremony. Mind you, the chairs now have cushions so lingering over lunch is no longer quite so numbing an experience. Service is pretty laid back but does get the job done, with just the occasional prompt required, while the menu exhibits a veritable hotchpotch of influences; expect to find everything from dim sum to risotto, burgers to pork belly and crab cakes to calves liver. The cooking is undertaken with more care than you expect and with these satisfying crowd-pleasers it's easy to see why the place is perennially busy.

Villandry

H1 **French** XX

170 Great Portland St ✉ W1W 5QB ⊖ Regent's Park
✆ (020) 7631 3131
Fax (020) 7631 3030
e-mail contactus@villandry.com
www.villandry.com

Closed 25-26 and 31 December, 1 January and Sunday dinner

Carte £25/41

It's almost a whole food village here as they've got most areas covered, from morning coffees to late drinks, snacks and plates of charcuterie to full meals. As such, it's worth coming in through the Great Portland entrance so as to walk past all the bounteous produce, rather than the Bolsover Street entrance which takes you straight into the restaurant. It has an appealing farmhouse-in-the-city kind of feel. The menu is quite extensive and its thrust is mostly French; there's a daily-changing plat du jour and a shellfish section but, in among the onion soups, cassoulets and terrines, you might also find a roast beef or a steak and ale pie. Bargain-hunters will be familiar with the Villandry outpost at Bicester Village.

Vineria

D0-1 **Italian** XX

1 Blenheim Terrace ✉ NW8 0EH ⊖ St John's Wood
✆ (020) 7328 5014
e-mail london@vineria.it
www.vineria.it

Closed Monday

Menu £20 (lunch) – Carte £28/39

The name has changed from Osteria Stecca to Vineria and the former number two in the kitchen has been promoted to head chef – otherwise little has changed at this neighbourhood Italian restaurant. The enclosed terrace at the front is a terrific spot in summer, while the small conservatory section can be a little draughty in winter. The enthusiastic application of white emulsion gives the main room a bright, clean feel. Service can sometimes be a little anxious. The menu covers all points of the country and the pasta section is one not to be ignored. Prices on the à la carte may seem quite high, especially in comparison to the good value lunch menu, but all dishes come fully garnished so there are no side orders to bump up that final bill.

The Wallace

G2 — French

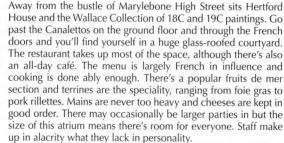

Hertford House,
Manchester Sq ✉ W1U 3BN
✆ (020) 7563 9505
e-mail reservations@thewallacerestaurant.com
www.thewallacerestaurant.com

⊖ Bond St
Closed 25 December – lunch only

Carte £26/32

VISA MC AE

Away from the bustle of Marylebone High Street sits Hertford House and the Wallace Collection of 18C and 19C paintings. Go past the Canalettos on the ground floor and through the French doors and you'll find yourself in a huge glass-roofed courtyard. The restaurant takes up most of the space, although there's also an all-day café. The menu is largely French in influence and cooking is done ably enough. There's a popular fruits de mer section and terrines are the speciality, ranging from foie gras to pork rillettes. Mains are never too heavy and cheeses are kept in good order. There may occasionally be larger parties in but the size of this atrium means there's room for everyone. Staff make up in alacrity what they lack in personality.

Zayna

F2 — Indian

25 New Quebec Rd ✉ W1H 7SF
✆ (020) 7723 2229
Fax (0870) 0420 022
e-mail info@zaynarestaurant.co.uk
www.zaynarestaurant.co.uk

⊖ Marble Arch

Carte £29/40

A/C VISA MC AE

When a restaurant is named after the owner's daughter you know there's going to be a lot of love around. Zayna reflects the personality of Riz Dar who spent his formative years around Kashmir and Punjab and whose first job was in his father's restaurant in Pakistan. It's no surprise then to find a menu of North Indian and Pakistani delicacies. It comes divided according to cooking method, from the pan, grill, tawa or oven; but look out for the refined street food using offal. He is passionate about produce: spices are roasted and ground in house and only halal meat and free-range chicken are used. Dishes come packed with flavour, although the final bill can quickly mount up. The ground floor is the more elegant of the two rooms.

Bloomsbury · Hatton Garden · Holborn

A real sense of history pervades this central chunk of London. From the great collection of antiquities in the British Museum to the barristers who swarm around the Royal Courts of Justice and Lincoln's Inn; from the haunts of Charles Dickens to the oldest Catholic church in Britain, the streets here are dotted with rich reminders of the past. Hatton Garden's fame as the city's diamond and jewellery centre goes back to Elizabethan times while, of a more recent vintage, Bloomsbury was home to the notorious Group (or Set) who, championed by Virginia Woolf, took on the world of art and literature in the 1920s.

A full-on encounter with **Holborn** is, initially, a shock to the system. Coming up from the tube, you'll find this is where main traffic arteries collide and a rugby scrum regularly ensues. Fear not, though; the relative calm of London's largest square, part-flanked by two quirky and intriguing museums, is just round the corner. The square is **Lincoln's Inn Fields,** which boasts a canopy of characterful oak trees and a set of tennis courts. On its north side is **Sir John Soane's Museum,** a gloriously eccentric place with twenty thousand exhibits where the walls open out like cabinets to reveal paintings by Turner and Canaletto. On its south side, the Hunterian Museum, refitted a few years ago, is a fascinating repository of medical bits and pieces. Visitors with a Damien Hirst take on life will revel in the likes of animal digestive systems in formaldehyde, or perhaps the sight of half of mathematician Charles Babbage's brain. Others not so fascinated by the gory might flee to the haunting silence of **St Etheldreda's church** in Ely Place, the only surviving example of thirteenth-century Gothic architecture in London. It survived the Great Fire of 1666, and Latin is still the language of choice.

Contemplation of a different kind takes centre stage in the adjacent **Hatton Garden.** This involves eager-eyed couples gazing at the glittering displays of rings and jewellery that have been lighting up the shop fronts here for many generations, ever since the leafy lane and its smart garden environs took the fancy of Sir Christopher Hatton, a favourite of Elizabeth I. After gawping at the baubles, there's liquid refreshment on hand at one of London's most atmospheric old pubs, the tiny Ye Old Mitre hidden down a narrow passageway. The preserved trunk of a cherry tree stands in the front bar, and, by all accounts, Elizabeth I danced the maypole round it (a legend that always seems more believable after the second pint).

Bloomsbury has intellectual connotations, and not just because of the writers and artists who frequented its townhouses in the twenties. This is where the University of London has its headquarters, and it's also home to the **British Museum,** the vast treasure trove of international artefacts that attracts visitors in even vaster numbers. As if the exhibits themselves weren't lure enough, there's also the fantastic glass-roofed Great Court, opened to much fanfare at the start of the Millennium, which lays claim to being the largest covered public square in Europe. To the north of here by the Euston Road is the **British Library,** a rather stark red brick building that holds over 150 million items and is one of the greatest centres of knowledge in the world. Meanwhile, Dickens fans should make for the north east corner of Bloomsbury for the great man's museum in **Doughty Street:** this is one of many London houses in which he lived, but it's the only one still standing. He lived here for three years, and it proved a fruitful base, resulting in Nicholas Nickleby and Oliver Twist. The museum holds manuscripts, letters and Dickens' writing desk. If your appetite for the written word has been truly whetted, then a good tip is to head back west half a mile to immerse yourself in the bookshops of Great Russell Street.

C. Eymenier / MICHELIN

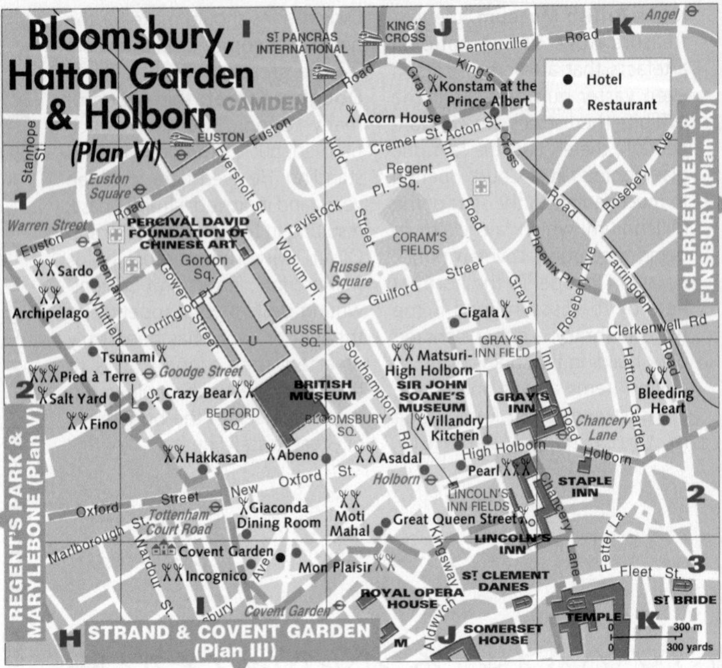
Bloomsbury, Hatton Garden & Holborn
(Plan VI)
Hotel
Restaurant
ST PANCRAS INTERNATIONAL
KING'S CROSS
EUSTON
CAMDEN
Euston Square
Warren Street
PERCIVAL DAVID FOUNDATION OF CHINESE ART
Gordon Sq.
RUSSELL SQ.
Russell Square
CORAM'S FIELDS
Regent Sq.
BRITISH MUSEUM
BEDFORD SQ.
BLOOMSBURY SQ.
SIR JOHN SOANE'S MUSEUM
GRAY'S INN FIELD
GRAY'S INN
Chancery Lane
STAPLE INN
LINCOLN'S INN FIELDS
LINCOLN'S INN
Holborn
Goodge Street
Tottenham Court Road
Covent Garden
ROYAL OPERA HOUSE
ST CLEMENT DANES
SOMERSET HOUSE
TEMPLE
ST BRIDE
Angel
Konstam at the Prince Albert
Acorn House
Sardo
Archipelago
Tsunami
Pied à Terre
Salt Yard
Crazy Bear
Fino
Hakkasan
Abeno
Asadal
Matsuri-High Holborn
Villandry Kitchen
Cigala
Bleeding Heart
Pearl
Giaconda Dining Room
Moti Mahal
Great Queen Street
Covent Garden
Incognico
Mon Plaisir
CLERKENWELL & FINSBURY (Plan IX)
REGENT'S PARK & MARYLEBONE (Plan V)
STRAND & COVENT GARDEN (Plan III)
300 m
300 yards

Abeno

I2 **Japanese**

47 Museum St ✉ WC1A 1LY
✆ (020) 7405 3211
Fax (020) 7405 3212
e-mail okonomi@abeno.co.uk
www.abeno.co.uk

⊖ Tottenham Court Road
Closed 1 January, 23-27 and 31 December

Menu £13 (lunch) – Carte £15/43

A/C VISA MC

Okonomi-yaki is the speciality of this modest but very charming little Japanese place. That's a pancake-like dish, prepared at your table, where you decide on which toppings you want. They are surprisingly rich so a side order of salad or pickle is worth considering but don't ignore the rest of the menu, nor the desserts – the green tea ice cream is particularly good. With only eight tables it can get busy, especially with the British Museum being just yards away but they are open all day and do take reservations. It's best to come with friends as it's a fun experience and the staff, in their natty red T-shirts, are sweet tempered and dextrous on that hotplate. The sake cocktails will get any party off to a flying start.

Acorn House

J0 **Modern European**

69 Swinton St ✉ WC1X 9NT
✆ (020) 7812 1842
e-mail bookings@acornhouserestaurant.com
www.acornhouserestaurant.com

⊖ King's Cross
Closed 25 December, Sunday and Bank Holidays

Carte £25/36

A/C VISA MC AE

However worthy the principles of a restaurant – and this restaurant has many worthy principles – the proof must always be in the pudding and fortunately at Acorn House that pudding tastes good. This is a joint venture between the Terence Higgins and Shoreditch Trusts and was London's first eco-friendly training restaurant. They buy local and organic, use renewable 'green' electricity, purify their water, compost waste and recycle. Their menu is teasingly understated, with just the mainstays of the dishes listed. What you get is healthy, generously proportioned, flavoursome seasonality on a plate, using a variety of culinary influences; who can resist kicking off with a rhubarb Bellini? The room has a bright, café-style feel.

Archipelago

H1 **Innovative** XX

110 Whitfield St ✉ W1T 5ED
✆ (020) 7383 3346
Fax (020) 7383 7181
e-mail info@archipelago-restaurant.co.uk
www.archipelago-restaurant.co.uk

⊖ Goodge Street
Closed 24-26 December, 1 January, Saturday lunch, Sunday and Bank Holiday Mondays

Carte £30/40

VISA MC AE

On a rainy night it takes on the atmosphere of a steamy colonial outpost and you half expect a hunter in a pith helmet to walk past your table. This restaurant is certainly not for the squeamish while those of an overly serious disposition may not get it either. 'Eclectic' is an oft-bandied word to describe hybrid cooking but here it's truly merited. Where else can you eat crocodile, zebra, kangaroo or wildebeest? Peacock has also recently appeared and scorpion has made the odd appearance in the past. The cooking itself often takes on an Asian element and the staff are all faultlessly well informed. Every surface is covered in feathers, trinkets and carvings, all for sale, and your local will seem very dull after this.

Asadal

J2 **Korean** XX

227 High Holborn ✉ WC1V 7DA
✆ (020) 7430 9006
e-mail info@asadal.co.uk
www.asadal.co.uk

⊖ Holborn
Closed 25-26 December, 1 January and Sunday lunch

Menu £12 (lunch) – Carte £13/20

A/C VISA MC AE

Every nationality of cuisine has enjoyed its moment in the spotlight and now Asadal, a basement restaurant adjacent to Holborn tube, successfully argues the case for Korean cooking to be given a higher profile. There may be a barbecue in the centre of most of the tables but there is so much more to Korean cooking. The philosophy is built upon harmony of taste, it's all made for sharing and there's even a health dividend to most of the specialities. Novices will find that the menu is helpfully descriptive but don't be shy about using the call buttons under the table to summon help. The room is perfectly comfortable, with lots of wood and plenty of partitions and there are quieter corners for those wishing to escape the general clamour.

Bleeding Heart

K2 French XX

Bleeding Heart Yard (off Greville St)
EC1N 8SJ
(020) 7242 8238
Fax (020) 7831 1402
e-mail bookings@bleedingheart.co.uk
www.bleedingheart.co.uk

Farringdon
Closed 23 December-4 January, Saturday, Sunday and Bank Holidays – booking essential

Carte £29/37

Head for the luminous hanging heart in the right-hand corner of the atmospheric 17C yard, pass the bustling bistro and terrace, and go downstairs for the full Bleeding Heart experience. You'll find a restaurant that's always busy, especially with those from the City - if you're after a more romantic dinner then come on a Friday night when the suits have long gone. The attractions for the regulars are the fast-paced service, the French food and the terrific wine list. The menu changes seasonally and has a traditional core, while the cooking is as well practised as the service and the sauces satisfyingly rich. The owners also have their own vineyard in Hawkes Bay and their highly impressive wine list has a bias towards New Zealand and France.

VISA

AE

Cigala

J1 Spanish X

54 Lamb's Conduit St WC1N 3LW
(020) 7405 1717
Fax (020) 7242 9949
e-mail tasty@cigala.co.uk
www.cigala.co.uk

Russell Square
Closed 24-26 December, 1 January and Easter – booking essential

Menu £18 (lunch) – Carte £24/35

Lamb's Conduit hustles and bustles these days and Cigala fits right in. It's quite stark and a bit echoey but once all the regulars pile in they create their own infectious vibe. They come for the authentic and appealingly priced Spanish cooking. The menu changes daily, the highlight being the long list of tapas/starters - two of these plus a main course should more than suffice. There are dishes for two, such as paella and arroz caldoso, that are worth waiting the 30 minutes and the Spanish drinks list is equally tempting. Owner Jake Hodges now spends a lot of his time in Spain and the kitchen can sometimes be lacking in a little lustre, but this is still a good place to spend a winter's evening when summer seems a long way off.

A/C

VISA

AE

Crazy Bear

12

Asian XX

26-28 Whitfield St ✉ W1T 2RG ⊖ Goodge Street
✆ (020) 7631 0088
Fax (020) 7631 1188
e-mail enquiries@crazybear-fitzrovia.co.uk
www.crazybeargroup.co.uk

Menu £15 – Carte £24/50

A/C VISA MC AE

The sign is still concealed but that probably adds to the sense of exclusivity and furtiveness. Crazy Bear's clientele are a young bunch, attracted by the chance to dress up for the busy basement bar and the ground floor restaurant. The lighting is moody and the tables are small, so some juggling is required if you want to share plates - and sharing is certainly the best option. The menu is a lengthy issue, covering a number of cuisines, from China to Thailand and from mild and comforting to larynx-laceratingly hot. Dim sum is served all day, and the menu is divided into starters, soups, salads, meat, seafood and curries, as well as eleven or twelve plate tasting menus. Ingredients are good and the choice sufficient to suit all tastes.

Fino

12

Spanish XX

33 Charlotte St (entrance on Rathbone St) ⊖ Goodge Street
✉ W1T 1RR
✆ (020) 7813 8010
Fax (020) 7813 8011
e-mail info@finorestaurant.com
www.finorestaurant.com

Closed 24-25 December, Saturday lunch, Sunday and Bank Holidays

Carte £22/34

VISA MC AE

They don't make it easy on themselves by giving their address as Charlotte Street when, in fact, the discreet entrance to this basement restaurant is actually on Rathbone Street. Perhaps that's the reason why, once you've descended the staircase, you'll find that it has something of a secretive and local vibe. Tapas is the order of the day although it's all structured slightly more formally than you'd find in Spain and the room itself is decidedly more stylish than you'd expect. Five or six dishes per couple to share should suffice, although set menus are available for the undecided. Try a sherry or something from the exclusively Spanish wine list. Helpful waitresses are more than willing to offer advice as well as a translation of unfamiliar words.

Giaconda Dining Room

I2 **Modern European**

9 Denmark Street WC2H 8LS — Tottenham Court Road
(020) 7240 3334
e-mail paulmerrony@gmail.com
www.giacondadining.com

Closed 1 week Christmas, 3 weeks August, Saturday, Sunday and Bank Holidays – booking essential

Carte £24/28

A/C VISA MC AE

In the shadow of Centrepoint lies a frayed little area that's 'not quite Soho.' Here you'll find Denmark Street - London's own historic Tin Pan Alley – now home to the Giaconda Dining Room. Aussies Paul and Tracey Merrony have a small but perfectly formed little place; spartanly decorated, busy from day one and great fun. Paul describes his cooking as "Frenchy, with day trips to Italy," which translates on the plate as confident, gutsy, no-nonsense and immeasurably satisfying. Tripe; steak tartare; pork sausage stew; risotto; a deconstructed pig's trotter and a daily changing fish or grilled dish special - there's something for everyone and, with most wine bottles in the £20s, it's all done at a credit-crunch busting price.

Great Queen Street

J2 **British**

32 Great Queen St
WC2B 5AA
(020) 7242 0622
Fax (020) 7404 9582

Holborn
Closed Christmas-New Year, Sunday dinner and Bank Holidays – booking essential

Menu £25 (Sunday lunch) – Carte £23/36

VISA MC

Great Queen Street is now an established point on the foodie trail and the lack of an obvious sign outside just adds to that sense of discovery and exclusivity. The look is appealingly down to earth and it's always full of noise, due to general merry-making and dodgy acoustics. Its popularity means staff are always under pressure but they are more practised these days and all share the kitchen's enthusiasm. The cooking is equally lusty and satisfying and sourcing is clearly a passion. It thrives on seasonality and is proudly British. Look out for the dishes for two, whether that's the mighty rib and chips or one of the enormous pies. The paintings are by Aldous Eveleigh, whose studio is above The Anchor and Hope, the owners' alma mater.

Hakkasan ✿

I2

Chinese XX

8 Hanway Place ✉ W1T 1HD

✆ (020) 7927 7000

Fax (020) 7907 1889

e-mail mail@hakkasan.com

www.hakkasan.com

⊖ Tottenham Court Road

Closed 24-25 December

Carte £32/109

A/C VISA MC AE

Hakkasan

The subterranean Hakkasan remains as cool and seductive as ever and its popularity shows no sign of slowing. Despite the size and general bustle, it is actually possible to have quite an intimate experience here, thanks to the clever lighting and good acoustics. Service can be a little hit and miss and depends largely on who your waiter is and their levels of enthusiasm although it does generally get better when the room reaches capacity. Lunchtime dim sum is a real highlight, although they sometimes appear curiously reluctant to offer you that particular menu. There are 20 chefs in the kitchen, many of whom are, like the head chef, from Singapore. The extensive menu is laid out clearly and logically, although there can be a marked difference in price between similar sounding dishes. Cantonese remains the starting point but the kitchen adds its own signature of inventiveness to give the dishes zip and the flavours depth. One thing the waiting staff do get right is telling you when you've unwittingly but understandably succumbed to over-ordering.

First Course

- Grilled quail with green mango and papaya salad.
- Scallop and prawn cake with dried scallop sauce.

Main Course

- Stir-fried Mongolian style venison.
- Silver cod with champagne and honey.

Dessert

- Chocolate ganache.
- Muscavado savarin with ginger tea ice cream.

Incognico

13 French XX

117 Shaftesbury Ave
✉ WC2H 8AD
✆ (020) 7836 8866
Fax (020) 7240 9525
e-mail incognicorestaurant@gmail.com
www.incognico.com

⊖ Tottenham Court Road
Closed Sunday and Bank Holidays

Menu £20 – Carte £28/39

A/C VISA MC AE

The smart brasserie look remains largely the same, thanks to its worn-in leather, art deco styling, panelling and neatly laid tables. Table 25, enveloped in an alcove, is still the table of choice for the romantically inclined and the service continues to be well organised. But the main change is the elusiveness of those good value set menus; there is a one available but you sometimes have to tease it out of them. The cooking has a French base but with prominent Italian influences and the menu is heavily supported by daily specials. It's frill-free and confidently executed but those side dishes are needed and can push up the final bill. It still beats all those tourist joints that this part of town attracts hands down.

Konstam at the Prince Albert

J0 Traditional X

2 Acton St ✉ WC1X 9NA
✆ (020) 7833 5040
e-mail princealbert@konstam.co.uk
www.konstam.co.uk

⊖ King's Cross St Pancras
Closed 24 December-2 January, Saturday lunch and Bank Holidays

Carte £26/35

VISA MC AE

Gentrification may remain elusive but at least King's Cross now offers a few dining options. Oliver Rowe took a shabby Victorian pub, named it after his great grandfather and kept the décor functional, save for a striking ornamental lighting feature. However, what makes this restaurant so unusual is that the produce is nearly all sourced from within the boundaries of the London transport network. Using local supplies is easy when you're in Devon but Central London throws up its own challenges and you'll spend most of the time wondering where exactly some of the ingredients on your plate came from. The open kitchen means that if curiosity gets the better of you, then the chefs are within questioning range.

Matsuri - High Holborn

J2 — Japanese XX

Mid City Pl, 71 High Holborn ✉ WC1V 6EA
✆ (020) 7430 1970
Fax (020) 7430 1971
e-mail eat@matsuri-restaurant.com
www.matsuri-restaurant.com

⊖ Holborn
Closed 25 December,1 January, Sunday and Bank Holidays

Menu £29/35 – Carte £19/75

VISA MC AE

This more modern branch of the Japanese Matsuri restaurants contrasts with the rather traditional feel of the Bury Street original. The shiniest part of the large room is the very long sushi bar to the right as you enter, while the main dining room is the darker area at the back; those who come for teppan-yaki – the third part of the operation – should head downstairs. The best plan for those in the dining room is to order one of the set menus, which includes a kaiseki option for those wanting the full Japanese experience. Otherwise, the soft shell crabs and the sashimi are highlights for anyone going down the à la carte route. Lunch is certainly the busiest part of the day, when staff are less inclined to stand around.

Mon Plaisir

I3 — French XX

19-21 Monmouth St ✉ WC2H 9DD
✆ (020) 7836 7243
Fax (020) 7240 4774
e-mail monplaisirrestaurant@googlemail.com
www.monplaisir.co.uk

⊖ Covent Garden
Closed 25 December-1 January, Saturday lunch, Sunday and Bank Holidays

Menu £17 (lunch) – Carte £29/47

VISA MC AE

London's oldest French restaurant is also one of its most gloriously unpretentious and individual. If you think the Eurostar transports you to France in an instant, try walking into Mon Plaisir, family run for over fifty years, where cries of 'Bonjour!' greet every arrival. The walls are decorated with a plethora of posters, pictures and paraphernalia and the bar is from a Lyonnais brothel. Regulars have their favourite of the numerous interconnecting rooms, all of which ooze unmistakeable Gallic charm. But this is no themed restaurant - this is as real as the coq au vin or cassolette d'escargots. The fixed price lunch and pre-theatre menus represent excellent value and periodically held evenings featuring a particular region of France are popular events.

Moti Mahal

J2 **Indian** XX

45 Great Queen St ✉ WC2B 5AA — ⊖ Holborn

✆ (020) 7240 9329 — Closed 25-28 December, New Year, Saturday lunch and Sunday

Fax (020) 7836 0790

e-mail reservations@motimahal-uk.com

www.motimahal-uk.com

Menu £15/20 – Carte £31/42

A/C · VISA · MC · AE

From the outside Moti Mahal looks more like a cocktail bar than an Indian restaurant, while inside they've clearly let the barman choose the music. It's divided between two floors: the lower level has great semi-circular booths but unfortunately this room is used more for private parties or as an overflow for the bright ground floor. The chefs perform their kitchen duties behind a large window which allows diners the chance to see the action and the star of the show is undoubtedly the tandoor oven. The innovative menu is ambitious in its reach and far removed from the usual standards; the ingredients are top-notch which means that prices are also higher than average. Service is keen and sincere.

Pearl

J2 **French** XXX

252 High Holborn ✉ WC1V 7EN — ⊖ Holborn

✆ (020) 7829 7000 — Closed last 2 weeks August, Saturday lunch, Sunday and Bank Holidays

Fax (020) 7829 9889

e-mail info@pearl-restaurant.com

www.pearl-restaurant.com

Menu £29/55

A/C · VISA · MC · AE

A room as grand as this has to be busy otherwise the tables feel a little cast adrift. This former banking hall is within what was once Pearl Assurance's HQ; its high ceiling, chandeliers and columns certainly add some grandeur to proceedings but they clearly didn't make life easy when it came to adding the lighting. Waiting staff come dressed in black and are an enthusiastic, well-drilled bunch who do a good job ensuring that the surroundings don't become the main event. Chef Jun Tanaka, who pulls in plenty of the customers himself thanks to his television appearances, offers a menu high in originality but grounded in a classical French base. The wine list is a particularly impressive tome in both its depth and variety.

Pied à Terre ✿✿

12

Innovative XXX

34 Charlotte St ✉ W1T 2NH
(020) 7636 1178
Fax (020) 7916 1171
e-mail info@pied-a-terre.co.uk
www.pied-a-terre.co.uk

⊖ Goodge Street
Closed 24 December-5 January, Saturday lunch and Sunday

Menu £33 (lunch)/69 – Carte approx. £70

A/C VISA AE

Pied à Terre

David Moore may be spending less time here in the restaurant as he continues his bourgeoning TV career and also looks after their other place, L'Autre Pied; but Shane Osborn is a chef who eschews the limelight in favour of getting on with what he likes doing best – cooking. That doesn't mean he is cocooned in his own world – he still spends time seeing what competitors are up to by sharing thoughts and ideas with other chefs around the country. The restaurant is very much the senior member in Charlotte Street but this is still somewhere with ambition and a will to improve. It is certainly not the most spacious place around and when customers are assailed by staff at the beginning it can feel a little claustrophobic but things do subsequently calm down. The cooking may appear quite elaborate on the plate but there is no jostling of flavours. Certain dishes, such as the seared and poached foie gras starter and the bitter chocolate tart dessert enjoy a perennial presence on the menu. The set lunch menu represents decent value.

First Course

- Crayfish and garlic gnocchi with Lardo di Colonnata.
- Seared and poached foie gras with Sauternes consommé.

Main Course

- Suckling pig with beetroot, girolles and cider sauce.
- Turbot with crab and chicken boudin.

Dessert

- Bitter sweet chocolate tart, stout ice cream and macadamia nut cream.
- Hazelnut financière with honey and vanilla poached apricots.

Rasa Samudra

12 **Indian** XX

5 Charlotte St ✉ W1T 1RE
✆ (020) 7637 0222
Fax (020) 7637 0224
www.rasarestaurants.com

⊖ Goodge Street
Closed 24 December-1 January, Sunday lunch and Bank Holidays

Menu £23/30 – Carte £13/24

VISA MC AE

So how best to draw attention to yourself when you're competing for business in a street filled with an abundance of restaurants and cafés? Full marks go to Rasa Samudra for painting their façade a shocking shade of pink, which certainly makes them stand out, although intriguingly they have also decided to paint the interior in the same hue. The front room fills up first but go through to the rooms at the back which are far more inviting. The restaurant is also decorated with silks, carvings and assorted Indian ornaments but the food's the main attraction, with a menu divided into two main parts: rich and creamy seafood specialities from Kerala and fragrant vegetarian dishes. Begin your meal by trying typical Keralan tea shop snacks.

Roka

12 **Japanese** XX

37 Charlotte St ✉ W1T 1RR
✆ (020) 7580 6464
Fax (020) 7580 0220
e-mail info@rokarestaurant.com
www.rokarestaurant.com

⊖ Tottenham Court Road
Closed 24-27 December and 1 January

Carte approx. £32

A/C VISA MC AE

Roka has one of those appealingly perceptible pulses that only really busy, well-run restaurants enjoy. It attracts a handsome crowd although they don't just come to glory in their mutual attractiveness but to share food that's original, easy to eat and just as pretty as they are. The kitchen takes the flavours, delicacy and strong presentation standards of Japanese food and adds its own contemporary touches. The menu can appear bewildering but just skip the set menus and order an assortment from the various headings; ensure you have one of the specialities from the on-view Robata grill. Sometimes too many dishes can arrive at once but the serving team are a friendly and capable bunch and they'll ease up on the delivery if you ask.

Salt Yard

Mediterranean

H2

54 Goodge St ✉ W1T 4NA
(020) 7637 0657
Fax (020) 7580 7435
e-mail info@saltyard.co.uk
www.saltyard.co.uk

⊖ Goodge Street
Closed 10 days Christmas, Saturday lunch, Sunday and Bank Holidays

Carte £20/36

The first thing you get is a smiley welcome and then it's a straight choice between the bar-like ground floor or the more traditionally laid out dining room downstairs; the former is usually more fun. You'll then have a few snacks with something from the mostly Italian wine list, work up to ordering some charcuterie and go from there. It's this kind of flexibility, as well as the competitive pricing, that makes this place so appealing. Spanish is obviously the main influence but the kitchen also adds some Italian specialities and these vibrant Mediterranean aromas fill the air in an enticing way. Flavours are punchy, varied and effective while puddings such as soft chocolate cake with frangelico ice cream, are prepared with care.

Sardo

Italian

H1

45 Grafton Way ✉ W1T 5DQ
(020) 7387 2521
Fax (020) 7387 2559
e-mail info@sardo-restaurant.com
www.sardo-restaurant.com

⊖ Warren Street
Closed Christmas, Saturday lunch and Sunday

Carte £26/34

It's worth booking as Sardo is nearly always full - entirely understandably, as this is the sort of restaurant whose regulars pitch up on an almost daily basis. The owner, chef and most of the kitchen hail from Sardinia and the island provides most of the influences. The ravioli and speciality pastas are made in-house and the kitchen uses particularly hard wheat imported from small suppliers in Sardinia. The cooking is fresh, unpretentious and uses a lot of char-grilling; the menu is helped out by the daily-changing blackboard specials. The wine list also remains faithful as Sardinian wines make up half the list. The room is neat and tables are simply laid; those at the back are slightly lighter, thanks to the ceiling window.

Tsunami

H2 **Japanese**

93 Charlotte St. ✉ W1T 4PY
✆ (020) 7637 0050
Fax (020) 7637 4411
e-mail westend@tsunamirestaurant.co.uk
www.tsunamirestaurant.co.uk

⊖ Goodge Street
Closed 25 December, Saturday lunch and Sunday

Menu £13 (lunch) – Carte £19/35

You'll never find anyone from Clapham in Nobu or Roka because they always insist they have their own cheaper version in Tsunami. Now we all have the opportunity of seeing what they mean because a second branch has opened in the West End. Appropriately enough, it is at the less showy end of Charlotte Street but is prettily decorated with lacquered walls and a floral motif, with colour changing lights and lounge music. Staff have good intentions but do tend to go missing at crucial moments but the contemporary Japanese food is carefully prepared and the menu covers all points and includes plenty of originality. Seafood, whether grilled, as tempura or a sashimi salad, is a highlight and plenty can be shared without breaking the bank.

Villandry Kitchen

J2 **French**

95-97 High Holborn ✉ WC1V 6LF
✆ (020) 7242 4580
e-mail holborn@villandrykitchen.com
www.villandry.com

⊖ Holborn
Closed 25 December

Carte £18/30

This is the third and most recent addition to the Villandry group and should give all the surrounding chains in Holborn a run for their money. It aims to attract customers from early morning to late evening, offering everything from a breakfast menu to assorted charcuterie, from children's menus and pizzas to comforting French classics – and all at a fair price, where service is not automatically added. There's a good selection of wine by glass and carafe, including a decent house wine from Languedoc. The place is too big to be considered a bistrot and its somewhat austere layout means that the noise bounces around, but it does have an appealingly rustic and honest feel. Service is friendly, if at times a little overconfident.

Bayswater · Maida Vale

There may not appear to be an obvious link between Maida Vale and Italy, but the name of this smart area to the west of central London is derived from a battle fought over two hundred years ago in Southern Italy, and the most appealing visitor attraction in the neighbourhood is the charming canalside **Little Venice.** To stroll around here on a summer's day brings to mind promenading in a more distant European clime; it's hard to believe that the ear-shattering roar of the Westway is just a short walk away. South of this iconic elevated roadway – a snaking route out from Marylebone to the western suburbs – is Bayswater, a busy area of imposing nineteenth century buildings that's the epicentre of London's Middle Eastern community.

During its Victorian heyday, **Bayswater** was a grand and glamorous address for affluent and elegant types who wanted a giant green space (Hyde Park) on their doorstep. The whole area had been laid out in the mid 1800s, when grand squares and cream stuccoed terraces started to fill the acres between Brunel's curvy Paddington station and the park. But during the twentieth century Bayswater's cachet nose-dived, stigmatised as 'the wrong side of the park' by the arrivistes of Knightsbridge and Kensington. Today it's still a backpacker's paradise: home to a bewildering number of shabby tourist hotels, bedsits and B&Bs, converted from the grand houses. But this tells only a fraction of the modern story, because the area is undergoing a massive facelift that will transform it forever. The hub of this makeover is the **Paddington Basin,** a gigantic reclamation of the old Grand Union Canal basin in the shadow of the rail terminus. From a ramshackle wasteground, it's now a shimmering zone of metal, steel and glass, a phantasmagoria of blue chip HQs, homes, shops and leisure facilities. Even the barges have been turned into permanently moored 'retail opportunities'. Tree-lined towpaths along the perimeter complete the picture of a totally modern waterscape.

Lovers of the old Bayswater can still relish what made it famous in the first place: radiating out from **Lancaster Gate,** away from Hyde Park, is a web of streets with handsome squares and tucked-away mews, and it still retains pockets of close-knit communities, such as Porchester Square, west of Paddington station. Meanwhile, the 'cathedral' of the area, Whiteleys shopping centre in **Queensway**, remains a pivotal landmark, as it has been for more than a century. Just beyond Whiteleys heading away from central London, **Westbourne Grove** is still reassuringly expensive, or at least the bit that heads determinedly towards Notting Hill. But the wind of change has rustled other parts of the neighbourhood: Connaught Street has evolved into a villagey quarter of boutiques, galleries and restaurants, while, further west, Craven Hill Gardens is the height of chic, courtesy of The Hempel, a boutique hotel.

Little Venice pretty much acts as a dividing line between Bayswater and Maida Vale. Technically, it's the point where the Paddington arm of the Grand Union Canal meets the **Regent's Canal,** but the name, coined by poet Robert Browning who lived close by, has come to encompass the whole area just to the north of the soaring Westway. Narrow boat moorings vie for attention alongside the cafés and pubs that mercifully lack the frantic high street buzz so typical of their kind away from the water's edge. The permanently moored boats were here a long time before those upstarts at Paddington Basin. This is where you can find old-time favourites including a floating art gallery and a puppet theatre barge, and all overseen by the Warwick Castle pub, a stalwart of the area that's a minute's walk from the canal. Suitably refreshed, a wander round the residential streets of Maida Vale is very pleasant, dominated by the impressive Edwardian blocks of flats that conjure up a distinctive well-to-do scene.

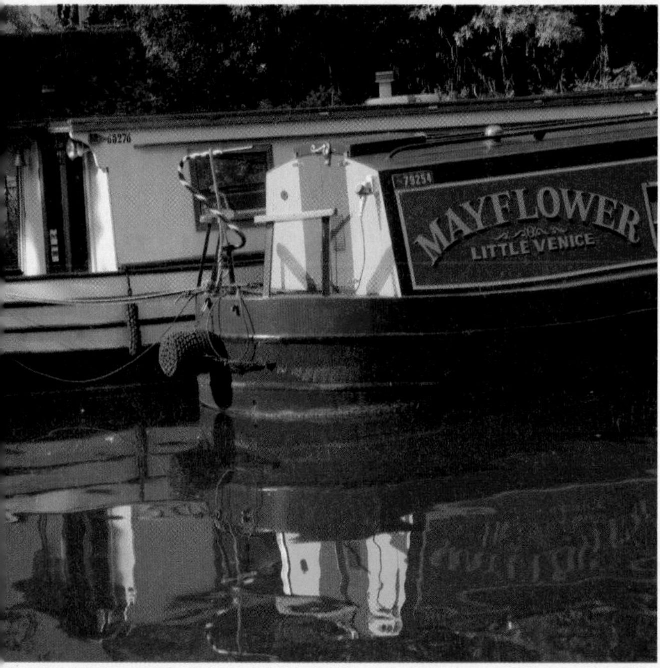

S. Ollivier / MICHELIN

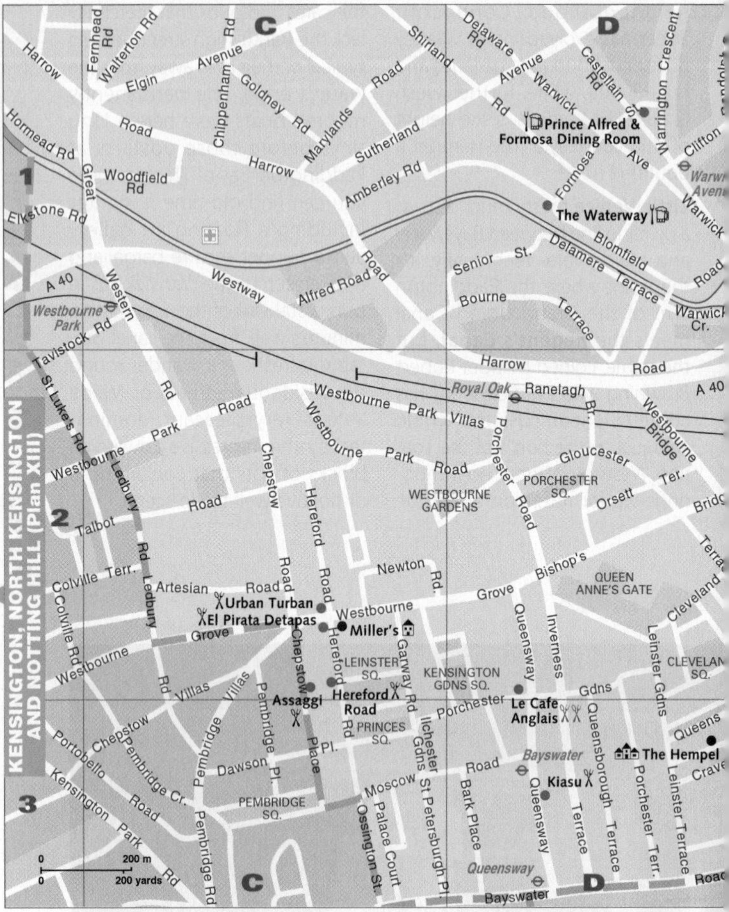
KENSINGTON, NORTH KENSINGTON AND NOTTING HILL (Plan XIII)
C
D
1
2
3
Prince Alfred & Formosa Dining Room
The Waterway
Urban Turban
El Pirata Detapas
Miller's
Assaggi
Hereford Road
Le Cafe Anglais
Kiasu
The Hempel
Westbourne Park
Royal Oak
Bayswater
Queensway
WESTBOURNE GARDENS
PORCHESTER SQ.
QUEEN ANNE'S GATE
LEINSTER SQ.
KENSINGTON GDNS SQ.
PRINCES SQ.
PEMBRIDGE SQ.
CLEVELAND SQ.
A 40
Westway
Harrow Road
Elgin Avenue
Sutherland Avenue
Westbourne Park Road
Westbourne Park Villas
Westbourne Grove
Chepstow Road
Hereford Road
Porchester Road
Queensway
Inverness Terrace
Bishop's Bridge Road
Moscow Road
Pembridge Villas
Ledbury Rd
Talbot Road
Great Western Rd
0 200 m
0 200 yards

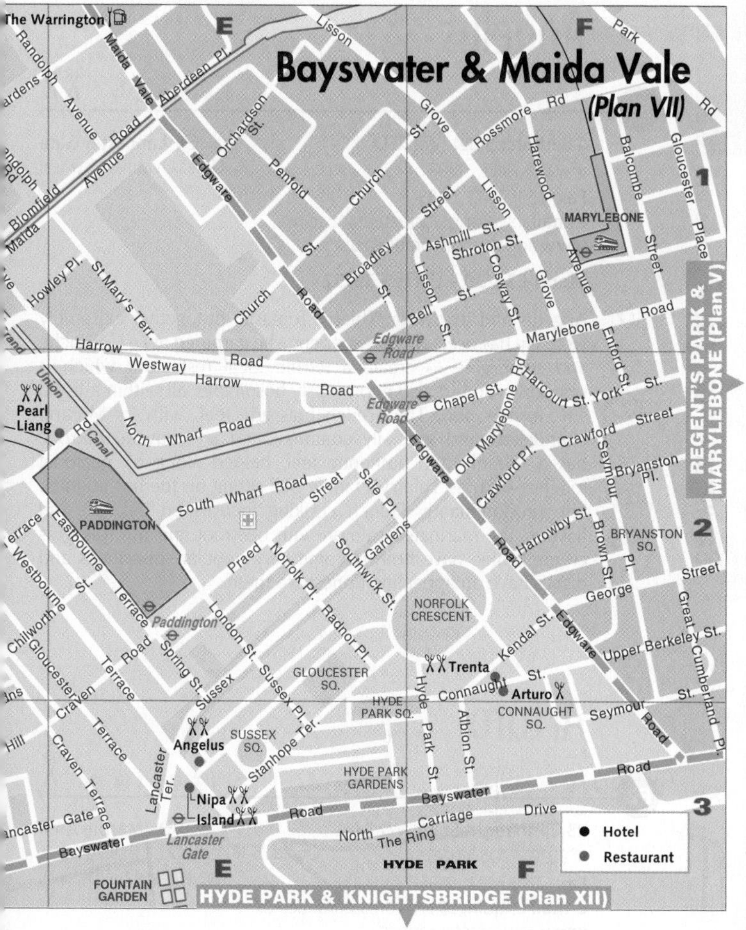

Bayswater & Maida Vale
(Plan VII)
The Warrington
E
F
Lisson
Park
Rd
Randolph
Gardens
Avenue
Maida
Vale
Aberdeen Pl.
Road
Avenue
Blomfield
Orchardson St.
Penfold
Edgware
Church
St.
Grove
Rossmore
Rd
Harewood
Lisson
Balcombe
Gloucester
Place
Street
MARYLEBONE
Ashmill St.
Shroton St.
Broadley
St.
Lisson
Cosway St.
Grove
Avenue
Street
Howley Pl.
St Mary's Terr.
Church
Road
Bell
St.
St.
Marylebone
Road
Edgware Road
Harrow
Westway
Road
Harrow
Road
Union
Canal
Pearl Liang
Rd
North
Wharf
Road
Edgware Road
Chapel St.
Old Marylebone Rd
Harcourt St.
York St.
Enford St.
Crawford
Street
Seymour
Bryanston Pl.
Crawford Pl.
REGENT'S PARK & MARYLEBONE (Plan V)
PADDINGTON
South Wharf Road
Street
Sale Pl.
Edgware
Road
Terrace
Westbourne
Eastbourne
Terrace
Praed
Norfolk Pl.
Southwick St.
Gardens
Harrowby St.
Brown St.
Pl.
BRYANSTON SQ.
1
2
3
Street
George
Chilworth
St.
Gloucester
Paddington
London St.
Radnor Pl.
NORFOLK CRESCENT
Kendal St.
Edgware
Road
Great Cumberland Pl.
Upper Berkeley St.
Road
Terrace
Craven
Spring St.
Sussex
Sussex Pl.
GLOUCESTER SQ.
Trenta
St.
Connaught
Arturo
St.
HYDE PARK SQ.
Hyde Park St.
Albion St.
CONNAUGHT SQ.
Seymour
Road
Terrace
Hill
Craven Terrace
Angelus
SUSSEX SQ.
Stanhope Ter.
Lancaster Ter.
HYDE PARK GARDENS
Road
Bayswater
Nipa
Island
Road
Carriage
Drive
Lancaster Gate
Terrace
Bayswater
Lancaster Gate
North
The Ring
HYDE PARK
Hotel
Restaurant
FOUNTAIN GARDEN
E
F
HYDE PARK & KNIGHTSBRIDGE (Plan XII)

Angelus

E3 — French XX

4 Bathurst St ✉ W2 2SD
✆ (020) 7402 0083
Fax (020) 7402 5383
e-mail info@angelusrestaurant.co.uk
www.angelusrestaurant.co.uk

⊖ Lancaster Gate
Closed Christmas-New Year

Menu £36/38 – Carte £36/52

A/C VISA MC AE

Angelus and its owner, Thierry Tomasin, fit together extremely well. He has used all the experience he garnered at Le Gavroche and Aubergine to create a terrific local restaurant which is smoothly run but also enormously hospitable, all within a listed 19C former pub. The French brasserie feel, with its Murano chandeliers and specially commissioned art nouveau mirrors, has a friendly and authentic feel, helped along by personal touches such as Thierry's family bell sitting on the bar counter. The predominantly French cooking focuses on balance and flavour; the marinated salmon with beetroot and the foie gras crème brûlée have both become very popular specialities and dishes have an appealing honesty to them.

Arturo

F2 — Italian X

23 Connaught St ✉ W2 2AY
✆ (020) 7706 3388
Fax (020) 7402 9195
e-mail enquiries@arturorestaurant.co.uk
www.arturorestaurant.co.uk

⊖ Marble Arch
Closed 25-26 December, 1 January, Easter, Saturday and Sunday lunch

Menu £17 – Carte £20/33

A/C VISA MC AE

Ubiquitous beige is the prevailing shade of this slickly designed neighbourhood restaurant, surrounded by antique and art emporia and the growing signs of gentrification. It's all clean and crisp inside, with the clear lines only interrupted by the unevenly shaped customers. Service is confident but phlegmatic. The menu offers up an unchallenging selection of fresh and colourfully presented Italian dishes. Seasoning can occasionally be a little hit and miss but pasta dishes are sensibly proportioned and desserts are nicely balanced. Those who don't mind eating early are rewarded with an inexpensive set menu with adequate choice, as are those coming for lunch. The exclusively Italian wine list keeps things affordable.

Assaggi

C2 **Italian** X

39 Chepstow Pl, (above Chepstow pub) ⊖ Bayswater
✉ W2 4TS
✆ (020) 7792 5501
e-mail nipi@assaggi.demon.co.uk
www.assaggi.com

Closed 2 weeks Christmas, Sunday and Bank Holidays – booking essential

Carte approx. £44

A/C VISA MC

Assaggi has always been about simplicity, from the pared-down surroundings of this room above a pub to the handwritten bill at the end. The cooking has also always been about honest flavours and quality produce but the creeping hand of complacency has seen some of the shine come off; dishes that were once full of vitality now seem duller in comparison and the kitchen appears to have lost a little of its verve and panache. This is a pity because Assaggi has always been a spirited and inclusive restaurant and has shown that good food need not be accompanied by great ceremony. Regulars, kissed on the way in and the way out, may treat the place like their local trattoria, but the prices represent a special night out for most of us.

Le Café Anglais

D2 **Modern European** XX

8 Porchester Gdns ✉ W2 4BD ⊖ Bayswater
✆ (020) 7221 1415
e-mail info@lecafeanglais.co.uk
www.lecafeanglais.co.uk

Closed 25-26 December and 1 January

Menu £20/25 – Carte £28/45

A/C VISA MC AE

The terminal blandness of Queensway received a boost back late 2007 when Rowley Leigh, formerly of Kensington Place, opened this vast brasserie within Whiteleys, the Grade II listed shopping centre. His place shares the same conviviality and culinary accessibility as 'KP' but on a bigger scale and with better acoustics. The art deco styling, leather banquettes and big windows may reflect Whiteleys 1911 roots but it's still best to take the lift up from the side entrance. Allow extra time for reading: the menu offers a huge range of brasserie classics, ranging from rabbit rillettes and parmesan custard to the daily specials and meats turning slowly on the rotisserie. The wine list is decidedly Old World.

Hereford Road

British

C2

3 Hereford Road ✉ W2 4AB
✆ (020) 7727 1144
e-mail info@herefordroad.org
www.herefordroad.org

⊖ Bayswater
Closed 24, 26, 31 December and 1 January – booking essential

Menu £16 (lunch) – Carte £27/30

The clues are all there: the adoption of the street name, unassuming décor, enthusiastic service and splendidly British cooking. Yes, Tom Pemberton was ordained by St John in Clerkenwell, and the locals should be delighted he's pitched up here. The first sight is the narrow open kitchen (this was once a butcher's) and the six tables for two with side-by-side seating. The main body is down a few steps, with the four booths being the prize seats. Dishes are as uncomplicated as their menu descriptions suggest and at prices commendably lower than at his alma mater. You might find duck hearts, calf's brains, braised rabbits, pork with fennel or brill with courgettes. Don't miss the dishes for two, such as a whole oxtail or roe shoulder.

Island

Modern European

E3

Lancaster Ter ✉ W2 2TY
✆ (020) 7551 6070
Fax (020) 7551 6071
e-mail eat@islandrestaurant.co.uk
www.islandrestaurant.co.uk

⊖ Lancaster Gate

Carte £27/46

The Island in question may be more 'traffic' than 'tropical' but there's no denying they've made the best of an unpromising location. It's actually part of the huge Royal Lancaster Hotel but you wouldn't know it if you approach this large glass structure from the park. Inside it's all very crisp and bright; there's a bar to one side with views of the park (and that traffic) but the atmosphere is relaxed and the staff demonstrate commendable enthusiasm. The menu tries to appeal to everyone by offering an easy mix of grilled steaks, European brasserie favourites, a bit of Asia here and some American there. So expect everything from crab cakes and burgers to sea bass and risotto, all prepared on view through the hatch into the kitchen.

Kiasu

D3 **Asian**

48 Queensway ✉ W2 3RY ⊖ Bayswater
✆ (020) 7727 8810
Fax (020) 7727 7220
e-mail info@kiasu.co.uk
www.kiasu.co.uk

Menu £6 (weekday lunch) – Carte £15/33

A/C VISA MC

Queensway is awash with similar looking restaurants, but when there's one named after the Hokkien Chinese word for 'afraid to be second best' then it must be worth exploring. The owner of Kiasu is Malaysian and the Strait of Malacca, a passageway between the Indian and Pacific oceans, is the inspiration behind his food. That means exotically sounding specialities like nasi lemak or otak-otak but also dishes from neighbouring countries like Indonesia and Singapore. Some are hot and spicy, others light and fragrant and this is food designed for sharing; as your dishes arrive in no particularly order and the tables are a little small, you may have to do some juggling. The place is always packed out; it's simply but brightly decorated and good fun.

Nipa

E3 **Thai**

Lancaster Ter ✉ W2 2TY ⊖ Lancaster Gate
✆ (020) 7551 6039
Fax (020) 7724 3191
e-mail nipa@lancasterlondon.com
www.niparestaurant.co.uk

Closed Christmas-New Year, Saturday lunch, Sunday and Bank Holidays

Menu £15/27 – Carte £26/37

A/C VISA MC AE

You'll find Nipa to be a little oasis of calm and hospitality, once you've made it up to the first floor of the Royal Lancaster and sidestepped the businessmen on their laptops in the adjacent lounge. Its teak panelling and ornaments are all imported from Thailand and they've done a convincing job of replicating the original Nipa in Bangkok's Landmark Hotel – if anything, it's even a little smarter. The menu is comprehensive, with a mix of the recognisable blended with more regional specialities. Dishes are marked 1-3 in chillies for their respective heat, come in decent sizes and the harmonious blend of flavours and textures successfully delivers what the aromas promise. Set menus are at the back and provide a convenient all-round experience.

Pearl Liang

E2 — **Chinese** XX

8 Sheldon Sq., Paddington Central
⊠ W2 6EZ
✆ (020) 7289 7000
www.pearlliang.co.uk

⊖ Paddington
Closed 24-25 December

Menu £23 – Carte £25/53

Pearl Liang is a largely windowless restaurant which, depending on your opinion of the corporate development that is Paddington Central, may be a good or bad thing. The interior of this large Chinese restaurant is also kept pretty business-like, both in the type of clientele it attracts and the style of service it provides them with. The kitchen delivers the promises of the menu and no more, but those menus are quite varied, from the 'Jade', 'Pearl' and 'Diamond' set menus to the extensive à la carte which blends the classics and more unusual choices, like jellyfish with sesame, pig's trotter and drunken chicken. Dishes from other Asian countries creep onto the menu but it's best to stick to the Chinese specialities.

El Pirata De Tapas

C2 — **Spanish** X

115 Westbourne Grove ⊠ W2 4UP
✆ (020) 7727 5000
e-mail info@elpiratadetapas.co.uk
www.elpiratadetapas.co.uk

⊖ Bayswater
Closed early January and Bank Holidays

Carte £14/23

Spanish restaurants and tapas-style eating satisfy our appetite for a shared, less structured dining experience and El Pirata is no exception. It's spread over two floors, although you wouldn't want to be the first table downstairs, and is decorated in a contemporary yet warm style. The staff give helpful advice on a menu that is quite lengthy but helpfully divided up into sections, from charcuterie to fish, croquettes to vegetarian, meat to paellas; there are also a couple of appealing and balanced set menus and the pricing structure is far from piratical. The kitchen shows respect for traditional flavours but is not afraid of trying new things or adding a note of playfulness to some dishes. A good place to come with friends.

Prince Alfred & Formosa Dining Room

D1 **Gastropub**

5A Formosa St ✉ W9 1EE ⊖ Warwick Avenue.
✆ (020) 7286 3287
e-mail princealfred@youngs.co.uk
www.theprincealfred.com

Carte £21/35

Original plate glass, panels and snugs make The Prince Alfred a wonderful example of a classic Victorian pub. Unfortunately, the eating is done in the Formosa Dining Room extension on the side but at least it's a lively room with capable cooking. There's a rustic theme running through the menu, with a strong British accent, so traditionalists will enjoy the fish pie, potted trout, steak and ale pie and calves liver but there are also risottos, parfaits and terrines for those of a more European bent. The open kitchen is not averse to sprucing up some classics, for example your burger arrives adorned with foie gras and truffles. Prices are realistic, even with a charge made for bread, and the friendly team cope well under pressure.

Trenta

F2 **Italian** XX

30 Connaught St ✉ W2 2AF ⊖ Marble Arch
✆ (020) 7262 9623
Fax (020) 7262 9636

Closed Christmas-New Year, Sunday and Bank Holidays – dinner only and lunch Thursday and Friday

Carte £23/31

The locals are doing their bit for the surrounding area by attempting to rechristen it 'Connaught Village.' That may be stretching things somewhat but, then again, places like the diminutive but engagingly run Trenta do offer a palpable sense of neighbourhood. The chef hails from Emilia Romagna and the richer cooking of this region informs his style. The set menu offers bags of choice; dishes come fully attired and generously proportioned and there's an honesty to the cooking. Desserts are steeped in the flavours of Italy and there's also a good affogati section. The wine list offers a concise but adequate tour across Italy. The restaurant is compact but bright, although try to avoid the less animated downstairs.

Urban Turban

C2 **Indian**

98 Westbourne Grove ✉ W2 5RU ⊖ Bayswater
✆ (020) 7243 4200
Fax (020) 7243 4080
e-mail info@urbanturban.uk.com
www.urbanturban.uk.com

Menu £10 (lunch) – Carte £22/27

A/C

VISA MC AE

Mumbai street food was the inspiration behind this venture from Vineet Bhatia. The idea is to order a number of not-so-small dishes, which arrive is no particularly order, and share them with friends. These range from tangy scallops and lamb kebabs to chicken tossed in spring onion and soya sauce, reflecting the influence of the Chinese on some of those street stalls. For the particularly gregarious there are whole platters to share while those who would no sooner share a fork than a dish should head straight for the 'classic helpings'. The ground floor is where the bustle is, along with the bar and the lounge music; the relatively calmer downstairs section is the far nicer spot for eating in. The name is at least easy to remember.

The Warrington

D1 **Gastropub**

93 Warrington Cres ✉ W9 1EH ⊖ Maida Vale.
✆ (020) 7592 7960 dinner only and lunch Friday-Sunday
Fax (020) 7592 1603
e-mail thewarrington@gordonramsay.com
www.gordonramsay.com

Carte £20/27

A/C

VISA MC AE

Nothing upsets a community more than when their favourite pub gets a makeover and thereafter attracts interlopers from outlying postcodes. The cleverness of The Warrington, which dates from 1857, is that the Gordon Ramsay group spent a few million on the place but the ground floor, with its art nouveau friezes, dark wood and pillars, retained its traditional flavour and remains the haunt of locals just in for a drink, a snack or a lunchtime pie. The main eating event is upstairs in the smarter but decidedly less characterful restaurant. The cooking keeps things relatively simple and is an appealing mix of British and French, with cullen skink or chicken and mushroom pie jostling for your attention with steak tartare or confit of duck.

The Waterway

D1 **Gastropub**

54 Formosa St ✉ W9 2JU — ⊖ Warwick Avenue.

✆ (020) 7266 3557
Fax (020) 7266 3547
e-mail info@thewaterway.co.uk
www.thewaterway.co.uk

Carte £30/40

Strictly speaking, The Waterway is not really a pub but it does always have lots of people standing outside with drinks in their hands. To see it at its best you have to arrive by narrowboat as the terrific canalside terrace is one of its great selling points. The dining area is beyond the bar and has a nicely balanced menu. For starters expect squid, scallops or risotto; main courses could include beef Bourguignon or duck breast with okra and dishes are executed with a certain degree of vim. There are more accessible choices available too, especially on the terrace, like the house burger, Caesar salad and rib-eye steak. The young team of servers can sometimes place too much emphasis on functionality at the expense of personality.

A/C VISA MC AE

City of London • Clerkenwell Finsbury • Southwark

Say what you like about London, **The City** is the place where it all started. The Romans developed this small area – this square mile – nearly two thousand years ago, and today it stands as the economic heartbeat of not only the capital, but the country as a whole. Each morning it's besieged with an army of bankers, lawyers and traders, and each evening it's abandoned to an eerie ghost-like fate. Of course, this mass exodus is offset by the two perennial crowd-pullers, **St Paul's** and the **Tower of London**, but these are both on the periphery of the area, away from the frenetic commercial zone within. The casual visitor tends to steer clear of the City, but for those willing to mix it with the daytime swarm of office workers, there are many historical nuggets hidden away, waiting to be mined. You can find here, amongst the skyscrapers, a tempting array of Roman ruins, medieval landmarks and brooding churches designed by Wren and Hawksmoor. One of the best ways of encapsulating everything that's happened here down the centuries is to visit the Museum of London, on London Wall, which tells the story of the city from the very start, and the very start means 300,000 BC.

For those seeking the hip corners of this part of London, the best advice is to head slightly north-west, using the brutalist space of the **Barbican Arts Centre** as your marker. You're now entering **Clerkenwell**. Sliding north/south through here is the bustling and buzzy **St John Street,** home to some of the funkiest eating establishments and gastropubs in London, their proximity to **Smithfield** meat market giving a clue as to much of the provenance. Clerkenwell's revivalist vibe has seen the steady reclamation of old factory space: during the Industrial Revolution, the area boomed with the introduction of breweries, print works and the manufacture of clocks and watches. After World War II decline set in, but these days city professionals and loft-dwellers are drawn to the area's zeitgeist-leading galleries and clubs, not to mention the wonderful floor-to-ceiling delicatessens. Clerkenwell is home to The Eagle, one of the city's pioneering gastropubs and still a local favourite, brimming over with newspaper journalists (it's near The Guardian offices). It even has its own art gallery upstairs. Meanwhile, the nearby **Exmouth Market** teems with trendy bars and restaurants, popular with those on their way to the perennially excellent dance concerts at Sadler's Wells Theatre.

The area was once a religious centre, frequented by monks and nuns; its name derives from the parish clerks who performed Biblical mystery plays around the Clerk's Well set in a nunnery wall. This can be found in **Farringdon Lane** complete with an exhibition explaining all. Close by in St John's

Lane is the 16C gatehouse which is home to the Museum of the Order of St John (famous today for its ambulance services), and chock full of fascinating objects related to the Order's medieval history.

Not too long ago, a trip over London Bridge to **Southwark** was for locals only, its trademark grimness ensuring it was well off the tourist map. These days, visitors treat it as a place of pilgrimage as three of London's modern success stories reside here. **Tate Modern** has become the city's most visited attraction, a huge former power station that generates a blistering show of modern art from 1900 to the present day, its massive turbine hall a must-see feature in itself. Practically next door but a million miles away architecturally is Shakespeare's **Globe,** a wonderful evocation of medieval showtime. Half a mile east is the best food market in London: **Borough Market.** Foodies can't resist the organic feel-good nature of the place, with its mind-boggling number of stalls selling produce ranging from every kind of fruit and veg to rare-breed meats, oils, preserves, chocolates and breads. And that's just for hors-d'œuvres…

C. Eymenier / MICHELIN

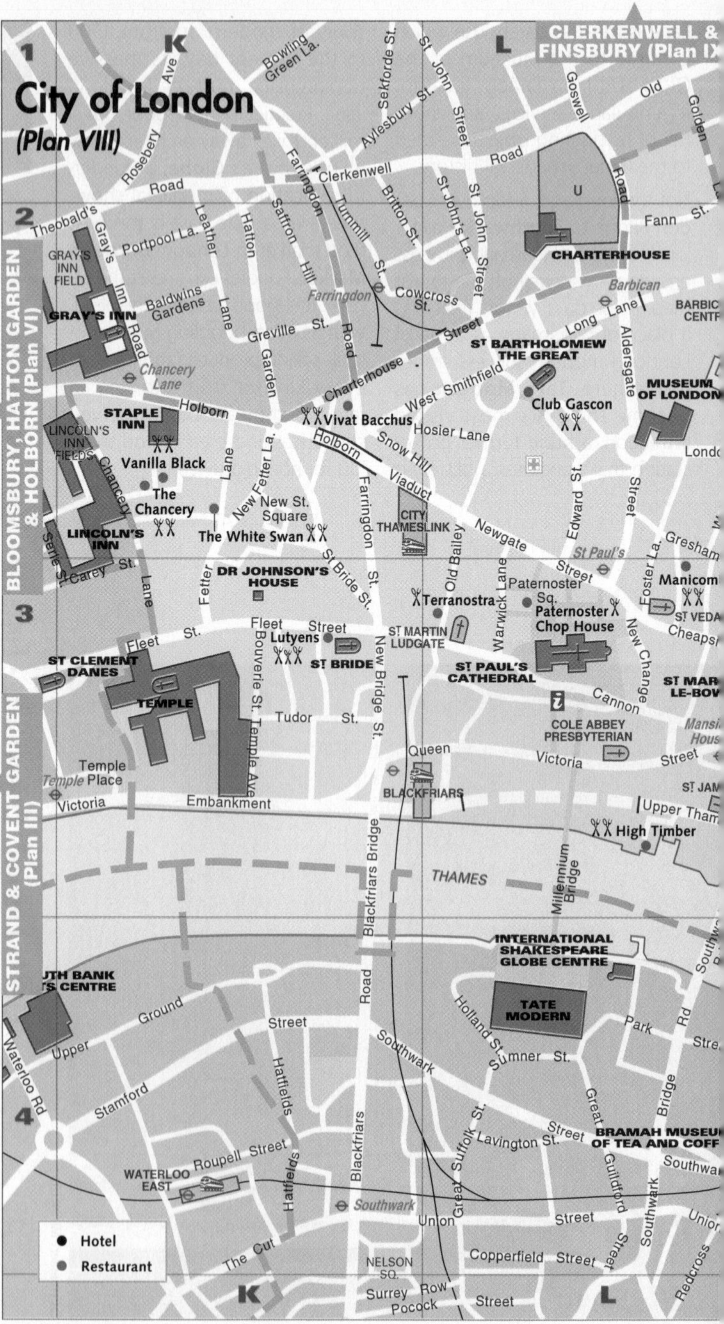
City of London
(Plan VIII)
CLERKENWELL & FINSBURY (Plan IX)
BLOOMSBURY, HATTON GARDEN & HOLBORN (Plan VI)
STRAND & COVENT GARDEN (Plan III)
K
L
1
2
3
4
Bowling Green La.
Sekforde St.
St John Street
Aylesbury St.
Rosebery Ave
Clerkenwell Road
Goswell Road
Old
Golden
Theobald's Road
Gray's Inn Road
Portpool La.
Leather Lane
Hatton Garden
Saffron Hill
Farringdon Road
Turnmill St.
Britton St.
St John's La.
Fann St.
CHARTERHOUSE
U
GRAY'S INN FIELD
GRAY'S INN
Baldwins Gardens
Greville St.
Farringdon
Cowcross St.
Charterhouse Street
Barbican
Long Lane
BARBICAN CENTRE
ST BARTHOLOMEW THE GREAT
Aldersgate Street
MUSEUM OF LONDON
Chancery Lane
Holborn
STAPLE INN
LINCOLN'S INN FIELDS
Vivat Bacchus
West Smithfield
Club Gascon
Hosier Lane
Snow Hill
Holborn Viaduct
London
Vanilla Black
The Chancery
New Fetter La.
New St. Square
Fetter Lane
CITY THAMESLINK
Old Bailey
Edward St.
Newgate Street
Gresham
St Paul's
LINCOLN'S INN
Serle St.
Carey St.
The White Swan
Farringdon St.
DR JOHNSON'S HOUSE
St Bride St.
Warwick Lane
Paternoster Sq.
Foster La.
Manicomi
ST VEDAST
Terranostra
Paternoster Chop House
Cheapside
New Change
Fleet St.
Fleet Street
Lutyens
ST BRIDE
ST MARTIN LUDGATE
ST PAUL'S CATHEDRAL
ST CLEMENT DANES
TEMPLE
Bouverie St.
New Bridge St.
Cannon
ST MARY LE-BOW
Tudor St.
COLE ABBEY PRESBYTERIAN
Mansion House
Temple Ave
Queen Victoria Street
Temple Place
Temple
BLACKFRIARS
ST JAMES
Victoria Embankment
Upper Thames
High Timber
Blackfriars Bridge
THAMES
Millennium Bridge
INTERNATIONAL SHAKESPEARE GLOBE CENTRE
SOUTH BANK ARTS CENTRE
Road
TATE MODERN
Holland St.
Park
Rd
Upper Ground
Street
Southwark Street
Sumner St.
Waterloo Rd
Hatfields
Great Guildford Street
Southwark Bridge
Stamford
Great Suffolk St.
Lavington St.
BRAMAH MUSEUM OF TEA AND COFFEE
Roupell Street
Blackfriars Road
WATERLOO EAST
Southwark
Union Street
Hotel
Restaurant
The Cut
NELSON SQ.
Copperfield Street
Redcross
Surrey Row
Pocock Street

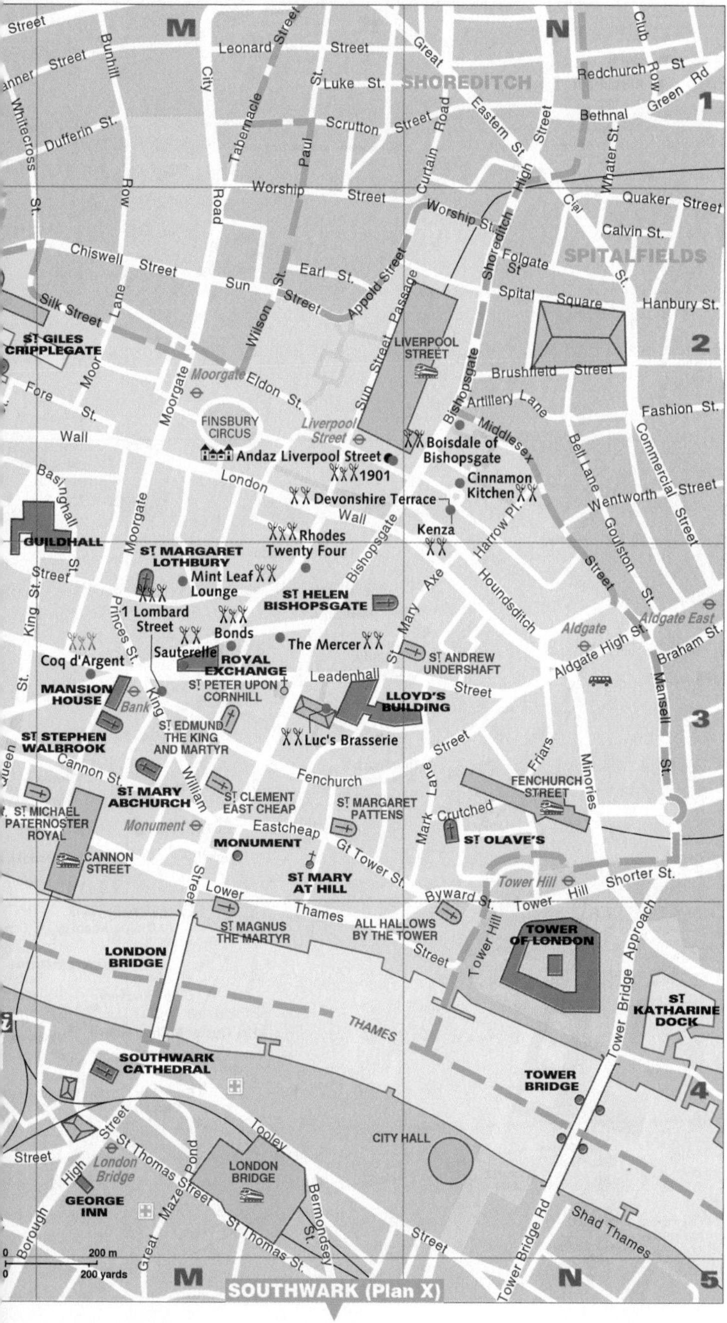

M
N
1
2
3
4
5
SHOREDITCH
SPITALFIELDS
Leonard Street
Street
Great Eastern St
St Luke St.
City Road
Tabernacle
Paul
Scrutton Street
Curtain Road
Bunhill Row
Whitecross St.
Dufferin St.
Worship Street
Worship St.
Club Row
Redchurch St
Bethnal Green Rd
Whater St.
Quaker Street
Calvin St.
Commercial Street
Shoreditch High Street
Chiswell Street
Earl St.
Sun Street
Appold Street
Sun Street Passage
Wilson St.
Folgate St
Spital Square
Hanbury St.
Silk Street
Moor Lane
ST GILES CRIPPLEGATE
LIVERPOOL STREET
Moorgate
Eldon St.
Brushfield Street
Artillery Lane
Fashion St.
Fore St.
Wall
FINSBURY CIRCUS
Liverpool Street
Bishopsgate
Middlesex
Andaz Liverpool Street
Boisdale of Bishopsgate
1901
London Wall
Cinnamon Kitchen
Devonshire Terrace
Bell Lane
Wentworth Street
Basinghall St.
Kenza
Harrow Pl.
Goulston St.
GUILDHALL
Moorgate
Rhodes Twenty Four
ST MARGARET LOTHBURY
Mint Leaf Lounge
Houndsditch
Gresham Street
ST HELEN BISHOPSGATE
King St.
Princes St.
1 Lombard Street
Bonds
The Mercer
St Mary Axe
Aldgate
Aldgate East
Aldgate High St.
Braham St.
Coq d'Argent
Sauterelle
ROYAL EXCHANGE
ST ANDREW UNDERSHAFT
Leadenhall Street
MANSION HOUSE
Bank
ST PETER UPON CORNHILL
LLOYD'S BUILDING
Mansell St.
King William Street
ST EDMUND THE KING AND MARTYR
ST STEPHEN WALBROOK
Luc's Brasserie
Queen St.
Cannon St.
Fenchurch Street
Mark Lane
Friars
Minories
ST MARY ABCHURCH
ST CLEMENT EAST CHEAP
ST MARGARET PATTENS
Crutched
FENCHURCH STREET
ST MICHAEL PATERNOSTER ROYAL
Monument
Eastcheap
ST OLAVE'S
MONUMENT
Gt Tower St.
CANNON STREET
ST MARY AT HILL
Tower Hill
Shorter St.
Lower Thames Street
Byward St.
ST MAGNUS THE MARTYR
ALL HALLOWS BY THE TOWER
TOWER OF LONDON
Tower Bridge Approach
LONDON BRIDGE
THAMES
ST KATHARINE DOCK
SOUTHWARK CATHEDRAL
TOWER BRIDGE
CITY HALL
Tooley Street
Street
St Thomas Street
London Bridge
Borough High Street
Pond
Maze
LONDON BRIDGE
Bermondsey St.
GEORGE INN
Great
St Thomas St.
Tower Bridge Rd
Shad Thames
0 200 m
0 200 yards
SOUTHWARK (Plan X)

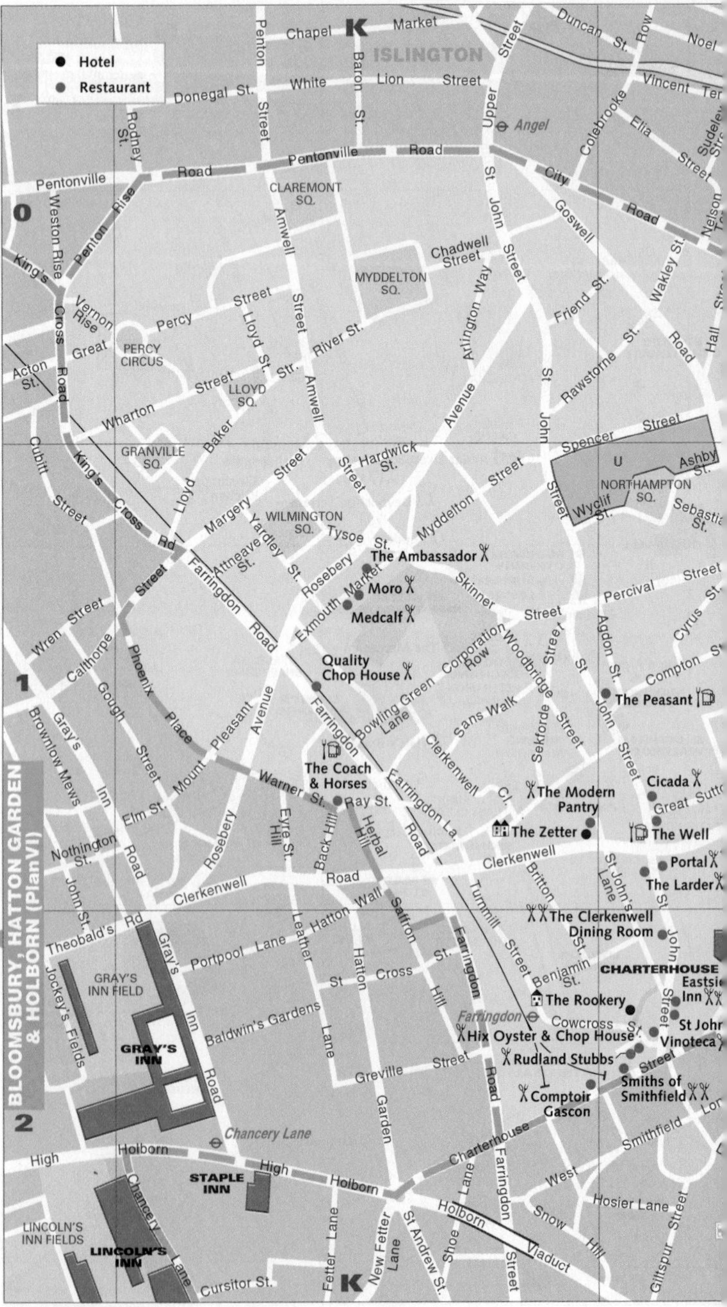
Hotel
Restaurant
ISLINGTON
K
O
1
2
BLOOMSBURY, HATTON GARDEN & HOLBORN (Plan VI)
Angel
Farringdon
Chancery Lane
CLAREMONT SQ.
MYDDELTON SQ.
PERCY CIRCUS
LLOYD SQ.
GRANVILLE SQ.
WILMINGTON SQ.
NORTHAMPTON SQ.
U
GRAY'S INN FIELD
GRAY'S INN
STAPLE INN
LINCOLN'S INN FIELDS
LINCOLN'S INN
CHARTERHOUSE
The Ambassador
Moro
Medcalf
Quality Chop House
The Peasant
The Coach & Horses
Cicada
The Modern Pantry
The Zetter
The Well
Portal
The Larder
The Clerkenwell Dining Room
The Rookery
Eastside Inn
St John Vinoteca
Hix Oyster & Chop House
Rudland Stubbs
Smiths of Smithfield
Comptoir Gascon
Chapel Market
White Lion Street
Donegal St.
Penton Street
Baron St.
Rodney St.
Pentonville Road
Upper Street
Duncan St.
Noel
Vincent Ter
Colebrooke Row
Elia Street
City Road
Goswell Road
St John Street
Weston Rise
Penton Rise
King's Cross Road
Vernon Rise
Great Percy Street
Lloyd St.
Amwell Street
River St.
Chadwell Street
Arlington Way
Friend St.
Wakley St.
Rawstorne St.
Acton St.
Wharton Street
Lloyd Baker Str.
Avenue
Spencer Street
Ashby St.
Wyclif St.
Sebastian St.
Cubitt Street
Hardwick St.
Margery Street
Yardley St.
Tysoe St.
Myddelton Street
Attneave St.
Rosebery Avenue
Exmouth Market
Skinner Street
Percival Street
Cyrus St.
Farringdon Road
Wren Street
Calthorpe
Phoenix Place
Corporation Row
Woodbridge Street
Agdon St.
Compton St.
Gough Street
Gray's Inn Road
Brownlow Mews
Mount Pleasant
Bowling Green Lane
Sans Walk
Sekforde Street
Clerkenwell Cl.
Warner St.
Ray St.
Farringdon La.
Great Sutton
Elm St.
Nothington St.
John St.
Eyre St. Hill
Back Hill
Herbal Hill
Clerkenwell Road
Britton St.
St John's Lane
Theobald's Rd
Portpool Lane
Leather Lane
Hatton Wall
Saffron Hill
Hatton Garden
Turnmill Street
Benjamin St.
Jockey's Fields
St Cross Street
Baldwin's Gardens
Cowcross St.
Greville Street
Charterhouse Street
Smithfield
Holborn
High Holborn
Chancery Lane
West Smithfield
Hosier Lane
Snow Hill
Holborn Viaduct
Giltspur Street
Fetter Lane
New Fetter Lane
St Andrew St.
Shoe Lane
Farringdon Street
Cursitor St.

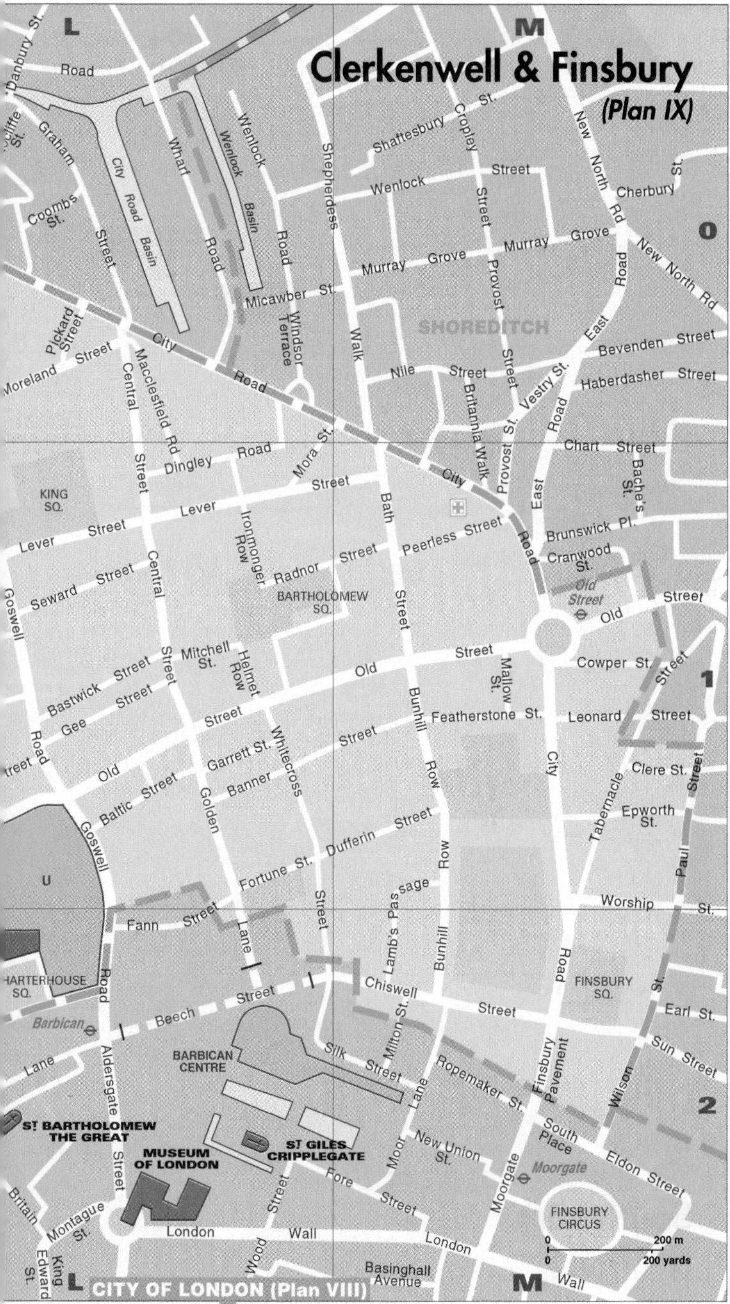
Clerkenwell & Finsbury
(Plan IX)
L
M
O
1
2
SHOREDITCH
KING SQ.
BARTHOLOMEW SQ.
U
CHARTERHOUSE SQ.
FINSBURY SQ.
FINSBURY CIRCUS
BARBICAN CENTRE
ST BARTHOLOMEW THE GREAT
MUSEUM OF LONDON
ST GILES CRIPPLEGATE
Barbican
Old Street
Moorgate
Danbury St.
Road
Graham
Coombs St.
Street
City Road Basin
Wharf Road
Wenlock Basin
Wenlock
Road
Shepherdess Walk
Shaftesbury
Cropley St.
Street
Wenlock
Street
New North Rd
Cherbury St.
Murray Grove
Murray Grove
Provost Street
New North Rd
Road
Micawber St.
Windsor Terrace
Pickard Street
Moreland Street
City Road
Central Street
Macclesfield Rd
East Road
Bevenden Street
Nile Street
Britannia Walk
Provost St.
Vestry St.
Haberdasher Street
Chart Street
Bache's St.
Dingley Road
Mora St.
Street
Bath Street
City Road
Lever Street
Lever Street
Ironmonger Row
Peerless Street
Brunswick Pl.
Cranwood St.
Radnor Street
Seward Street
Goswell Road
Old Street
Mitchell St.
Helmet Row
Bunhill Row
Mallow St.
Cowper St.
Bastwick Street
Gee Street
Featherstone St.
Leonard Street
Garrett St.
Whitecross Street
Old Street
Clere St.
Paul Street
Baltic Street
Golden Lane
Banner Street
Tabernacle Street
Epworth St.
Dufferin Street
Fortune St.
Lamb's Passage
Bunhill Row
Worship St.
Fann Street
Chiswell Street
Milton St.
Finsbury Pavement
Earl St.
Wilson St.
Beech Street
Aldersgate Street
Lane
Silk Street
Sun Street
Ropemaker St.
Moor Lane
South Place
Eldon Street
New Union St.
Fore Street
Wood Street
Moorgate
Britain
Montague St.
London Wall
King Edward St.
Basinghall Avenue
London Wall
0
200 m
0
200 yards
CITY OF LONDON (Plan VIII)

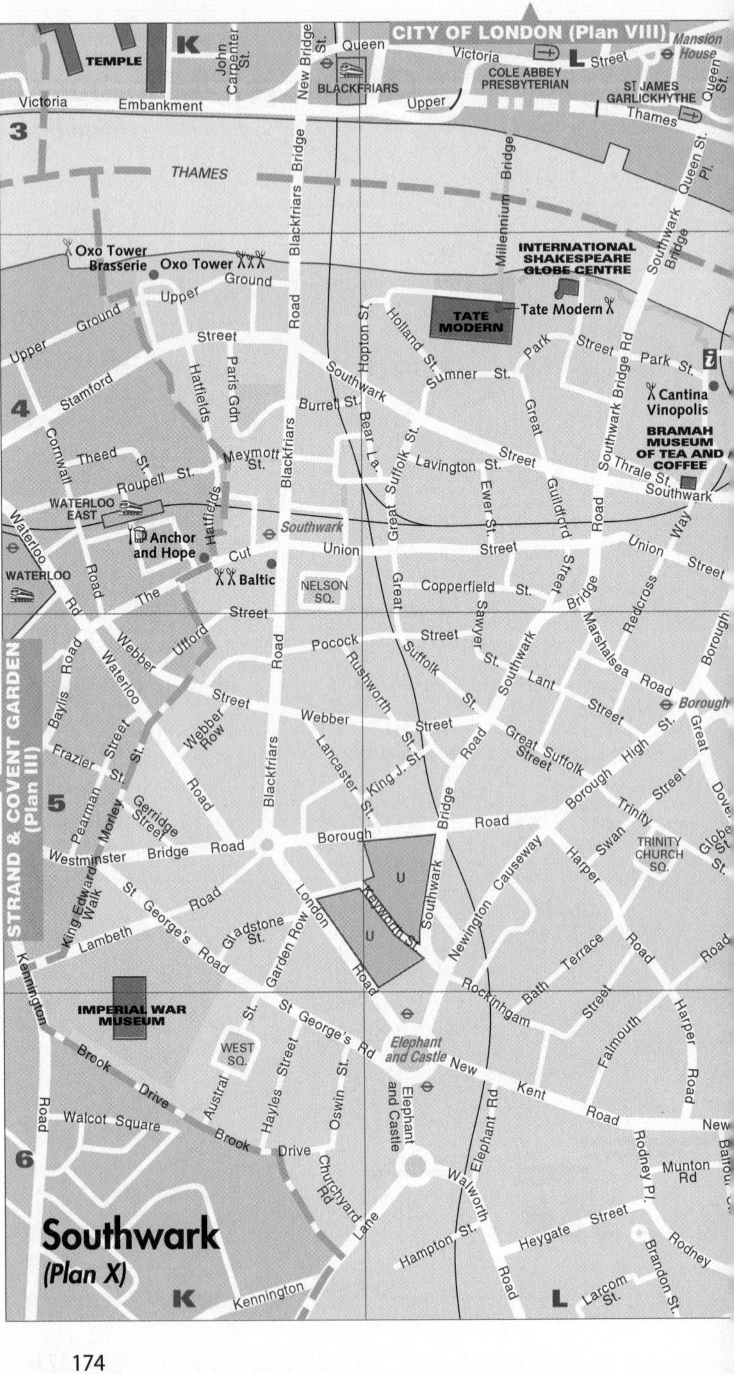
Southwark
(Plan X)
CITY OF LONDON (Plan VIII)
STRAND & COVENT GARDEN (Plan III)
K
L
3
4
5
6
TEMPLE
BLACKFRIARS
Mansion House
COLE ABBEY PRESBYTERIAN
ST JAMES GARLICKHYTHE
THAMES
Victoria Embankment
Upper Thames Street
Queen Victoria Street
New Bridge St.
John Carpenter St.
Queen St.
Queen St. Pl.
Blackfriars Bridge
Millennium Bridge
Southwark Bridge
Oxo Tower Brasserie
Oxo Tower
INTERNATIONAL SHAKESPEARE GLOBE CENTRE
TATE MODERN
Tate Modern
Cantina Vinopolis
BRAMAH MUSEUM OF TEA AND COFFEE
Upper Ground
Stamford Street
Hatfields
Paris Gdn
Hopton St.
Holland St.
Sumner St.
Park Street
Park St.
Southwark Street
Burrell St.
Bear La.
Great Suffolk St.
Lavington St.
Ewer St.
Great Guildford Street
Southwark Bridge Road
Thrale St.
Theed St.
Roupell St.
Meymott St.
Cornwall
WATERLOO EAST
WATERLOO
Waterloo Road
Anchor and Hope
The Cut
Baltic
Southwark
Union Street
NELSON SQ.
Copperfield St.
Redcross Way
Marshalsea Road
Borough
Borough High St.
Sawyer St.
Lant Street
Pocock Street
Rushworth St.
Webber Street
Webber Row
Ufford St.
Baylis Road
Frazier St.
Pearman Street
Morley St.
Gerridge Street
Lancaster St.
King J. St.
Westminster Bridge Road
Borough Road
Trinity Street
Swan St.
TRINITY CHURCH SQ.
Harper Road
Globe St.
Dover St.
Causeway
Newington
Keyworth St.
London Road
Garden Row
Gladstone St.
St George's Road
Lambeth Road
King Edward Walk
Kennington Road
IMPERIAL WAR MUSEUM
U
Terrace
Bath Terrace
Rockingham Street
Falmouth Road
Elephant and Castle
New Kent Road
WEST SQ.
St. George's Rd
Austral St.
Hayles Street
Oswin St.
Brook Drive
Walcot Square
Churchyard Rd
Elephant Rd
Walworth Road
Rodney Pl.
Rodney Road
Munton Rd
Balfour St.
Heygate Street
Hampton St.
Brandon St.
Larcom St.
Kennington Lane

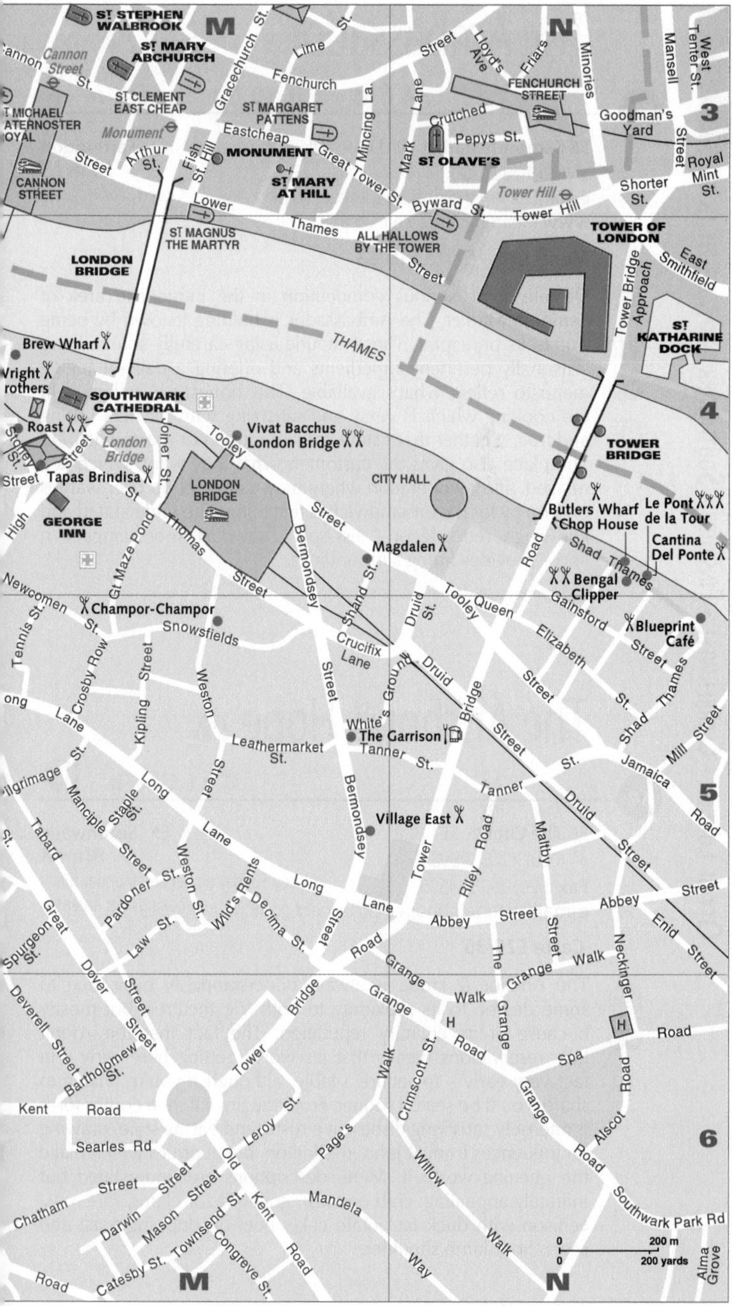
M
N
3
4
5
6
ST STEPHEN WALBROOK
ST MARY ABCHURCH
ST CLEMENT EAST CHEAP
ST MARGARET PATTENS
MONUMENT
ST MARY AT HILL
ST OLAVE'S
CANNON STREET
FENCHURCH STREET
Cannon Street
Monument
Tower Hill
ST MAGNUS THE MARTYR
ALL HALLOWS BY THE TOWER
LONDON BRIDGE
TOWER OF LONDON
ST KATHARINE DOCK
THAMES
TOWER BRIDGE
CITY HALL
SOUTHWARK CATHEDRAL
GEORGE INN
London Bridge
Brew Wharf
Roast
Tapas Brindisa
Vivat Bacchus London Bridge
Magdalen
Butlers Wharf Chop House
Le Pont de la Tour
Cantina Del Ponte
Bengal Clipper
Blueprint Café
Champor-Champor
The Garrison
Village East
Lime St.
Fenchurch Street
Gracechurch St.
Eastcheap
Great Tower St.
Mincing La.
Mark Lane
Crutched Friars
Lloyd's Ave
Minories
Mansell Street
West Tenter St.
Goodman's Yard
Pepys St.
Byward St.
Tower Hill
Royal Mint St.
Shorter St.
East Smithfield
Tower Bridge Approach
Lower Thames Street
Arthur St.
Fish St. Hill
Tooley Street
Joiner St.
St Thomas Street
Bermondsey Street
Shad St.
Druid St.
Queen Elizabeth Street
Shad Thames
Gainsford Street
Crucifix Lane
White's Grounds
Snowsfields
Newcomen St.
Gt Maze Pond
Tennis St.
Crosby Row
Kipling Street
Weston Street
Leathermarket St.
Tanner St.
Long Lane
Manciple Street
Staple St.
Pardoner St.
Weston St.
Wild's Rents
Decima St.
Law St.
Tower Bridge Road
Riley Road
Maltby Street
Jamaica Road
Mill Street
Abbey Street
Enid Street
Neckinger
The Grange
Grange Walk
Grange Road
Spa Road
Alscot Road
Crimscott St.
Willow Walk
Page's Walk
Great Dover Street
Spurgeon St.
Tabard St.
Pilgrimage St.
Deverell Street
Bartholomew St.
Kent Road
Searles Rd
Old Kent Road
Leroy St.
Mandela Way
Chatham Street
Darwin Street
Mason Street
Townsend St.
Congreve St.
Catesby St.
Southwark Park Rd
Alma Grove
0 200 m
0 200 yards

The Ambassador

Modern European

K1

55 Exmouth Market ✉ EC1R 4QL
(020) 7837 0009
e-mail clive@theambassadorcafe.co.uk
www.theambassadorcafe.co.uk

Farringdon
Plan IX
Closed Bank Holidays

Menu £16 – Carte £19/33

VISA MC AE

Despite some serious competition in the immediate area of Exmouth Market, The Ambassador is holding its own by being true to its principles. These include using carefully sourced and seasonally pertinent ingredients and offering a daily-changing menu to reflect what's available. This honesty is reflected in the cooking which is gutsy and satisfying with flavours lasting and true, whether that's slow-cooked mutton or roasted halibut. The place also gives the customers what they want, which is a relaxed, all-day operation where they can meet up over waffles or drop by for bacon sandwiches first thing. The understated and knowingly retro décor – less spit 'n sawdust, more languor 'n lino – provides fitting surroundings.

The Anchor & Hope

British

K4

36 The Cut ✉ SE1 8LP
(020) 7928 9898
Fax (020) 7928 4595
e-mail anchorandhope@btconnect.com

Southwark.
Plan X
Closed Sunday dinner and Monday lunch – bookings not accepted

Carte £20/35

VISA MC

The Anchor & Hope is always understandably busy, due to some degree to its proximity to both Vic theatres, but mostly because of its culinary reputation. The fact that they don't take reservations means that it's worth getting here early - in fact very early – to secure a table, although if you're willing to share, you'll be seated sooner. From the tiny kitchen comes forth immensely satisfying dishes, in a rustic and earthy style, drawing on influences from St John in Islington, but at prices which make the queuing worth it. Menu descriptions are understated but infinitely appealing: crab on toast, grilled razor clams, rare roast venison with duck fat potato cake, beef on dripping toast and seven hour lamb shoulder.

Baltic

K4 **Eastern European** XX

74 Blackfriars Rd ✉ SE1 8HA ⊖ Southwark
✆ (020) 7928 1111 **Plan X**
Fax (020) 7928 8487 Closed 25-26 December
e-mail info@balticrestaurant.co.uk
www.balticrestaurant.co.uk

Menu £18 – Carte £20/30

The façade may be a little unprepossessing but persevere and you'll find yourself in a slick bar. If you can resist the tempting array of vodkas, including some appealingly original home-made flavours, then proceed further and you'll end up in the arresting space of the restaurant. Alcoves around the edge and, above, a wooden trussed ceiling with vaulted glass combine with bright white walls to give this former industrial space a vividly modernist feel. At this point you'll probably expect some sort of pan-Asian fusion thing but fortunately Baltic enjoys the same ownership as Wódka, so the cooking here covers the altogether more muscular cuisines of Eastern Europe and the Baltic states. It is robust, full of flavour and requires an appetite.

Bengal Clipper

N4 **Indian** XX

Cardamom Building, Shad Thames, ⊖ London Bridge
Butlers Wharf ✉ SE1 2YR **Plan X**
✆ (020) 7357 9001
Fax (020) 7357 9002
e-mail mail@bengalclipper.co.uk
www.bengalclipper.co.uk

Menu £15 – Carte £23/29

Set among the converted wharves and warehouses by the part of the Thames where cargoes of Indian teas and spices were once traded, you'll find, fittingly enough, Bengal Clipper, a firmly established Indian restaurant whose reputation has been based on reliable cooking and big, bustling surroundings. The size means that the restaurant is often the chosen venue of larger parties and tables so the atmosphere, particularly in the evenings, is usually fairly hectic, although the smartly kitted out staff are an unflappable lot. Specialities from all parts of India are showcased, along with several originally conceived dishes which includes, in honour of the building in which the restaurant sits, a chicken curry flavoured with cardamom.

Blueprint Café

N5 **Modern European**

Design Museum, Shad Thames, Butlers Wharf ✉ SE1 2YD
✆ (020) 7378 7031
e-mail blueprintcafe@danddlondon.com
www.danddlondon.com

⊖ London Bridge
Plan X
Closed 25 December and Sunday dinner

Menu £23/28 s – Carte £26/40 s

VISA MC AE

The first thing one notices is the great views of Tower Bridge and The Thames, which, thanks to the restaurant's raised position, are terrific - and on sunny days, the windows fully retract. The Blueprint Café forms an integral part of the Design Museum, which opened back in 1989, and it enjoys its own shiny and sleek simplicity; the atmosphere is never less than breezy. The cooking is very much of the no-nonsense, what-you-read-is-what-you-get school and the long-standing chef uses flavours that are pronounced, sunny and seasonal. Dishes from his daily-changing menu, such as smoked eel with horseradish, veal with girolles and lemon posset, come with confident simplicity and, as a result, are easy to eat.

Boisdale of Bishopsgate

N2 **Scottish**

Swedeland Court, 202 Bishopsgate
✉ EC2M 4NR
✆ (020) 7283 1763
Fax (020) 7283 1664
e-mail info@boisdale-city.co.uk
www.boisdale.co.uk

⊖ Liverpool Street
Plan VIII
Closed 25 December-4 January, Saturday, Sunday and Bank Holidays

Menu £29/37 – Carte £26/43

A/C VISA MC AE

It's easy to miss and the ground floor is a popular spot for those who like some champagne and oysters on their way home; but follow the tartan carpet down to the relative calm of the cosy and characterful restaurant, complete with live music. That carpet was a clue as this is all about Scotland. Admittedly some of the accents are as unconvincing as Mel Gibson's but there is no denying that the food is the real thing. The large menu is made up of plenty of Scottish specialities and reminds us just how spectacular the produce is north of the border. Salmon, shellfish, beef and, of course, haggis are the perennial favourites but so are the daily specials of game, fish and assorted pies. You'll leave with an urge to hike somewhere.

Bonds

Modern European XXX

M3

5 Threadneedle St ✉ EC2R 8AY
✆ (020) 7657 8088
Fax (020) 7657 8089
e-mail bonds@theetongroup.com
www.theetoncollection.com

⊖ Bank
Plan VIII
Closed Saturday, Sunday and Bank Holidays

Menu £16 (lunch) – Carte £33/42

A/C VISA MC AE

Bonds repays the investment of its customers by providing plenty of interest, in both the menu choice and the surroundings. This former banking hall dates from the 1850s and its marble, pillars and panelling make it a grand old room in which to house a restaurant. The cooking is equally bold and the experienced kitchen produce well-versed dishes that are unfussy and keep their roots largely within Europe. Slow-cooking is a popular technique and is used with veal shin, rump of lamb and pork belly, while fish from Newhaven is handled deftly. Service is up to speed at lunch; dinner is less frenzied, when the lower lighting helps create a more intimate atmosphere. The cocktail list makes the adjacent bar worth visiting.

Brew Wharf

Traditional X

M4

Brew Wharf Yard, Stoney St ✉ SE1 9AD
✆ (020) 7378 6601
Fax (020) 7940 5997
e-mail brewwharf@vinopolis.co.uk
www.brewwharf.com

⊖ London Bridge
Plan X
Closed Christmas-New Year and Sunday

Carte £19/29

A/C VISA MC AE

If you're been fighting the crowds at Borough Market and don't fancy eating on the hoof or queuing for a table then head over to Brew Wharf; it's conveniently located just around the corner under the railway arches. It's a bar, restaurant and micro brewery combined, so there should have something that appeals. These beers, along with an extensive range of imported bottles, prove to be the main draw for many, especially the weekday after-work crowd, and the menu, which doubles as a place mat, provides just the right sort of no-nonsense food you'll fancy when you've got a beer in your hand. This includes rotisserie dishes such as marinated whole or half chickens, rib-eye steak sandwiches, Caesar salads and pints of prawns.

Butlers Wharf Chop House

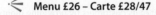

N4

British

36e Shad Thames, Butlers Wharf
SE1 2YE
(020) 7403 3403
Fax (020) 7940 1855
e-mail bwchophouse@danddlondon.com
www.chophouse.co.uk

London Bridge
Plan X
Closed 1-3 January and Sunday dinner in winter

Menu £26 – Carte £28/47

"Location, location, location" as every estate agent has said. A little summer sunshine and few restaurants in London can rival Butlers Wharf's delightful spot on the river. However, those terrace tables can't be booked – just join the queue at the bar. The menu reads like a roll-call of Britishness: expect potted shrimps, prawn cocktail, grilled lemon sole with Jersey Royals and the classic mixed grill. While the kitchen doesn't always quite deliver on the promise of the menu, dishes are generally satisfying. Seasonal offerings, such as the long list of strawberry dessert creations in June, are usually worth exploring. Levels of noise and general merriment are high and staff just about cope with the high numbers of customers.

VISA MC AE

Cantina Del Ponte

N4

Italian

36c Shad Thames, Butlers Wharf
SE1 2YE
(020) 7403 5403
e-mail cantinareservations@danddlondon.com
www.cantina.co.uk

London Bridge
Plan X

Menu £14/19 – Carte £25/37

A refurbishment a few years back made this Italian stalwart a little darker and more atmospheric, although they wisely kept the mural. The best tables on a summer's day remain those on the riverside terrace under the bright orange awning. The menu was also tweaked: it was out with the pizzas and in with a greater degree of authenticity. The focus is on appealing and flavoursome dishes and the set menu, which is available until 7pm, represents very good value. The à la carte offers an appealing selection, from recognisable standards to others displaying greater originality. Those flavours are well defined and portions are bigger than expected. The wine list covers all of Italy and there's a good choice by the glass.

VISA MC AE

Cantina Vinopolis

L4 **International**

No.1 Bank End ✉ SE1 9BU
☎ (020) 7940 8333
Fax (020) 7089 9339
e-mail cantina@vinopolis.co.uk
www.cantinavinopolis.com

⊖ London Bridge
Plan X
closed Sunday dinner and Bank Holidays

Menu £30 – Carte £23/34

A/C VISA AE

Southwark is becoming something of a Utopia for today's gastronauts. Food supplies can be garnered at the wonderful Borough Market and oenologists will find relief and fulfilment at Vinopolis, the wine merchant and museum. Cantina Vinopolis is the wine attraction's public restaurant and is housed under vast, magnificent Victorian arches that lend a palpable sense of history and atmospherics to the whole place. The exposed kitchen offers a menu that flits between continents and, as one would expect, the wine list offers an interesting and correspondingly diverse selection with many well priced bottles. The styling and comforts are simple and uncomplicated and the service is smoothly effective.

Champor-Champor

M5 **Asian**

62-64 Weston St
✉ SE1 3QJ
☎ (020) 7403 4600
e-mail mail@champor-champor.com
www.champor-champor.com

⊖ London Bridge
Plan X
Closed 1 week Easter, 1 week Christmas, Sunday and Bank Holidays – booking essential – dinner only

Menu £32

A/C VISA AE

Spirits cannot fail to be lifted as soon as you find yourself in this beguiling restaurant with its exuberant and vibrant decoration; any Malay speakers out there will instantly appreciate the name, which roughly translates as 'mix-and-match'. That certainly applies to the two rooms into which it is divided and where no two tables are the same. The rooms are festooned with everything from Buddha statues to tribal artefacts, from masks to carvings and all with the added exoticism of incense fragrance in the air and flickering candle light. The cooking also comes with a mix of influences and equal amounts of colour, panache and vitality, and is a fusion of Malaysian and assorted Asian cuisines.

The Chancery

K2 **Modern European** XX

9 Cursitor St ✉ EC4A 1LL
✆ (020) 7831 4000
Fax (020) 7831 4002
e-mail reservations@thechancery.co.uk
www.thechancery.co.uk

⊖ Chancery Lane
Plan VIII
Closed 25 December, Saturday and Sunday

Menu £34

A/C VISA MC AE

Surrounded by the law courts, The Chancery, open only during the week, provides the perfect spot for that last meal of freedom or the post-trial celebratory acquittal. It is the sister restaurant to The Clerkenwell Dining Room and the bright main room benefits from the large picture windows and understated decoration. This is the room in which to reserve your table, rather than the basement which can lack something in atmosphere. Service is sufficiently fleet of foot and efficient to reassure those with an eye on the adjournment. The cooking also comes suitably well-judged and is modern in style but underpinned by a solid understanding of the ingredients. The wine list has some well-chosen bottles under £25.

Cicada

L1 **Asian** X

132-134 St John St ✉ EC1V 4JT
✆ (020) 7608 1550
Fax (020) 8608 1551
e-mail cicada@rickerrestaurants.com
www.rickerrestaurants.com

⊖ Farringdon
Plan IX
Closed Sunday and Bank Holidays

Menu £11/15 – Carte approx. £23

VISA MC AE

You'll need to book ahead to guarantee a table at this busy, noisy and infectiously entertaining Pan-Asian restaurant, which was the first in Will Ricker's London-wide chain. The semi-booth seating and open style kitchen add to the general drama and the bar is more than just an addendum to the restaurant. A pot of knives, forks and chopsticks on each table allow you to decide just how authentic you want the experience to be. The varied and lengthy menu changes often but perennial favourites like chilli salt squid are constants. The Chinese element is quite strong and dim sum forms a large part but there's also more Japanese influence than in the other branches, which comes in the form of sashimi, maki rolls and tempura.

Cinnamon Kitchen

N2 **Indian** XX

9 Devonshire Square ✉ EC2M 4YL ⊖ Liverpool St
✆ (020) 7626 5000 **Plan VIII**
Fax (020) 7397 9611
e-mail info@cinnamon-kitchen.com
www.cinnamon-kitchen.com

Closed 25-26 December, 1 January, Saturday lunch, Sunday and Bank Holidays

Menu £18 s – Carte £31/50 s

Having successfully established Westminster's Cinnamon Club and made it a popular choice with those who run the country, the team behind it opened a second branch here in the City, to appeal to those who own, or once thought they owned, the country. This is all about contemporary Indian dining: the cooking is creative and original, the surroundings light and unobtrusive and the service keen and sprightly. The menu bears little resemblance to the usual Indian fare and includes ingredients like quinoa, red deer and scallops. The arresting presentation doesn't come at the expense of the punchy flavours. The grill section is worth exploring and enthusiastic amateur cooks should position themselves at the Tandoor Bar to watch all the action.

A/C VISA MC AE

The Clerkenwell Dining Room

L2 **French** XX

69-73 St John St ✉ EC1M 4AN ⊖ Farringdon
✆ (020) 7253 9000 **Plan IX**
Fax (020) 7253 3322
e-mail reservations@theclerkenwell.com
www.theclerkenwell.com

Closed 25 December, Saturday lunch, Sunday and Bank Holidays

Carte £25/35

The chef owner of this smart and surprisingly sizeable place has a classically French background so that means you can expect sound cooking techniques from his kitchen and be safe in the knowledge that the food will be free from any unusual or challenging combinations. Nonetheless, this is dining that comes with all the bells and whistles such as amuse bouche and you'll certainly feel fed by the end, although the most successful dishes are those in a simpler style. The room to your left as you enter is the nicer spot. The service is slick and smooth but this contributes to the mildly schizophrenic personality of the restaurant as it cannot decide whether it is a rather serious-minded operation or a more casual neighbourhood eaterie.

A/C VISA MC AE

Club Gascon ✿

L2

French XX

57 West Smithfield ✉ EC1A 9DS
✆ (020) 7796 0600
Fax (020) 7796 0601
e-mail info@clubgascon.com
www.clubgascon.com

⊖ Barbican
Plan VIII
Closed Christmas-New Year, Saturday lunch, Sunday and Bank Holidays – booking essential

Menu £28/42 – Carte £43/68

A/C · VISA · MC · AE

Club Gascon

The rich bounty of France's southwest region is celebrated in the bourgeoning empire of Pascal Aussignac and Vincent Labeyrie but their pre-eminent creation remains Club Gascon. The restaurant is now over a decade old but some subtle changes have prepared it for the next chapter. The colour-coordinated redesign has allowed the original marble to become more of a feature and the cooking has also developed. Traditional dishes such as cassoulet and the like are now available at their 'comptoir' nearby and this in turn allows the energetic Aussignac – who even creates the dramatic floral displays himself – to be a little more daring in the kitchen here. The southwest remains his greatest influence but these days he pushes a little at the boundaries. The size of the portions has also grown slightly, although the seasonal menu, with or without suggested wine pairings, is often the best way to go. Service always begins well but can sometimes wobble a little when the room reaches capacity, but it is very hard to leave Club Gascon without feeling a little better about life.

First Course

- Abalone and razor clams à la plancha with parsnip and seaweed tartare.
- Duck foie gras club.

Main Course

- Cappuccino of black pudding and lobster.
- Dover sole with bordelaise sauce, morels and garlic.

Dessert

- Rhubarb and champagne sorbet, rose Chantilly.
- White chocolate bon-bon with raspberries and pistachio.

The Coach & Horses

K1

Italian influences

26-28 Ray St ✉ EC1R 3DJ
(020) 7837 1336
Fax (020) 7278 1478
e-mail info@thecoachandhorses.com
www.thecoachandhorses.com

⊖ Farringdon.
Plan IX
Closed Christmas to New Year, Easter, Saturday lunch, Sunday dinner and bank holidays

Carte £22/28

VISA MC AE

The Coach and Horses may have a palpable sense of its own Victorian heritage but it's still moving with the times. A recent refreshment of the dining room has turned it into a very pleasant environment. Here, the menu is a reflection of the self-taught chef's enthusiasm for all things European, especially its sunnier Mediterranean parts. There are Spanish and Italian influences aplenty, with everything from osso bucco to polenta, chorizo to chilled soups. But our own British contribution to cuisine is not forgotten, especially in the bar where the appealing list of snacks includes Scotch eggs with mustard – surely a near perfect accompaniment to a pint. Any summer warmth provokes a stampede for the enclosed decked yard.

Comptoir Gascon

K2

French

61-63 Charterhouse St ✉ EC1M 6HJ
(020) 7608 0851
Fax (020) 7608 0871
e-mail info@comptoirgascon.com
www.comptoirgascon.com

⊖ Farringdon
Plan IX
Closed Christmas-New Year, Sunday and Monday – booking essential

Carte £16/26

A/C VISA MC AE

This buzzy restaurant should be subsidised by the French Tourist Board as it does more to illustrate one component of Gascony's famed douceur de vivre – sweetness of life – than any glossy brochure. The wines, breads, foie gras, duck and cheeses all celebrate SW France's reputation for earthy, proper man-food. The menu is divided into 'mer', 'vegetal' and 'terre'; be sure to order duck, whether as rillettes, confit or in a salade Landaise. After these big flavours, it'll come as a relief to see that the desserts, displayed in a cabinet, are delicate little things. The prices are also commendable; even the region's wine comes direct from the producers to avoid the extra mark-up. There's further bounty on the surrounding shelves.

Coq d'Argent

M3 **French** XXX

✉ EC2R 8EJ ⊖ Bank
✆ (020) 7395 5000 **Plan VIII**
Fax (020) 7395 5050 Closed Christmas, Easter and Bank Holidays
e-mail coqdargent@danddlondon.com – booking essential
www.coqdargent.co.uk

Menu £29 – Carte £31/46

There a few London restaurants offering great views and fewer still that look like a bow of a ship when you gaze up at them. Not only does Coq d'Argent look down over the Square Mile but it also has a great terrace and fantastic roof garden. The bar may get a regular pounding but the noise levels are contained. Service in the restaurant is slick and well-organised but they are so used to busy lunches that dinner can sometimes be served at too quick a pace. The cooking is regional French and dishes come with a certain refinement. There's a good balance between the traditional and more contemporary, with shellfish a popular option. The à la carte prices can also be a little lofty, especially as the main courses require side dishes.

Devonshire Terrace

N2 **Modern European** XX

Devonshire Sq ✉ EC2M 4WY ⊖ Liverpool Street
✆ (020) 7256 3233 **Plan VIII**
Fax (020) 7256 3244 Closed Saturday, Sunday and Bank Holidays
e-mail info@devonshireterrace.co.uk
www.devonshireterrace.co.uk

Carte £18/39

Devonshire Terrace is all about flexibility. Not only is it open from 7am until midnight, but the idea is to create your own main course by choosing the sauce and the side dishes to accompany your tiger prawns, veal chop, fishcakes or other brasserie-style offering. For those who would no sooner create their own main course than offer to help wash-up can choose salad or pastas dishes which come fully dressed. Apart from the two terraces, one of which is an all-year affair within the atrium, try to snare one of the booths in the bright restaurant with its high ceiling and open kitchen. The elephant motif? This was once an ivory store for the East India Company and the restaurant sponsors an elephant in South Africa.

Eastside Inn

Innovative XXX

L2

40 St John St ✉ EC1M 4AY
✆ (020) 7490 9230
Fax (0207) 7490 9234
e-mail reservations@esilondon.com
www.esilondon.com

⊖ Barbican
Plan IX
Closed 9-18 April, 23 August-5 September, 24 December-9 January, Saturday, Sunday and Bank Holidays

Menu £35/70

A/C VISA MC AE

The first thing you notice is the open-plan kitchen from where owner-chef Bjorn van der Horst directs operations. To one side is a formal, cream-coloured 'fine-dining' restaurant and on the other, a more relaxed 'bistro moderne' with recognisable classics. In the former, service is formal and mostly French and the cooking has a classical French foundation with plenty of inventive and highly original touches. Whilst there is no doubting the provenance of the prime ingredients or the technical skill and craft of the kitchen, not all the dishes work: some of the flavour partnerships make dishes soar, while others seem misconceived. In an area known for the casual style of its restaurants, will Eastside Inn be able to buck the trend?

The Garrison

Gastropub

M5

99-101 Bermondsey St ✉ SE1 3XB
✆ (020) 7089 9355
e-mail info@thegarrison.co.uk
www.thegarrison.co.uk

⊖ London Bridge.
Plan X
Closed 25-26 December and 1 January – booking essential at dinner

Menu £14 – Carte £28/45

A/C VISA MC AE

Close to the owners' other place, Village East, sits The Garrison, part shabby-chic gastropub, part boho brasserie. The pub's full of bustle and life and the ideal venue for meeting up with friends, especially if you can snare one of the booths. If you're an even bigger party then consider hiring the downstairs room which doubles as a mini cinema. There's a refreshing wholesomeness to the cooking; there are blackboard specials, everything's homemade except for the quince paste which comes with the cheese and the menu changes every eight weeks. Dishes display this no-nonsense approach by being full in flavour and decent in size, whether that's a meatloaf with purple sprouting broccoli or a smoked haddock with bubble and squeak.

High Timber

L3 **Modern European** XX

8 High Timber St ✉ EC4V 3PA
✆ (020) 7248 1777
e-mail info@hightimber.com
www.hightimber.com

⊖ Mansion House
Plan VIII
Closed 25 December-3 January, Saturday lunch and Sunday

Menu £18 (lunch) – Carte £24/44

Surprisingly few restaurants in London overlook the river, especially on the north side, so High Timber is already off to a good start. Add an impressive wine cellar with over 900 bins, including much from the owners' homeland of South Africa, and you've virtually guaranteed a good night out. Heavy wood tables and slate floors lend a slightly rustic look to what is the ground floor of a purpose-built office block. But the room has a fluid feel, as diners are encouraged to visit the cellar or indeed the cheese room to make their choice. The highlight of the concise, seasonal menu is the beef from the grill; they use 28 day matured Cumbrian beef, cut to order from the bone. Dishes have a muscular vigour and come served on slate or chopping boards.

Hix Oyster and Chop House

L2 **British** X

36-37 Greenhill Rents
✉ EC1M 6BN
✆ (0207) 017 1930
Fax (0207) 549 3584
e-mail chophouse@restaurantsetcltd.co.uk
www.hixoysterandchophouse.co.uk

⊖ Farringdon
Plan IX
Closed 25-26 December, 1 January, Saturday lunch and Bank Holidays

Menu £35 (Sunday lunch) – Carte £28/58

Utilitarian surroundings, seasonal British ingredients, plenty of offal and prissy-free cooking: this may sound like a description of St John but is in fact the solo venture of Mark Hix, the chef who made The Ivy more than just a celebrity love-in. Smithfield Market seems an appropriate location for a restaurant that not only celebrates Britain's culinary heritage with old classics like rabbit brawn, nettle soup and beef and oyster pie but also reminds us of our own natural bounty, from sand eels and asparagus, whiting to laver bread. It's also called an Oyster & Chop House for a reason, with four types of oyster on offer as well as plenty of meat, including Aberdeen beef aged for 28 days and served on the bone.

Kenza

N2 **Lebanese** XX

10 Devonshire Square ✉ EC2M 4YP ⊖ Liverpool Street
✆ (020) 7929 5533 **Plan VIII**
Fax (020) 7929 0303
e-mail info@kenza-restaurant.com
www.kenza-restaurant.com

Closed 25 December-4 January, Saturday lunch, Sunday and Bank Holidays

Menu £28 – Carte £26/37

A/C, VISA, MC, AE

The newly regenerated Devonshire Square may not appear that mysterious but descend the stairs down into Kenza and you'll be transported into the exotic Levant. The name, Arabic for 'treasure,' is well chosen and the floor tiles, lamps, carvings, colourful candles and satin cushions were all imported from Morocco. Moroccan and Lebanese cooking are the two main influences; the choices include samboussek pastries, kibbeh parcels, pureés and chargrills. There are also 'feast' menus for larger parties and the cooking is accurate and authentic; finish with theatrically poured mint tea and baklava. There's belly dancing, pumping music and large tables but the kitchen proves that a party atmosphere and good food are not mutually exclusive.

The Larder

L1 **Modern European** XX

91-93 St John St ✉ EC1M 4NU ⊖ Farringdon
✆ (020) 7608 1558 **Plan IX**
e-mail info@thelarderrestaurant.com
www.thelarderrestaurant.com

Closed 24 December-2 January, Easter, Sunday, Monday lunch and Bank Holidays

Menu £17 (lunch) – Carte £23/34

A/C, VISA, MC, AE

An appropriate name as there is bounty galore. On one side is the bakery with plenty of artisanal breads and cakes. The restaurant, meanwhile, is one of those large, semi-industrial places with exposed brick and pipes and an open kitchen at the back. This kind of hard-edged space can push up the decibels but that's part of its appeal. Think modern European comfort food, from moules marinière to roast salmon with pumpkin ravioli, but alongside the halloumi you might find Lancashire cheese and next to the chicken breast with Puy lentils could be a Barnsley chop, so the Union flag is raised occasionally (the owners are from Leeds). A side dish to accompany the main course is recommended and some thought has gone into them.

Luc's Brasserie

French XX

M3

17-22 Leadenhall Market ✉ EC3V 1LR
✆ (020) 7621 0666
Fax (020) 7623 8516
e-mail info@lucsbrasserie.com
www.lucsbrasserie.com

⊖ Bank
Plan VIII
Closed 25 December-04 January, Friday-Monday dinner, Saturday-Sunday and Bank Holidays – booking essential at lunch

Menu £19 – Carte £29/41

VISA MC AE

Go into Leadenhall Market and look up – that's Luc's Brasserie, a restaurant which first appeared in the late 1890s and was reinvigorated and re-launched in 2006. The top floor is fairly sedate but the main room- from where you can admire the Victorian splendour of the market – is where the action is. The menu is an unapologetic paean to all things French, from snails to steak tartare, confit of duck to crème brûlée. The kitchen wisely sticks to conventional and classic recipes and it's easy to see why ties are quickly loosened. Staff do their bit by getting on with things but do so with a smile. As one would expect, the mood relaxes somewhat on the three nights they open for dinner, when a fixed price menu is also available.

Lutyens

Modern European XXX

K3

85 Fleet St ✉ EC4 1AE
✆ (020) 7583 8385
Fax (020) 7583 8386
e-mail info@lutyens-restaurant.com
www.lutyens-restaurant.com

⊖ St Paul's
Plan VIII
Closed lunch Saturday and Sunday

Carte £29/43

A/C VISA MC AE

Having built one restaurant empire, Sir Terence Conran appears to have embarked on creating another. Lutyens opened in 2009 following the success of Boundary, and boasts that unmistakeable Conran look: timeless and effortless good looks mixed with functionality. He also found another building of note: the restaurant is within what was the HQ of Reuters and is named after its architect, Sir Edwin. The menu is an appealing Anglo-French affair, with an assortment of classics ranging from parfaits and fruits de mer to Dover sole and roast grouse, along with dishes from the rotisserie; sushi even makes an incongruous appearance. Service is clued-up but perhaps a little more formal than it needs to be. There's a busy bar on the Fleet Street side.

Magdalen

M4 **British**

152 Tooley St ✉ SE1 2TU
✆ (020) 7403 1342
Fax (020) 7403 9950
e-mail info@magdalenrestaurant.co.uk
www.magdalenrestaurant.co.uk

⊖ London Bridge
Plan X
Closed last 2 weeks August, 24 December - 4 January, Saturday lunch and Sunday

Menu £19 (lunch) – Carte £27/45

A/C VISA MC AE Diners

How you pronounce it may depend on your education, but what is certain is that Magdalen is an appealing addition to this part of town. Owned by a triumvirate of chefs, the place is divided between two floors (no bookings are taken on the ground floor) and has the look of a French brasserie about it. The cooking, however, looks closer to home for influence; what you read is, laudably, what you get, and you'll find hugely appealing words like 'roast', 'potted' and 'dripping' appearing regularly. This is all about being fancy-free and full of flavour; there's still the odd Gallic flavour but even the snails come with a nettle soup. There are also dishes made for two, like whole calves kidney or custard tart. Service is pitched just right.

Manicomio

L3 **Italian**

6 Gutter Lane ✉ EC2V 8AS
✆ (020) 7726 5010
Fax (020) 7726 5011
e-mail gutterlane@manicomio.co.uk
www.manicomio.co.uk

⊖ St Paul's
Plan VIII
Closed Christmas-New Year, Saturday, Sunday and Bank Holidays

Carte £29/47

A/C VISA MC AE

This sibling to the King's Road branch opened in the summer of 2008 and is on the first floor of a Norman Foster-designed building. On the ground floor is the deli/café while the bar is kept separately on the top floor, away from the restaurant which makes a nice change in this part of town. The owners' other business is importing Italian produce so they know their cipollas. There's also plenty of British meat, game and fish but prepared in an Italian way, with top notch Italian accompaniments. The cooking covers many regions, with daily specials; one or two side dishes are needed for the main course and these, together with the bread, may bump the bill up. The room has a bright, fresh feel; all the furniture is imported from Italy.

Medcalf

K1 **British**

40 Exmouth Market ✉ EC1R 4QE
(020) 7833 3533
e-mail mail@medcalfbar.co.uk
www.medcalfbar.co.uk

⊖ Farringdon
Plan IX
Closed 23 December-5 January, Sunday dinner and Bank Holidays – booking essential

Carte £22/34

There is something very 'proper' about Medcalf: maybe that's the no-frills décor that celebrates the original butcher's shop that was here from 1912 (the lights are held up by meat hooks); maybe it's the loud and buzzy pub-like atmosphere, with the good range of draught beers, wines by the glass and assorted snacks or maybe it's the fresh, appealing and very seasonal British cooking, with dishes like Barnsley chop or calves liver, which has a satisfyingly robust, masculine feel to it. Whatever it is, it works as the restaurant gets very busy, very quickly. Those who think jellies and foams should only be found at children's playtime rather than on a dinner plate will find much to celebrate here at Medcalf.

The Mercer

M3 **Modern European**

34 Threadneedle St ✉ EC2R 8AY
(020) 7628 0001
Fax (020) 7588 2822
e-mail info@themercer.co.uk
www.themercer.co.uk

⊖ Bank
Plan VIII
Closed 25 December-2 January, Saturday, Sunday and Bank Holidays

Carte £27/38

The credit crunch means it's even less likely that a restaurant will ever be converted into a bank so, at the moment, the trend remains from bank to restaurant; here at The Mercer you can even see where the tellers used to sit. The high ceilings and windows let in plenty of light and the place has a pleasingly animated brasserie feel, with service that is slick and well paced. Open from breakfast, the kitchen concentrates on familiar flavours and comforting classics. While the cooking may not always live up to the promise of the menu, it is nonetheless satisfying. Scottish beef features in the Grill section and there are daily specials which could be corned beef hash or a fish pie. There's a huge choice of wines by the glass or carafe.

Mint Leaf Lounge

M3 **Indian** XX

12 Angel Court, Lothbury ✉ EC2R 7HB ⊖ Bank
✆ (020) 7600 0992 **Plan VIII**
Fax (020) 7600 6628 Closed 25-26 December, 1 January, Easter, Saturday and Sunday
e-mail reservations@mintleaflounge.com
www.mintleaflounge.com

Menu £16 (lunch) – Carte £27/41

This was formerly NatWest's HQ and has been turned into a stylish and slick Indian restaurant. The bar is bigger and the dining area smaller than the original branch in St James's, but with the stock market the way it's been, you can't blame them for that. The menu cleverly allows for flexibility in that many of the dishes are available in both starter and main course size and the presentation on the plate is quite contemporary. The majority of influences come from the more southerly parts of India and dishes demonstrate genuine care in preparation. Fish, meat or vegetarian platters are available and there's a good value set lunch menu. Knowledgeable staff in ubiquitous black provide nicely paced service.

The Modern Pantry

K2 **International** X

47-48 St John's Sq ✉ EC1V 4JJ ⊖ Farringdon
✆ (020) 7553 9210 **Plan IX**
e-mail enquiries@themodernpantry.co.uk Closed 24-28 December and 1 January – booking advisable
www.themodernpantry.co.uk

Menu £23 (lunch) – Carte £22/37

Anna Hansen, formerly of The Providores, opened her own restaurant in a Georgian building that's been everything from a foundry to a carpentry workshop. Bold and zingy flavours full of vitality are the hallmarks of her cooking; its roots are fusion but tempered with an understanding of when to leave alone. The small plates, such as chorizo and feta fritters, are perfectly formed nibbles and full-bodied main courses like the rabbit stew can pack an unexpected chilli punch. Earl Grey or rosewater provide original flavours to desserts. The communal feel and café style of the ground floor is the best place to be; the atmosphere upstairs is a little more restrained although the same menu is served on both floors.

Moro

K1

Mediterranean X

34-36 Exmouth Market ✉ EC1R 4QE
✆ (020) 7833 8336
Fax (020) 7833 9338
e-mail info@moro.co.uk
www.moro.co.uk

⊖ Farringdon
Plan IX
Closed Easter, 1 week Christmas-New Year and Bank Holidays – booking essential

Carte £28/36

A/C VISA MC AE

Despite being a feature of Exmouth market for over a decade, Moro remains one of the busiest restaurants around, but anyone left frustrated by not getting a table should consider just pitching up and sitting at the zinc-topped bar: it's a great spot for tapas and some wonderful sherries, you'll get the full benefit of the wondrous aromas from the open kitchen and be able to watch the chefs in action. Moorish cooking is the draw which means Spain and the Muslim Mediterranean. The wood-burning oven and charcoal grill provide the smokiness and charring to improve and enhance the poultry, meat and sourdough bread. The cooking is colourful and invigorating and the menu changes fully every two weeks.

1901

M2

French XXX

Liverpool St ✉ EC2M 7QN
✆ (020) 7618 7000
Fax (020) 7618 5035
e-mail london.restres@andaz.com
www.andaz.com

⊖ Liverpool Street
Plan VIII

Menu £22 (lunch) – Carte £32/41

A/C VISA MC AE

1901 is the redecorated, rebranded and relaunched version of what was previously called Aurora. It's one of several restaurants within the Andaz hotel and is very much their flagship. This is a hugely impressive room, which they've painted white to make the eye-catching cupola even more striking. A cocktail bar has been added, along with a cheese and wine room; the cheeses being of predominantly British provenance. The cooking is mostly French in preparation and technique but stoutly British in terms of the ingredients it uses. A refined and delicate touch is evident in dishes such as poached halibut with saffron potatoes and the smoked haddock boudin. There is an army of staff on hand who are well-practiced but also friendly.

1 Lombard Street

M3 **International** XXX

1 Lombard St ✉ EC3V 9AA
✆ (020) 7929 6611
Fax (020) 7929 6622
e-mail hb@1lombardstreet.com
www.1lombardstreet.com

⊖ Bank
Plan VIII
Closed Saturday, Sunday and Bank Holidays – booking essential at lunch

Carte £49/62

A/C VISA MC AE

The contrast between the two restaurants at Lombard Street couldn't be greater. The brasserie is the more boisterous of the two, with its busy bar beneath an impressive domed skylight and a menu of classics like coq au vin. If you want a more subdued atmosphere, then fight through the crowds to the rear restaurant. Here everything, from the menu to the service, is taken far more seriously. Dishes are mostly traditional at their core but finished with a contemporary flourish; they are more obvious in their ambition and busier in their presentation. The dishes for two are worth considering. The discreet service and smartly dressed room make it popular with those who are making, planning or closing a deal.

Oxo Tower

K4 **Modern European** XXX

(8th floor), Oxo Tower Wharf,
Barge House St ✉ SE1 9PH
✆ (020) 7803 3888
Fax (020) 7803 3838
e-mail oxo.reservations@harveynichols.com
www.harveynichols.com

⊖ Southwark
Plan X
Closed 25-26 and dinner 24 December

Carte £34/53

A/C VISA MC AE

The Oxo Tower Restaurant is the smarter, more serious and ambitious sibling to the next door brasserie but both share terrific views and wonderful terraces from their location on the 8th floor of the iconic former Oxo riverside factory. The restaurant appears to be permanently busy and this means staff are sometimes a little too eager to tell you what time you have to vacate your table rather than making you feel welcome. The place is roomy, bright and open, with plenty of bustle; the cooking is contemporary and mostly European in influence while the kitchen uses plenty of top-end ingredients. Those views really are great but, on a clear day, you can see plenty of more reasonably priced restaurants.

Oxo Tower Brasserie

Modern European

(8th floor), Oxo Tower Wharf,
Barge House St ✉ SE1 9PH
✆ (020) 7803 3888
Fax (020) 7803 3838
e-mail oxo.reservations@harveynichols.com
www.harveynichols.com

⊖ Southwark
Plan X
Closed 25 -26 and dinner 24 December

Menu £25 (lunch) – Carte £26/45

If you've never asked for a window table before, then now is the time to start. Better still, ask for the terrace and face east towards St Paul's for the best views. The light-filled, glass-encased brasserie on the eighth floor of the iconic Oxo Tower makes much of its riverside location but that's not to say that this is just a spot for a summer's day. The bold, zingy flavours and influences from around the globe ensure that the cooking is bright and sunny even when it's dull outside. Staff do their bit by being a responsive bunch and the place really rocks in the evenings when there's live music and the open kitchen becomes more of a feature. It's much more fun than the restaurant and the prices are friendlier too.

L3

Paternoster Chop House

British

Warwick Court, Paternoster
Square ✉ EC4M 7DX
✆ (020) 7029 9400
Fax (020) 7029 9409
e-mail paternosterr@dandlondon.com
www.paternosterchophouse.com

⊖ St Paul's
Plan VIII
Closed 2 weeks Christmas, Saturday, Sunday dinner and Bank Holidays

Menu £25 – Carte £31/43

In the shadow of St Paul's lies this updated version of a chop house. Enter when it's busy and you'll be assailed by a wall of noise from the bar, dining room and even the open kitchen at the back. Tables are set close together, adding to the general bonhomie; the room is crisp and uncluttered and the chairs unforgiving to loiterers. However busy, service copes well and the young team are an organised bunch. The menu is large and the cooking determinedly British, hearty and classic. Shellfish is popular; the kitchen does its own butchery and there's plenty of comfort food, from cottage pie to Bakewell tart. Not only is there a fish of the day, usually from Cornwall, but also a daily beast such as Galloway beef.

The Peasant

L1 **Gastropub**

240 St John St ✉ EC1V 4PH
✆ (020) 7336 7726
Fax (020) 7490 1089
e-mail eat@thepeasant.co.uk
www.thepeasant.co.uk

⊖ Farringdon.
Plan IX
Closed 25 December to 1 January and bank holidays except Good Friday – booking essential

Menu £35 (dinner) – Carte £23/30

Originally called the George & Dragon, it changed to The Peasant to celebrate Wat Tyler's revolting ones of 1381 who gathered near this spot. However, what really made the name of this classic Victorian pub was its being in the vanguard of the original gastro-pub movement. The busy ground floor bar, with its tiles, arched windows, high ceiling and mosaics is a great place for some heartening fare, from sausage and mash to plates of charcuterie or meze, to go with your beer. Upstairs, it's more your proper restaurant experience with decoration courtesy of a fairground/circus theme and a more formal feel. Here, you'll find a degree of originality in the cooking, but the kitchen is at its best when it keeps things relatively simple.

Le Pont de la Tour

N4 **French**

36d Shad Thames,
Butlers Wharf ✉ SE1 2YE
✆ (020) 7403 8403
Fax (020) 7940 1835
e-mail lepontres@danddlondon.com
www.lepontdelatour.co.uk

⊖ London Bridge
Plan X

Menu £32/43

The regeneration of the River and Butlers Wharf were there for all to see in 1991 when Le Pont de la Tour opened and its glamorous reputation was done no harm when Tony Blair entertained Bill Clinton here in 1997. The elegant room provides diners with terrific views of Tower Bridge and the activity on the river, especially from the delightful terrace, while the menu offers a comprehensive selection of dishes that borrow heavily from France, all served by a well-drilled team. For those after less formal surroundings then head for the Bar & Grill which specialises in crustaceans and fruits de mer while those wanting something to take home are catered for by an impressive array of produce in the adjacent food store.

Portal

L1 **Mediterranean** XX

88 St John St ✉ EC1M 4EH
✆ (020) 7253 6950
Fax (020) 7490 5836
e-mail reservations@portalrestaurant.com
www.portalrestaurant.com

⊖ Farringdon
Plan IX
Closed 1-6 January, Saturday lunch, Sunday and Bank Holidays

Menu £26 (lunch) – Carte £27/47

A/C VISA MC AE

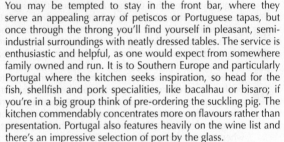

You may be tempted to stay in the front bar, where they serve an appealing array of petiscos or Portuguese tapas, but once through the throng you'll find yourself in pleasant, semi-industrial surroundings with neatly dressed tables. The service is enthusiastic and helpful, as one would expect from somewhere family owned and run. It is to Southern Europe and particularly Portugal where the kitchen seeks inspiration, so head for the fish, shellfish and pork specialities, like bacalhau or bisaro; if you're in a big group think of pre-ordering the suckling pig. The kitchen commendably concentrates more on flavours rather than presentation. Portugal also features heavily on the wine list and there's an impressive selection of port by the glass.

Quality Chop House

K1 **British** X

92- 94 Farringdon Rd ✉ EC1R 3EA
✆ (020) 7837 5093
Fax (020) 7833 8748
e-mail enquiries@qualitychophouse.co.uk
www.qualitychophouse.co.uk

⊖ Farringdon
Plan IX
Closed 25 December

Carte £23/39

A/C VISA MC AE

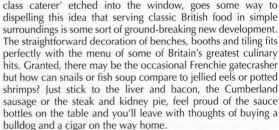

This late 19C chop house, with the words 'Progressive working class caterer' etched into the window, goes some way to dispelling this idea that serving classic British food in simple surroundings is some sort of ground-breaking new development. The straightforward decoration of benches, booths and tiling fits perfectly with the menu of some of Britain's greatest culinary hits. Granted, there may be the occasional Frenchie gatecrasher but how can snails or fish soup compare to jellied eels or potted shrimps? Just stick to the liver and bacon, the Cumberland sausage or the steak and kidney pie, feel proud of the sauce bottles on the table and you'll leave with thoughts of buying a bulldog and a cigar on the way home.

Rhodes Twenty Four ✿

British XXX

M3

24th floor, Tower 42, 25 Old Broad St
EC2N 1HQ
(020) 7877 7703
Fax (020) 7877 7788
e-mail reservations@rhodes24.co.uk
www.rhodes24.co.uk

Liverpool Street
Plan VIII
Closed Christmas-New Year, Saturday, Sunday and Bank Holidays

Carte £38/60

A/C VISA MC AE

Rhodes Twenty Four

It's still all a bit of a palaver getting into Tower 42, what with the metal detectors and the security checks, but at least the views from the 24th floor are worth it and no one's going to gawp at you from outside while you eat. The suits still pack in at lunchtime but the mood is altogether more measured and relaxing in the evening. Despite economic challenges, Rhodes 24 has maintained its standards and the kitchen continues to display a firm understanding of fine cooking: the strength of each dish lies in its outward simplicity which, in turn, owes much to the kitchen's ability and confidence in knowing when to leave alone. This can be done when you have absolute respect for the ingredients, of which most are British, and know how to get the best out of them. Just order the beef and onion suet pudding and, as the waiter approaches with it, watch the covetous glances from fellow diners. The sauces, both sweet and savoury, are prepared with a deft hand and, what's more, the waiter will leave you the jug.

First Course
- Seared scallops, mashed potato and shallots.
- Pigeon and cep tart with white onion sauce.

Main Course
- Saddle of venison with globe artichokes and truffle.
- Skate wing with langoustines, leeks and ham.

Dessert
- Apricot tart with mint syrup and apricot sorbet.
- Warm coffee and chocolate pudding.

Roast

M4 **British** XX

The Floral Hall, Borough Market ⊖ London Bridge
✉ SE1 1TL **Plan X**
✆ (0845) 034 7300
Fax (0845) 034 7301
e-mail info@roast-restaurant.com
www.roast-restaurant.com

Closed 25-26 December, 1-2 January and Sunday dinner – booking essential

Carte £32/63

A/C VISA MC AE

It's in the one place where you don't look when you find yourself in the deliciously enticing surroundings of Borough Market – up. Jump into the lift and upstairs you'll be greeted and led into a vast room; the best seats are in the raised section beyond the bar. The place is always busy and the young team are a friendly bunch, although they can sometimes appear to be a man down. The food is all about being British and proud of it, reflecting the values of the market below and the importance of provenance. Start with the cocktail of the week, move on to Cornish herring or Arbroath smokie followed by roast lamb or steak and onion pudding and finish with a Bakewell tart or rhubarb crumble. You'll leave whistling 'Land of Hope and Glory'.

Sauterelle

M3 **French** XX

The Royal Exchange ✉ EC3V 3LR ⊖ Bank
✆ (020) 7618 2483 **Plan VIII**
www.restaurantsauterelle.com

Closed Saturday and Sunday

Menu £21 – Carte £33/43

A/C VISA MC AE

Opened original in 1565, The Royal Exchange may have been rebuilt twice, most recently in 1842, but today it is one of the great rousing landmarks in the City. Within the Exchange and to complement the Grand Bar and Café, one finds Sauterelle on its mezzanine level; now five years old and another in the D&D collection of restaurants. From its lofty position, Sauterelle (meaning 'grasshopper' in French) provides slick and comfortable surroundings and the well-drilled staff make light of the busy lunchtimes. The menu concentrates on classic bourgeois French cooking, with rillettes, marmites and saucissons to the fore. Expect scallops with Jerusalem artichoke, magret of duck and, to finish, a crème brûlée.

St John ✿

British

L2

26 St John St ✉ EC1M 4AY
✆ (020) 7251 0848
Fax (020) 7251 4090
e-mail reservations@stjohnrestaurant.com
www.stjohnrestaurant.com

Carte £22/39

⊖ Barbican
Plan IX
Closed Christmas-New Year, Easter, Saturday lunch, Sunday dinner and Bank Holidays – booking essential

A/C · VISA · MC · AE

St John

The walls, painted in a shade of detention centre white, add to the utilitarian feel of the room which was once a smokehouse in the 19C. There's no standing on ceremony; indeed no ceremony at all, and that makes dining at St John such a joyful experience as the focus is entirely directed at the food. You can play it safe and go for some crab and then roast beef but this is the place to try new flavours, whether that's the cuttlefish or the ox tongue. Game is a real favourite and the only gravy will be the blood of the bird – this is natural, 'proper' food. Seasonality is at its core – the menu is rewritten for each service – and nothing sums up the philosophy more than the potatoes and greens: they are always on the menu but the varieties and types change regularly. The waiters all dress in chef's jackets and some spend time in the kitchen so they know what they're talking about. There are dishes for two as well as magnums of wine for real trenchermen – and be sure to order a dozen warm madeleines to take home.

First Course
- Roast bone marrow and parsley salad.
- Black cuttlefish and onions.

Main Course
- Middle white pork, swede and pickled walnut.
- Rabbit with mustard and bacon.

Dessert
- Eccles cake and Lancashire cheese.
- Iced yoghurt slice with blueberries.

Skylon

J4 **Modern European** XXX

1 Southbank Centre, Belvedere Rd ✉ SE1 8XX ⊖ Waterloo
Plan III
✆ (020) 7654 7800
Fax (020) 7654 7801
Closed 25 December
e-mail skylonreservations@danddlondon.com
www.skylonrestaurant.co.uk

Menu £18/43 – Carte £25/35

The dining flagship in the revamped Royal Festival Hall offers a choice: a Grill to one side, with a raised cocktail bar making the most of the river views, and a Restaurant to the other, where things are a little more sedate and a tad more comfortable. This was the first project from D&D London following their management buy-out of Conran Restaurants and the 1950s styling and imaginative design made it a natural addition to the existing portfolio. The Grill offers an easy-to-eat menu, from eggs Benedict to bowls of pasta, as well as pre and post performance menus and something for the kids. The restaurant offers up more ambitious dishes that display a greater degree of complication, finer ingredients and higher prices.

Smiths of Smithfield

L2 **Modern European** XX

Top Floor, 67-77 Charterhouse St ✉ EC1M 6HJ ⊖ Barbican
Plan IX
✆ (020) 7251 7950
Fax (020) 7236 5666
Closed 24 December-2 January and Saturday lunch
e-mail reservations@smithsofsmithfield.co.uk
www.smithsofsmithfield.co.uk

Carte £35/47

If you ever arrange a get-together with a friend here just remember to be a little precise in your meeting spot. Smiths is housed in a vast building where all four of its floors are given over to eating, drinking and general merry making. As a rule of thumb, prices and levels of formality go up the higher up you go yourself. The ground floor is a relaxed bar with an exposed brick warehouse feel and easy, snacky menu. Then it's the cocktail bar, followed by the large and lively 'dining room' which is actually more a brasserie and finally the 'top floor' which has a more corporate, groomed feel and boasts terrific views of the surrounding rooftops. Cooking is decidedly modern with well sourced meats something of a speciality.

Tapas Brindisa

M4 **Spanish**

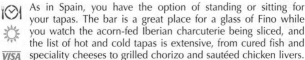

18-20 Southwark St, Borough Market ⊖ London Bridge
SE1 1TJ **Plan X**
(020) 7357 8880
e-mail office@tapasbrindisa.com
www.brindisatapaskitchens.com

Carte £21/35

As in Spain, you have the option of standing or sitting for your tapas. The bar is a great place for a glass of Fino while you watch the acorn-fed Iberian charcuterie being sliced, and the list of hot and cold tapas is extensive, from cured fish and speciality cheeses to grilled chorizo and sautéed chicken livers. It all happens on the edge of Borough Market in what was once a potato warehouse; the owners spent years importing Spanish produce so they know what they're talking about. With its tightly packed tables and convivial atmosphere, it does get very busy and as they don't take reservations, be prepared to wait; if they are full then ask nicely and you can put your name down and then wander around the market.

VISA MC AE

Tate Modern (Restaurant)

L4 **British**

7th Floor, Tate Modern, Bankside SE1 9TG ⊖ Southwark
(020) 7887 8888 **Plan X**
Fax (020) 7401 5171
Closed 24-26 December – lunch only
e-mail tate.modernrestaurant@tate.org.uk
www.tate.org.uk/modern/eatanddrink

Menu £20 (lunch) – Carte dinner £23/33

Floor to ceiling windows on two sides and a large mural on a third allow light and colour to fill this large restaurant on the 7th floor of the Tate Modern and balance all that black. Even if you don't get a window table you'll still get a great view of St. Paul's. There's seating for 145 but they stop taking reservations when they get to 100 to allow for the impulse diner. Lunch starts at 11.30 and ends at 3pm so there's every possibility of getting in but waiting at the bar is no hardship. The menu is an appealing mix of light, seasonal, fresh and zesty dishes, with a daily fish from Newlyn. The influences are mostly British, with the occasional Italian note. There's a good choice of wines by the glass and carafe as well as interesting soft drinks.

VISA MC AE

Terranostra

L3

Italian

27 Old Bailey ✉ EC4M 7HS
✆ (020) 3201 0077
e-mail info@terranostrafood.co.uk
www.terranostrafood.co.uk

⊖ St Paul's
Plan VIII
Closed Christmas, Easter, Saturday lunch, Sunday and Bank Holidays – booking advisable at lunch

Menu £18 – Carte £23/32

VISA MC AE

The City, and especially the area around the Old Bailey, is an area not exactly known for its cheery spirit and bonhomie. So praise be for Terranostra, because its informal, relaxed style and sweet-natured service could brighten up anyone's day. The food is honest, light and fresh and comes in generous sizes. The menu is nicely balanced and has appealing Sardinian leanings, which means malloreddus and fregola pastas, the sausage known as salsiccia sarda, rich and golden bottarga and plenty of moreish, crisp bread. On sunny days the French doors open onto the pavement terrace and those on a celebratory lunch from the courtrooms virtually opposite might find added resonance in D.H. Lawrence's view that Sardinia was "like freedom itself".

Vanilla Black

K2

Vegetarian

17-18 Tooks Court ✉ EC4A 1LB
✆ (020) 7242 2622
www.vanillablack.co.uk

⊖ Chancery Lane
Plan VIII
Closed 2 weeks Christmas, Saturday, Sunday and Bank Holiday Mondays

Menu £23/30 – Carte £23/30

A/C VISA MC AE

Those who think vegetarian food is all nut cutlets and knitted muesli should get along to Vanilla Black. Run by a Teesside couple who had a restaurant of the same name in York, they prove that vegetarian food can be varied, flavoursome and filling. The room is neat but quite stark and crisp in its decoration; sufficient warmth comes from the owner and her team of waiting staff. The set priced menu represents fair value and the cooking displays sufficient originality and imagination. Certainly no one leaves hungry as the flavoursome dishes use liberal amounts of cheese and potato. This is a proper restaurant that could heal the wounds of any carnivore scarred in their youth by an unpleasant vegetarian experience.

Village East

M5 **Modern European**

171-173 Bermondsey St ✉ SE1 3UW ⊖ London Bridge
✆ (020) 7357 6082 **Plan X**
Fax (020) 7403 3360 Closed 24-27 December
e-mail info@villageeast.co.uk
www.villageeast.co.uk

Menu £13 (2 course lunch)/30 – Carte £26/37

A/C VISA MC AE

Clever name - sounds a bit downtown Manhattan. But while Bermondsey may not be London's East Village, what Village East does is give this part of town a bit more 'neighbour' and a little less 'hood'. It's tricky to find so look for the glass façade and you'll find yourself in one of the bars, still wondering if you've come to the right place. Once, though, you've seen the open kitchen you know the dining area's not far away. Wood, brick, vents and large circular lamps give it that warehouse aesthetic. The menu is laid out a little confusingly but what you get is ample portions of familiar bistro style food, as well as some interesting combinations. The separately priced side dishes are not really needed and can push the bill up.

Vinoteca

L2 **Modern European**

7 St John St ✉ EC1M 4AA ⊖ Farringdon
✆ (020) 7253 8786 **Plan IX**
e-mail enquiries@vinoteca.co.uk Closed 23 December - 3 January
www.vinoteca.co.uk and Sunday dinner

Carte £20/30

VISA MC

Vinoteca, a self-styled 'bar and wine shop', comes divided into two tiny rooms and is always so busy that you'll almost certainly have to wait for a table. But what makes this frenetic place so special is the young and very passionate team who run it so well. The wine list is thrilling: it is constantly evolving and covers all regions, including less familiar territories along with the organic and the biodynamic. In circumstances such as these, the food can often be an afterthought but here it isn't. Alongside the cheeses and the cured meats that are available all day are classic dishes like pear, chicory and Roquefort salad; potted shrimps; bavette steak and panna cotta; all fresh tasting, well-timed and enjoyable.

Vivat Bacchus

K2 **Traditional** XX

(basement) 47 Farringdon St ✉ EC4A 4LL ⊖ Farringdon
✆ (020) 7353 2648 **Plan VIII**
Fax (020) 7353 3025
e-mail info@vivatbacchus.co.uk
www.vivatbacchus.co.uk

Closed 24 December-5 January, Saturday and Sunday

Menu £14/20 – Carte £19/35

A/C VISA MC AE

The wine list is just a teaser: they actually have 750 labels, 20,000 bottles and five cellars. Glory to the god of wine indeed. And few things complement wine better than red meat and cheese – the two other specialities here. The large premises are mostly taken up with the wine bar and deli, with an appealing selection of platters, cheeseboards and tapas. For a more intimate experience head to the basement for a menu of two halves: one modern European, the other specialising in meats. Côte de boeuf is for two brave people with similar appetites while the presence of Springbok, and the huge number of South African wines, reveals the nationality of the owner. Customers are welcome to tour the cellars and the impressive cheese room.

Vivat Bacchus London Bridge

M4 **Traditional** XX

(basement) 4 Hays Lane ✉ SE1 2HB ⊖ London Bridge
✆ (0207) 234 0891 **Plan X**
Fax (0207) 357 7021
e-mail londonbridge@vivatbacchus.co.uk
www.vivatbacchus.co.uk

Closed Christmas-New Year, Sunday and Bank Holidays

Menu £12 (lunch) – Carte £21/34

VISA MC AE

The owners have sensibly avoided the temptation to tamper with a winning formula and so their second branch closely follows the style of the original in The City. That means a packed wine bar on the ground floor where city types quaff wines with relish and feast on 'world platters' from assorted countries. This then leads down to a slightly industrial looking basement restaurant, with a fantastic cellar and cheese room. Buying 'en primeur', they have created an impressive list with a large South African section and such is their enthusiasm that staff almost drool over oenophiles. The food is appropriately robust and also contains South African specialities, including the excellent roast springbok. Be sure to sample the cheese.

The Well

L1

Gastropub

180 St John St ✉ EC1V 4JY
✆ (020) 7251 9363
Fax (020) 7253 9683
e-mail drink@downthewell.co.uk
www.downthewell.com

⊖ Farringdon.
Plan IX
Closed 25 December

Carte £20/40

VISA, MC, AE

The Well is perhaps more of a locals' pub than many others found around these parts. It's all quite small inside but, thanks to some huge sliding glass windows, has a surprisingly light and airy feel, and the wooden floorboards and exposed brick walls add to the atmosphere of a committed metropolitan pub. Monthly changing menus offer modern dishes ranging from potted shrimps, to foie gras and chicken liver parfait, or sea trout and samphire, as well as classic English puddings like Eton Mess and some particularly good cheeses. The downstairs bar with its seductive lighting and fish tank is only available for private hire; check out the picture of a parched desert and a well which follows the curve of the wall on your way down.

The White Swan

K2

Modern European XX

108 Fetter Lane ✉ EC4A 1ES
✆ (020) 7242 9696
Fax (020) 7404 2250
e-mail info@thewhiteswanlondon.com
www.thewhiteswanlondon.com

⊖ Temple
Plan VIII
Closed 25-26 December, Saturday and Sunday

Menu £29 (lunch) – Carte £30/36

A/C, VISA, MC, AE

You'll find something akin to an assault course at the White Swan because to get to the first floor restaurant you have to fight your way through the drinkers in the ground floor bar and, at lunch time, this is more challenging than you think. Once upstairs, you'll find a small but neat room and service that is polite and friendly but also well paced and professional. The mirrored ceiling and large windows add plenty of light, although the closeness of the tables can make private conversation tricky. However, the cooking is good enough to induce the odd contented silence. It is classical in its base but with the occasional contemporary tweak and dishes display a certain refinement. Pricing is also fair when one considers the location.

Wright Brothers

M4

Seafood

11 Stoney St, Borough Market ✉ SE1 9AD ⊖ London Bridge
✆ (020) 7403 9554
Fax (020) 7403 9558
e-mail reservations@wrightbros.eu.com
www.wrightbros.eu.com

Plan X
Closed Christmas - New Year, Sunday and Bank Holidays

Carte £20/33

VISA MC AE

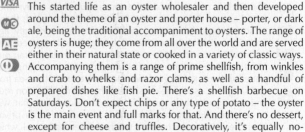

This started life as an oyster wholesaler and then developed around the theme of an oyster and porter house – porter, or dark ale, being the traditional accompaniment to oysters. The range of oysters is huge; they come from all over the world and are served either in their natural state or cooked in a variety of classic ways. Accompanying them is a range of prime shellfish, from winkles and crab to whelks and razor clams, as well as a handful of prepared dishes like fish pie. There's a shellfish barbecue on Saturdays. Don't expect chips or any type of potato – the oyster is the main event and full marks for that. And there's no dessert, except for cheese and truffles. Decoratively, it's equally no-nonsense and the atmosphere is all the better for it.

THE ARTISTRY OF CHAMPAGNE
MAISON FONDÉE EN 1776
BRUT PREMIER
LOUIS ROEDERER
CHAMPAGNE
BRUT
REIMS
12% vol.
750 ml
www.louis-roederer.co

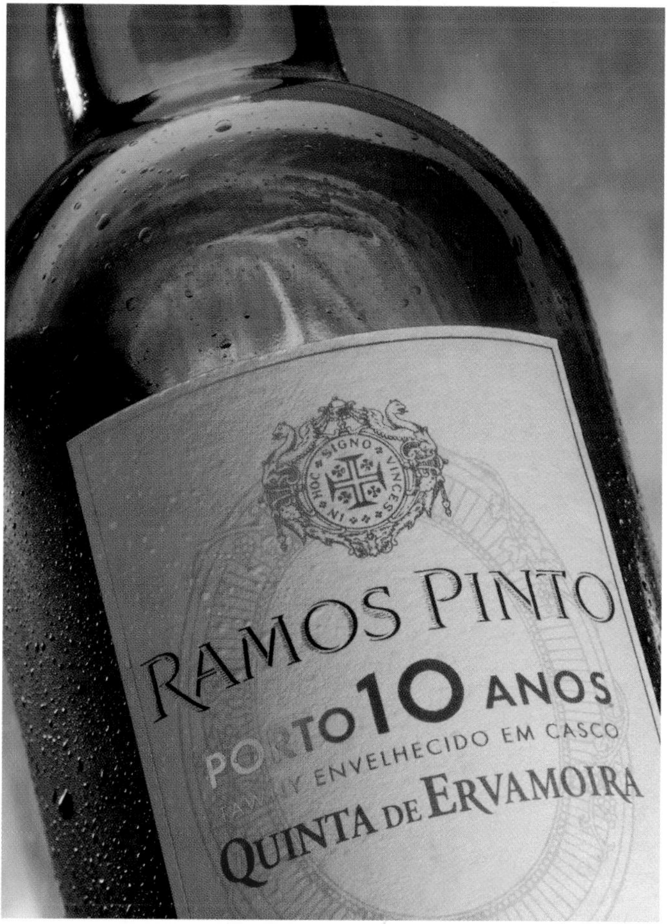

IN HOC SIGNO VINCES

RAMOS PINTO
Est. 1880

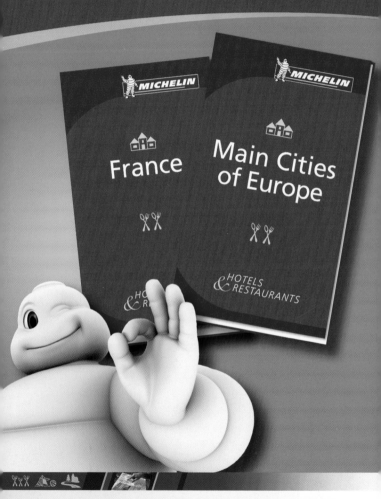

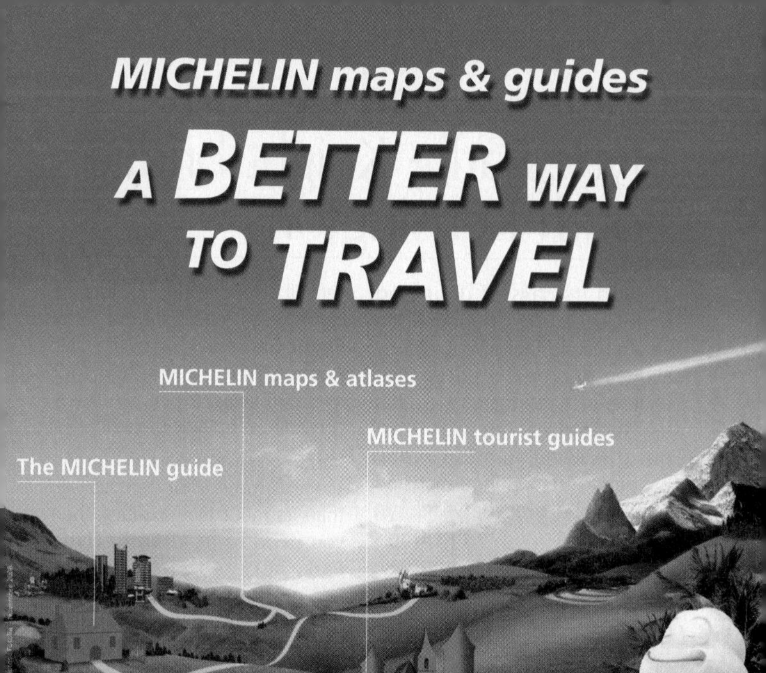
MICHELIN maps & guides
A BETTER WAY TO TRAVEL
MICHELIN maps & atlases
MICHELIN tourist guides
The MICHELIN guide

MICHELIN
Great Britain & Ireland 2010
MICHELIN
GREAT BRITAIN & IRELAND 2010
MICHELIN
Great Britain
MICHELIN
eating out in pubs
2010
MICHELIN
Great Britain & Ireland

Chelsea · Earl's Court · Hyde Park · Knightsbridge · South Kensington

Though its days of unbridled hedonism are long gone - and its 'alternative' tag is more closely aligned to property prices than counter-culture - there's still a hip feel to **Chelsea.** The place that put the Swinging into London has grown grey, distinguished and rather placid over the years, but tourists still throng to the **King's Road,** albeit to shop at the chain stores which have steadily muscled out SW3's chi-chi boutiques. It's not so easy now to imagine the heady mix of clans that used to sashay along here, from Sixties mods and models to Seventies punks, but for practically a quarter of a century, from the moment in 1955 when Mary Quant opened her trend-setting Bazaar, this was the pavement to parade down.

Chelsea's most cutting-edge destination these days is probably the gallery of modern art that bears the name of Margaret Thatcher's former favourite, Charles Saatchi. Which isn't the only irony, as Saatchi's outlandishly modish exhibits are housed in a one-time military barracks, the Duke of York's headquarters. Nearby, the traffic careers round **Sloane Square,** but it's almost possible to distance yourself from the fumes by sitting amongst the shady bowers in the centre of the square, or watching the world go by from a prime position in one of many cafés. Having said that, *the* place to get away from it all, and yet still be within striking distance of the King's Road, is the delightful **Physic Garden,** down by the river. Famous for its healing herbs for over 300 years, it's England's second oldest botanic garden.

Mind you, if the size of a green space is more important to you than its medicinal qualities, then you need to head up to **Hyde Park,** the city's biggest. Expansive enough to accommodate trotting horses on Rotten Row, swimmers and rowers in the Serpentine, up-to-the-minute art exhibitions at the Serpentine Gallery, and ranting individualists at Speakers' Corner, the park has also held within its borders thousands of rock fans for concerts by the likes of the Rolling Stones, Simon and Garfunkel and Pink Floyd.

Just across from its southern border stands one of London's most imperious sights, The **Royal Albert Hall,** gateway to the cultural hotspot that is South Kensington. Given its wings after the 1851 Great Exhibition, the area round **Cromwell Road** invested heavily in culture and learning, in the shape of three world famous museums and three heavyweight colleges. But one of its most intriguing museums is little known to visitors, even though it's only a few metres east of the Albert Hall: the Sikorski is, by turns, a moving and spectacular showpiece for all things Polish.

No one would claim to be moved by the exhibits on show in nearby **Knightsbridge,** but there are certainly spectacular credit card transactions made here. The twin retail shrines of Harvey Nichols and Harrods are the proverbial honey-pots to the tourist bee, where a 'credit crunch' means you've accidentally trodden on your visa. Between them, in **Sloane Street,** the world's most famous retail names line up like an A-lister's who's who. At the western end of Knightsbridge is the rich person's Catholic church of choice, the Brompton Oratory, an unerringly lavish concoction in a baroque Italianate style. Behind it is the enchanting Ennismore Gardens Mews, a lovely thoroughfare that dovetails rather well with the Oratory.

Further west along Old Brompton Road is **Earl's Court,** an area of grand old houses turned into bedsits and spartan hotels. An oddly bewitching contrast sits side by side here, the old resting alongside the new. The old in this case is Brompton Cemetery, an enchanting wilderness of monuments wherein lie the likes of Samuel Cunard and Emmeline Pankhurst. At its southwest corner, incongruously, sits the new, insomuch as it's the home of a regular influx of newcomers from abroad, who are young, gifted and possessed of vast incomes: the players of Chelsea FC.

C. Eymenier/MICHELIN

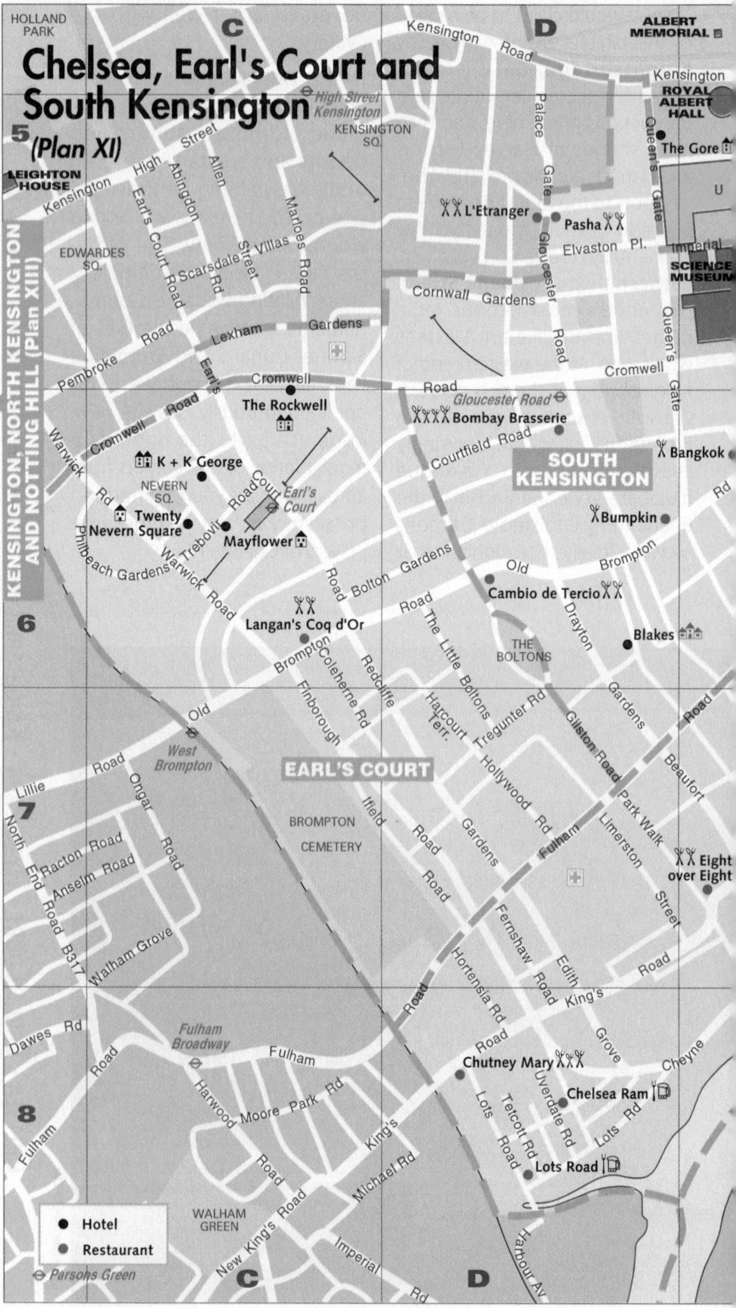
Chelsea, Earl's Court and South Kensington
(Plan XI)
HOLLAND PARK
LEIGHTON HOUSE
EDWARDES SQ.
KENSINGTON SQ.
High Street Kensington
ALBERT MEMORIAL
ROYAL ALBERT HALL
The Gore
L'Etranger
Pasha
SCIENCE MUSEUM
Imperial
KENSINGTON, NORTH KENSINGTON AND NOTTING HILL (Plan XIII)
The Rockwell
K + K George
NEVERN SQ.
Twenty Nevern Square
Earl's Court
Mayflower
Gloucester Road
Bombay Brasserie
Bangkok
SOUTH KENSINGTON
Bumpkin
Cambio de Tercio
Blakes
THE BOLTONS
Langan's Coq d'Or
West Brompton
EARL'S COURT
BROMPTON CEMETERY
Eight over Eight
Fulham Broadway
Chutney Mary
Chelsea Ram
Lots Road
WALHAM GREEN
Parsons Green
Hotel
Restaurant
Kensington Road
Kensington High Street
Abingdon
Allen
Earl's Court Road
Scarsdale Villas
Marloes Road
Palace Gate
Queen's Gate
Elvaston Pl.
Gloucester Road
Cornwall Gardens
Lexham Gardens
Pembroke Road
Cromwell Road
Warwick Rd
Courtfield Road
Philbeach Gardens
Trebovir Rd
Warwick Road
Bolton Gardens
Old Brompton Road
Drayton Gardens
The Little Boltons
Coleherne Rd
Redcliffe Road
Finborough Road
Harcourt Terr.
Tregunter Rd
Gilston Road
Hollywood Rd
Park Walk
Beaufort
Lillie Road
Ongar Road
North End Road B317
Racton Road
Anselm Road
Walham Grove
Ifield Road
Redcliffe Gardens
Fulham Road
Limerston Street
Fernshaw Road
Hortensia Rd
Edith Grove
King's Road
Dawes Rd
Fulham Road
Harwood Road
Moore Park Rd
Michael Rd
New King's Road
Imperial Rd
Lots Road
Tetcott Rd
Uverdale Rd
Cheyne
Harbour Av
C
D
5
6
7
8

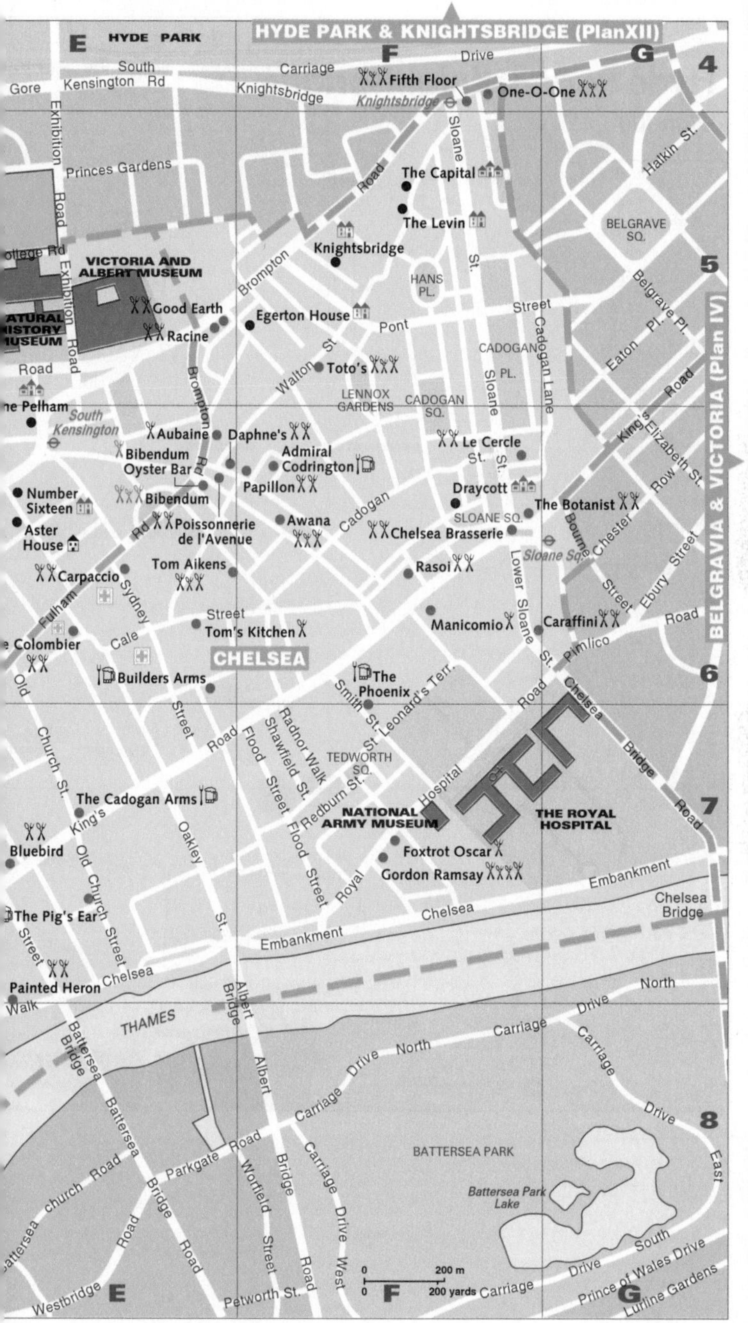
HYDE PARK & KNIGHTSBRIDGE (PlanXII)
E
F
G
4
5
6
7
8
HYDE PARK
South Carriage Drive
Kensington Rd
Gore
Knightsbridge
Knightsbridge
Fifth Floor
One-O-One
Exhibition Road
Princes Gardens
Sloane St.
The Capital
The Levin
Knightsbridge
Brompton Road
Halkin St.
BELGRAVE SQ.
College Rd
VICTORIA AND ALBERT MUSEUM
NATURAL HISTORY MUSEUM
Good Earth
Racine
Egerton House
HANS PL.
Pont Street
Cadogan Lane
Belgrave Pl.
Eaton Pl.
CADOGAN PL.
Walton St.
Toto's
LENNOX GARDENS
CADOGAN SQ.
Sloane St.
Road
BELGRAVIA & VICTORIA (Plan IV)
The Pelham
South Kensington
Aubaine
Daphne's
Le Cercle
King's Road
Elizabeth St.
Bibendum Oyster Bar
Admiral Codrington
Number Sixteen
Bibendum
Papillon
Draycott
Row
Aster House
Poissonnerie de l'Avenue
Awana
Cadogan St.
Chelsea Brasserie
The Botanist
SLOANE SQ.
Sloane Sq.
Bourne Street
Chester
Ebury Street
Tom Aikens
Carpaccio
Rasoi
Lower Sloane St.
Fulham Rd
Sydney Street
Tom's Kitchen
Manicomio
Caraffini
Pimlico Road
Le Colombier
Cale
CHELSEA
Builders Arms
The Phoenix
Old Church St.
Smith St.
St Leonard's Terr.
Chelsea Bridge Road
Radnor Walk
Shawfield St.
Flood Street
TEDWORTH SQ.
Hospital Road
The Cadogan Arms
King's Road
Redburn St.
NATIONAL ARMY MUSEUM
THE ROYAL HOSPITAL
Bluebird
Oakley St.
Foxtrot Oscar
Gordon Ramsay
Royal
Embankment
Chelsea Bridge
The Pig's Ear
Old Church Street
Chelsea Embankment
Painted Heron
Chelsea Walk
North
Albert Bridge
THAMES
Carriage Drive
Battersea Bridge
North Carriage Drive
Carriage Drive
Albert Bridge Road
Battersea Bridge Road
Parkgate Road
Worfield Street
Carriage Drive West
BATTERSEA PARK
East
Battersea Park Lake
Battersea church Road
South
Westbridge Road
Petworth St.
0 200 m
0 200 yards
Carriage Drive
Prince of Wales Drive
Lurline Gardens

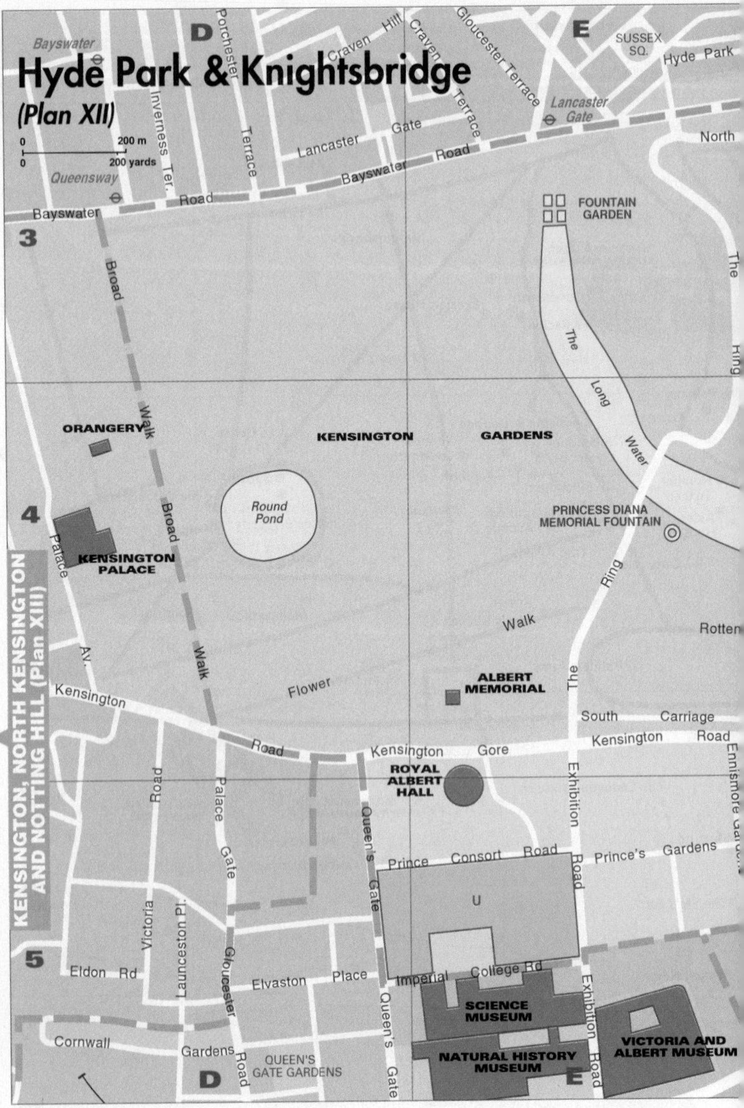

Hyde Park & Knightsbridge
(Plan XII)
0 200 m
0 200 yards
D
E
3
4
5
Bayswater
Queensway
Lancaster Gate
Porchester Terrace
Inverness Ter.
Craven Hill
Craven Terrace
Gloucester Terrace
SUSSEX SQ.
Hyde Park
Lancaster Gate
Bayswater Road
North
FOUNTAIN GARDEN
The Ring
Broad Walk
ORANGERY
KENSINGTON GARDENS
The Long Water
Round Pond
PRINCESS DIANA MEMORIAL FOUNTAIN
KENSINGTON PALACE
Palace Av.
Flower Walk
Rotten
ALBERT MEMORIAL
South Carriage
Kensington Road
Kensington Gore
ROYAL ALBERT HALL
Exhibition Road
Ennismore Gardens
Prince Consort Road
Prince's Gardens
Palace Gate
Queen's Gate
U
Victoria Road
Launceston Pl.
Gloucester Road
Eldon Rd
Elvaston Place
Imperial College Rd
SCIENCE MUSEUM
NATURAL HISTORY MUSEUM
VICTORIA AND ALBERT MUSEUM
Cornwall Gardens
QUEEN'S GATE GARDENS
KENSINGTON, NORTH KENSINGTON AND NOTTING HILL (Plan XIII)

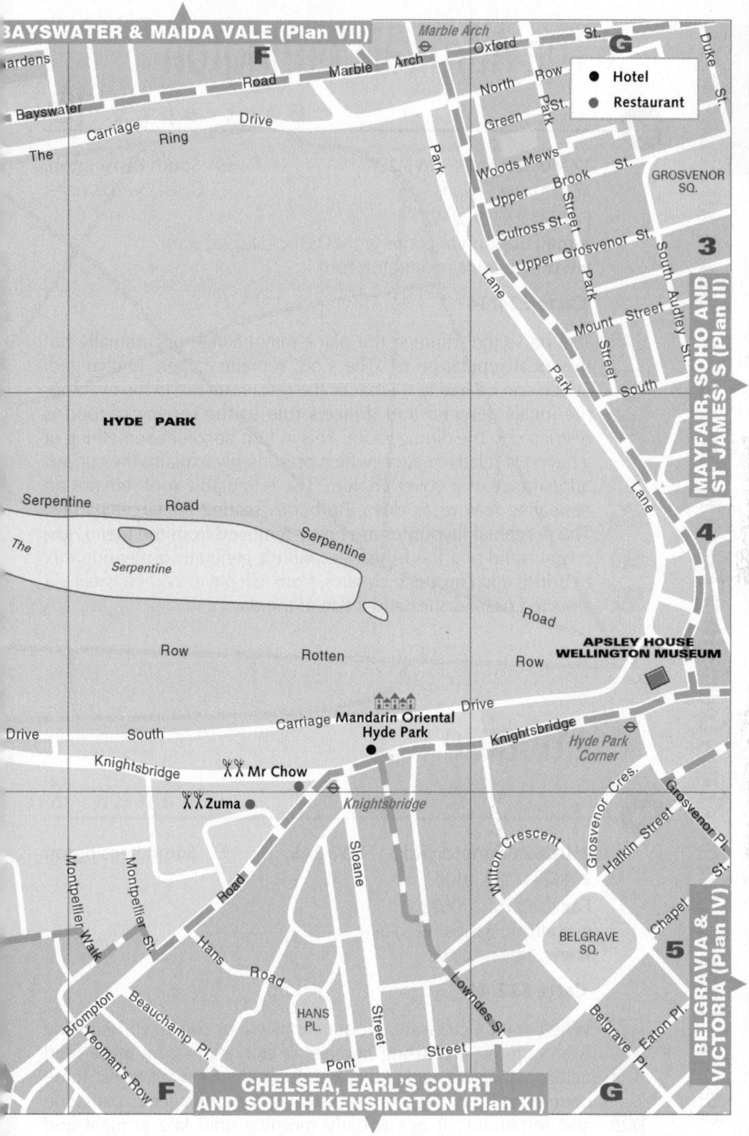
BAYSWATER & MAIDA VALE (Plan VII)
MAYFAIR, SOHO AND ST JAMES'S (Plan II)
BELGRAVIA & VICTORIA (Plan IV)
CHELSEA, EARL'S COURT AND SOUTH KENSINGTON (Plan XI)
F
G
3
4
5
Hotel
Restaurant
Marble Arch
Oxford St.
Marble Arch
Bayswater Road
Duke St.
North Row
Park St.
Green St.
Park Lane
Woods Mews
Upper Brook St.
GROSVENOR SQ.
Culross St.
Upper Grosvenor St.
South Audley St.
Park Street
Mount Street
South
The Ring
Carriage Drive
HYDE PARK
Serpentine Road
The Serpentine
Serpentine Road
Rotten Row
APSLEY HOUSE WELLINGTON MUSEUM
South Carriage Drive
Mandarin Oriental Hyde Park
Knightsbridge
Hyde Park Corner
Mr Chow
Zuma
Knightsbridge
Grosvenor Cres.
Wilton Crescent
Halkin Street
Grosvenor Pl.
Chapel St.
BELGRAVE SQ.
Sloane Street
Montpellier Walk
Montpellier St.
Brompton Road
Hans Road
HANS PL.
Lowndes St.
Belgrave Pl.
Eaton Pl.
Beauchamp Pl.
Yeoman's Row
Pont Street

The Admiral Codrington

F6 **Gastropub**

17 Mossop St ✉ SW3 2LY ⊖ South Kensington.
✆ (020) 7581 0005 Closed 25-26 December
Fax (020) 7589 2452
e-mail theadmiral-codrington@333holdingsltd.com
www.theadmiralcodrington.com

Carte £24/34

A/C VISA MC AE

The personnel running the place may change occasionally but the local reputation of 'The Cod' remains largely unchanged. Lunch can be had in the bar or the restaurant but in the evenings the locals descend and drinkers rule so the serving of food is restricted to the dining room. This in turn becomes something of a haven of relative peace (which presumably explains the curious appearance of a cover charge). The retractable roof remains an appealing feature as does the booth seating for larger parties. The perennial favourites are never removed from the menu, like crispy squid and the fishcakes, and it's generally a pleasing mix of British and European classics, from fish pie to veal Holstein via assorted pasta dishes and a fish of the day.

Aubaine

E6 **French**

260-262 Brompton Rd ✉ SW3 2AS ⊖ South Kensington
✆ (020) 7052 0100
Fax (020) 7052 0622
e-mail info@aubaine.co.uk
www.aubaine.co.uk

Carte £22/44

A/C VISA MC AE

Whether it's a croissant, croque monsieur or coq au vin, Aubaine is among the increasing number of operations of a more fluid nature which recognise that we don't always want to eat three courses at 1pm. Describing itself as a 'boulangerie, patisserie and restaurant', it opens early morning until late at night and offers a comprehensive choice of French specialities to satisfy all appetites at all times with the location making it especially busy during shopping hours. The breads are baked here and the 'shop' section does a roaring trade. The dining area fuses country and city; dressers, flowers and distressed wooden tables are juxtaposed with the modernity of exposed air-con vents and it all opens out onto the pavement in summer.

Awana

F6 **Malaysian** XXX

85 Sloane Ave ✉ SW3 3DX
✆ (020) 7584 8880
Fax (020) 7584 6188
e-mail info@awana.co.uk
www.awana.co.uk

⊖ South Kensington
Closed 25-26 December and 1 January – booking essential

Menu £15 (lunch) – Carte £21/44

A/C VISA MC AE

Eddie Lim, the owner, has over 70 restaurants around the world so clearly knows what he's doing. Awana is no exception; a charming welcome and endearing service are the norm, the food is fresh and invigorating and the room comfortable, particularly the stylish bar. If you sit at the satay bar for the house speciality then ensure you chat to the chef who's a font of information about Malaysian cuisine. Curries, grills and stir-fries are the mainstays of the main menu; the curries are almost soup-like with their sauces so make sure you order plenty of roti canai, the wonderful bread; the grills include whole sea bass or rack of lamb, while the stir-fries will make us realise the inadequacies of what we all knock up these days at home.

Bangkok

E6 **Thai** X

9 Bute St ✉ SW7 3EY
✆ (020) 7584 8529
www.bankokrestaurant.co.uk

⊖ South Kensington
Closed Christmas-New Year, Sunday and Bank Holidays

Carte £20/32

A/C VISA MC

Bangkok has been going strong for years and, for that, we should all be grateful. It is an honest, unpretentious neighbourhood restaurant and one of the first in the capital to offer Londoners a taste of Thailand in the days before gap years, package holidays and our discovery of woks. The menu's not overlong; starters include quite a few soups but the beef and chicken satay are particularly good. Main courses are helpfully divided into beef, pork and chicken; highlights include the beef with crispy Thai basil, while the noodles are very light and moreish. The prices are decidedly unKensington-like and the ladies go about their service with organised efficiency. The multitudinous following ensures there's always a bubbly atmosphere.

Bibendum

E6 French XXX

Michelin House,
81 Fulham Rd ✉ SW3 6RD
✆ (020) 7581 5817
Fax (020) 7823 7925
e-mail reservations@bibendum.co.uk
www.bibendum.co.uk

⊖ South Kensington
Closed 24-26 December and 1 January

Menu £30 (lunch and Sunday dinner) – Carte £40/60

Bibendum is now well into its twenties but very little has changed over those years, which is why it remains a favourite restaurant for so many. Matthew Harris' cooking continues to produce the sort of food that Elizabeth David would adore – it's mostly French but with a subtle British point of view. The set lunch menu has now been joined by a small à la carte selection; evening menus are handwritten and the roast chicken with tarragon for two remains a perennial presence. Side dishes can bump the final bill up further than expected but the food is easy to eat and satisfying. The striking character of Michelin's former HQ, dating from 1911, is perhaps best appreciated at lunch when the sun lights up the glass Bibendum - the Michelin Man.

Bibendum Oyster Bar

E6 Seafood X

Michelin House,
81 Fulham Rd ✉ SW3 6RD
✆ (020) 7589 1480
Fax (020) 7823 7925
e-mail reservations@bibendum.co.uk
www.bibendum.co.uk

⊖ South Kensington
Closed 24-26 December and 1 January – bookings not accepted

Carte £20/33

The plateau de fruits de mer, for two, is the house speciality here. It includes crab, langoustines, prawns, oysters, winkles and whelks and will leave anyone being satisfied and, when the sun is shining, pleased with the world in general. You'll find other satisfying classics, from potted shrimps to egg mayonnaise, assorted salads and, predictably enough, a selection of oysters. The accessible wine list includes 460ml pots. It is all served in a relaxed continental-style café, with a mosaic floor and colourful ceramic tiles depicting the early days of French motoring – as befits any establishment located in the former foyer of Michelin House. The crustacea stall and florist at the front of the building attract plenty of passers-by.

Bluebird

British XX

E7

350 King's Rd ✉ SW3 5UU ⊖ Sloane Square
✆ (020) 7559 1000
Fax (020) 7559 1115
e-mail enquiries@bluebird-restaurant.co.uk
www.bluebird-restaurant.com

Menu £21 – Carte £32/52

The last refurbishment may have softened the huge space a little but Bluebird still delivers the atmosphere and excitement one expects from such a large industrial space. A former garage built in 1923; it houses everything from a wine store and café to a food shop and private members club, with the restaurant as the centrepiece. The kitchen champions British produce and highlights their provenance, be it Herdwick mutton, Cumbrian beef or Goosnargh chicken. It also features British cheeses along with seasonal fruit and veg. That being said, not all the dishes are so Anglo-centric: there are assorted pasta choices and the occasional French classic. Sunday roasts and a children's menu ensure that all bases are covered.

Bombay Brasserie

Indian XXXX

D6

Courtfield Rd ✉ SW7 4QH ⊖ Gloucester Road
✆ (020) 7370 4040
Fax (020) 7835 1669
e-mail bombay1brasserie@aol.com
www.bombaybrasserielondon.com

Closed 25-26 December – booking advisable at dinner

Menu £22 (weekday lunch buffet) – Carte £34/47

Going strong since 1982, The Bombay Brasserie has always been one of the smartest Indian restaurants around but it began 2009 with a brand new look which revitalised the whole place. Plushness abounds, from the deep carpet and huge chandeliers of the large main room to the show kitchen of the conservatory and the very smart bar. The staff also got a new look with their burgundy waistcoats, but they continue to offer very charming and professional service. The menu hasn't been forgotten either and was overhauled by Hemant Oberoi. They replaced the predictable with the more creative, while at the same time respecting traditional philosophies; influences are a combination of Bori, Parsi, Maharashtrian and Goan cuisine.

The Botanist

F6 **Modern European** XX

7 Sloane Square ✉ SW1W 8EE ⊖ Sloane Square
✆ (020) 7730 0077 Closed 25 December
Fax (020) 7730 7177
e-mail info@thebotanistonsloanesquare.com
www.thebotanistonsloanesquare.com

Carte £28/41

A/C VISA MC AE

Tom and Ed Martin have found themselves another great spot to woo both the drink-after-work crowd and the local dining market. Getting through those drinkers can be a bit of bunfight but you'll be rewarded by a sleek and swish restaurant that occupies the other half of this corner establishment; try to sit near the back, next to the botanical backdrop. It's open from early breakfast until late dinner and the menus are modern European in their influence and tone; the kitchen has the confidence to eschew over-embellishment and flavours are true and distinctive. On a summer's night the windows open up all around, creating a very pleasant atmosphere. Service captures the mood but not at the expense of attentiveness.

Builders Arms

E6 **Gastropub**

13 Britten St ✉ SW3 3TY ⊖ South Kensington
✆ (020) 7349 9040
e-mail buildersarms@geronimo-inns.co.uk
www.geronimo-inns.co.uk

Carte £25/30

A/C VISA MC AE

The Builders Arms is very much like a packed village local - the only difference being that, in this instance, the village is Chelsea. They adopt a simple but effective approach to cooking – there's an easy to read menu, supplemented by a daily specials blackboard, which always includes a soup and fresh fish. Dishes range from devilled kidney on toast to herb-crusted lamb; others, such as the corn-fed peri-peri chicken are designed for sharing. Presentation has an appealingly rustic edge; portions are appropriately pub-size and prices are kept realistic. There's a weekly Bordeaux selection as well as regular wine promotions. Bookings are only taken for larger parties but just tell the staff that you're here to eat and they'll sort you out.

Bumpkin

British

D6

102 Old Brompton Road ✉ SW7 3RD ⊖ Gloucester Road
✆ (020) 7341 0802
Fax (020) 7835 0714
e-mail mike@bumpkinuk.com
www.bumpkinuk.com

Carte £26/38

A/C · VISA · MC · AE

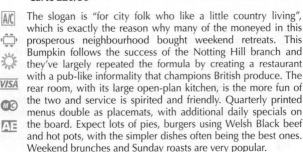

The slogan is "for city folk who like a little country living", which is exactly the reason why many of the moneyed in this prosperous neighbourhood bought weekend retreats. This Bumpkin follows the success of the Notting Hill branch and they've largely repeated the formula by creating a restaurant with a pub-like informality that champions British produce. The rear room, with its large open-plan kitchen, is the more fun of the two and service is spirited and friendly. Quarterly printed menus double as placemats, with additional daily specials on the board. Expect lots of pies, burgers using Welsh Black beef and hot pots, with the simpler dishes often being the best ones. Weekend brunches and Sunday roasts are very popular.

The Cadogan Arms

Gastropub

E7

298 King's Rd ✉ SW3 5UG ⊖ South Kensington
✆ (020) 7352 6500 booking advisable at dinner
e-mail nadia@etmgroup.co.uk
www.thecadoganarmschelsea.com

Carte £24/37

A/C · VISA · MC · AE

The Martin Brothers seem to have the King's Road covered, with The Botanist at the Sloane Square end and now The Cadogan Arms at the other. The tiled entrance step reads 'Luncheon, bar and billiards' which sounds appealingly like a lost afternoon and it is clear that this pub is 'pubbier' and more blokey than their others. The upstairs billiard tables are available by the hour and, while you eat, you'll feel the beady eyes of the various stuffed and mounted animals on the walls. The cooking is appropriately gutsy and full-on. Juicy Aberdeen Angus rib-eye, golden-fried haddock, Dexter Beef and Welsh lamb are all staples of the menu. Starters and desserts are a little showier – perhaps something for the ladies? Service is charming.

Cambio de Tercio

D6 **Spanish** XX

163 Old Brompton Rd ✉ SW5 0LJ
(020) 7244 8970
Fax (020) 7373 2359
e-mail alusa@btconnect.com
www.cambiodetercio.co.uk

⊖ Gloucester Road
closed 2 weeks Christmas

Carte £27/39

The concept works well: choose 3 or 4 tapas each from the left side of the menu and they'll arrive in an orderly fashion so that sharing can be done at a leisurely pace. But if you feel that the tapas size just doesn't hit the spot or you haven't liked sharing since childhood then the dishes on the right hand side are pretty much the same except they come in regular main course size. Definitely start with Iberica ham and include the spicy patatas bravas and the sticky and rich oxtail in red wine. The chef uses his toys to good effect with the more contemporary desserts. Lots of vintages from Vega Sicilia and Pingus wines feature, along with Alion and Roda. Service gets better the more you visit. They also own the tapas bar across the road.

Caraffini

F6 **Italian** XX

61-63 Lower Sloane St ✉ SW1W 8DH
(020) 7259 0235
Fax (020) 7259 0236
e-mail info@caraffini.co.uk
www.caraffini.co.uk

⊖ Sloane Square
Closed 25 December, Easter, Sunday and Bank Holidays – booking essential

Carte £23/39

One doesn't have to look far to see why Paolo Caraffini's restaurant is always so busy: it has a wonderfully genial host, smooth service, reliably good Italian food and a highly hospitable atmosphere. Just watching the number of regulars Paolo greets as friends, from Chelsea art dealers to King's Road shoppers, will make you want to become a part of the club. Warm and cosy in winter, bright and sunny in summer with pavement tables for alfresco dining, this really is a place for all seasons. Daily specials supplement the already balanced menu that covers many regions of Italy and any requests to veer off-menu are satisfied without fuss or fanfare. Caraffini is proof that good hospitality is very much alive and kicking.

Carpaccio

E6 **Italian** XX

4 Sydney St ✉ SW3 6PP — ⊖ South Kensington
✆ (020) 7352 3435 — Closed Bank Holidays
Fax (020) 7622 8304
e-mail carpacciorest@aol.com
www.carpacciorestaurant.co.uk

Carte £24/35

A/C VISA MC AE

Ladies-who-lunch may have colonised much of Chelsea but, here at Carpaccio, the decoration is far more blokey: there are stills from assorted James Bond films and, reflecting the owner's passion for all things related to Formula 1, the cockpit of an Ayrton Senna racing car. It's a lively place with animated service from an all-Italian crew and it attracts a wide range of customer; the best seats are at the back under a large skylight. Pizzas have been added to the menu, and they are done well and the daily specials are always worth considering – as are the varied veal dishes. Aptly enough, carpaccio of meat and fish is a speciality and Sunday lunches are real family affairs. The wine list is exclusively Italian, with a fair choice by the glass.

Le Cercle

F6 **French** XX

1 Wilbraham Pl ✉ SW1X 9AE — ⊖ Sloane Square
✆ (020) 7901 9999 — Closed Christmas - New Year, Sunday and Monday
Fax (020) 7901 9111
e-mail info@lecercle.co.uk
www.lecercle.co.uk

Menu £15/18 – Carte £20/35

A/C VISA MC AE

It was originally going to be a swimming pool hence the unusual basement layout; the somewhat repetitive procedures on arrival highlight some of the logistical problems. But don't miss the seductive little bar halfway down the stairs, from where you can survey the scene; there's another, louder one around a fireplace. As this is an offshoot of Club Gascon, expect appealing tasting plates that are still bigger than your average tapas. The 'terroir' French cooking means flavours are distinctive and dishes satisfyingly rich. The wine list focuses on Bordeaux and Alsace and wines are paired with the dishes. Staff are a patient and clued-up lot. As many regard this as more of a winter destination, look out for tempting summer promotions.

Chelsea Brasserie

F6 **French** XX

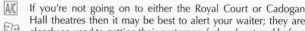

7-12 Sloane Sq. ✉ SW1W 8EG ⊖ Sloane Square
✆ (020) 7896 9988
Fax (020) 7751 4211
e-mail rob@chelsea-brasserie.co.uk
www.sloanesquarehotel.co.uk

Menu £25 – Carte £32/40

A/C, VISA, MC, AE, D

If you're not going on to either the Royal Court or Cadogan Hall theatres then it may be best to alert your waiter; they are clearly so used to getting their customers fed and watered before curtain up that they sometimes find it hard to shift down a gear later on. It's no surprise that it is so busy early evening because their theatre menus represent excellent value. The menus, like the waiters, are mostly French born with some intercontinental experience. Vegetarians get plenty of choice and carnivores should be satisfied with the selection from the grill. The cooking has a breezy confidence and hits the spot. The front section of the restaurant attached to the bar is more fun, while tables are the back are quieter.

Chelsea Ram

D8 **Gastropub**

32 Burnaby St ✉ SW10 0PL ⊖ Fulham Broadway.
✆ (020) 7351 4008
e-mail bookings@chelsearam.co.uk

Menu £18 (dinner) – Carte £19/24

A/C, VISA, MC

This stalwart of the London dining scene remains as popular as ever; book or arrive early for lunch as they only have 17 tables and they get snapped up quickly, particularly the two by the fire. There's full table service and whilst it all chills out a little at dinner, timings from the kitchen are generally spot-on. Comforting classics and honest home-cooking is how the chef describes his food: homemade soup comes with crusty bread, lamb chops with bubble and squeak, sausages with mash and rib-eye with dauphinoise potatoes; there are pies and casseroles and even some mean snacks to accompany a pint. You can also get a proper pudding, not a dessert, and these could include sticky banana or a crumble.

Chutney Mary

D8 **Indian** XXX

535 King's Rd ✉ SW10 0SZ — ⊖ Fulham Broadway
✆ (020) 7351 3113
Fax (020) 7351 7694
e-mail chutneymary@realindianfood.com
www.realindianfood.com

Closed dinner 25 December – dinner only and lunch Saturday – Sunday

Menu £22 (lunch) – Carte £29/39

If you can't find it, ask a cabbie, as the precise location of Chutney Mary is reputed to form part of 'The Knowledge'. This long-standing Indian restaurant has always been more West End sophisticate than local eatery and was at the vanguard when Indian restaurants came of age in London. Silk wall hangings from Jaipur are the latest addition to the decoration which gets regularly refreshed, while the conservatory remains a favoured spot. The cooking has become slightly lighter recently and the flavours more subtle. Newer dishes include dabba gosht made with lamb, halibut in a mustard sauce and steamed bream in a banana leaf, but kebabs and tandoor and grilled dishes remain popular. Wine from the glass-fronted cave plays a large part.

Le Colombier

E6 **French** XX

145 Dovehouse St ✉ SW3 6LB — ⊖ South Kensington
✆ (020) 7351 1155
Fax (020) 7351 5124
e-mail lecolombier1998@aol.com
www.le-colombier-restaurant.co.uk

Menu £25 (lunch) – Carte £29/43

Le Colombier is as warm and welcoming as it is honest and reliable and thereby offers proof that being a good neighbourhood restaurant takes more than just being in a good neighbourhood. French influences abound, from the accents of the staff and the menu content to the inordinate amount of double cheek kissing that occurs – most of the customers appear to know one another or feel they should like to know one another. In summer, when the full-length windows fold back, the terrace is the place to sit although the under-floor heating ensures the place is equally welcoming in winter. Oysters, game in season, veal in various forms and regional cheeses are the highlights, as are the classic desserts from crêpe Suzette to crème brûlée.

Daphne's

E6 **Italian** XX

112 Draycott Ave ✉ SW3 3AE ⊖ South Kensington
✆ (020) 7589 4257
Fax (020) 7225 2766
e-mail reservations@daphnes-restaurant.co.uk
www.daphnes-restaurant.co.uk

Closed 25-26 December and 1 January – booking essential

Menu £19 (lunch) – Carte £31/50

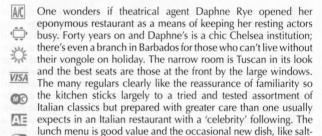

One wonders if theatrical agent Daphne Rye opened her eponymous restaurant as a means of keeping her resting actors busy. Forty years on and Daphne's is a chic Chelsea institution; there's even a branch in Barbados for those who can't live without their vongole on holiday. The narrow room is Tuscan in its look and the best seats are those at the front by the large windows. The many regulars clearly like the reassurance of familiarity so the kitchen sticks largely to a tried and tested assortment of Italian classics but prepared with greater care than one usually expects in an Italian restaurant with a 'celebrity' following. The lunch menu is good value and the occasional new dish, like salt-baked sea bass, gets in under the radar.

Eight over Eight

E7 **Asian** XX

392 King's Rd ✉ SW3 5UZ ⊖ Gloucester Road
✆ (020) 7349 9934
Fax (020) 7351 5157
e-mail eightovereight@rickerrstaurants.com
www.rickerrestaurants.com

Closed 25-26 December, 1 January and Sunday lunch

Menu £15 (lunch) – Carte £27/39

What was once the Man in the Moon pub is now a fiercely fashionable pan-Asian restaurant, proving that the King's Road is not all high street chains and baby shops and can still cut it with the fashionistas. The menu has a fairly wide remit to cover much of South East Asia with Chinese, Japanese, Malaysian, Korean and Thai influences all featuring and most dishes designed for sharing. Don't hesitate to ask for help from the charming, and alarmingly attractive, staff. The room is all moody and cool, with a slick bar at the front and the restaurant at the back. Chocolate coloured leather seating and two shades of oak on the walls contrast with the delicate silk parasol styled lamps. (There was a major fire here as we went to print.)

L'Etranger

D5 **Innovative** XX

36 Gloucester Rd ✉ SW7 4QT — ⊖ Gloucester Road
✆ (020) 7584 1118 — Closed 25 December and Saturday lunch – booking essential
Fax (020) 7584 8886
e-mail etranger@etranger.co.uk
www.circagroupltd.co.uk

Menu £20 (lunch) – Carte £33/89

When free from the tyranny of traditional recipes, French émigrés are generally more open to the idea of culinary experimentation. Add to the mix the French colony of South Kensington and you end up with a restaurant like L'Etranger: a French restaurant which incorporates influences from Japanese cuisine. The fact that it works owes much to the respect the kitchen has for the ingredients, cooking techniques and flavours of both cultures. The various menus demand detailed examination and include a champagne and fish menu for those really indulging themselves. Finish off, but not literally, with their 'Death by Chocolate'. Silks and lilacs create a stylish, atmospheric space; ask for one of the corner tables. The wine and sake list is impressive.

Fifth Floor at Harvey Nichols

F4 **Modern European** XXX

109-125 Knightsbridge ✉ SW1X 7RJ — ⊖ Knightsbridge
✆ (020) 7235 5250 — Closed Christmas, Easter and Sunday dinner
Fax (020) 7823 2207
e-mail reception@harveynichols.com
www.harveynichols.com

Menu £20 (lunch) – Carte £29/58

Those weak-willed in the face of shopping opportunities can bypass the department store by taking the express lift to the Fifth Floor, but even there one might find it hard to avoid the epicurean treats of the food hall or the similarly arresting sirens in the bar. The restaurant was made-over in 2007 and its pod-like shape and coloured lighting give it a space-age chicness. Table size is generous but the room retains a sense of intimacy. The menu is modern European with the focus on France. The kitchen has a delicate touch and there are occasional flashes of originality. The Market Menu at lunch is good value and the wine list is an impressive work, with particular emphasis on French and dessert wines, as well as champagne.

Foxtrot Oscar

F7

Traditional

79 Royal Hospital Rd ✉ SW3 4HN
(020) 7352 4448
Fax (020) 7592 1603
e-mail foxtrotoscar@gordonramsay.com
www.gordonramsay.com

⊖ Sloane Square
Closed 10 days Christmas, Monday-Tuesday and lunch Wednesday-Thursday – booking essential

Carte £26/34

This Chelsea institution was created by Michael Proudlock nearly 30 years ago when he returned from New York with tales of burgers and eggs Benedict. Years later Gordon Ramsay and his chefs from up the road became regulars and so he jumped at the change of buying it. Fast forward to the present and even though it's part of the Ramsay empire, Michael is still there, greeting his regulars. It's taken a couple of goes but they're steadily getting the feel of the place and the style of service right. Meanwhile, the kitchen effortlessly captures the essence of comfort food for which the restaurant is known. Expect pies, cassoulet and coq au vin alongside fishcakes and potted duck. And they still do a pretty good burger and eggs Benedict.

Good Earth

E5

Chinese

233 Brompton Rd ✉ SW3 2EP
(020) 7584 3658
Fax (020) 7823 8769
e-mail goodearthgroup@aol.com
www.goodearthgroup.co.uk

⊖ Knightsbridge
Closed 23-31 December

Menu £12/36 – Carte £26/37

The Brompton Road branch of this small chain has been a reliable constant for many a year and is suitably authentic on all levels: the service is brisk, the menu lengthy, cooking is dependable and desserts are not worth bothering with. There is no particular bias, save for a few Sichuan dishes, but they do use plenty of higher-end ingredients like scallops and Dover sole. Included among the set menus is the Lobster Dinner, a reminder of the restaurant's location and target market. More unusual dishes are often introduced but it's the old favourites and classic combinations that sell. Unlike most restaurants spread over two floors, here the basement level is actually the busier and more popular choice than the ground floor.

Gordon Ramsay ✿✿✿

French XXXXX

F7

68-69 Royal Hospital Rd ✉ SW3 4HP
✆ (020) 7352 4441
Fax (020) 7352 3334
www.gordonramsay.com

Menu £45/90

⊖ Sloane Square
Closed 25-26 December, 1 January, Saturday and Sunday – booking essential

A/C · VISA · MC · AE

Gordon Ramsay Holdings

Those who come looking for a rant and a rave, an eff or a blind, will leave disappointed because Gordon Ramsay's flagship restaurant is the antithesis of his TV persona: here, all is calm, ordered and scrupulously courteous. That's not to say there isn't passion here because there clearly is – this is a kitchen on top of its game. Clare Smyth has settled comfortably into her role as head chef and, while there is clearly the Gordon Ramsay signature to certain dishes, such as the ravioli of lobster, langoustine and salmon or the Best End of Cornish lamb with a confit of shoulder, she has added a subtle sense of rural sincerity to what could be called urbane city food. The kitchen understands the true worth of each ingredient, finds their rightful partners and knows when to leave alone, such as with the roast duck breast with creamed cabbage and beetroot, or the scallops partnered with new season peas. The elegant simplicity of the room works very well and the serving team glide effortlessly around it, led by the modest Jean-Claude who is now the daddy of London maitre d's.

First Course

- Pressed foie gras with Madeira jelly, smoked duck, peach and almond crumble.
- Scallops with peas, bacon and baby gem lettuce.

Main Course

- Roasted fillet of turbot with langoustines, linguine and wild mushrooms.
- Barbary duck breast with cabbage, beetroot and caramelised shallots.

Dessert

- Cherry soufflé with chocolate sorbet and crystallised pistachios.
- Pineapple ravioli with mango and raspberries.

Langan's Coq d'Or

C6 **Traditional**

254-260 Old Brompton Rd ✉ SW5 9HR ⊖ Earl's Court
✆ (020) 7259 2599
Fax (020) 7370 7735
e-mail admin@langansrestaurant.co.uk
www.langansrestaurants.co.uk

Closed 25-26 December and 1 January

Menu £26 – Carte approx. £29

The celebrated restaurateur Peter Langan may no longer be with us, but Richard Shepherd created a restaurant of which his friend would no doubt have approved. He also named it in honour of the original moniker of Langan's in Stratton Street. It is almost two restaurants in one: the glass enclosed front section goes by the name of the 'bar and grill', is more informal in style and opens out onto the street in summer while beyond is the main restaurant, whose walls are filled with a huge collection of artwork. The menu is a no-nonsense celebration of the best of British combined with what Europe can offer. So, expect bangers and mash alongside rack of lamb. For the incurably louche, breakfast is served until early evening.

Lots Road & Pub Dining Room

D8 **Gastropub**

114 Lots Rd ✉ SW10 0RJ ⊖ Fulham Broadway.
✆ (020) 7352 6645
e-mail lotsroad@foodandfuel.co.uk
www.lotsroadpub.com

Carte £20/31

Lots Road and its customers are clearly happy with one another as the pub has introduced a customer loyalty scheme, whereby anyone making their fifth visit is rewarded with a discount. Lunch is geared more towards those just grapping a quick bite but dinner sees a choice that includes oysters, mussels and a savoury tart of the day; the Perthshire côte de boeuf is the house speciality. There are also pies and casseroles, in appropriate pub-like sizes and even some salads. Service remains bright and cheery, even on those frantic Thursday nights when the pub offers 'Thursday Treats' with wine tasting and nibbles. The only disappointment is the somewhat ordinary bread for which they make a not insubstantial charge.

Manicomio

F6 **Italian** X

85 Duke of York Sq,
King's Rd ✉ SW3 4LY
✆ (020) 7730 3366
Fax (020) 7730 3377
e-mail info@manicomio.co.uk
www.manicomio.co.uk

⊖ Sloane Square
closed 25-26 December and 1 January

Carte £28/41

With the Saatchi Gallery next door, Manicomio has really hit the jackpot: the King's Road looks to be on the rise again and Duke of York Square could turn out to be one of its most fashionable quarters. The restaurant has bedded in nicely – another branch has opened in The City – and its terrace is deservedly popular on warm days. The deli occupies one half; the restaurant the other, and the cooking is Italian and wholesome. The pasta dishes are a meal in themselves and the kitchen keeps flavours natural and dishes simple and reliable. Service never loses its sense of fun, even when creaking slightly under the pressure of being busy. The restaurant has a warm and relaxed feel with exposed brick walls, modern artwork and a bar on one side.

Marco

T2 **Traditional** XX

Stamford Bridge,
Fulham Rd ✉ SW6 1HS
✆ (020) 7915 2929
Fax (020) 7915 2931
e-mail info@marcorestaurant.co.uk
www.marcorestaurant.co.uk

⊖ Fulham Broadway
Plan XVIII
Closed 25 December, Sunday and Monday
except match days – dinner only

Carte £34/59

A section of Manchester United fans was once derided as being prawn sandwich eaters; London expectations being what they are, at Chelsea's ground you get a restaurant from Marco Pierre White. Some will inevitably cry foul and shed a tear for football's working class roots; others will cheer for this evidence of our growing culinary maturity. Both sides, though, should applaud the menu, which offers British classics and 'bloke' food galore, from classically prepared liver and bacon to fish and chips and rib-eyes with assorted accompaniments. This being a polyglot club means other nationalities are also represented, in this case a bit of Italy and France, and more sophisticated fare such as foie gras terrine or duck confit is also available.

Mr Chow

F4 **Chinese** XX

151 Knightsbridge ✉ SW1X 7PA
✆ (020) 7589 7347
Fax (020) 7584 5780
e-mail mrchowuk@aol.com
www.mrchow.com

⊖ Knightsbridge
Closed 24 to 26 December, 1 January, Easter Monday and Monday lunch

Menu £23/38 – Carte £42/63

Chinese food, Italian waiters, swish surroundings, steep prices and immaculately coiffured regulars: it's an unusual mix that clearly works because Mr Chow has already celebrated its fortieth birthday. Even if you're not recognisable, you'll get a friendly welcome and the champagne chariot will be wheeled towards you. The laminated menu is long but clearly divided between sections entitled 'from the sea', 'from the land' and 'from the sky'; chickens will be pleased to find themselves in this last category. The cooking is far better than you expect, with genuine care shown. The desserts are thoroughly European and come on a trolley, with tarts the speciality. Your final bill won't be clearly itemised but this doesn't seem to bother anyone.

One-O-One

F4 **Seafood** XXX

101 Knightsbridge ✉ SW1X 7RN
✆ (020) 7290 7101
Fax (020) 7235 6196
e-mail oneoone@luxurycollection.com
www.oneoonerestaurant.com

⊖ Knightsbridge
Closed 25-26 December and 1 January

Menu £19/38 – Carte £49/62

Walking past the Sheraton Park Tower hotel, one of London's less majestic buildings, you'd never know there was a restaurant behind those heavy net curtains, and a rather good one to boot. Granted, the room size and shape mean an animated atmosphere remains elusive and staff, pleasant though they are, have little presence. But the food is good and that food is mostly fish. They've found a balance between offering a traditional à la carte menu and a list of 'petits plats', 6 of which, taken together, will satisfy the fiercest of appetites. Much of the produce comes from Brittany and Norway; the latter gives us the King crab legs which are the stars of the show. The kitchen is not afraid of adding a little playfulness to its classical base.

Painted Heron

Indian XX

E7

112 Cheyne Walk ✉ SW10 0DJ
✆ (020) 7351 5232
www.thepaintedheron.com

⊖ Gloucester Road
closed 25 December, 1 January and Saturday lunch

Menu £32 – Carte £33/40

They call their style "modern Indian" which, in essence, means the kitchen's influences come from across the land; from Kashmir and Rajasthan to Kerala and Goa. Fish, largely from Hastings, is handled dextrously and much is made of seasonal game, whether that's the tandoor pigeon breasts, the partridge with red chilli paste or grouse in a southern stew. Flavours tend to be well-defined and balanced. The room is bigger than you think and has quite a formal feel, thanks largely to the style of service from the young team, but it's broken up into nooks and crannies and hence quite intimate. The open courtyard is an attractive feature and, despite its tiny entrance and tucked away location, the restaurant always appears to be busy.

Papillon

French XX

F6

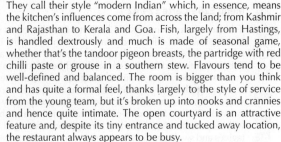

96 Draycott Ave ✉ SW3 3AD
✆ (020) 7225 2555
Fax (020) 7225 2554
e-mail info@papillonchelsea.co.uk
www.papillonchelsea.co.uk

⊖ South Kensington
Closed Sunday dinner

Menu £20 (lunch) – Carte £35/47

Ask for one of the large round tables by the French windows that open onto the pavement patio for that authentic brasserie experience. Papillon is the genuine French article: the mirrors, lamps and animated conversations are all there. The kitchen, too, makes its mark on classic regional recipes: snails with garlic, steak tartare and Mediterranean fish soup can be followed by roast turbot with truffle sauce, saddle of lamb with Lyonnaise potato or Chateaubriand Rossini. There are also plenty of thoughtfully-created salads for those who prefer to keep things light – this is Chelsea, after all. The wine list is also mainly Gallic, with Italy and Spain getting a little look-in. Lunch and early evening see a keenly-priced menu.

Pasha

D5 **Moroccan**

1 Gloucester Rd ✉ SW7 4PP ⊖ Gloucester Road
✆ (020) 7589 7969 Closed 24-25 December and 1 January
Fax (020) 7581 9996
e-mail info@pasha-restaurant.co.uk
www.pasha-restaurant.co.uk

Menu £28 – Carte £24/42

If the prosaic surroundings of Gloucester Road leave you in need of more colourful fillip to your love-life then try buying into the whole Pasha experience: the exotic scent of incense and the rich, romantic and velvety décor should be enough to arouse anyone's ardour. Downstairs is the place to be, in one of the semi-private booths in particular, where rose petals are strewn seductively over the tables and service is appropriately sweet-natured. Choose from one of the 'feast' menus and the food will keep on coming, including kemia (Moroccan small plates), tagines and sweet pastries. By the end your more corpulent figure may leave you feeling less romantically inclined so be thankful to the belly dancers for buying you some time.

The Phoenix

F6-7 **Gastropub**

23 Smith St ✉ SW3 4EE ⊖ Sloane Square
✆ (020) 7730 9182 Closed 25-26 December
e-mail thephoenix@geronimo-inns.co.uk
www.geronimo-inns.co.uk

Carte £23/30

The Phoenix may be part of an ever-expanding group of pubs but you'd never know it. It's a rather chic little number, close enough to the King's Road to be a useful pit-stop but also something of a local destination. The largest part of the pub is taken over by those very civilised locals, relaxing in the squashy sofas, enjoying a Welsh rarebit with their drinks. But work your way through to the back and you'll find the dining room, refurbished in 2008, where the murmur from the bar reminds you you're still in a pub. The food is tasty and satisfying, whether that's eggs Benedict, Portland crab on toast or steak and hand-cut chips which arrive in sweet enamel pie dishes. The seasonal specials on the blackboard get snapped up quickly.

The Pig's Ear

Gastropub

E7

35 Old Church St ✉ SW3 5BS
✆ (020) 7352 2908
Fax (020) 7352 9321
e-mail thepigsear@hotmail.co.uk
www.thepigsear.com

⊖ Sloane Square
Closed Sunday dinner

Carte £25/40

VISA MC AE

This foodie pub off the King's Road, with its board games and newspapers, is a great spot for whiling away a weekend hour or three. The owners' love of cinema and music is evident in the plethora of posters and photos; a jug of Bloody Mary sits proudly on the bar and bottles of Bréton cider are served alongside the beers and wines. It can feel as if all of Chelsea has come out to play, so book ahead for the panelled dining room, or alternatively, ask if you can commandeer the Blue Room – a cosy, curtained off area with a real fire. The menu is modern British meets the Med, with dishes like beef marrow, lamb stew and dumplings, or Cornish crab Thermidor. Charcuterie is a staple and the great bread comes from The Flour Station in Battersea.

Poissonnerie de l'Avenue

French

E6

82 Sloane Ave ✉ SW3 3DZ
✆ (020) 7589 2457 / 577 4
Fax (020) 7581 3360
e-mail peterr@poissonerle.co.uk
www.poissonneriedelavenue.co.uk

⊖ South Kensington
Closed 25 December and 1 January

A/C

Menu £26 (lunch) – Carte £28/43

VISA MC AE

Poissonnerie de l'Avenue is a trusty Chelsea institution with a loyal band of followers. Refreshing unmoved by the dictates of fashion, the restaurant comes divided into three classically decorated rooms with wood panelling, seafaring-themed oil paintings and a decidedly grown-up atmosphere. The regulars prefer the newer far room. As the name suggests, it is all about fish here, whether that's the confident and robust Mediterranean-inspired main courses or the new season oysters one can enjoy in the bar. The fish is supremely fresh, exceptionally well sourced and comes unmasked in flavour and undisguised in presentation. Enough to make one almost forget the 15% service charge on top of a cover charge.

Racine

E5 **French** XX

239 Brompton Rd ✉ SW3 2EP
✆ (020) 7584 4477
Fax (020) 7584 4900
e-mail jon@racine-restaurant.com
www.racine-restaurant.com

⊖ South Kensington
Closed 25 December

Menu £18/20 (lunch and early dinner) – Carte £28/44

It's all change again at the top. Now it is Henry Harris who is back running the kitchen and the show in general, and Eric Garnier, his erstwhile partner, who has left. However, Racine has such a loyal following that it virtually runs itself – or gives that impression. Most other elements remain unchanged and that authentic French brasserie feel couldn't be more bedded in: the brown leather now has a real lived-in look, the wood has darkened and the mirrors have gone a smoky opaque. There are good value menus for lunch and early dinner and from the à la carte you can expect a comprehensive selection of bourgeois classics, from tête de veau to steak tartare and crème caramel, although the 14½ % service charge can push up the final bill.

A/C · VISA · MC · AE

Tom's Kitchen

E6 **French** X

27 Cale St ✉ SW3 3QP
✆ (020) 7349 0202
Fax (020) 7823 3652
e-mail info@tomskitchen.co.uk
www.tomskitchen.co.uk

⊖ South Kensington
Closed 25 December and 1 January

Carte £27/52

The Tom is Tom Aikens and this is a simpler but immeasurably worthy addendum to his eponymous restaurant around the corner. What was previously The Blenheim pub has an industrial-lite feel, with eating on the ground floor, a bar on the second and private dining at the top. Once you've found the right door to get in you'll be welcomed by an enthusiastic team and those without reservations are steered to the counter. Open from breakfast to very late, the menu offers uncomplicated but carefully prepared comfort food. French is the main influence, with such classics as steak tartare and confit of duck, but Britain supplies the majority of the ingredients as well as the occasional dish, while Italy turns up too with the odd risotto or panna cotta.

VISA · MC · AE

Rasoi ✿

F6

Indian XX

10 Lincoln St ✉ SW3 2TS
✆ (020) 7225 1881
Fax (020) 7581 0220
e-mail info@rasoirestaurant.co.uk
www.rasoirestaurant.co.uk

⊖ Sloane Square
Closed 25 -26 December, 1 January, Saturday lunch and Sunday

Menu £26/55

A/C
VISA
AE

Rasoi

Part of the appeal of Vineet Bhatia's Rasoi is that it's found in an archetypal Chelsea townhouse and that the atmosphere inside is usually far warmer and more intimate than anything one usually experiences in an Indian restaurant. This is often despite, rather than because of, the staff, who bring a mix of nationalities and varying degrees of competency to the operation. Proof that most people are really here for the food comes in the fact that the 'gourmand' menu is by far the most popular choice. It has been reduced from an unwieldy nine courses to a more manageable seven. The cooking is inventive and the kitchen proves that Indian food can be just as open to interpretation as other cuisines. But what makes it all work is the quality of the ingredients used and the deft, controlled spicing. Tea drinkers will find much to savour in the range and the ritual. Sit in the bigger room at the back which has more personality than the one at the front. Larger parties should consider one of the more opulent private rooms upstairs.

First Course

- Grilled prawn, coconut and chilli panna cotta with brown shrimp chutney.
- Almond tikki with spicey chickpea masala and tamarind chutney sorbet.

Main Course

- Baked sea bass, tandoori crushed potatoes and crispy okra.
- Tandoori black spice chicken, chilli khichdi and milk fritters.

Dessert

- Blueberry and black cardamom kulfi.
- Fruit and champagne terrine.

Tom Aikens ✿

E6

Innovative XXX

43 Elystan St ✉ SW3 3NT
✆ (020) 7584 2003
Fax (020) 7589 2107
e-mail info@tomaikens.co.uk
www.tomaikens.co.uk

⊖ South Kensington
Closed 25-26 December, New Year, Easter Monday, Saturday lunch, Sunday, Monday and Bank Holidays

Menu £29 (lunch) – Carte £29/65

A/C
VISA
MC
AE

Tom Aikens

Financial difficulties off the pitch, as they say in football parlance, impacted somewhat on the squad and the adverse publicity that arose from going into administration also had a knock-on effect on groups of supporters. 2009 was not a particularly good year for many; it was a terrible one for Tom Aikens and his suppliers and the backlash reverberated for a long time. So, having lost much of his sheen, the best route back for him when the restaurant immediately reopened was to return to what he does well – cooking. His food is best when it is restrained; when he lets his ingredients – which are very seasonal and largely from the British Isles – shine through. He handles fish particularly adroitly and accompanying flavours are always complementary. Desserts are usually slightly more experimental in their construction. The room is elegant and neat without being showy. If they can also inject some more personality into the service, there is no reason why 2010 could not be the year of forgiveness.

First Course

- Tartare of scallops with almond gazpacho.
- Pickled artichoke salad with potato and truffle.

Main Course

- Fillet of beef with summer truffle and red wine sauce.
- John Dory with almonds, endive and orange dressing.

Dessert

- Pistachio meringue, parfait and cassonade.
- Chocolate dacquoise with peanut mousse and milk ice cream.

Toto's

F5 **Italian** XXX

Walton House, Walton St ✉ SW3 2JH
✆ (020) 7589 0075
Fax (020) 7581 9668

⊖ Knightsbridge
Closed 25-27 December – booking essential at dinner

Menu £24 (lunch)
Carte £34/45

Any restaurant this busy but without a website, still including a cover charge and beyond the jurisdiction of the fashion police, must be doing something right. Walton House is home to Toto's, with the entrance on the cobbled Lennox Garden Mews. It is old-fashioned in the best sense of the word: you'll feel genuinely looked after. The ground floor is where the action is but tables on the balcony offer more privacy. Despite the smart surroundings, the Italian food is decidedly earthy and rustic. Freshness and consistency are the hallmarks of the kitchen and there's a simplicity and honesty to the cooking. The handmade pasta is a strength and those daunted by a middle course can merely ask for a reduced portion.

Zuma

F5 **Japanese** XX

5 Raphael St ✉ SW7 1DL
✆ (020) 7584 1010
Fax (020) 7584 5005
e-mail info@zumarestaurant.com
www.zumarestaurant.com

⊖ Knightsbridge
Closed 25-26 December and 1 January

Carte approx. £26

Japanese food meets Contemporary Japanese food at this stylish Knightsbridge restaurant, popular with the glittering and the glitterati and ideally located for those seeking a little respite from the strain of shopping or being photographed doing so. The place is certainly eye catching in its design, with a plethora of granite, stone, marble and wood creating a restaurant that successfully blends east with west. Choose from a variety of seating options, from the bustle of the main dining area to the theatre afforded by the sushi counter. The menu offers up an intriguing mix of the traditional with the ultra modern, all expertly crafted and delicately presented. Lovers of sake will find over thirty varieties available.

Kensington · North Kensington · Notting Hill

It was the choking air of 17C London that helped put **Kensington** on the map: the little village lying to the west of the city became the favoured retreat of the asthmatic King William III who had Sir Christopher Wren build **Kensington Palace** for him. Where the king leads, the titled follow, and the area soon became a fashionable location for the rich. For over 300 years, it's had no problem holding onto its cachet, though a stroll down Kensington High Street is these days a more egalitarian odyssey than some more upmarket residents might approve of.

The shops here mix the everyday with the flamboyant, but for a real taste of the exotic you have to take the lift to the top of the Art Deco Barkers building and arrive at the Kensington Roof Gardens, which are open to all as long as they're not in use for a corporate bash. The gardens are now over seventy years old, yet still remain a 'charming secret'. Those who do make it up to the sixth floor discover a delightful woodland garden and gurgling stream, complete with pools, bridges and trees. There are flamingos, too, adding a dash of vibrant colour.

Back down on earth, Kensington boasts another hidden attraction in **Leighton House** on its western boundaries. The Victorian redbrick façade looks a bit forbidding as you make your approach, but step inside and things take a dramatic turn, courtesy of the extraordinary Arab Hall, with its oriental mosaics and tinkling fountain creating a scene like something from ***The Arabian Knights.*** Elsewhere in the building, the Pre-Raphaelite paintings of Lord Leighton, Burne-Jones and Alma-Tadema are much to the fore. Mind you, famous names have always had a hankering for W8, with a particular preponderance to dally in enchanting **Kensington Square,** where there are almost as many blue plaques as buildings upon which to secure them. William Thackeray, John Stuart Mill and Edward Burne-Jones were all residents.

One of the London's most enjoyable green retreats is **Holland Park,** just north of the High Street. It boasts the 400 year-old Holland House, which is a fashionable focal point for summer-time al fresco theatre and opera. Holland Walk runs along the eastern fringe of the park, and provides a lovely sojourn down to the shops; at the Kyoto Garden, koi carp reach hungrily for the surface of their pool, while elsewhere peacocks strut around as if they own the place.

Another world beckons just north of here – the seedy-cum-glitzy environs of **Notting Hill.** The main drag itself, Notting Hill Gate, is little more than a one-dimensional thoroughfare only enlivened by second hand record shops, but to its south are charming cottages with pastel shades in leafy streets, while to the north the appealing **Pembridge Road** evolves into the boutiques of Westbourne Grove. Most people heading in this direction are making for the legendary Portobello Road market – particularly on Saturdays, which are manic. The market stretches on for more than a mile, with a chameleon-like ability to change colour and character on the way: there are antiques at the Notting Hill end, followed further up by food stalls, and then designer and vintage clothes as you reach the Westway. Those who don't fancy the madding crowds of the market can nip into the Electric Cinema and watch a movie in supreme comfort: it boasts two-seater sofas and leather armchairs. Nearby there are another two film-houses putting the hip into the Hill – the Gate, and the Coronet, widely recognised as one of London's most charming 'locals'.

Hidden in a mews just north of **Westbourne Grove** is a fascinating destination: the Museum of Brands, Packaging and Advertising, which does pretty much what it says on the label. It's both nostalgic and evocative, featuring thousands of items like childhood toys, teenage magazines…and HP sauce bottles.

S. Ollivier / MICHELIN

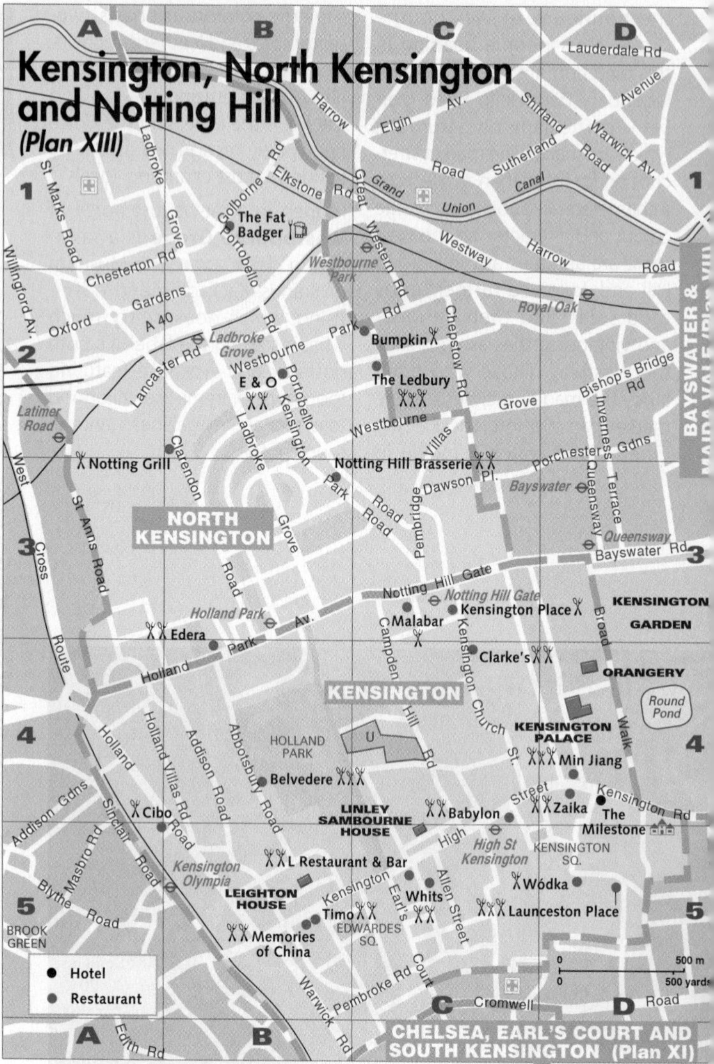
Kensington, North Kensington and Notting Hill
(Plan XIII)
A
B
C
D
1
2
3
4
5
The Fat Badger
Bumpkin
The Ledbury
E & O
Notting Grill
Notting Hill Brasserie
NORTH KENSINGTON
Edera
Malabar
Kensington Place
Clarke's
KENSINGTON
KENSINGTON GARDEN
ORANGERY
Round Pond
KENSINGTON PALACE
Min Jiang
Zaika
The Milestone
Babylon
Belvedere
Cibo
LINLEY SAMBOURNE HOUSE
L Restaurant & Bar
LEIGHTON HOUSE
Whits
Wódka
Launceston Place
Timo
Memories of China
HOLLAND PARK
BROOK GREEN
Hotel
Restaurant
BAYSWATER &
CHELSEA, EARL'S COURT AND SOUTH KENSINGTON (Plan XI)
Westbourne Park
Royal Oak
Ladbroke Grove
Latimer Road
Bayswater
Queensway
Notting Hill Gate
Holland Park
High St Kensington
Kensington Olympia
Lauderdale Rd
Elgin Av.
Shirland Road
Sutherland Avenue
Warwick Av.
Grand Union Canal
Harrow Road
Westway
Elkstone Rd
Golborne Rd
Ladbroke Grove
Portobello Rd
St Marks Road
Chesterton Rd
Oxford Gardens
A 40
Willingford Av.
Lancaster Rd
Westbourne Park Rd
Westbourne Grove
Great Western Rd
Chepstow Rd
Bishop's Bridge Rd
Inverness Terrace
Porchester Gdns
Queensway
Bayswater Rd
Kensington Park Road
Pembridge Villas
Dawson Pl.
Clarendon Road
St Anns Road
West Cross Route
Notting Hill Gate
Holland Park Av.
Campden Hill Rd
Kensington Church St.
Broad Walk
Kensington Rd
Holland Road
Holland Villas Rd
Addison Road
Abbotsbury Road
Addison Gdns
Sinclair Road
Masbro Rd
Blythe Road
Kensington High Street
Earl's Court Rd
Allen Street
Pembroke Rd
Warwick Rd
Edith Rd
Cromwell Road
EDWARDES SQ.
KENSINGTON SQ.
0
500 m
0
500 yards

Babylon

C4 — **Modern European** XX

99 Kensington High St (entrance on Derry St) ✉ W8 5SA

⊖ High Street Kensington

Closed 24 December - 2 January and Sunday dinner

✆ (020) 7368 3993

Fax (020) 7368 3995

e-mail babylon@roofgardens.virgin.com

www.roofgardens.virgin.com

Menu £20 (lunch) – Carte £46/57

The challenge is to find the entrance which is secreted on the right as you walk down Derry Street; then it's the lift up to the 7th floor and suddenly you're surrounded by trees. There's no doubting that this is quite a spot and while the gardens just below may not be 'hanging' they are an understandably appealing place for a party. The restaurant is a long, narrow affair whose contemporary décor reflects the leafy outdoors and the terrace takes some beating in summer. Influences on the menu remain largely within Europe and the cooking shows a degree of perkiness and ambition. The lunch time set menu is priced to appeal to local businesses while the à la carte can get a little expensive. The wine list plants its flag firmly in the New World.

Belvedere

B4 — **French** XXX

Holland House, off Abbotsbury Rd ✉ W8 6LU

⊖ Holland Park

Closed 26 December, 1 January and Sunday dinner

✆ (020) 7602 1238

Fax (020) 7610 4382

e-mail info@belvedererestaurant.co.uk

www.belvedererestaurant.co.uk

Menu £20 (lunch) – Carte £26/49

Built in 17C as the summer ballroom to the Jacobean Holland House, The Belvedere sits in a stunning position in Holland Park. It's hard to believe you're still in London but check the location first as signposts within the park are a little elusive. The ground floor is the more glittery, with mirrors, glass balls and a small bar area. Upstairs is more traditional in style and leads out onto the charming terrace which is well worth booking in summer. Service remains decidedly formal. The menu covers all bases from eggs Benedict to even the occasional Thai, but it's worth sticking to the more classical, French influenced dishes as these are kitchen's strength. Produce is well sourced and dishes nicely balanced. France dominates the wine list.

Bumpkin

D6 **British**

209 Westbourne Park Rd ✉ W11 1EA ⊖ Westbourne Park
✆ (020) 7243 9818 Closed 25-26 December, 1 January and August Bank Holiday
Fax (020) 7229 1826
e-mail reservations@bumpkinuk.com
www.bumpkinuk.com

Menu £12 (2 course lunch) – Carte £24/39

The aim was to create a clubby place with a wholesome, homespun feel and for that they chose a derelict pub with a dubious past. It works, largely because they have eschewed the gastropub in favour of creating something a little different. The ground floor is a brasserie with an appealing menu of light bites, pots, pies and grills with satisfying dishes ranging from macaroni cheese to liver and bacon. Those wanting something equally gutsy, but slightly more refined, can head to the first floor restaurant for dishes such as osso bucco or wild sea bass. Both kitchens share an emphasis on seasoning, sourcing and buying organic where possible. The other floors are taken up with private dining and whisky tasting.

Cibo

A5 **Italian**

3 Russell Gdns ✉ W14 8EZ ⊖ Kensington Olympia
✆ (020) 7371 6271 Closed Christmas-New Year, Saturday lunch and Sunday dinner
Fax (020) 7602 1371
e-mail ciborestaurant@aol.com
www.ciborestaurant.net

Carte £25/39

Cibo has long been a familiar landmark in Holland Park and its constituency appears to be mostly regulars whom the owner greets effusively, although any event at nearby Olympia will bring in a few interlopers. It's always felt a little claustrophobic inside, the décor is now looking a little weary and service can be a little distracted if the boss is away but the food still merits attention. Start with some great bresaola with goat's cheese, followed by the huge grilled seafood and shellfish platter – it may be expensive but does include everything from clams and prawns to squid and swordfish and will satisfy the biggest appetite. The best part of the dessert menu is the selection of interesting and original ice creams.

Clarke's

C4 **Modern European** XX

124 Kensington Church St ✉ W8 4BH ⊖ Notting Hill Gate
✆ (020) 7221 9225
Closed 2 weeks Christmas-New Year and Bank Holidays
Fax (020) 7229 4564
e-mail restaurant@sallyclarke.com
www.sallyclarke.com

Menu £40 (dinner) – Carte lunch £29/35

A/C VISA MC AE

Sally Clarke spent a few years in California and those who know Alice Waters' Chez Panisse will recognise the concept: crisp, seasonal produce, a minimal amount of interference from the kitchen and clean, fresh flavours. As the restaurant approaches its quarter of a century it's clear that it doesn't have to be warm and sunny outside to appreciate this type of cooking. The only significant change happened a few years back when customers were given a choice at dinner: for many years there had been a set menu with no alternative. The downstairs is a good spot to watch the kitchen in action; upstairs is more intimate. The long-standing manager keeps things rolling along nicely and knows his regulars. There's bounty galore in the shop next door.

E&O

B2 **Asian** XX

14 Blenheim Crescent ✉ W11 1NN ⊖ Ladbroke Grove
✆ (020) 7229 5454
Closed 25-26 December and August Bank Holiday
Fax (020) 7229 5522
e-mail eando@rickerrestaurants.com
www.rickerrestaurants.com

Carte £22/44

A/C VISA MC AE

Once you've sidestepped the full-on bar of this Notting Hill favourite, a step from Portobello Road, you'll find yourself in a moodily sophisticated restaurant packed with the beautiful and the hopeful. The room is understatedly urbane, with slatted walls, large circular lamps and leather banquettes, while noise levels are at the party end of the auditory index. Waiting staff are obliging, pleasant and often among the prettiest people in the room. E&O stands for Eastern and Oriental and the menu journeys across numerous Asian countries, dividing itself into assorted headings which include dim sum, salads, tempura, curries and roasts. Individual dishes vary in size and price, so sharing, as in life, is often the best option.

Edera

B4 **Italian** XX

148 Holland Park Ave ✉ W11 4UE ⊖ Holland Park
✆ (020) 7221 6090
Fax (020) 7313 9700
e-mail edera@btconnect.com

Carte £31/44

A/C VISA MC AE

No restaurant can survive without the support of regulars and few restaurants demonstrate the importance of customer loyalty more than Edera. In an area not overburdened with exciting choices, Edera maintains decent numbers by focusing its attentions on its regulars. The room may not have too much character but the atmosphere is local and congenial. Meanwhile, the kitchen does what all good Italians do: it uses superior ingredients, eschews fads and doesn't crowd the plate. There is a subtle Sardinian element to the menu here – you'll find malloreddus pasta, the bottarga comes as carpaccio or with spaghetti and there's often suckling pig available at weekends – while the desserts display an appealing lightness of touch.

The Fat Badger

B1 **British**

310 Portobello Road ✉ W10 5TA ⊖ Ladbroke Grove
✆ (020) 8969 4500
e-mail fat_badger@me.com
www.thefatbadger.com

Carte £20/29

VISA MC AE

The Fat Badger treads the line between being worn in and worn out. Stuffing sprouts from sofas and chips and scuffs abound but the locals seem to like the general raggedness. Use of the upstairs restaurant is largely dependent on enough punters requesting it and, besides, the same menu is served in the bar. The one decorative element that really stands out is the patterned wallpaper which only reveals its true nature on close inspection. Service can be hit and miss as not all members of staff share the same attitude towards customer service. But the food is good: the kitchen doesn't try to reinvent anything but also displays a light touch, whether in the crisp cuttlefish and chorizo, the roast chicken breast or the panna cotta.

Kensington Place

Modern European

C3

201-209 Kensington Church St
W8 7LX
(020) 7727 3184
Fax (020) 7792 8388
e-mail kpr-res-adm@danddlondon.com
www.kensingtonplace-restaurant.co.uk

Notting Hill Gate
Restricted opening Christmas-New Year – booking essential

Menu £17/23 – Carte £31/42

When Kensington Place opened in 1987, it broke the mould by showing Londoners that good food could be served in a relaxed style and for that we should all be grateful. Now, some twenty-three years later it finds itself being something of an elder statesman. Rowley Leigh may have long gone but the current team, under the ownership of D&D, are not reinventing any wheels. The cooking remains unfussy, seasonal and decently proportioned. Classics like foie gras with a sweet corn pancake and scallops with pea purée remain and accompaniments to the main courses are well chosen. The wine list is lengthy and listed by grape variety and style. The acoustics are still terrible but the atmosphere remains fun.

Launceston Place

Modern European

D5

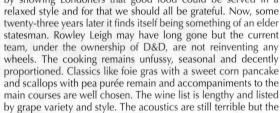

1a Launceston Pl W8 5RL
(020) 7937 6912
Fax (020) 7938 2412
e-mail lpr_res@dandlondon.com
www.launcestonplace-restaurant.co.uk

Gloucester Road
Closed 24-30 December, 1 January, 4 January, Monday lunch and Bank Holidays

Menu £18/42

Launceston Place now forms part of the D&D group and is largely unrecognisable from its former days. The last, much needed reincarnation made the walls darker, the lighting moodier and the ambition more evident but the best thing it that the appealing neighbourhood feel has not been lost, even with service that takes itself seriously. Tristan Welch, who previously worked with Marcus Wareing, is the confident young chef at the helm and his cooking is original but also well grounded and balanced. He's also a keen champion of home-grown produce: about 80% of the ingredients come from within the British Isles and he's planning to increase this figure further. The Tasting Menu is priced not far north of the à la carte and showcases his talent well.

The Ledbury ✿✿

C2 **French** XXX

127 Ledbury Rd ✉ W11 2AQ
✆ (020) 7792 9090
Fax (020) 7792 9191
e-mail info@theledbury.com
www.theledbury.com

⊖ Notting Hill Gate
Closed lunch over Christmas and 28-31 August

Menu £25 (lunch £40 Sunday)/60 (dinner) – Carte lunch £38/47

VISA MC AE

The Ledbury

The Ledbury has been quietly going about its business, getting better and better. The Australian head chef, Brett Graham, is one of the more intelligent chefs around and his passion for quality ingredients really shines through. He is constantly on the lookout for new supplies and suppliers and knows what to do when he gets them. Hebridean lambs arrive whole and are then butchered, with every part of the beast used; game is also one of the kitchen's strengths – Brett is a keen shot. The kitchen is also firmly grounded in technique so that whenever a slightly unusual flavour or a little tease is introduced, it is done merely to enhance the dish. This is bravado cooking but without affectation. Even though Brett was involved in the opening of The Harwood Arms in 2009, he didn't take his eye off the ball here. Along with The Ashes, let's hope he stays on this side of the world. The room is elegant without being overdressed and the serving team are well organised and professional but they never forget that fundamentally this is a neighbourhood restaurant.

First Course

- Pheasant and herb tea with pheasant canapés.
- Lasagne of rabbit with morels and watercress.

Main Course

- Skate wing in brown butter with asparagus and langoustines.
- Shoulder of lamb with celery and pomme purée.

Dessert

- Passion fruit soufflé with Sauternes ice cream.
- Gingerbread with crème chantilly and apple.

L Restaurant & Bar

C5 **Spanish** XX

2 Abingdon Rd ✉ W8 6AF
✆ (020) 7795 6969
Fax (020) 7795 6699
e-mail info@l-restaurant.co.uk
www.l-restaurant.co.uk

⊖ High Street Kensington
Closed Monday lunch and Bank Holidays

Carte £26/34

A/C · VISA · MC · AE

This is a bright Spanish restaurant that's well supported by the locals, many of whom just pop into the front bar for some tapas and a cocktail. But go through and you'll find yourself in a surprisingly large space, with a mezzanine floor, glass roof and mirrored wall that make it seem even bigger. The best seats are on the upper level as those beneath are a little claustrophobic; celebrity photos by Patrick Lichfield line the walls. The menu is divided between hot and cold tapas on one side, an à la carte the other. Although the paella for two is a popular choice, having the tapas is the best option; about five dishes per person should suffice. Occasional live music helps the atmosphere along, as does the reasonably priced wine list.

Malabar

C3 **Indian** X

27 Uxbridge St ✉ W8 7TQ
✆ (020) 7727 8800
e-mail feedback@malabar-restaurant.co.uk
www.malabar-restaurant.co.uk

⊖ Notting Hill Gate
Closed 1 week Christmas and August Bank Holiday – buffet lunch Sunday

Menu £24 s – Carte £23/44 s

A/C · VISA · MC · AE

Malabar celebrated 25 years back in 2008 and it is not difficult to see why it has lasted so long: it's tucked away in a residential part of Notting Hill and has a friendly neighbourhood atmosphere; it gets a regular coat of fresh paint; the service is sweet natured and the cooking is both carefully prepared and good value. The menu is nicely balanced, not too long and focuses on more northerly regions of India. The starters are particularly interesting and vary from succulent marinated chops to tandoori monkfish. Main courses are generously sized, subtly spiced and are served on warm metal thalis; tender lamb dishes are done especially well and the breads are excellent. The buffet lunch on Sunday, when children under 12 go free, is terrific value.

Memories of China

B5 **Chinese** XX

353 Kensington High St
✆ (020) 7603 6951
Fax (020) 7603 0848
e-mail mocken@londonfinedininggroup.com
www.memories-of-china.co.uk

⊖ High Street Kensington
Closed Christmas-New Year and Sunday lunch – booking essential

Carte £26/48

A/C VISA MC AE

Memories of China is a well established Chinese restaurant which pulls in both the locals, many of whom will never have a bad word said about the place, and those staying in one of the surrounding hotels. As such, it's always busy so it's well worth coming secure in the knowledge that you're made a reservation. The menu, rather like the room, is relatively compact and keeps things on the straight and narrow by focusing on classic Cantonese and Szechuan cooking. Set menus are available for groups or those who prefer others to make their decisions for them. The glass façade of this corner restaurant chimes with the bright and modern décor of the interior with Chinese themed murals and calligraphy.

Min Jiang

D4 **Chinese** XXX

Royal Garden Hotel, 10th Floor,
2-24 Kensington High St ✉ W8 4PT
✆ (020) 7361 1988
Fax (020) 7361 1991
e-mail reservations@minjiang.co.uk
www.minjiang.co.uk

⊖ High Street Kensington

Menu £20/48 – Carte £40/61

A/C VISA MC AE

Restaurants with views are rare in London so it's no surprise that this Chinese restaurant, found on the 10th floor of the Royal Garden Hotel, makes the most of its position overlooking Kensington Palace and Gardens. Named after the Min River of Sichuan, an area which influences the menu, it's an offshoot from the original in the group's Singapore hotel. The lunchtime dim sum is done particularly well, while the speciality of the à la carte is the Beijing duck which is roasted in a wood fired oven. The presence of lobster, abalone and shark fin can somewhat distort the prices of the appealing menu. The room is a long, stylish one, with vases influenced by the Ming Dynasty and photos of assorted Chinese scenes.

Notting Hill Brasserie

B3 French XX

92 Kensington Park Rd ✉ W11 2PN
✆ (020) 7229 4481
Fax (020) 7221 1246
e-mail info@nottinghillbrasserie.com
www.nottinghillbrasserie.com

⊖ Notting Hill Gate
Closed 27-29 December

Menu £23/30 (lunch) – Carte £40/53

A/C

VISA

MC

AE

The lighting is flatteringly dim and there's always a good smattering of locals but this restaurant, housed within an Edwardian townhouse, is hardly what one expects from somewhere calling itself a brasserie. It's got a large bar, where the jazz musos perch themselves each evening and the dining room is divided up between smaller rooms, each with their own individual character and this adds to the intimacy. Service is a real strength and the staff are all generally clued-up. The menu reads very well, with each dish headlined by the single main component and influences stretch across the Mediterranean. When those dishes arrive they look very appealing, although flavours can sometimes be a little timid.

Timo

B5 Italian XX

343 Kensington High St
✉ W8 6NW
✆ (020) 7603 3888
Fax (020) 7603 8111
e-mail timorestaurant@fsmail.net
www.timorestaurant.net

⊖ High Street Kensington
Closed 25 December, Sunday and Bank Holidays

Menu £18 (lunch) – Carte dinner £29/44

A/C

VISA

MC

AE

At the Olympia end of Kensington High Street sits this warm and inviting Italian restaurant. The colours of cream and beige, matched with summery paintings of garden landscapes, lend a sunny feel, whatever the season outside. The tables are as smartly dressed as the waiters, who provide conscientious service and the suited owner does the rounds and knows his regulars. The set menu comes divided into the typically Italian four courses, although the impressive looking bread basket will test your powers of self-restraint. Daily specials to supplement the menu are temptingly described and the desserts merit particular investigation. This is a solidly reliable neighbourhood restaurant which sensibly doesn't try to reinvent anything.

Whits

C5 **Modern European** XX

21 Abingdon Rd ✉ W8 6AH
✆ (020) 7938 1122
Fax (020) 7938 1122
e-mail info@whits.co.uk
www.whits.co.uk

⊖ High Street Kensington
Closed 23 December-6 January, Sunday and Monday

Menu £19/24
Carte dinner £29/38

A/C VISA MC

Privately-owned restaurants with a couple at the helm are becoming something of a rarity but there is a certain kind of service one only gets from an owner of a restaurant; it is usually a combination of concern, confidence, pride and sincerity. Eva at Whits is a case in point – she's one of life's natural hosts who puts all customers at ease and the relaxed atmosphere is the restaurant's great strength. Her partner Steve's cooking certainly doesn't pull any punches; combinations are tried and tested, techniques are classic and flavours bold and upfront. The presentation on the plate is somewhat elaborate but diners all leave eminently satisfied, thanks to some generous portioning. There's a good value set menu alongside the à la carte.

Wódka

D5 **Polish** X

12 St Albans Grove ✉ W8 5PN
✆ (020) 7937 6513
Fax (020) 7937 8621
e-mail info@wodka.co.uk
www.wodka.co.uk

⊖ High Street Kensington
Closed 25-26 December – dinner only

Menu £19 – Carte £23/30

VISA MC AE

Once through the velvet curtain you're be struck instantly by the warmth of both the restaurant itself and the charming young Polish ladies who run it so well. It's divided into two rooms – the one furthest from the bar is the more intimate – and has a unpretentious, local feel. The enticing menu is full of Eastern European promise and the kitchen delivers with its full-bodied and gutsy cooking. There's plenty of game on show in season alongside the heartening soups, as well as favourites like blinis with salmon through to caviar. But the kitchen can do more than just put hairs on your chest: desserts such as an excellent pear tart reveal an unexpected lightness of touch. There are chilled or warm vodkas galore, along with Polish beers.

Zaika

D4 **Indian** XX

1 Kensington High St ✉ W8 5NP
☏ (020) 7795 6533
Fax (020) 7937 8854
e-mail info@zaika-restaurant.co.uk
www.zaika-restaurant.co.uk

⊖ High Street Kensington
Closed 25-26 December, 1-2 January and Monday lunch

Menu £25 (lunch)
Carte £30/40

A/C VISA MC AE

Chef Sanjay Dwivedi is making his mark here at Zaika and choosing from his menu can take time as there are plenty of things on it that sound different and interesting. His judicious use of spicing ensures that the main ingredient of each dish is never overwhelmed and while his cooking has a refined and sophisticated quality that's a far cry from most Indian restaurants, those dishes still arrive in generous proportions. To see what the kitchen can really do, try one of the tasting menus. Perhaps to disguise its previous incarnation as a bank, the room has been decorated in a theatrical and flamboyant way, with plenty of drapes and lots of colour. The bar is a fun spot for drinks and service is unobtrusive and efficient.

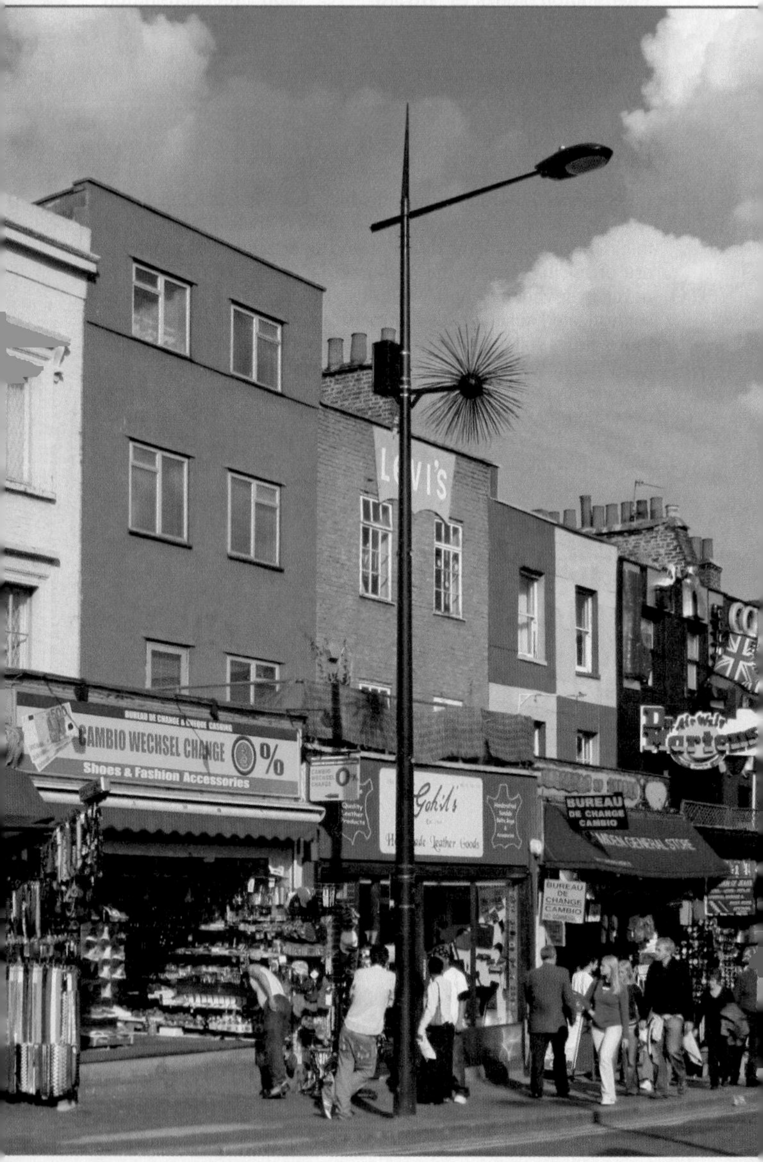
CAMBIO WECHSEL CHANGE
0%
Shoes & Fashion Accessories
BUREAU DE CHANGE CAMBIO
BUREAU DE CHANGE CAMBIO

Greater London

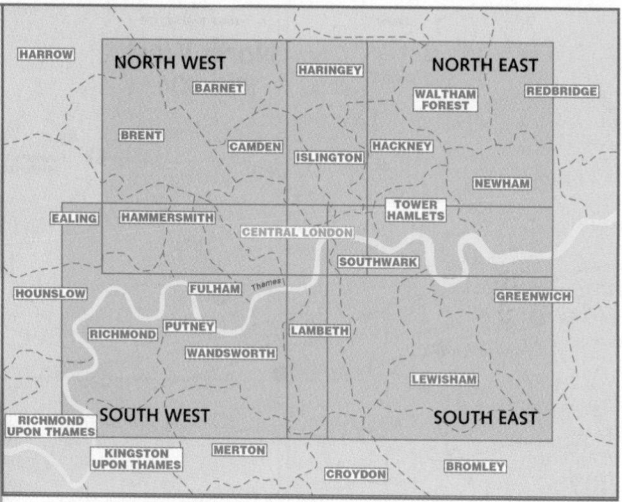

- ▶ North-West 258
- ▶ North-East 278
- ▶ South-East 296
- ▶ South-West 310

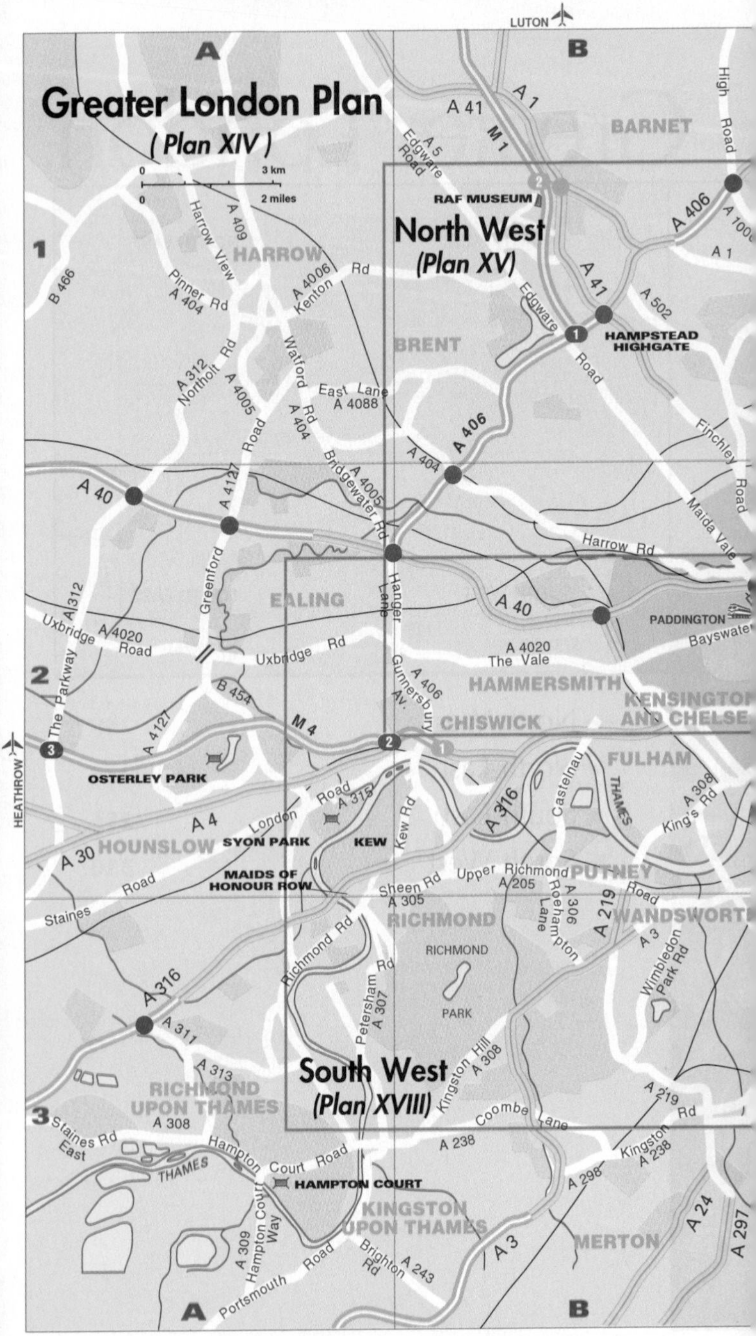

Greater London Plan
(Plan XIV)
0 3 km
0 2 miles
LUTON
HEATHROW
A
B
1
2
3
North West
(Plan XV)
South West
(Plan XVIII)
BARNET
HARROW
BRENT
EALING
HAMMERSMITH
KENSINGTON AND CHELSEA
CHISWICK
FULHAM
HOUNSLOW
PUTNEY
WANDSWORTH
RICHMOND
RICHMOND PARK
RICHMOND UPON THAMES
KINGSTON UPON THAMES
MERTON
RAF MUSEUM
HAMPSTEAD HIGHGATE
PADDINGTON
OSTERLEY PARK
SYON PARK
KEW
MAIDS OF HONOUR ROW
HAMPTON COURT
THAMES
A 41
A 1
M 1
A 5 Edgware Road
High Road
A 406
A 1000
A 502
Edgware Road
Finchley Road
Maida Vale
Harrow Rd
A 40
A 404
Bridgewater Rd
A 4005
Hanger Lane
Harrow View
A 409
B 466
Pinner Rd A 404
A 4006 Kenton Rd
Watford Rd A 404
A 312 Northolt Rd
A 4005 Road
East Lane A 4088
A 4127
Greenford Rd
A 312
Uxbridge Road A 4020
Uxbridge Rd
The Parkway
B 454
A 4020 The Vale
Bayswater
A 406 Gunnersbury Av.
M 4
A 4
London Road
A 315
Kew Rd
A 30
Staines Road
A 316
Castelnau
A 308 King's Rd
Upper Richmond Road
Sheen Rd A 305
A 205
A 306 Roehampton Lane
A 219
A 3
Wimbledon Park Rd
Richmond Rd
Petersham Rd A 307
Kingston Hill A 308
A 311
A 313
A 308
Staines Rd East
Hampton Court Road
Coombe Lane
A 238
A 219 Rd
Kingston A 238
A 298
A 24
A 297
A 309 Hampton Court Way
Portsmouth Road
Brighton Rd A 243

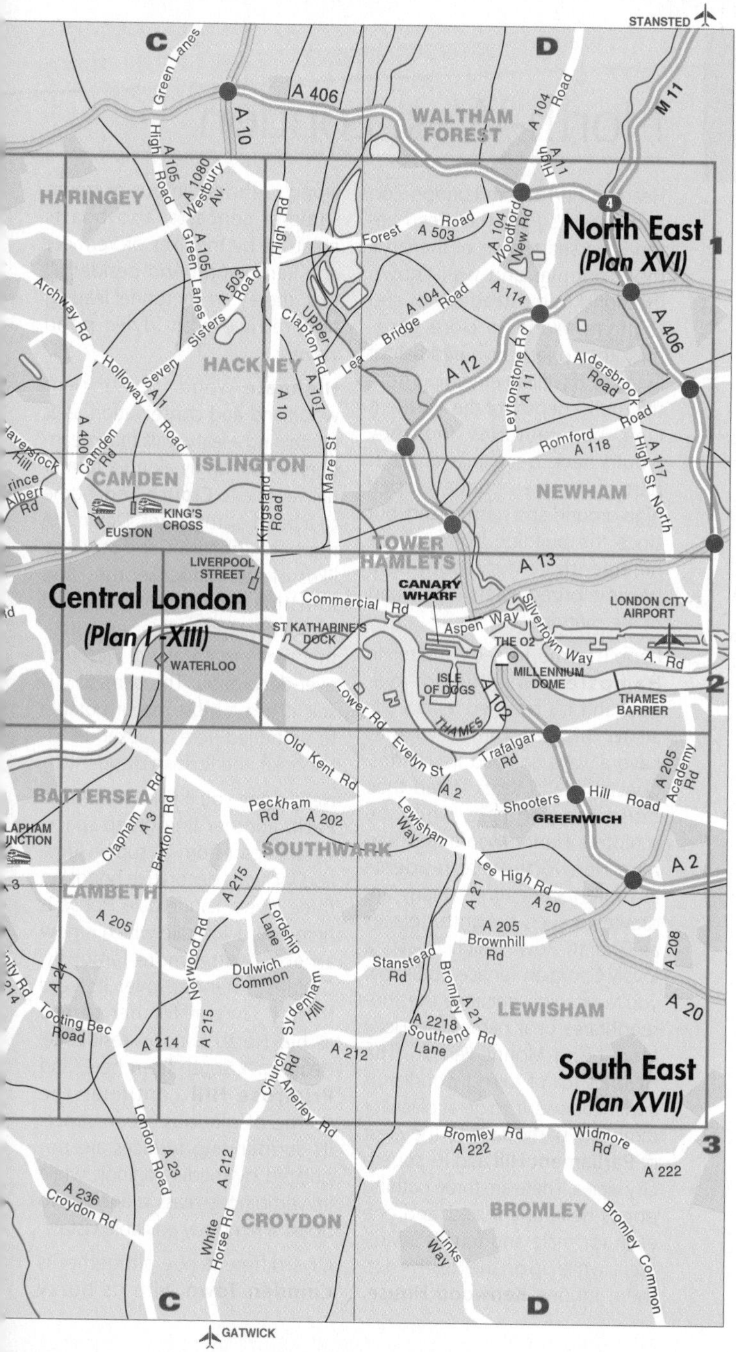
STANSTED
GATWICK
C
D
1
2
3
North East
(Plan XVI)
Central London
(Plan I -XIII)
South East
(Plan XVII)
HARINGEY
WALTHAM FOREST
HACKNEY
ISLINGTON
CAMDEN
TOWER HAMLETS
NEWHAM
BATTERSEA
LAMBETH
SOUTHWARK
GREENWICH
LEWISHAM
CROYDON
BROMLEY
EUSTON
KING'S CROSS
LIVERPOOL STREET
WATERLOO
CANARY WHARF
ST KATHARINE'S DOCK
ISLE OF DOGS
THE O2
MILLENNIUM DOME
THAMES BARRIER
LONDON CITY AIRPORT
THAMES
Green Lanes
A 406
A 10
A 104 Road
M 11
A 105 High Road
A 1080 Westbury Av.
High Rd
Forest A 503 Road
A 104 Woodford New Rd
High A 11
A 105 Green Lanes
Seven Sisters A 503 Road
Archway Rd
Holloway A 1 Road
Upper Clapton Rd A 107
Lea Bridge A 104 Road
A 114
A 12
Leytonstone Rd A 11
Aldersbrook Road
A 406
A 10
Mare St
A 400 Camden Rd
Haverstock Hill
Prince Albert Rd
Kingsland Road
Romford A 118 Road
A 117 High St North
A 13
Commercial Rd
Aspen Way
Silvertown Way
A. Rd
Lower Rd
A 102
Evelyn St
Trafalgar Rd
Old Kent Rd
A 2
Peckham Rd A 202
Lewisham Way
Shooters Hill Road
A 205 Academy Rd
Clapham A 3 Rd
Brixton Rd
A 215
Lee High Rd A 20
A 21
A 205 Brownhill Rd
A 208
A 2
A 205
Lordship Lane
Norwood Rd
Dulwich Common
Stanstead Rd
Bromley A 21 Rd
A 20
A 24
Tooting Bec Road
A 214
A 215
Sydenham Hill
A 2218 Southend Lane
A 212
Church Rd
Anerley Rd
Bromley Rd A 222
Widmore Rd
A 222
London Road A 23
A 236 Croydon Rd
A 212 White Horse Rd
Links Way
Bromley Common
CLAPHAM JUNCTION

North-West London

Heading north from London Zoo and Regent's Park, the green baton is passed to two of the city's most popular and well-known locations: Hampstead Heath and Highgate Wood. In close proximity, they offer a favoured pair of lungs to travellers emerging from the murky depths of the Northern Line. Two centuries ago, they would have been just another part of the area's undeveloped high ground and pastureland, but since the building boom of the nineteenth century, both have become prized assets in this part of the metropolis.

People came to seek shelter in **Hampstead** in times of plague, and it's retained its bucolic air to this day. Famous names have always enjoyed its charms: Constable and Keats rested their brush and pen here, while the sculptors Henry Moore and Barbara Hepworth were residents in more recent times. Many are drawn to such delightful places as Church Row, which boasts a lovely Georgian Terrace. You know you're up high because the thoroughfares bear names like Holly Mount and Mount Vernon. The Heath is full of rolling woodlands and meadows; it's a great place for rambling, particularly to the crest of **Parliament Hill** and its superb city views. There are three bathing ponds here, one mixed, and one each for male and female swimmers, while up on the Heath's northern fringes, **Kenwood House,** along with its famous al fresco summer concerts, also boasts great art by the likes of Vermeer and Rembrandt. And besides all that, there's an ivy tunnel leading to a terrace with idyllic pond views.

Highgate Wood is an ancient woodland and conservation area, containing a leafy walk that meanders enchantingly along a former railway line to **Crouch End,** home to a band of thespians. Down the road at Highgate Cemetery, the likes of Karl Marx, George Eliot, Christina Rossetti and Michael Faraday rest in a great entanglement of breathtaking Victorian over-decoration. The cemetery is still in use – most recent notable to be buried here is Alexander Litvinenko, the Russian dissident.

Next door you'll find **Waterlow Park,** another fine green space, which, apart from its super views, also includes decorative ponds on three levels. Lauderdale House is here, too, a 16C pile which is now an arts centre; more famously, Charles II handed over its keys to Nell Gwynn for her to use as her North London residence. Head back south from here, and **Primrose Hill** continues the theme of glorious green space: its surrounding terraces are populated by media darlings, while its vertiginous mass is another to boast a famously enviable vista.

Of a different hue altogether is **Camden Town** with its buzzy edge, courtesy of a renowned indie music scene, goths, punks, and six earthy markets selling everything from tat to exotica. Charles Dickens grew up here, and he was none too complimentary; the area still relishes its seamy underside. A scenic route out is the **Regent's Canal,** which cuts its way through the market and ambles to the east and west of the city. Up the road, the legendary Roundhouse re-opened its arty front doors in 2006, expanding further the wide range of Camden's alt scene.

One of the music world's most legendary destinations, the **Abbey Road** studios, is also in this area and, yes, it's possible to join other tourists making their way over that zebra crossing. Not far away, in Maresfield Gardens, stands a very different kind of attraction. The Freud Museum is one of the very few buildings in London to have two blue plaques. It was home to Sigmund during the last year of his life and it's where he lived with his daughter Anna (her plaque commemorates her work in child psychiatry). Inside, there's a fabulous library and his working desk. But the pivotal part of the whole house is in another corner of the study – the psychiatrist's couch!

S. Ollivier/ MICHELIN

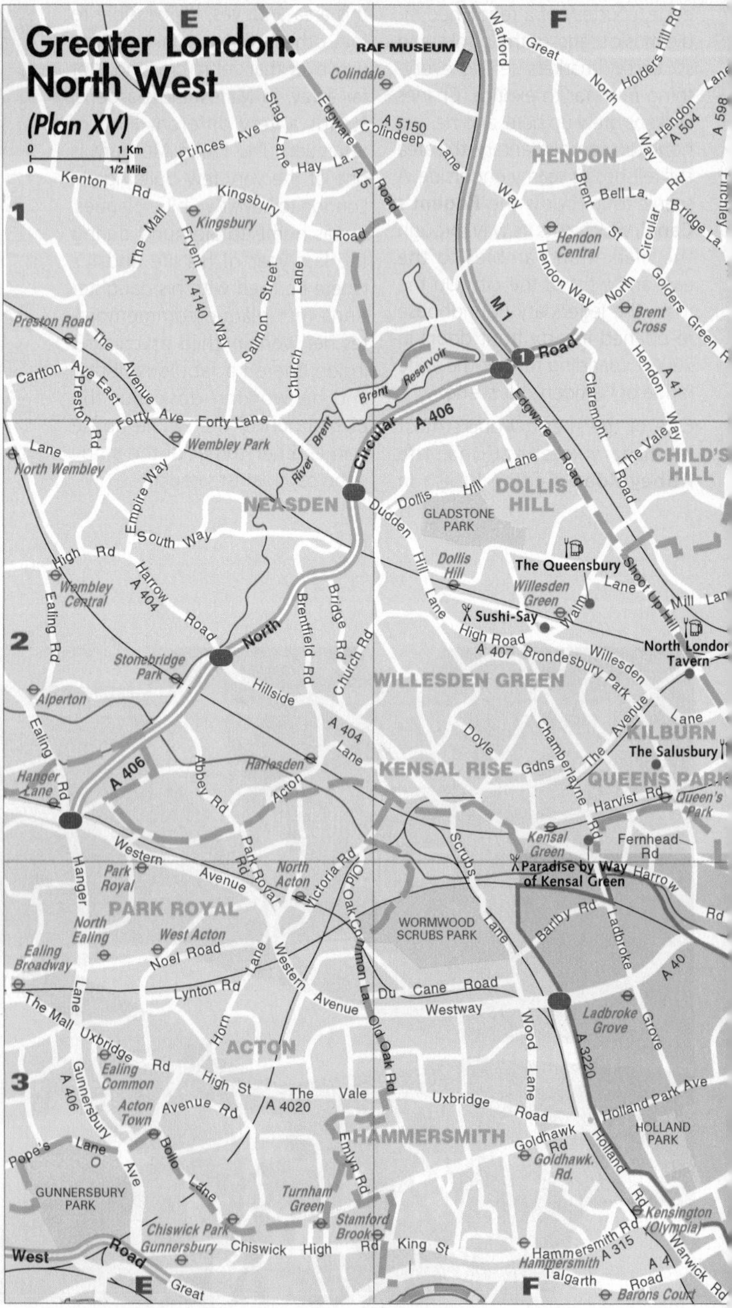
Greater London: North West
(Plan XV)
0 1 Km
0 1/2 Mile
E
F
1
2
3
RAF MUSEUM
Colindale
Kingsbury
Hendon Central
Brent Cross
HENDON
Preston Road
Wembley Park
North Wembley
NEASDEN
Brent Reservoir
River Brent
DOLLIS HILL
GLADSTONE PARK
Dollis Hill
The Queensbury
Willesden Green
Sushi-Say
North London Tavern
Wembley Central
Stonebridge Park
Alperton
WILLESDEN GREEN
KILBURN
The Salusbury
QUEENS PARK
Queen's Park
KENSAL RISE
Kensal Green
Paradise by Way of Kensal Green
Harlesden
Hanger Lane
CHILD'S HILL
North Acton
PARK ROYAL
Park Royal
North Ealing
West Acton
Ealing Broadway
WORMWOOD SCRUBS PARK
Ladbroke Grove
ACTON
Ealing Common
Acton Town
HAMMERSMITH
HOLLAND PARK
Goldhawk Rd.
Kensington (Olympia)
GUNNERSBURY PARK
Turnham Green
Stamford Brook
Chiswick Park
Gunnersbury
Hammersmith
Barons Court
M 1
A 406
A 5
A 5150
A 4140
A 404
A 407
A 41
A 504
A 598
A 40
A 3220
A 4020
A 315
A 4
North Circular Road
Edgware Road
Watford Way
Great North Way
Western Avenue
Westway
Uxbridge Road
Harrow Road
Chiswick High Rd
King St
Talgarth Road
West Road
Great

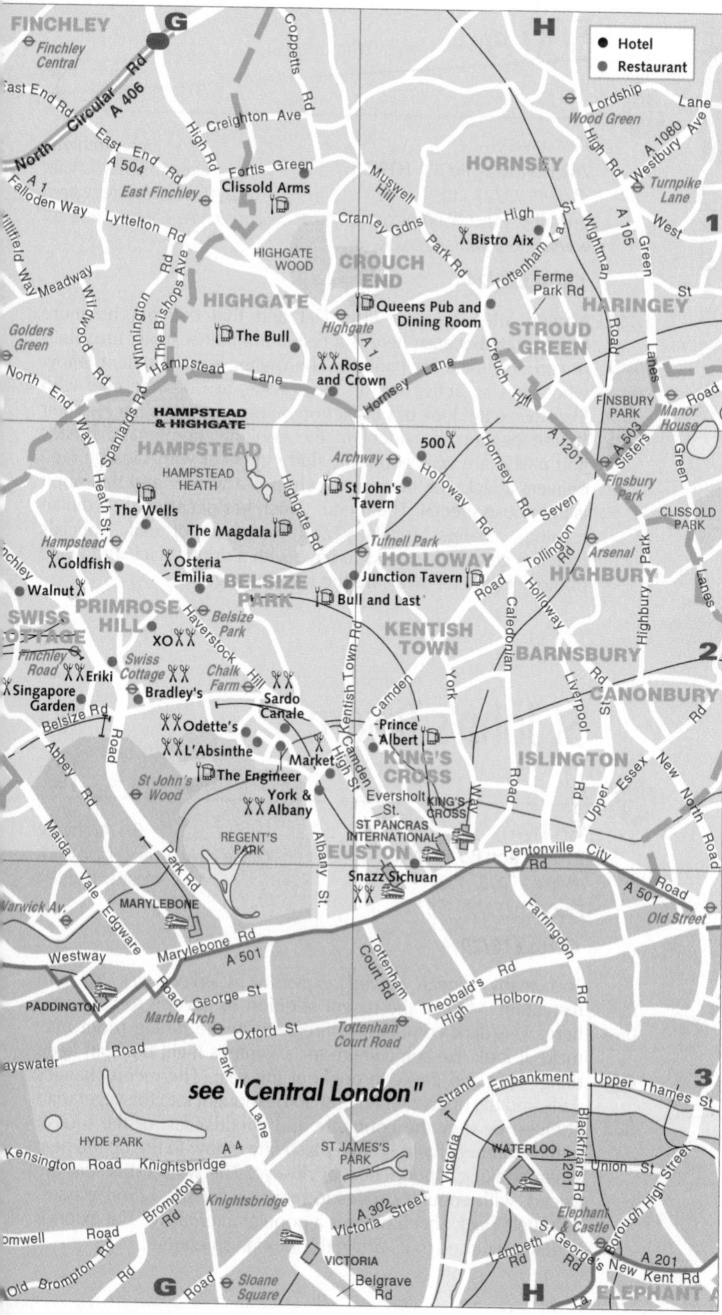
Hotel
Restaurant
G
H
1
2
3
FINCHLEY
Finchley Central
North Circular Rd
A 406
East End Rd
A 504
A 1
Falloden Way
Lyttelton Rd
East Finchley
Coppetts Rd
Creighton Ave
High Rd
Fortis Green
Clissold Arms
HIGHGATE WOOD
Muswell Hill
Cranley Gdns
Park Rd
CROUCH END
Bistro Aix
HORNSEY
Lordship Lane
Wood Green
High Rd
A 1080
Westbury Ave
Turnpike Lane
West
High St
Tottenham La.
Wightman
A 105
Green
Lanes
Ferme Park Rd
HARINGEY
STROUD GREEN
Queens Pub and Dining Room
HIGHGATE
Highgate
A 1
The Bull
Rose and Crown
Hornsey Lane
Crouch Hill
Golders Green
Meadway
Wildwood Rd
Winnington Rd
The Bishops Ave
Hampstead Lane
North End Way
Spaniards Rd
HAMPSTEAD & HIGHGATE
HAMPSTEAD
HAMPSTEAD HEATH
Highgate Rd
FINSBURY PARK
Manor House
Road
Sisters
A 503
A 1201
Finsbury Park
Green
CLISSOLD PARK
500
Archway
Holloway Rd
Hornsey Rd
Seven
St John's Tavern
Heath St.
The Wells
The Magdala
Hampstead
Goldfish
Osteria Emilia
Walnut
Tufnell Park
HOLLOWAY
Tollington Rd
Arsenal
HIGHBURY
Highbury Park
Lanes
BELSIZE PARK
Junction Tavern
Road
Bull and Last
SWISS COTTAGE
PRIMROSE HILL
Belsize Park
Haverstock Hill
XO
Kentish Town Rd
KENTISH TOWN
Holloway
Caledonian
BARNSBURY
Finchley Road
Eriki
Swiss Cottage
Chalk Farm
Singapore Garden
Bradley's
Sardo Canale
Camden
York
Liverpool Rd
St
CANONBURY
Rd
Belsize Rd
Odette's
L'Absinthe
Market
Camden High St
Prince Albert
KING'S CROSS
ISLINGTON
Abbey Rd
Road
The Engineer
St John's Wood
York & Albany
Eversholt St.
KING'S CROSS
Way
Road
Upper
Essex
New North Road
Maida Vale
REGENT'S PARK
Albany St.
ST PANCRAS INTERNATIONAL
EUSTON
Pentonville Rd
City Road
A 501
Park Rd
Snazz Sichuan
Farringdon Rd
Old Street
Warwick Av.
MARYLEBONE
Edgware
Marylebone Rd
A 501
Westway
Tottenham Court Rd
PADDINGTON
Road
George St
Theobald's Rd
Holborn
High
Marble Arch
Oxford St
Tottenham Court Road
Bayswater Road
Park Lane
see "Central London"
Strand
Embankment
Upper Thames St
HYDE PARK
A 4
ST JAMES'S PARK
Victoria
WATERLOO
A 201
Blackfriars Rd
Union St
Borough High Street
Kensington Road
Knightsbridge
Brompton Rd
Knightsbridge
A 302
Victoria Street
Elephant & Castle
Cromwell Road
Old Brompton Rd
Rd
VICTORIA
Lambeth Rd
St George's Rd
New Kent Rd
A 201
Road
Sloane Square
Belgrave Rd
La.
ELEPHANT

500

Italian

H2

Archway
782 Holloway Rd ✉ N19 3JH
✆ (020) 7272 3406
e-mail contact@500restaurant.co.uk
www.500restaurant.co.uk

⊖ Archway
Closed 2 weeks summer, 10 days Christmas, Sunday lunch and Monday – booking essential

Carte £20/24

VISA MC AE

Named after the cute little Fiat and that couldn't be more appropriate because here is a restaurant that is small, fun, well-priced and ideal for London. The owner is an ebullient fellow who takes an active role in the service, as does the chef who likes to see the look of satisfaction on his customers' faces. Their shared passion is evident in the cooking: homemade breads and pastas are very good; the fluffy gnocchi with sausage ragu delivers a kick; the tender veal chop is a winner and the rabbit is the house special. The menu, which has occasional Sardinian leanings, changes regularly and the sheet of daily specials includes great little snacks to have with a drink. Black and white photos of old Holloway are the only incongruity.

St John's Tavern

Gastropub

H2

Archway
91 Junction Rd ✉ N19 5QU
✆ (020) 7272 1587
Fax (020) 7272 1587

⊖ Archway
Closed 25-26 December and lunch Monday-Thursday

Carte £18/29

VISA MC AE

Too many diners arrived expecting Clerkenwell's St John restaurant – hence the recent addition of 'tavern' to the name here. The dark colours and fireplace in the dining room may make it look like somewhere for a winter's night but staff keep things light and perky throughout the year. The menu changes daily and the open kitchen puts some thought into the vegetarian choices, be they the courgette and cheddar tart or the squash and halloumi parcels; but they also know how to fire up the heat when cooking a pork chop or rib-eye. The wine list is sensibly priced, with enough carafes to make up for the 125ml glasses, although Black Sheep bitter is a popular alternative. The exterior is being returned to its original Victorian splendour.

Osteria Emilia

G2 — Italian X

Belsize Park

85b Fleet Road ✉ NW3 2QY

✆ (020) 7433 3317

e-mail osteriaemilia@giacobazzis.co.uk

⊖ Belsize Park

Closed 2 weeks summer, Christmas to New Year, Sunday and Monday

Carte £26/35

A/C VISA MC AE

The Giacobazzi family have run the deli across the road for 18 years so when they opened this Italian restaurant in mid 2008 there was plenty of goodwill in the neighbourhood. They hail originally from near Bologna and so the name refers to the region of Emilia-Romagna, the 'bread basket' of Italy and it is this area which informs the menu. The kitchen not only eschews the usual generic Italian fare but is also unafraid of doing things differently: expect ravioli stuffed with sea bass or saltimbocca made with rabbit rather than veal; the grilled polenta is a good way to start things off. The 44 seater restaurant is spread over two floors (ask for upstairs) and its white, bright, pared-down simplicity works well.

XO

G2 — Asian XX

Belsize Park

29 Belsize Lane ✉ NW3 5AS

✆ (020) 7433 0888

Fax (020) 7794 3474

e-mail xo@rickerrestaurants.com

www.rickerrestaurants.com/xo

⊖ Belsize Park

Closed 25-26 December and 1 January

Carte £19/36

A/C VISA MC AE

Who knew Belsize Park was so trendy? Apart from estate agents, obviously. This branch of Will Ricker's small chain of glossy pan-Asian restaurants may not be quite as frenetic as the others but it still attracts plenty of shiny happy people, many of whom are holding hands. It follows the same theme as the others: a busy front bar that serves decent cocktails, behind which is the slick, uncluttered restaurant in shades of lime. The menu trawls through most of Asia; start with some warm edamame while reading through it. Highlights include the ever-popular crispy squid and the tender and tasty Indonesian lamb rendang curry but tempura is done with too heavy a hand. Sharing is the key, especially as those who come in large parties get the booths.

Market

British

G2

Camden Town

43 Parkway ✉ NW1 7PN
(020) 7267 9700
www.marketrestaurant.co.uk

⊖ Camden Town
Closed 25 December-2 January, Sunday dinner and Bank Holidays – booking essential

Menu £10 (2 course lunch weekdays) – Carte £25/29

A/C VISA MC AE

Naming a restaurant in Camden 'Market' may open up all manner of "who's on first base?" confusion but the mere fact that a decent restaurant is doing well here is cause for celebration. The pared-down look of exposed brick walls, zinc-topped tables and old school chairs works well but it is in the cooking where the appeal lies. While there may be the occasional pasta, the best thing about the daily-changing menu is the Britishness of it all. Pre-starter nibbles, like the glorious mutton dripping on toast, hint at what's to follow. Start with salt beef salad or devilled kidneys follow up with lemon sole, Barnsley chop or a chicken and ham pie and you can finish with a treacle sponge or pear crumble. The prices are pretty decent too.

Prince Albert

Gastropub

H2

Camden Town

163 Royal College St ✉ NW1 0SG
(020) 7485 0270
Fax (020) 7713 5994
e-mail info@princealbertcamden.com
www.princealbertcamden.com

⊖ Camden Town.
booking essential

Menu £11/12 – Carte £19/32

VISA MC AE

Albert had only been Prince Consort for three years when this pub opened in 1843. In 1863 work began down the road on St. Pancras and it seems appropriate that the reopening of this Gothic Victorian masterpiece has coincided with the rebirth of the pub. The Prince Albert has kept much of its character but now comes with an appealing neighbourhood feel. The simpler lunch menu is served throughout the pub but in the evening the upstairs restaurant gets it own menu. Decent olives and homemade soda bread are on hand while choosing from a selection of satisfyingly filling dishes, where traceability is given every respect. The wine list is on the back of the menu and offers over a dozen labels by the glass and plenty of choice for under £20.

York & Albany

G2 **Modern European** XX

Camden Town

⊖ Camden Town
booking essential

127-129 Parkway ✉ NW1 7PS
✆ (020) 7388 3344
Fax (020) 7592 1603
e-mail yorkandalbany@gordonramsay.com
www.gordonramsay.com/yorkandalbany

Menu £18 (lunch) – Carte £28/41

Hard to believe that this 1820s John Nash coaching inn lay virtually derelict before Gordon Ramsay Holdings resuscitated and relaunched it. The terrific front bar offers a more civilised environment than is usually the case in Camden and leads into the restaurant at the back. Don't come expecting pub grub: the cooking here is quite neat and refined in its makeup, but without being fussy, and is designed to be enjoyed as three courses. The menu is not overly long and keeps its influences mostly within Europe. If you want to watch how it's all done then ask for a table in the basement level where you'll find the open kitchen. Service can still be a little hit and miss but the overall atmosphere and look of the place add extra appeal.

Bistro Aix

J1 **French** X

Crouch End

Closed Monday – dinner only

54 Topsfield Par, Tottenham Lane
✉ N8 8PT
✆ (020) 8340 6346
e-mail bistroaix@hotmail.co.uk
www.bistroaix.co.uk

Menu £15 (lunch and weekday dinner) – Carte £19/33

The location may be Crouch End, the chef-owner may be American but for a couple of hours this little bistro will whisk you off to the verdant French countryside. The high ceiling, mustard coloured walls, dressers, plants and mirrors all add to that rustic feel, while two specially commissioned paintings of cooks and pastoral scenes tell you this is a place run by, and for, those with a genuine love of food. Francophiles will find plenty of contentment in the vast majority of the menu, which features all the favourites from classic onion soup or seared foie gras to steak frites or rack of lamb, but there are other dishes whose origins owe more to Italian cooking. Look out for the good value weekday set menu.

The Queens Pub and Dining Room

Gastropub

H1

Crouch End

26 Broadway Par ✉ N8 9DE
✆ (020) 8340 2031
e-mail queens@foodandfuel.co.uk
www.thequeenscrouchend.co.uk

Carte approx. £25

VISA MC AE

It would be hard to find a more striking example of Victoriana than The Queens Pub and Dining Room. From the original mahogany panelling to the beautiful stained glass windows and ornate ceiling, this pub has it all. The dining room is particularly stunning – ask for tables 105 or 106 on the raised section. The open kitchen recognises that some will only want classic pub food in this environment – so you'll find beef and mushroom pie, rib-eye, plaice goujons and various sausages – while others want something slightly more ambitious, hence the likes of risotto, plates of smoked meats, sea bass and assorted choices of a more Mediterranean persuasion. Selected dishes are highlighted to form part of the affordable 'This week we love…' menu.

Bull and Last

Gastropub

G2

Dartmouth Park

168 Highgate Road
✉ NW5 1QS
✆ (020) 7267 3641
e-mail info@thebullandlast.co.uk

⊖ Tufnell Park.
Closed 25 December – booking essential

Carte £26/32

VISA MC

You'll be thankful that Parliament Hill is so close because you'll need the exercise – portions at the reinvigorated Bull and Last are man-sized and that man was clearly hungry. It was taken over in 2008 by the team behind Putney's Prince of Wales and they've kept plenty of character. It's bright and breezy and hugely popular so book first. Suppliers are name-checked on boards behind the bar which tells you they take their food seriously. Animals are taken whole and butchered accordingly so expect lots of terrines and homemade charcuterie, along with everything from oysters to smoked eel; the menu can change twice a day depending on available produce. There's an upstairs room used at weekends that's like a taxidermist's showroom.

Snazz Sichuan

H2-3

Chinese XX

Euston

37 Chalton St ✉ NW1 1JD
✆ (020) 7388 0808
www.newchinaclub.co.uk

⊖ Euston

Carte £10/40

VISA MC AE

The Sichuan Province in the southwest of China is known for its foggy conditions and rare sightings of the sun. To compensate for this lack of heat from the big yellow orb, Sichuan cooking provides its own heat in the form of the Sichuan pepper: a fierce and fiery little number. Pork is another speciality and these two elements form a large part of the menu here which is simply split between cold and hot dishes: hot in every sense. Stir-fry is the favoured form of cooking and the meal traditionally ends in rice - so ask if you want it earlier. Window seats are the best, loudness and laughter are positively encouraged and the restaurant virtually doubles as the Sichuan tourist board as it also houses a gallery and traditional tea room.

Clissold Arms

G1

Gastropub

Fortis Green

Fortis Green Rd ✉ N2 9HR
✆ (020) 8444 4224
e-mail ianshepherd-clissoldarms@btconnect.com
www.jobo-developments.com

⊖ East Finchley.
Closed 1 January

Carte £21/34

VISA MC

The Clissold Arms reputedly played host to The Kinks' first gig – conveniently so, as Ray Davies once lived across the street. The majority of the space is now given over to those eating – drinkers are buffeted into the front section. The menu offers a daily-changing list of interesting dishes; terrines are something of a house speciality, as are the whole sea bass, the ribs of beef and the 32-day aged steaks. Come for lunch and you'll encounter more typical pub grub such as steak and ale pie, alongside the potted crab. Cooking is soundly done and portions are suitably generous. The staff just about keep their smiles when it gets busy, which it does frequently so it's prudent to book ahead. There's a terrace for lazing on a sunny afternoon.

Goldfish

Asian

G3

Hampstead ⊖ Hampstead

82 Hampstead High St. ✉ NW3 1RE Closed 24-25 December

✆ (020) 7794 6666

www.goldfish-restaurant.co.uk

Menu £16 (lunch) – Carte £15/30

VISA MC AE

Hampstead has seen quite a few restaurants come and go over the years; Goldfish is the latest to try its luck and may yet buck the trend and prove to be a stayer. This sweet place calls its cooking 'modern Chinese' but really the kitchen looks to influences from across Asia. The à la carte menu is lengthy but highlights include anything involving crab, the fish dishes and some of the chef's own creations, such as the very rich Mocha ribs. Prices at lunch are very reasonable, especially the dim sum which pulls in plenty of punters at weekends. The place is divided into three little rooms which all have their own style. Staff have their hearts in the right place and they remember their regulars, of whom there are growing numbers.

The Magdala

Gastropub

G2

Hampstead ⊖ Belsize Park.

2A South Hill Park ✉ NW3 2SB

✆ (020) 7435 2503

Fax (020) 7435 6167

e-mail themagdala@hotmail.co.uk

www.the-magdala.com

Carte £19/28

VISA MC

The Magdala has its place in history as it was outside this pub where Ruth Ellis, the last woman to be hanged in Britain, shot her paramour in 1955. To its credit, the pub doesn't let this episode define it but instead concentrates on its community feel, general air of friendliness and decent food. The owner worked here for several years before buying it in 2007 and she certainly keeps her eye on the ball. The concise but balanced menu keeps its heart and influences mostly within the British Isles. There are also interesting snacks and sharing plates, like antipasti, on the supplementary blackboard. Wisely, no great risks are taken in preparation; this is about decent pub food. The menu lengthens at weekends when the upstairs room comes into play.

The Wells

G2 Gastropub

Hampstead ⊖ Hampstead.
30 Well Walk ✉ NW3 1BX
✆ (020) 7794 3785
Fax (020) 7794 6817
e-mail info@thewellshampstead.co.uk
www.thewellshampstead.co.uk

Carte £20/33

London pubs can be loud, hysterical affairs but The Wells is a more sober beast, as one would expect from a pub in the middle of Hampstead village. Being so near the Heath makes it feel like a country pub but, then again, it's equally close to the High Street which adds a dose of urban poise. Downstairs is usually pretty busy but head up to the neat, first floor dining room that's divided into three, with the brightest - the blue room - looking down over the spring blossom. The cooking reflects the pub: it's hearty but with a sophisticated finish. You'll find duck confit or rump of lamb, scallops and wood pigeon but also veggie shepherd's pie and Sunday roasts. Puddings are big and they do a good apple and rhubarb crumble.

Rose and Crown

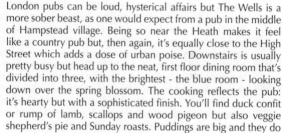

G1 Modern European XX

Highgate ⊖ Archway
86 Highgate St ✉ N6 5HX
✆ (020) 8340 0770
e-mail jess@roseandcrownhighate.co.uk
www.roseandcrownhighgate.co.uk

Closed Sunday dinner and Monday lunch

Menu £20 (dinner) – Carte £21/30

An attractive white façade, illuminated at night, highlights what was once a pub but is now most definitely a restaurant. There's some 18C cornicing still there but the theme is now contemporary and all black and white. The bar remains but is now where you sit deliberating over the menu and the dining tables are smartly laid with linen. This may all give the impression of a formal restaurant but in fact the atmosphere is relaxed and inclusive, thanks largely to the confident and genial staff. The influences on the kitchen are mostly European, although the original touches are not quite as daring as they suggest. Overall the cooking is soundly executed and the prices more than fair, especially on the weekly changing set menu.

The Bull

G1

Gastropub

Highgate
13 North Hill ✉ N6 4AB
✆ (0845) 456 5033
e-mail info@inthebull.biz
www.themeredithgroup.co.uk

⊖ Highgate.
Closed Monday in winter

Menu £15 – Carte £21/30

If the first thing you notice is a drinks trolley then you know you're not in your, or anyone else's, local boozer. It's all about the food here, which is modern European with a dominant French gene running through it. Dishes are seasonally pertinent and the construction, ingredients and execution are aimed more at the 'serious' end of the dining pub scale, although there is a good value lunch menu available. The home-baked breads are excellent. Those who have a boat they wish to push out will find their task aided by the wine list, which does also offer plenty of affordable bottles. Weekends welcome more of a family atmosphere, with brunch offered. The room is bright, service is on the ball and Thursday night is music night.

VISA
MC
AE

Paradise by way of Kensal Green

F2

Gastropub

Kensal Green
19 Kilburn Lane ✉ W10 4AE
✆ (020) 8969 0098
e-mail shelley@thecolumbogroup.com
www.theparadise.co.uk

⊖ Kensal Green.
Closed August bank holiday

Menu £15/30 – Carte £24/31

A/C

"For there is good news yet to hear and fine things to be seen / before we go to Paradise by way of Kensal Green", so ended a poem by G.K.Chesterton; writer, philosopher, theologian and vegetarian-loather. The pub reminds us that there's more to the local area than a cemetery. It's appealingly bohemian, with mismatched furniture, Murano chandeliers, old portraits and even the odd birdcage. Burlesque shows, comedy and live music all happen upstairs. The bar menu ranges from Welsh rarebit to plates of charcuterie but the main menu appears in the evening in the restaurant. Mostly British ingredients come with enduring partners, like asparagus with butter, York ham with Cumberland sauce and lemon sole with Jersey Royals. Portions are man-sized.

VISA
MC

North London Tavern

Gastropub

F2

Kilburn

375 Kilburn High Rd
NW6 7QB
(020) 7625 6634
e-mail northlondontavern@realpubs.co.uk
www.realpubs.co.uk

Kilburn.
Closed 25 December, lunch 26 December and 1 January and Monday

Carte £19/29

VISA MC

The dining room is separated from the bar by a red curtain and glass panelling and, like the bar, it can quickly fill up. Old church seats, mismatched tables, high ceilings and chandeliers add a little gothic character. Lunch is a simpler affair in the bar but at dinner the printed menu, which is rather needlessly repeated verbatim on a large blackboard, offers a comprehensive selection of gastropub greatest hits, from belly pork to rib-eye, tuna niçoise to apple crumble, plus a couple of veggie options. The crusty bread is terrific and each dish arrives fully garnished and appetisingly presented on big white plates. There's a whole roast beast at weekends and the wine list keeps things mostly under £20.

L'Absinthe

French

G2

Primrose Hill

40 Chalcot Road NW18LS
(020) 7483 4848
e-mail info@labsinthe.co.uk

Chalk Farm
Closed 2 weeks Christmas, August and Monday

Menu £13 (weekday lunch) – Carte £19/28

A/C VISA MC AE

40 Chalcot Road has long been Primrose Hill's Bermuda Triangle: many restaurants have tried this corner and all have failed. The current owner gave many years of his life to Marco Pierre White as a manager so who would begrudge him success with his own place, especially when he's clearly so passionate? He's created your classic French bistro, right down to the Belle Epoque posters, tightly packed little tables and cries of bonjour! The menu also ticks all the right boxes, from onion soup and steak frites, Lyonnais salad to duck confit. The place is jumping, lunch is a steal and the exclusively French wine list comes with a commendable pricing structure, with corkage charged on the retail price. Whisper it, but maybe this time…

The Engineer

G2 **Gastropub**

Primrose Hill

⊖ Chalk Farm.

65 Gloucester Ave ✉ NW1 8JH
✆ (020) 7722 0950
Fax (020) 7483 0592
e-mail info@the-engineer.com
www.the-engineer.com

Carte £20/35

The Engineer was at the vanguard of London's gastropub movement and remains a classic example of the genre. The Grade II listed pub, with its stuccoed Italianate façade, dates from around 1850. The restaurant is wrapped around the front bar and the whole place appears to be in a permanent state of noisy excitement. The staff are young and enthusiastic although they can occasionally get stretched but fortunately customers never appear to be in any hurry either. The kitchen shows a healthy respect for the provenance of its meats and balances more modern influences with pub favourites; it's always worth ordering a bowl of those fabulous Baker fries on the side. Dishes come in fairly strapping proportions and flavours have plenty of oomph.

VISA · MC

Odette's

G2 **Modern European**

Primrose Hill

⊖ Chalk Farm
Closed Christmas and Monday

130 Regent's Park Rd ✉ NW1 8XL
✆ (020) 7586 8569
Fax (020) 7586 8362
e-mail info@odettesprimrosehill.com
www.odettesprimrosehill.com

Menu £18 (lunch) – Carte £31/41

Bryn Williams, who rose to prominence through his appearance on the 'Great British Menu' TV programme, took over the reigns here in Primrose Hill back in 2008. He had his work cut out, as this venerable Primrose institution has often been perceived locally as being a bit too smart and expensive, hence he's made some price adjustments. His menu does contain many ingredients from his Welsh homeland, such as the beef and the cheeses, but he also knows those locals have sophisticated tastes so you'll find plenty of game, some offal and a degree of complexity to some of the dishes. Decoratively, the restaurant remains awash with yellow and there's a nice enclosed terrace at the back. Service sometimes struggles to get the tone right.

A/C · VISA · MC · AE

Sardo Canale

G2 **Italian** XX

Primrose Hill

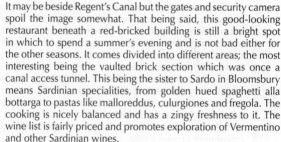

42 Gloucester Ave ✉ NW1 8JD
✆ (020) 7722 2800
Fax (020) 7722 0802
e-mail info@sardocanale.com
www.sardocanale.com

⊖ Chalk Farm
Closed Christmas and Monday

Menu £13 (lunch) – Carte £25/33

It may be beside Regent's Canal but the gates and security camera spoil the image somewhat. That being said, this good-looking restaurant beneath a red-bricked building is still a bright spot in which to spend a summer's evening and is not bad either for the other seasons. It comes divided into different areas; the most interesting being the vaulted brick section which was once a canal access tunnel. This being the sister to Sardo in Bloomsbury means Sardinian specialities, from golden hued spaghetti alla bottarga to pastas like malloreddus, culurgiones and fregola. The cooking is nicely balanced and has a zingy freshness to it. The wine list is fairly priced and promotes exploration of Vermentino and other Sardinian wines.

The Salusbury

F2 **Gastropub**

Queens Park

50-52 Salusbury Road ✉ NW6 6NN
✆ (020) 7328 3286
e-mail thesalusburypub@btconnect.com

⊖ Queens Park.
Closed 25-26 December,
1 January and Monday lunch

Menu £22/25

The Salusbury is a pleasingly down-to-earth pub; one side is for drinking, the other hosts a laid-back dining room. The Italian menu is a model of understatement and it's not until the food arrives that one realises how seriously this pub takes its cooking. There's plenty of choice, including about five pasta dishes that can be taken as starters or main courses. Dishes are as generous in size as they are in flavour. The crisp Sardinian guttiau bread comes with aubergine and pecorino and is a great way of starting proceedings; the pappardelle with the tender duck ragu is very tasty; an impressive array of fish go into the fritto misto and the tiramisu would shame many a smart Italian restaurant. The wine list offers plenty for under £20.

Bradley's

G2 **Modern European** XX

Swiss Cottage
25 Winchester Rd ✉ NW3 3NR
(020) 7722 3457
Fax (020) 7435 1392
e-mail bradleysnw3@btinternet.com
www.bradleysnw3.co.uk

⊖ Swiss Cottage
Closed 25 December, Easter, Saturday lunch and Sunday dinner

Menu £17/23 – Carte £27/36

A/C, VISA, MC, AE

Bradley's has matured nicely over the years and the rejuvenated Hampstead Theatre has given it an extra shot in the arm. The cooking is uncomplicated and nimble; it's grounded in France but with ingredients from across the British Isles, whether that's crab from Dorset, beef from Orkney or a daily fish delivery from Looe. The fixed price menu, run alongside the more extensive à la carte, represents excellent value, as does the wine list which offers the majority of bottles under £30. Service is well marshalled by the owner and the kitchen dispatches dishes promptly, which is sensible when the theatre crowd form a major part of the business. The room is light and open, although sound can bounce around a little.

Eriki

G2 **Indian** XX

Swiss Cottage
4-6 Northways Parade,
Finchley Rd ✉ NW3 5EN
(020) 7722 0606
Fax (020) 7722 8866
e-mail info@eriki.co.uk
www.eriki.co.uk

⊖ Swiss Cottage
Closed 25-26 December, 1 January, Saturday lunch and Bank Holidays

Carte £20/30

A/C, VISA, MC, AE

Eriki eschews tired old standards and instead offers a diverse and contrasting gastronomic tour around all parts of India, from Goan curries to Punjabi-style prawns, Hariyali scallops to Lucknowi lamb. The cooking is fresh and invigorating; vegetarians will be in clover and the breads are good. The cutlery is imported from Rajasthan and the carved tables and heavy chairs add a sense of permanence. The staff are a pleasant bunch, although this vibrantly coloured restaurant can go from quiet to full in a matter of moments so get your order in quickly. Eriki is so much more than your typical neighbourhood Indian restaurant, a fact not lost on its many regulars. The only negative is the less than inspiring view of drab old Finchley Road.

Singapore Garden

G2 — Asian XX

Swiss Cottage

83 Fairfax Road ✉ NW6 4DY
✆ (020) 7328 5314
Fax (020) 7624 0656
www.singaporegarden.co.uk

⊖ Swiss Cottage
Closed Christmas

Menu £20/28 – Carte £27/46

A/C VISA MC AE

Singapore Garden has been a stalwart of Swiss Cottage for many a year but a relatively recent refurbishment and relaunch has widened its appeal even further. The room is now bright and smart, although the tables for two are set very close together. Service has an endearing enthusiasm. The menu is the usual lengthy affair but just ignore the more generic dishes and head to the back page for the Singaporean and Malaysian specialities for here is where the kitchen's expertise lies. These dishes are supplemented by a list of seasonal specials so, whether you start with some roti canai with curry, try a laksa, a ho jien omelette or a vibrant rojak, you'll find cooking full of zingy freshness and vitality.

Junction Tavern

G2 — Gastropub

Tufnell Park

101 Fortess Rd ✉ NW5 1AG
✆ (020) 7485 9400
Fax (020) 7485 9401
www.junctiontavern.co.uk

⊖ Tufnell Park.
Closed 24-26 December and 1 January

Carte £21/27

VISA MC

Tufnell Park has always appealed to young professionals because, along with its Victorian terraces, it has a belligerent edge to add a little credibility. The Junction Tavern fits in well. The menu changes daily and portion size has been slightly reduced to give more balance to the menu as a whole; the cooking remains unfussy and relies on good flavours. There's plenty of choice, from light summer dishes such as grilled sardines and seared tuna to the more robust rib-eye and pork belly. Staff are a chatty bunch who know their beers – they offer weekly changing guest beers and hold a popular beer festival; the 'pie and a pint' choice remains a favourite. Commendably, they also offer tap water without being prompted.

Walnut

Traditional

G2

West Hampstead

⊖ West Hampstead
Closed Monday – dinner only

280 West End Lane, Fortune Green
✉ NW6 1LJ
✆ (020) 7794 7772
e-mail info@walnutwalnut.com
www.walnutwalnut.com

Carte £25/34

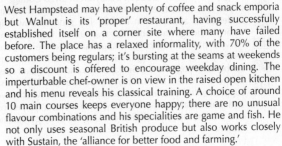

West Hampstead may have plenty of coffee and snack emporia but Walnut is its 'proper' restaurant, having successfully established itself on a corner site where many have failed before. The place has a relaxed informality, with 70% of the customers being regulars; it's bursting at the seams at weekends so a discount is offered to encourage weekday dining. The imperturbable chef-owner is on view in the raised open kitchen and his menu reveals his classical training. A choice of around 10 main courses keeps everyone happy; there are no unusual flavour combinations and his specialities are game and fish. He not only uses seasonal British produce but also works closely with Sustain, the 'alliance for better food and farming.'

The Queensbury

Gastropub

F2

Willesden Green

⊖ Willesden Green.

110 Walm Lane ✉ NW2 4RS
✆ (020) 8452 0171
e-mail info@thequeensbury.net
www.thequeensbury.net

Carte £19/25

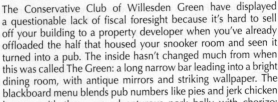

The Conservative Club of Willesden Green have displayed a questionable lack of fiscal foresight because it's hard to sell off your building to a property developer when you've already offloaded the half that housed your snooker room and seen it turned into a pub. The inside hasn't changed much from when this was called The Green: a long narrow bar leading into a bright dining room, with antique mirrors and striking wallpaper. The blackboard menu blends pub numbers like pies and jerk chicken burgers with the more adventurous pork belly with chorizo; Parma ham with celeriac remoulade comes on a wooden board and desserts appear to be a strength of the kitchen. There's brunch at weekends and further snacky choices available in the bar.

Sushi-Say

F2 — Japanese

Willesden Green

33B Walm Lane ✉ NW2 5SH
☎ (020) 8459 2971
Fax (020) 8907 3229

⊖ Willesden Green
Closed 25-26 December, 1 January, 2 weeks March-April, 1 week August, Monday and Tuesday following Bank Holiday – dinner only

Menu £17/37
Carte £16/40

VISA MC

One of the delights of Willesden Green must surely be this long-standing Japanese restaurant which has never looked back since being revamped back in 2007 and which is nearly always full. As the name suggests, sushi is the reason why many come and a seat at the counter, watching owner Mr Shimizu's expertise with his knife, is the place to be; if you're tempted to supplement your selection with some creamy uni or rich, warmed unagi then just ask him and he'll oblige. If you prefer other styles of Japanese cookery then you'll find plenty of choice; it's often worth considering the monthly specials menu; the yakitori is particularly good and there's a well-priced selection of sake and shochu. Mrs Shimizu leads her team with alacrity and efficiency.

North-East London

If northwest London is renowned for its leafy acres, then the area to its immediate east has a more urban, brick-built appeal. Which has meant, over the last decade or so, a wholesale rebranding exercise for some of its traditionally shady localities. A generation ago it would have been beyond the remit of even the most inventive estate agent to sell the charms of Islington, Hackney or Bethnal Green. But then along came Damien Hirst, Tracey Emin et al, and before you could say 'cow in formaldehyde' the area's cachet had rocketed.

Shoreditch and **Hoxton** are the pivotal points of the region's hip makeover. Their cobbled brick streets and shabby industrial remnants were like heavenly manna to the artists and designers who started to colonise the old warehouses twenty years ago. A fashionable crowd soon followed in their footsteps, and nowadays the area around **Hoxton Square** positively teems with clubs, bars and galleries. Latest must-see space is the year-old Rivington Place, a terrific gallery that highlights visual arts from around the world. Nearby are Deluxe (digital installations), AOP (photographic shows) and Hales (Spencer Tunick's acres of gooseflesh… etc).

Before the area was ever trendy, there was the Geffrye Museum. A short stroll up Hoxton's **Kingsland Road,** it's a jewel of a place, set in elegant 18C almshouses, and depicting English middle-class interiors from 1600 to the present day. Right behind it is St. Mary's Secret Garden, a little oasis that manages to include much diversity including a separate woodland and herb area, all in less than an acre. At the southern end of the area, in Folgate Street, Dennis Severs' House is an original Huguenot home that recreates 18 and 19C life in an original way – cooking smells linger, hearth and candles burn, giving you the impression the owners have only just left the place. Upstairs the beds remain unmade: did a certain local artist pick up any ideas here?

When the Regent's Canal was built in the early 19C, **Islington's** fortunes nose-dived, for it was accompanied by the arrival of slums and over-crowding. But the once-idyllic village managed to hold onto its Georgian squares and handsome Victorian terraces through the rough times, and when these were gentrified a few years ago, the area ushered in a revival. **Camden Passage** has long been famed for its quirky antique emporiums, while the slinky Business Design Centre is a flagship of the modern Islington. Cultural icons established themselves around the Upper Street area and these have gone from strength to strength. The **Almeida** Theatre has a habit of hitting the production jackpot with its history of world premieres, while the King's Head has earned itself a reputation for raucous scene-stealing; set up in the seventies, it's also London's very first theatre-pub. Nearby, the Screen on the Green boasts a wonderful old-fashioned neon billboard.

Even in the 'bad old days', Islington drew in famous names, and at Regency smart **Canonbury Square** are the one-time homes of Evelyn Waugh (no.17A) and George Orwell (no.27). These days it houses the Estorick Collection of Modern Italian Art; come here to see fine futuristic paintings in a Georgian villa. To put the history of the area in a proper context, head to St. John Street, south of the City Road, where the Islington Museum's shiny new headquarters tells the story of a colourful and multi-layered past.

Further up the A10, you come to **Dalston,** a bit like the Islington of old but with the buzzy Ridley Road market and a vibrant all-night scene including the blistering Vortex Jazz Club just off Kingsland Road. A little further north is **Stoke Newington,** referred to, a bit unkindly, as the poor man's Islington. Its pride and joy is Church Street, which not only features some characterful bookshops and eye-catching boutiques, but also lays claim to Abney Park Cemetery, an enchanting old place with a wildlife-rich nature reserve.

C. Eymenier / MICHELIN

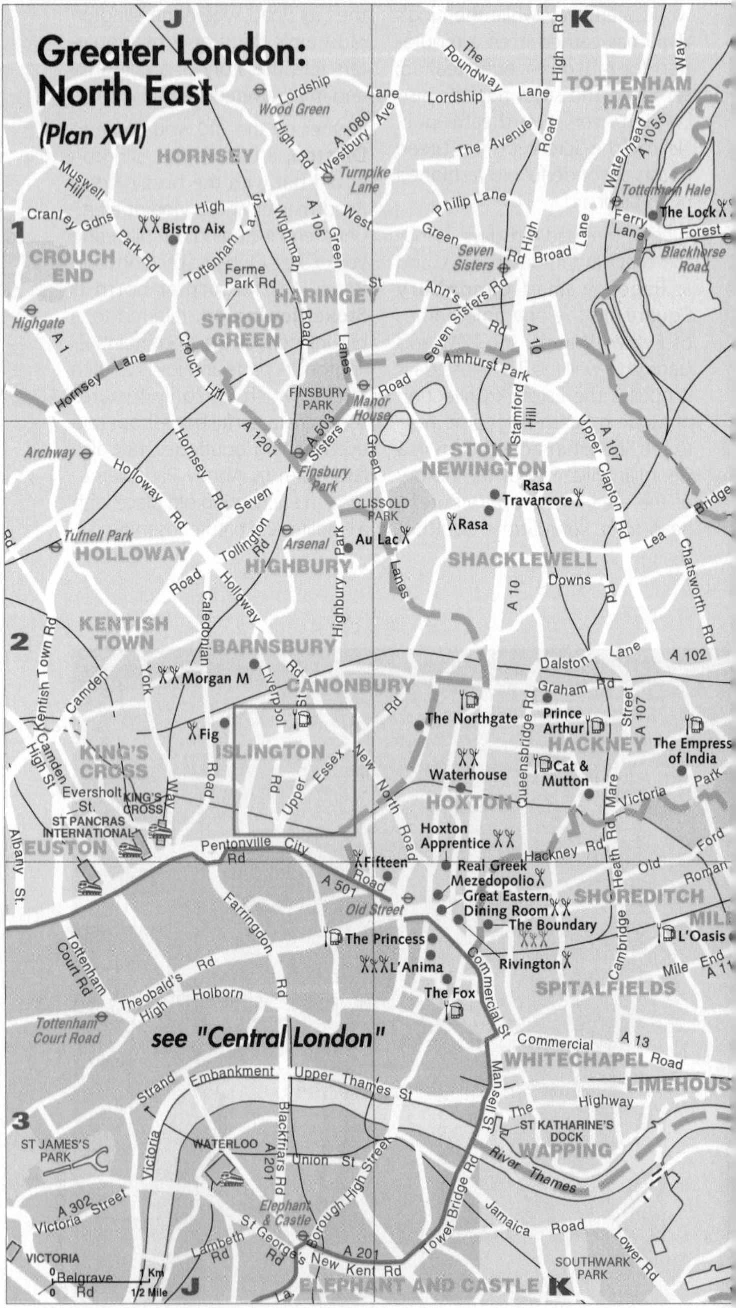
Greater London: North East
(Plan XVI)
HORNSEY
CROUCH END
Highgate
STROUD GREEN
HARINGEY
FINSBURY PARK
Manor House
Finsbury Park
Archway
Tufnell Park
HOLLOWAY
Arsenal
HIGHBURY
KENTISH TOWN
BARNSBURY
CANONBURY
KING'S CROSS
ISLINGTON
EUSTON
ST PANCRAS INTERNATIONAL
KING'S CROSS
TOTTENHAM HALE
Tottenham Hale
Seven Sisters
Blackhorse Road
Wood Green
Turnpike Lane
STOKE NEWINGTON
CLISSOLD PARK
SHACKLEWELL
HACKNEY
HOXTON
SHOREDITCH
Old Street
SPITALFIELDS
WHITECHAPEL
LIMEHOUS
WAPPING
ST KATHARINE'S DOCK
Tottenham Court Road
see "Central London"
WATERLOO
Elephant & Castle
ELEPHANT AND CASTLE
ST JAMES'S PARK
VICTORIA
SOUTHWARK PARK
River Thames
Bistro Aix
The Lock
Rasa Travancore
Rasa
Au Lac
Morgan M
Fig
The Northgate
Prince Arthur
The Empress of India
Waterhouse
Cat & Mutton
Hoxton Apprentice
Fifteen
Real Greek Mezedopolio
Great Eastern Dining Room
The Boundary
The Princess
L'Anima
Rivington
The Fox
L'Oasis
1 Km
1/2 Mile

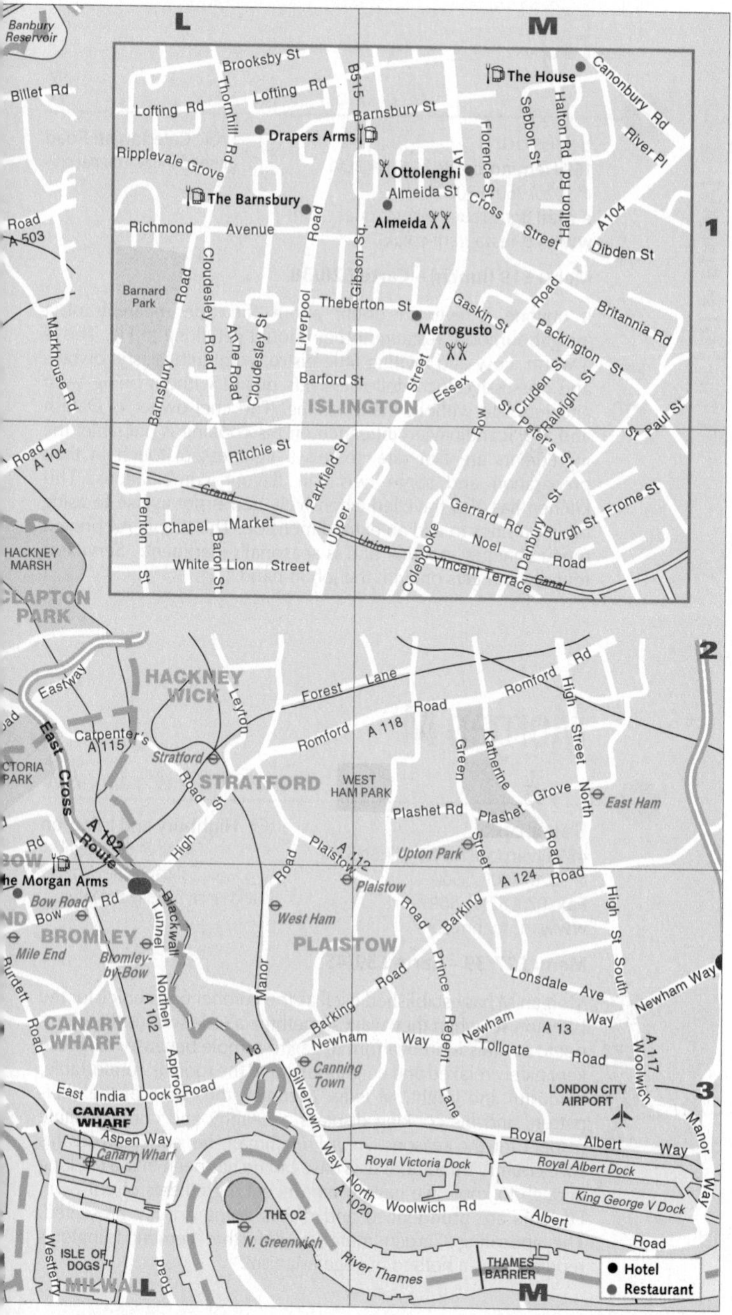

L
M
The House
Drapers Arms
Ottolenghi
The Barnsbury
Almeida
Metrogusto
ISLINGTON
HACKNEY MARSH
CLAPTON PARK
HACKNEY WICK
STRATFORD
WEST HAM PARK
PLAISTOW
BROMLEY
CANARY WHARF
The Morgan Arms
LONDON CITY AIRPORT
Royal Victoria Dock
Royal Albert Dock
King George V Dock
THE O2
THAMES BARRIER
River Thames
ISLE OF DOGS
MILWALL
1
2
3
Hotel
Restaurant

Fig

J2 **Modern European**

Barnsbury
169 Hemingford Rd ✉ N1 1DA
✆ (020) 7609 3009
e-mail figrestaurant@btconnect.com
www.fig-restaurant.co.uk

⊖ Caledonian Road
Closed Sunday – dinner only

Menu £19 (lunch) – Carte £28/38

If anyone is ever in doubt about the true meaning of a 'neighbourhood' restaurant they should get along to Fig. This is a warm, cosy and inviting little bistro, with enthusiastic owners and possessive local followers. It's quaint without being twee and intimate without being stifling. The chef-owner is Danish and the Scandinavian influence on his cooking is palpable: the ingredients are first rate, there's a lightness of touch in their preparation and some twists in flavour combinations. This kitchen has also travelled extensively and is not averse to using other cuisines to add an extra dimension. The simple A4 printed menu changes monthly and is seasonally pertinent. Service is friendly and gets on with the job in hand.

Morgan M

J2 **French**

Barnsbury
489 Liverpool Rd ✉ N7 8NS
✆ (020) 7609 3560
Fax (020) 8292 5699
www.morganm.com

⊖ Highbury and Islington
Closed 24-30 December, Sunday dinner, Monday and lunch Tuesday and Saturday

Menu £27/39 – Carte £39/45

Morgan M has established itself as the number one choice for the Islington set when they want something a little serious. But that's not to say this is an overformal gastro-temple because things are kept nicely relaxed and neighbourly and the room is comfortable, colourful and bright. M is for Meunier, the name of the chef-patron, and his cooking displays a healthy and commendable respect for the seasons. As a Frenchman, his cooking uses his own country's traditions as a base but he has been in the UK long enough to know we have some decent ingredients of our own. Flavours are pronounced and dishes come artfully presented. The appealing Garden menus will further cement Islington's reputation as a hotbed of vegetarianism.

The Morgan Arms

L3 Gastropub

Bow

43 Morgan St ✉ E3 5AA
(020) 8980 6389
e-mail themorgan@geronimo-inns.co.uk
www.geronimo-inns.co.uk

⊖ Bow Road.
Closed 25-26 December – bookings not accepted

Carte £20/31

A/C VISA AE

This former boozer's clever makeover respects its heritage while simultaneously bringing it up to date. The bar's always busy while the dining area is more subdued. You'll find the kitchen keeps its influences mostly within Europe but also understands just what sort of food works well in a pub. The daily-changing menu usually features pasta in some form and staples like whitebait - which come devilled in this instance - assorted tarts and the perennial favourite, fishcakes accompanied by a poached egg. What's more, prices are kept at realistic levels which, together with their policy of not taking bookings, makes this pub appealing to those who live nearby and who like a little spontaneity in their lives.

The House

M1 Gastropub

Canonbury

63-69 Canonbury Rd ✉ N1 2DG
(020) 7704 7410
Fax (020) 7704 9388
e-mail info@inthehouse.biz
www.themeredithgroup.co.uk

⊖ Highbury and Islington.
Closed Monday lunch

Menu £15 (lunch) – Carte £26/35

VISA AE

The House is one of the smarter pubs around; indeed, with its attractive terrace it can look more like a restaurant from the outside but step inside and you'll find sufficient numbers of regulars relaxing around the bar exuding a general sense of localness. Even the eating area towards the rear has that reassuringly hotchpotch feel and, while the service is clearly on the button, it is also friendly and chatty. The menu covers all corners, from the classics like shepherd's pie and apple crumble to other more elaborate choices such as sea bass with artichoke purée and peppered venison with spiced red cabbage. Cooking is clean, crisp and confident and there's an emphasis on good quality, organic ingredients.

Cat & Mutton

British

K2

Hackney
76 Broadway Market ✉ E8 4QJ
(020) 7254 5599
Fax (020) 7986 1444
e-mail catandmutton@yahoo.co.uk
www.catandmutton.co.uk

⊖ Bethnal Green.
Closed 25-26 December, 1 January and Monday lunch

Carte £22/60

VISA MC AE

The Cat and Mutton is your typical early Victorian corner pub with a bona fide London feel; it is a drinking pub that does decent food, rather than vice versa. It can take a hammering with the after-work crowd and has a rough and ready vibe, with exposed brick walls and a resolute lack of decorative embellishment. Such uncompromising surroundings make it an unlikely spot in which to find good food but that's exactly what The Cat and Mutton delivers, although it's still not the place for a romantic dinner à deux. The blackboard offers around five choices per course, which could include anything from chilli squid to a steak. Using some ingredients garnered from the local market, the cooking is full-bodied and satisfying.

The Empress of India

Gastropub

K2

Hackney
130 Lauriston Rd, Victoria Park ✉ E9 7LH
(020) 8533 5123
Fax (020) 7404 2250
www.theempressofindia.com

⊖ Mile End.
Closed 25 December

Carte £19/29

VISA MC AE

The building dates from the 1880s and has enjoyed various past incarnations as a nightclub and a floristry training school. Now a smart, open-plan pub with the emphasis firmly on dining, it's brightly lit with high ceilings, mosaic flooring, red leather banquettes and eye-catching murals picturing Indian scenes. The seasonally-evolving menu is classically based with some Mediterranean influences, and blends the robust with the more refined. The patrons use rare breeds for their meats and poultry, and these can often be temptingly seen and smelt cooking on the rotisserie. It's also open all day, with the Empress Afternoon tea offering an interesting selection of leaf teas. Kids have their own menu which they can colour in.

Prince Arthur

K2 **Gastropub**

Hackney
95 Forest Rd ✉ E8 3BH
✆ (020) 7249 9996
Fax (020) 7249 7074
e-mail info@theprincearthurlondonfields.com
www.theprincearthurlondonfields.com

⊖ Bethnal Green.
Closed 25-26 December, Monday-Tuesday lunch

Carte £20/27

VISA MC

The Prince Arthur is less gastropub, more your favourite little local serving proper pub grub. Much of the old character remains but the owners, brothers Tom & Ed Martin, have added some ironic touches, from stuffed animals to a collection of saucy seaside postcards. It's also for locals, with the occasional corduroyed Martin Amis enthusiast thrown in. The menu is appealingly unaffected. Soup comes with crusty bread, prawns by the pint and there are pub classics like cottage pie. Desserts should really be written as 'puddings' as they are of the weigh-you-down-but-make-you-feel-good variety. That being said, the deep-fried jam sandwich with carnation milk ice cream appears to be more of an attention-grabber than a culinary breakthrough.

Au Lac

J2 **Vietnamese**

Highbury
82 Highbury Park ✉ N5 2XE
✆ (020) 7704 9187
Fax (020) 7704 9187

⊖ Arsenal
dinner only

Carte £8/21

A/C VISA MC

Au Lac may look a little ordinary from the outside, but that just adds to its appeal. Run enthusiastically by two brothers – one's in the kitchen, the other's out front – it provides proof of why Vietnamese cooking is considered one of Asia's healthiest cuisines: it involves lots of quick stir-frying, uses plenty of fresh herbs like mint and basil and keeps vegetables crisp. Specialities here include 'Pho' noodle soup with rare beef and chargrilled sea bass with banana leaves but they also regularly introduce new dishes on the menu. Portions are on the more-than-generous side so sharing is necessary and, while there are a few Chinese dishes on the menu to attract the less adventurous, it's best to stick to what they do best.

Fifteen London

Italian

K3

Hoxton
13 Westland Pl ✉ N1 7LP
✆ (0871) 3301 515
Fax (020) 7251 2749
www.fifteen.net

⊖ Old Street
Closed dinner 24 and 25 December

Menu £25 (weekday lunch)/60 – Carte £33/42

This is the original branch of Jamie Oliver's charitable 'Fifteen' restaurants and it's already on its eighth intake of trainees. Their programme lasts for 18 months and they receive schooling in all departments of the restaurant while being closely monitored by the experienced full-time staff. There are two operations here: the buzzy ground floor trattoria and a slightly more formal basement restaurant. The Italian cooking bears the unmistakeable signature of Jamie Oliver and the students are clearly being taught that most valuable of lessons: buy the best quality, seasonal ingredients and don't mess them about too much. This laudable project makes worrying about the occasional lapse seem somewhat mean-spirited.

Great Eastern Dining Room

Asian

K3

Hoxton
54 Great Eastern St ✉ EC2A 3QR
✆ (020) 7613 4545
Fax (020) 7613 4137
e-mail greateastern@rickerrestaurants.com
www.rickerrestaurants.com

⊖ Old Street
Closed Sunday
and Bank Holidays

Menu £15/19 – Carte £15/45

Will Ricker's flourishing group of hip restaurants came into its own here in Great Eastern Street and coincided with Hoxton's own emergence onto the fashion radar. The format here is similar to the others in the group: the bar, given equal billing as the restaurant, occupies most of the front section and it's usually so packed even a sardine would think twice. The noise spills into the restaurant, adding a lively vibe to the place. It's all great fun. The kitchen's influences spill across South East Asia, with dim sum, curries, roasts and tempura all carefully prepared. Helpfully, the reverse of the menu carries a glossary of Asian culinary terms. The serving team are a sassy and well-informed bunch.

Hoxton Apprentice

K2-3 **Modern European**

Hoxton
16 Hoxton Sq ✉ N1 6NT
✆ (020) 7749 2828
e-mail info@hoxtonapprentice.com
www.hoxtonapprentice.com

⊖ Old Street
Closed 23 December-3 January, Sunday dinner and Monday

Carte £20/27

Despite the severe parking restrictions, Hoxton Square has become quite a dining quarter and Hoxton Apprentice stands out from others for two reasons. Firstly, it was set up by a charity, Training for Life, to give opportunities to the unemployed or homeless with all the profits going back into the charity and, secondly, the cooking is rather good. This is not merely a restaurant for the community minded - the restaurant stands up in its own right. The apprentices work alongside pros and the kitchen uses decent, seasonal ingredients; the wine is competitively priced and the service is both conscientious and considerate. Housed in a former Victorian school, the room retains a relaxed and easy feel, with French windows opening out onto the terrace.

Real Greek Mezedopolio

K3 **Greek**

Hoxton
14-15 Hoxton Market ✉ N1 6HG
✆ (020) 7739 8212
Fax (020) 7739 4910
e-mail hoxton@therealgreek.com
www.therealgreek.co.uk

⊖ Old Street
Closed 25-26 December and 1 January

Carte £15/20

What were previously two distinct neighbouring restaurants, the Real Greek and Mezedopolio, are now one, which focuses on providing a very relaxed environment, where the emphasis is on an unstructured, shared eating experience. The menu is divided between cold and hot meze, souvlaki and large plates for 'sharers', which could be fish, meat or vegetarian, and it's all very fresh and healthy. The idea is to chat, drink and order a few plates – like barrel-aged feta, flatbread, grilled kalamari or loukaniko sausage – then have a few more drinks, followed by more chat and more ordering. It's all housed within a 1913 Christian Mission, with the large marble bar the best place to sit if you're just in for a quick bite after work.

Water House

Italian influences XX

K2

Hoxton

10 Orsman Rd ✉ N1 5QJ
✆ (020) 7033 0123
e-mail eat@waterhouserestaurant.co.uk
www.waterhouserestaurant

⊖ Essex Road Station
Closed 25 December-8 January, Sunday dinner and Monday

Carte £15/22

VISA MC AE

Acorn House's eco-friendly credentials reaped plenty of interest and the charitable trust behind it has now opened a second project, Water House. The ambitions here are even greater, for the restaurant not only harnesses renewable power, thanks to its canal-side location, but also seeks practical ways of reducing its carbon footprint. Moreover, it trains local people, aims to help regenerate a hitherto unfashionable part of town and plays a part in local life to boot. These virtuous goals would count for little if the cooking was not so satisfying. It is Italian in influence and style; the menu is refreshingly succinct and seasonal; ingredients are not mucked about with; flavours are natural and the prices are fair.

Almeida

French XX

M1

Islington

30 Almeida St ✉ N1 1AD
✆ (020) 7354 4777
Fax (020) 7354 2777
e-mail sharonw@danddlondon.com
www.almeida-restaurant.co.uk

⊖ Angel
Closed 1 January, Monday lunch and Sunday dinner

Menu £32 (dinner) – Carte lunch £18/28

A/C VISA MC AE

If you're not here for a pre-theatre bite before going to the Almeida theatre opposite then try not to arrive around 7-7.30pm as you'll find yourself in the midst of an almighty exodus which leaves the restaurant in a degree of disarray and the waiters looking shell-shocked. They then dim the lights and take a deep breath but it's usually a while before the atmosphere builds again. Prices at this crisply decorated restaurant are more realistic these days, especially at lunch when the room really benefits from the two large new windows. The menu's French influence is a little less pronounced but dishes still use intelligent combinations, like venison with pumpkin and lamb with artichoke. Look out for some interesting French regional wines.

The Barnsbury

L1 **Gastropub**

Islington
209-211 Liverpool Rd
N1 1LX
(020) 7607 5519
Fax (020) 7607 3256
e-mail info@thebarnsbury.co.uk
www.thebarnsbury.co.uk

Highbury and Islington.
Closed 24-26 December and 1 January

Carte £26/29

VISA
AE

The Barnsbury may not look much like a typical pub from outside but it ticks all the boxes within: the wooden floorboards, the big central bar and the scattering of locals all nursing pints. Add in some originality such as chandeliers fashioned from wine glasses and a cabinet of Mamod steam-powered boys' toys and you have another worthy Islington pub, complete with a little garden at the back. The menu's printed on grease-proof paper and offers something for everyone; starters could be foie gras with quince or moules marinière, main courses pumpkin risotto or rump of lamb. There are useful 500ml carafes available and a good value, pre-7pm menu. You'll find a cactus on each table, a reflection of the somewhat prickly service.

The Drapers Arms

L1 **British**

Islington
44 Barnsbury St N1 1ER
(020) 7619 0348
e-mail info@thedrapersarms.com
www.thedrapersarms.com

Highbury and Islington.

Carte £18/30

VISA
AE

This handsome Georgian pub was rescued, revived and reopened in 2009 by new owners, one of whom is the son of restaurant critic Fay Maschler. The chef is an alumnus of St John but, while his experience informs his cooking, that doesn't make it a facsimile. It does place the same emphasis on seasonality, on unfussy 'proper' British cooking and on the use of less familiar cuts, but there's also an acknowledgement that this is a local pub first and foremost. Reservations are only taken for the somewhat starkly decorated upstairs dining room but you'll find the same menu in the bar, where it's more fun, with its shelves of Penguin Classics and board games as well as a further menu of dishes such as oysters, devils on horseback and whelks.

Metrogusto

M1

Italian XX

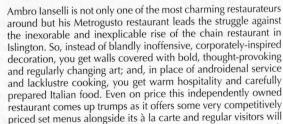

Islington
13 Theberton St ✉ N1 0QY
✆ (020) 7226 9400
Fax (020) 7226 9400
e-mail ambroianeselli@btconnect.com
www.metrogusto.co.uk

⊖ Angel
Closed 25-26 December and 1 January
– dinner only

Menu £19 (dinner) – Carte £24/36

A/C VISA MC AE

Ambro Ianselli is not only one of the most charming restaurateurs around but his Metrogusto restaurant leads the struggle against the inexorable and inexplicable rise of the chain restaurant in Islington. So, instead of blandly inoffensive, corporately-inspired decoration, you get walls covered with bold, thought-provoking and regularly changing art; and, in place of androidenal service and lacklustre cooking, you get warm hospitality and carefully prepared Italian food. Even on price this independently owned restaurant comes up trumps as it offers some very competitively priced set menus alongside its à la carte and regular visitors will never get bored thanks to the daily changing pasta, risotto, 'catch of the day' and 'butcher's cut'.

The Northgate

K2

Gastropub

Islington
113 Southgate Rd ✉ N1 3JS
✆ (020) 7359 7392
Fax (020) 7359 7393
e-mail thenorthgate@hotmail.co.uk

⊖ Dalston Kingsland (rail).
dinner only

Carte £20/27

VISA MC AE

The Northgate is decked out in the usual gastropub aesthetic of mismatched furniture and local artists' work for sale on the walls; at the back you'll find tables laid up for dining and an open kitchen. You'll also find an extraction fan that's so strong you can feel its tug. Staff are pretty laid back, at times almost to the point of somnolence; go with a similarly relaxed frame of mind to avoid irritation. Where the pub scores is in the food: there's a strong Mediterranean influence on the vast blackboard. You'll find merguez and chorizo sausages, assorted pastas, a bit of Greek and some French – all in generously sized proportions with the emphasis on flavour. Finish with something a little closer to home like treacle tart.

Ottolenghi

M1 **Mediterranean**

Islington
287 Upper St ✉ N1 2TZ
✆ (020) 7288 1454
Fax (020) 7704 1456
e-mail upper@ottolenghi.co.uk
www.ottolenghi.co.uk

⊖ Highbury and Islington
Closed 25-26 December, 1 January and Sunday dinner – booking essential

Carte £29/34

A/C VISA MC AE

Coming with friends and sharing is the key at Ottolenghi. It's primarily a deli, with tempting piles of meringues and salads in its window, but morphs into a little restaurant at night, with communal tables, speedy but sociable service and a fun atmosphere. Dishes come either 'from the counter', where a waitress will go and dish up for you – so be nice – or 'from the kitchen' which involves some heating up. The menu changes daily and influences come from all parts of the wider Mediterranean: this is all about good fresh ingredients yielding plenty of flavour – and Veggies will be in clover. Three dishes per person are too many, yet two are not enough, so sharing is the key. The desserts are especially good and if you think you know salad, think again.

L'Oasis

K3 **Gastropub**

Mile End
237 Mile End Rd ✉ E1 4AA
✆ (020) 7702 7051
e-mail info@loasisstepney.co.uk
www.loasisstepney.co.uk

⊖ Stepney Green.

Carte £20/30

A/C VISA MC AE

The sign at the door confidently proclaims 'proper food cooked by proper chefs'. Few would dispute that there's something very warm and sincere about L'Oasis and much of that is down to the affable owner, John Cleary, who has created a welcoming neighbourhood spot. This may be quite a narrow Victorian pub but the ornate high ceiling adds a feeling of space and local artists' work lends some colour. Regulars insist that certain dishes remain perennials: the meze trays (including a vegetarian one), the New York strip steak, the house burger and the assorted sausages and pies that come with gravy and mash are the locals' favourites. It all works very well and L'Oasis is as good an example as anywhere of a real London pub.

L'Anima

K3 — Italian XXX

Shoreditch

1 Snowden St ✉ EC2 2DA
✆ (0207) 422 7000
Fax (0207) 422 7077
e-mail info@lanima.co.uk
www.lanima.co.uk

⊖ Liverpool St
Closed 24 December dinner-4 January, Saturday lunch and Sunday – booking essential

Menu £37 (lunch) – Carte £26/58

A/C VISA MC AE

L'Anima is an extremely handsome restaurant that looks as though it should be located somewhere slightly more glamorous than the edge of The City. A glass wall separates the bar from the restaurant, where you find limestone walls, impeccably laid tables, white leather chairs and clever lighting; ask for one of the tables on the raised section at the back. The mood is sophisticated and the look smart and stylish. The chef may come from Calabria but his team have arrived from all parts of Italy. His menu is appealing and balanced, offering a mix of classic and less familiar dishes; and there's a helpful glossary of terms for the unfamiliar. The emphasis is on flavour and most dishes deliver that in spades. Service is smooth but also personable.

Boundary

K3 — French XXX

Shoreditch

2-4 Boundary St ✉ E2 7JE
✆ (020) 7729 1051
Fax (020) 7729 3061
e-mail reservations@theboundary.co.uk
www.theboundary.co.uk

⊖ Old St
Closed Monday and Saturday lunch and Sunday dinner

Menu £24 (lunch) – Carte £35/55

A/C VISA MC AE

When the management team took over his restaurant group, many thought Sir Terence Conran's days of opening restaurants were over. Not a bit of it, because he was soon back with a bang with Boundary. As is his way, he has taken an interesting building, in this case a large warehouse and former printworks, and turned into a veritable house of fun. From the top, you have a roof terrace with an open fire; Albion is a ground floor 'caff' alongside a shop and bakery and Boundary is the French-inspired 'main' restaurant below it. The room is stylish, good-looking and works well, while the kitchen serves up reassuringly familiar cross-Channel treats, including fruits de mer. The fourth part of the equation are the comfy, individually designed bedrooms.

The Fox

K3 **Gastropub**

Shoreditch

28 Paul St ✉ EC2A 4LB
✆ (020) 7729 5708
e-mail thefoxpublichouse@thefoxpublichouse.co.uk
www.thefoxpublichouse.co.uk

⊖ Old Street.
Closed Christmas-New Year, Saturday lunch, Sunday dinner and Bank Holidays – booking essential

Carte £24/34

VISA MC AE

Friday lunchtime and it'll be like a rugby scrum at the bar, but head upstairs for the contrasting serenity of the first floor dining room, where you'll also find a delightful roof terrace. Four choices per course form the set menu, although there's no pressure exerted to have the full three-courser. Dish descriptions are refreshingly concise and this no-nonsense simplicity is reflected in the rustic cooking with specialities of either a British or Mediterranean persuasion. The dining room boasts an appealingly thrown-together quality and, in between their constant sprints up and down the stairs from the kitchen, the waiting staff pitch the tone of service perfectly.

The Princess of Shoreditch

K3 **Gastropub**

Shoreditch

76-78 Paul St ✉ EC2A 4NE
✆ (020) 7729 9270
e-mail info@theprincessofshoreditch.com
www.theprincessofshoreditch.com

⊖ Old Street.
Closed 24-26 December, Saturday lunch and Sunday dinner

Carte £24/35

VISA MC AE

The old girl may change hands now and then but she remains as popular as ever. The ground floor is your proper pub; drinkers are the mainstay but they get an appealing and appropriate menu where platters of sausage, charcuterie and cheese are the highlights, along with pies of the cottage or pork variety. For more mellow surroundings follow the fairy lights up to a warm, candlelit room. Here, the menu displays greater ambition. The cooking is more European in its influence and, despite the occasional affected presentation, it's clear the kitchen has confidence and ability. Flavours are good, techniques are sound and parfaits are a real highlight. The pub prides itself on the friendliness of its staff and upstairs is no different.

Rivington Grill

K3 **British**

Shoreditch
28-30 Rivington St ✉ EC2A 3DZ
✆ (020) 7729 7053
www.rivingtongrill.co.uk

⊖ Old Street
Closed dinner 24 December, 25-26 December and 1 January

Menu £19 (weekend lunch) – Carte £21/47

A converted warehouse surrounded by design studios, galleries and printing premises means not only that this place is popular with artistically inclined types but that it also shows work itself, including a Tracey Emin neon "Life without you, never". However, it is also close to The City so head left when you enter as suited groups tend to occupy the tables on the right. The British menu will fill you with patriotic fervour – if this was what John Major had meant when he referred to 'back-to basics' there wouldn't have been such derision. There's a section 'on toast' and oysters are a speciality; there are pies, chops and faggots, even fish fingers and bubble and squeak. There are also plenty of bottles under £30 and special offers for weekend lunches.

Rasa

K2 **Indian**

Stoke Newington
55 Stoke Newington Church St
✉ N16 0AR
✆ (020) 7249 0344
www.rasarestaurants.com

Closed 24-26 December and 1 January – booking essential – dinner only

Menu £16 – Carte £9/13

Stoke Newington Church Street offers a plethora of restaurants but Rasa clearly stands out and that's not just because of the shocking pink paint. The locals are drawn here for both the satisfying cooking and the munificence of the pricing. Kerala and the south west coast of India provide the influence for the cooking which is vegetarian and full of flavour. The pickles and chutneys tell you straight off that this is somewhere different and the spicing is added with a sure hand. Specialities include deep-fried patties and dosa pancakes and Kerala's great produce such as bananas, coconut, cardamom and cashew also feature in the desserts which are well worth trying. Try getting a table in the back as it offers a little more room.

Rasa Travancore

K2 **Indian**

Stoke Newington

Closed 23-30 December – dinner only

56 Stoke Newington Church St
N16 0NB
(020) 7249 1340
www.rasarestaurants.com

Carte approx. £12

Virtually opposite Rasa is its sister Rasa Travancore. It also offers specialities from the Kerala region of India, but this time carnivores are catered for as it celebrates the unique cooking found within the Christian Syrian communities. Meat and fish play a large part and the menu offers a balanced selection, from steamed prawns to chicken stews and lamb curries. Despite having a basement kitchen, the dishes arrive piping hot and portions are in manageable sizes, so be sure to try some of the pre-meal snacks. Ornamentation within the two dining rooms is relatively limited but the delightful and charming service more than compensates. Everyone involved in the restaurant hails from Kerala and they're all rightly proud of their cuisine.

The Lock

K1 **Modern European**

Tottenham

Tottenham Hale
Closed 31 December, Saturday lunch, Sunday dinner and Monday

Heron House, Hale Wharf, Ferry Lane
N17 9NF
(020) 8885 2829
Fax (020) 8885 1618
e-mail thelock06@btconnect.com
www.thelockrestaurant.com

Menu £15 – Carte £22/33

A stark looking restaurant next to an ugly office development in the outer reaches of Tottenham doesn't sound like much of a sure thing but The Lock is proving to be stayer. This has been achieved by adhering to the aphorism of our time: the prices represent value for money. The chef-owner's food is artistically presented and comes with a certain Mediterranean élan, with a few twists thrown in for good measure. There is a tendency towards over-elaboration but the ingredients are good and the execution sound. Service is affable and friendly and also makes up for a lack of character to the room. The local corporate trade, grateful they don't have to hack into the West End for a decent meal, are taken with The Lock.

South-East London

Once considered not only the wrong side of the tracks, but also most definitely the wrong side of the river, London's southeastern chunk has thrived in recent times courtesy of the Docklands Effect. As the gleaming glass peninsula of **Canary Wharf** (ironically, just north of the Thames) sprouted a personality of its own – with bars, restaurants, slinky bridges and an enviable view, not to mention moneyed residents actually putting down roots – the city's bottom right hand zone began to achieve destination status on a par with other parts of London. You only have to stroll around the glossy and quite vast **Limehouse Basin** – a slick marina that was once a hard-grafting East End dock – to really see what's happened here.

Not that the area hasn't always boasted some true gems in the capital's treasure chest. **Greenwich,** with fabulous views across the water to the docklands from its delightfully sloping park, has long been a favourite of kings and queens: Henry VIII and Elizabeth I resided here. The village itself bustles along with its market and plush picturehouse, but most visitors make their way to the standout attractions, of which there are many. The **Royal Observatory** and the Meridian Line draw stargazers and hemisphere striders in equal number, while the palatial Old Royal Naval College is a star turn for lovers of Wren, who designed it as London's answer to Versailles. On the northern edge of Greenwich Park, the **National Maritime Museum** has three floors of sea-faring wonders; down by the pier, the real thing exists in the rather sorry-looking shape of the **Cutty Sark,** devastated by fire in 2007. Up on the peninsula, the O2 Arena's distinctive shape has become an unmistakable landmark, but if you fancy a contrast to all things watery, the Fan Museum on Crooms Hill has more handheld fans (over 3,000 of them) than anywhere else on earth. Strolling south from Greenwich park you reach **Blackheath,** an alluring suburban village, whose most striking feature is the towering All Saints' Church, standing proud away from the chic shops and restaurants.

Of slightly less spectacular charms, but a real crowd-pleaser nevertheless, is **Dulwich Village,** hidden deeper in the southeastern enclaves. It's a leafy oasis in this part of the world, with a delightful park that boasts at its western end, next to the original buildings of the old public school, the Dulwich Picture Gallery. This will soon reach its 200th birthday, and its pedigree is evident in works by the likes of Rembrandt, Rubens, Van Dyck and Canaletto. Half an hour's walk away across the park is the brilliant Horniman Museum, full of natural history and world culture delights – as well as a massive aquarium that seems to take up much of southeast London.

A bit further east along the South Circular, there's the unexpected gem of Eltham Palace, originally the childhood home of Henry VIII with a magnificent (and still visible) Great Hall. What makes it unique is the adjacent Art Deco mansion built for millionaires in the 1930s in Ocean Liner style. It's the closest you'll ever get to a setting fit for hog roast and champagne. Heading back towards London, a lifestyle of bubbly and banquets has never really been **Peckham**'s thing, but it boasts a couple of corkers in the shape of the South London Gallery with its zeitgeist-setting art shows, and the Peckham Library, a giant inverted 'L' that after a decade still looks like a lot of fun to go into.

Back in the luxury flat-lands of the **Docklands, Wapping** has become an interesting port of call, its new-build architecture mixing in with a still Dickensian feel, in the shape of glowering Victorian warehouses and Wapping New Stairs, where the bodies of pirates were hanged from a gibbet until seven tides had showered their limp bodies. You can catch a fascinating history of the whole area in the nearby Museum in Docklands.

C. Eymenier / MICHELIN

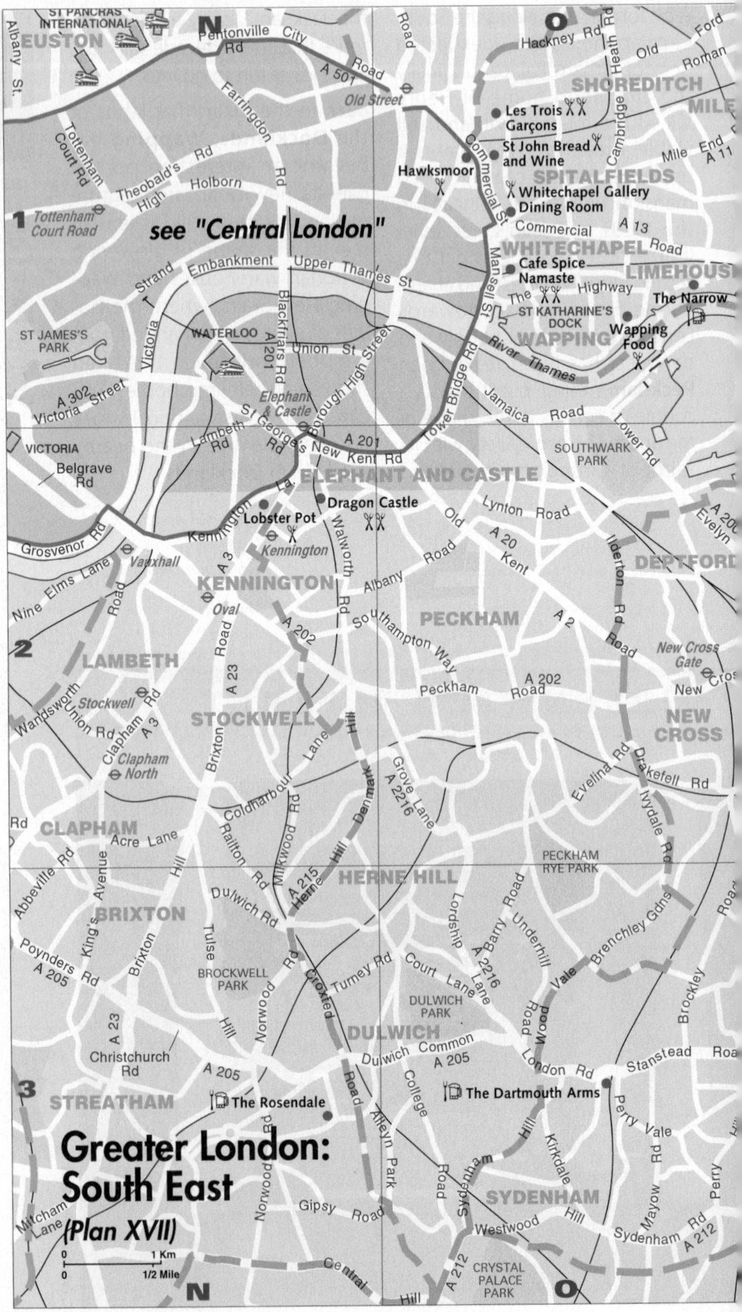

Greater London: South East
(Plan XVII)

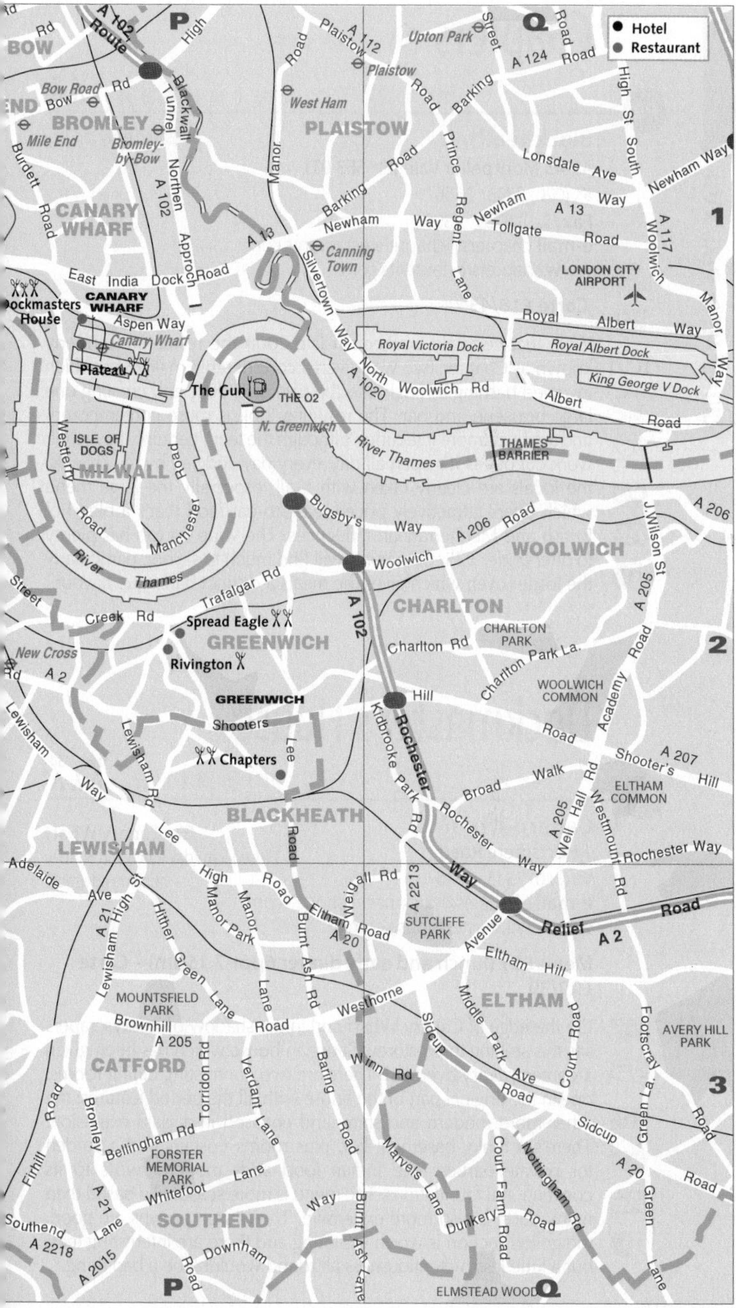
Hotel
Restaurant
P
Q
1
2
3
BOW
BROMLEY
Bow Road
Bow
Mile End
Bromley-by-Bow
CANARY WHARF
PLAISTOW
West Ham
Plaistow
Upton Park
A 112
A 124
A 102
Route
Blackwall Tunnel
Northern Approch
Manor Road
Barking Road
Prince Regent Lane
Lonsdale Ave
High St South
Newham Way
A 13
Newham Way
Tollgate Road
A 117
Woolwich Manor Way
Canning Town
Silvertown Way
East India Dock Road
LONDON CITY AIRPORT
Dockmasters House
Aspen Way
Canary Wharf
Plateau
The Gun
THE O2
N. Greenwich
Royal Albert Way
Royal Victoria Dock
Royal Albert Dock
King George V Dock
North Woolwich Rd
A 1020
Albert Road
THAMES BARRIER
River Thames
ISLE OF DOGS
MILWALL
Westferry Road
Manchester Road
Bugsby's Way
A 206 Road
A 206
J. Wilson St
WOOLWICH
Woolwich
Street
Trafalgar Rd
Creek Rd
Spread Eagle
GREENWICH
CHARLTON
CHARLTON PARK
Charlton Rd
Charlton Park La.
A 205
Academy Road
New Cross
A 2
Rivington
GREENWICH
Shooters Hill Road
WOOLWICH COMMON
Lewisham Way
Lewisham Rd
Chapters
Lee
Kidbrooke Park Rd
Rochester Way
A 207
Shooter's Hill
ELTHAM COMMON
Broad Walk
Well Hall Rd
Westmount Rd
Rochester Way
BLACKHEATH
Road
LEWISHAM
Lee High Road
Adelaide Ave
A 21
Lewisham High St
Hither Green Lane
Manor Park
Manor Lane
Burnt Ash Rd
Eltham Road
A 20
Weigall Rd
A 2213
SUTCLIFFE PARK
Avenue
Relief Road
A 2
Eltham Hill
ELTHAM
Middle Park Ave
Court Road
Footscray Road
AVERY HILL PARK
MOUNTSFIELD PARK
Brownhill Road
A 205
Westhorne
Sidcup Road
Winn Rd
CATFORD
Torridon Rd
Verdant Lane
Baring Road
Green La.
Bromley Road
Bellingham Rd
FORSTER MEMORIAL PARK
Whitefoot Lane
Firhill
A 21
Southend Lane
A 2218
SOUTHEND
Way
Downham
A 2015
Road
Burnt Ash Lane
Marvels Lane
Dunkery Road
Court Farm Road
Nottingham Rd
A 20
Green Lane
ELMSTEAD WOOD

Chapters

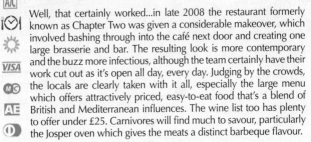

Modern European XX

P2

Blackheath

Closed early January

43-45 Montpelier Vale ✉ SE3 0TJ
✆ (020) 8333 2666
Fax (020) 8355 8399
e-mail chapters@chaptersrestaurants.com
www.chaptersrestaurants.com

Carte £18/43

A/C

VISA

AE

Well, that certainly worked...in late 2008 the restaurant formerly known as Chapter Two was given a considerable makeover, which involved bashing through into the café next door and creating one large brasserie and bar. The resulting look is more contemporary and the buzz more infectious, although the team certainly have their work cut out as it's open all day, every day. Judging by the crowds, the locals are clearly taken with it all, especially the large menu which offers attractively priced, easy-to-eat food that's a blend of British and Mediterranean influences. The wine list too has plenty to offer under £25. Carnivores will find much to savour, particularly the Josper oven which gives the meats a distinct barbeque flavour.

Dockmaster's House

Indian XXX

P1

Canary Wharf

⊖ Canary Wharf
Closed Saturday lunch and Sunday – booking advisable

1 Hertsmere Road
✆ (020) 7345 0345
e-mail enquiries@dockmastershouse.com
www.dockmastershouse.com

Menu £21 (lunch and early dinner 6pm-7.15pm) – Carte £29/39

VISA

AE

On the edge of Canary Wharf and in the shadow of its skyscrapers sits this striking three-storey Georgian house which has been given a contemporary overhaul. There are two contrasting dining rooms: one in the original part of the house with all the period features; the other more modern and shiny and encased in a glass extension. There's a funky basement bar, plus rooms upstairs and a garden for private parties. The Indian food adds modern twists to its conventional foundations. The menu is more seasonally based than many but it is also more expensive. The saffron prawns are good, the grilled section is worth exploring and there are interesting teas; but a little less pretentiousness all round wouldn't be a bad thing.

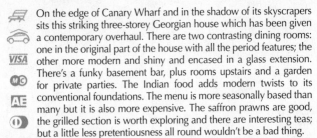

The Gun

P1 — **Gastropub**

Canary Wharf

27 Coldharbour ✉ E14 9NS
✆ (020) 7515 5222
Fax (020) 7515 4407
e-mail info@thegundocklands.com
www.thegundocklands.com

⊖ Blackwall (DLR).
Closed 25 December

Carte £21/30

This is a thoughtfully restored 18C pub with a long connection to the river and was where Lord Nelson conducted his trysts with Lady Emma Hamilton. But sit on the terrace or in the back with the locals and the views are of the O2 Arena. The concise menu is a balanced selection of European based dishes, prepared with a light yet assured touch. Fish is a key component of the blackboard daily specials and comes from Billingsgate, no further than a hefty cast away. Those side dishes can push up the final bill and there are plenty of temptations on the wine list, but this is a pub for those who know their food. There are jazz nights on Sundays; news that will attract and repel in equal measure but bite the bullet and get down to The Gun.

VISA · MC · AE · ①

Plateau

P1 — **Modern European**

Canary Wharf

(4th floor) Canada Place, Canada Square
✉ E14 5ER
✆ (020) 7715 7100
Fax (020) 7715 7110
e-mail raffaelef@danddlondon.com
www.plateaurestaurant.co.uk

⊖ Canary Wharf
Closed 25-26 December, 1 January, Sunday and Bank Holidays

Menu £35 – Carte £29/40

In a building that wouldn't look out of place in Manhattan is a restaurant that harks back to a time when bankers ruled the world. It is still, though, an impressive open-plan space and the dramatic glass walls and ceilings make the surrounding monolithic office blocks look strangely appealing. The striking 1970s retro design also seems to fit perfectly. There are two choices: the Grill where, as the name suggests, the choice is from rotisserie meats and classic grilled dishes, or the formal restaurant beyond with its comfortable surroundings. Here, the range is more eclectic and dishes are constructed with more global influences. They also come in ample sizes, though, so ignore the enthusiastic selling of the side dishes.

A/C · VISA · MC · AE · ①

Quadrato

Italian XXX

P1

Canary Wharf

⊖ Canary Wharf

Westferry Circus ✉ E14 8RS
✆ (020) 7510 1999
Fax (020) 7510 1998

Menu £25 – Carte £27/44

Instead of a fish tank there's a large enclosed kitchen with the chefs on display and, in summer, it is all about the elegant terrace, overlooking the river. This is a restaurant for those who enjoy feelings of luxury, space, comfort and general extravagance – qualities one would expect from any restaurant housed within a Four Seasons hotel. That also means that this perhaps is not the first choice for anyone looking for a bustling and buzzy atmosphere. Service is undertaken by a smart and professional bunch of young Italians. The cooking also takes itself seriously and offers diners a sophisticated meander around most regions of Italy, stopping awhile in Tuscany and Northern Italy. It is clear, precise and well presented.

A/C VISA MC AE

Dragon Castle

Chinese XX

N2

Elephant and Castle

⊖ Elephant and Castle
Closed 24-25 December

114 Walworth Rd ✉ SE17 1JL
✆ (020) 7277 3388
e-mail dragoncastle@hotmail.com
www.dragoncastle.eu

Menu £23 – Carte £20/44

Those unused to searching for restaurants around the Elephant and Castle should look out for a large blue building and a red studded door. The Dragon Castle is a huge and decoratively understated Chinese restaurant that may well represent the first phase of the area's planned rebirth. The staff are all enthusiastic, obliging and seemingly impervious to their unflattering uniforms. The cooking is Cantonese and, if you're a little more adventurous and want something different from the usual crowd pleasers, then go for what the Chinese clientele are having. This way you'll find yourself with very generously sized plates of authentic and enticing specialities, such as eel or hotpots of pork. The daytime dim sum is proving very popular.

A/C VISA MC AE

The Dartmouth Arms

O3 British

Forest Hill

7 Dartmouth Road ✉ SE23 3HN

✆ (020) 8488 3117

Fax (020) 8699 9946

e-mail info@thedartmouthamrs.com

www.thedartmoutharms.com

⊖ Forest Hill (rail).
Closed 25-26 December and 1 January

Menu £17 (dinner Monday-Thursday) – Carte £19/29

VISA

The Dartmouth Arms' position opposite Forest Hill train station meant that this was once the sort of pub whose main selling point was as somewhere to dive into for a swift one on the way home. But these days it is just the sort of place in which to spend the whole evening. The couple running the show know what their customers want and the menu offers an appealing mix of dishes. Many have more of a restaurant pedigree than your average pub grub, but there's stout Britishness in evidence here, as well as a healthy regard for seasonality. So expect to see Barnsley chops, asparagus, samphire and Jersey Royals at certain times of the year. There's also some invention so you'll find the black pudding in a risotto and crab beignets with chilli jam.

Rivington Grill

P2 British

Greenwich

178 Greenwich High Rd

✉ SE10 8NN

✆ (020) 8293 9270

www.rivingtongrill.co.uk

⊖ Greenwich (DLR)
Closed 25-26 December, 1 January, Monday, dinner 24 December,and lunch Tuesday and Wednesday

Menu £19/22 (lunch) – Carte £30/47

A/C

VISA

AE

It's open from breakfast until late and the menu changes every two weeks so they can introduce seasonal specials; the 'on toast' section is a local favourite and includes Welsh rarebit and devilled kidneys. Steaks are from Scotland; the prosperous can upgrade their fish and chips to lobster and chips and the puds are rich and satisfying. The wine list is sensibly priced and includes beers and Somerset brandies. It's spread over two floors, with the ground floor being the more casual; it attracts a younger, hipper crowd than the Shoreditch branch and has a more local feel; and it gets swamped with look-alikes whenever there's a pop siren playing the O2 arena. Tables of up to four people can get a discount at the next door cinema.

Spread Eagle

P2 — French XX

Greenwich — ⊖ Greenwich (DLR)

1-2 Stockwell St ✉ SE10 9FN
✆ (020) 8853 2333
Fax (020) 8293 1024
e-mail istuan.sram@greenwich-inc.com
www.spreadeaglerestaurant.co.uk

Menu £30 (lunch) – Carte £29/49

A/C, VISA, MC

Forming part of a 17th century coaching inn, the Spread Eagle in its current incarnation has been part of the Greenwich dining scene since 1966 and, in that time, has remained proudly impervious to changing design and decorative tastes. There are a number of different sitting areas, the best being the two semi-private booths on the ground floor, but the more able-bodied should try upstairs, via the original spiral staircase. On a winter's night the place really comes into its own with its log fire, panelling, antiques and dim lighting all adding to the well-mannered atmosphere. The kitchen attempts a modern interpretation of rustic French cooking and offers tasting menus, one of which is vegetarian, accompanied by chosen wines.

Lobster Pot

N2 — French X

Kennington — ⊖ Kennington

3 Kennington Lane ✉ SE11 4RG — Closed Sunday and Monday
✆ (020) 7582 5556
www.lobsterpotrestaurant.co.uk

Carte £34/54

A/C, VISA, MC, AE

Ignore the fairly shabby exterior, dive straight in and you'll think you've stumbled onto a French film set. Fish tanks, portholes, the cries of seagulls and the hoots of ferries…the place has the lot and it's hard to avoid getting caught up in the exuberance of it all. It's no surprise that it's also all about fish. The chef-owner, from Vannes in Brittany, goes to Billingsgate each morning and he knows what he's doing: his menu is classical and appetising, with fruits de mer, plenty of oysters, a lobster section and daily specials on the blackboard. Be sure to make room for the crêpes, which are great. It's not cheap but it is an experience. Underlining the family nature of the business, the son has opened a brasserie next door.

The Narrow

01 **Gastropub**

Limehouse

44 Narrow Street ✉ E14 8DP
✆ (020) 7592 7950
Fax (020) 7592 1603
e-mail thenarrow@gordonramsay.com
www.gordonramsay.com

⊖ Limehouse (DLR).
booking essential

Carte £21/27

Despite receiving some negative publicity in 2009 when it was revealed that certain dishes in Gordon Ramsay's pubs are prepared in a central kitchen, The Narrow does not seem any less frenetic. This 'logistical cooking', as they describe it, is used for dishes requiring a lengthy cooking process, such as the slow-roasted pork belly or beef braised in Guinness. However it gets there, the food on the plate is tasty, seasonal and laudably British, be it devilled kidneys, Morecambe Bay brown shrimps, a chicken pie or a sherry trifle. What is also certain is that no other London pub has better views, as one would expect from a converted dockmaster's house; just be sure to request a table in the semi-permanent conservatory.

Hawksmoor

01 **Beef specialities**

Spitalfields

157 Commercial Rd ✉ E1 6BJ
✆ (0207) 247 7392
e-mail info@thehawksmoor.com
www.thehawksmoor.com

⊖ Shoreditch
Closed 25 December, Saturday lunch, Sunday and Bank Holidays – booking advisable

Carte £27/70

Hawksmoor was a 17C architect and student of Sir Christopher Wren so you could expect this steakhouse to be housed in a building of note rather than in this modern edifice of little aesthetic value. Inside is equally unremarkable but no matter because this place is all about beef and, more specifically, British beef which has been hung for 35 days. It comes from Longhorn cattle raised by Ginger Pig in the heart of the North Yorkshire Moors and the quality and depth of flavour is exceptional. Just choose your preferred weight – go for 400g if you're hungry. Starters and puds don't come close in quality but again, no matter, because when you've got some fantastic red meat in front of you, all you need is a mate and a bottle of red wine.

Les Trois Garcons

01 French XX

Spitalfields
1 Club Row ✉ E1 6JX
✆ (020) 7613 1924
Fax (020) 7012 1236
e-mail info@lestroisgarcons.com
www.lestroisgarcons.com

⊖ Shoreditch
Closed 16-31 August, 23 December-10 January, Sunday and most Bank Holidays – dinner only

Menu £31 – Carte £50/68

A/C · VISA · MC · AE

The surrounding streets may be somewhat drab but the three friends (hence the name) who own this former pub are also antique dealers (hence the eccentric and exuberant decoration that resembles a theatrical props department). There are stuffed animals, beads, handbags and assorted objets d'art; heavy velvet curtains ensure that the lighting is dim and atmospheric. The kitchen, on the other hand, uses fairly classical French cooking techniques and flavour combinations, although the majority of ingredients are British. The menus change seasonally and presentation on the plate is neat and appetising. The early-in-the-week set menu is good value; the à la carte somewhat expensive. Service can occasionally veer from the efficient to the over-confident.

St John Bread and Wine

01 British X

Spitalfields
94-96 Commercial St ✉ E1 6LZ
✆ (020) 7251 0848
Fax (020) 7247 8924
e-mail reservations@stjohnbreadandwine.com
www.stjohnbreadandwine.com

⊖ Shoreditch
Closed Christmas-New Year and Bank Holidays

Carte £23/27

A/C · VISA · MC · AE

Less famous but by no means less loved than its sibling, this English version of a classic comptoir is the sort of place we would all like to have at the end of our road. Just the aroma as you enter is enough to get the appetite going. As the name suggests, this is a wine shop and a bakery but also a local restaurant. The menu changes twice a day and depends on what's in season; the Britishness of its ingredients and its promotion of forgotten recipes will enthuse everyone, not just culinary genealogists. But it's not all man-food like roast pig spleen or 'raw Angus'; there are lighter dishes such as plaice with samphire; and the Eccles cakes are a must. From breakfast to supper, certain dishes are only ready at certain times, so do check first.

Wapping Food

Modern European

O1

Wapping

Wapping Wall ✉ E1W 3SG
✆ (020) 7680 2080
e-mail office@thewappingproject.com
www.thewappingproject.com

⊖ Wapping
Closed 23 December-3 January, Sunday dinner and Bank Holidays

Carte £25/39

VISA · MC · AE

For some reason industrial spaces make great backdrops to restaurants and this Victorian former hydraulic power station, which was used to light up the West End theatres, is certainly no exception. It has been going for a decade and you can not only sit amongst the abandoned machinery but you're also surrounded by monthly-changing art exhibitions. The owner is an Aussie and her wine list is an exclusively Australian affair, while the cooking is equally unfussy and straightforward. The kitchen rightly relies on the quality of the produce to carry the dish, to which they add some Mediterranean or occasionally Asian touches. The serving team are a friendly bunch and they all know the answers to any questions relating to the history of the place.

The Rosendale

Gastropub

N3

West Dulwich

65 Rosendale Rd ✉ SE21 8EZ
✆ (020) 8670 0812
e-mail dine@therosendale.co.uk
www.therosendale.co.uk

⊖ West Dulwich (rail).
Closed 1 January

Menu £24 (Thursday-Sunday) – Carte £14/29

A/C · VISA · MC

Included among the many things that stand out about The Rosendale are that they make their own butter as well as their own bread and have a wine list that is remarkable in its breadth, depth and affordability. This vast former coaching inn dates from the 1820s and has a soaring ceiling and plenty of original features. There are two menus - the front bar has a grill menu, with more of your typical pub food. Go through to the dining room at the back and the menu there is of a more ambitious nature. It can appear even more complicated on the plate but there is no denying the quality of the ingredients and sourcing is clearly taken seriously. Fish is delivered daily from Cornwall; they hang their own meat and smoke their own fish.

Cafe Spice Namaste

Indian XX

01

Whitechapel

16 Prescot St ✉ E1 8AZ

✆ (020) 7488 9242

Fax (020) 7481 0508

e-mail info@cafespice.co.uk

www.cafespice.co.uk

⊖ Tower Hill

Closed Christmas-New Year, Saturday lunch, Sunday and Bank Holidays

Menu £30 – Carte £25/37

A/C VISA MC AE

This red-bricked Victorian building was once a magistrate's court. That information hardly prepares you for the sheer vivaciousness of the interior. Cyrus Todiwala's vibrant and ebullient restaurant has been going strong now for more than a decade, having been at the vanguard of the new wave of Indian restaurants. It comes divided into two large, high-ceilinged rooms separated by the bar. If there is a colour that hasn't been used in the fabrics or on the walls it's because it hasn't yet been created. Don't be surprised to see game and other classic British ingredients on the menu - the cooking here has moments of real innovation. All dishes come fragrantly spiced and nicely balanced, but look out for the Parsee specialities.

Whitechapel Gallery Dining Room

Mediterranean X

01

Whitechapel

77-82 Whitechapel High St ✉ E1 7QX

✆ (0207) 7522 7896

Fax (0207) 7522 7896

e-mail info@whitechapelgallery.org

www.whitechapelgallery.com

⊖ Aldgate East

Closed 24 December-2 January, Sunday dinner and Monday – booking advisable

Menu £20 (lunch) – Carte £26/31

VISA MC AE

The Whitechapel Gallery, founded in 1901 and best known for exhibiting Picasso's 'Guernica', has recently undergone a major refit and expansion into the former library next door. Not only did this double the available space but it also allowed for the creation of this very sweet restaurant. It's a bright, well-lit room, with tightly packed tables and lots of wood and mirrors. The seasonal British ingredients are invigorated with Mediterranean flavours and influences, so that pork belly comes with shaved fennel and a tomato salad, while sea bass is joined by squid, chilli and oregano. For dessert, great things are done with plums. The menu changes often and is refreshingly short; the four starters and main courses include a veggie option.

D. Chapuis / MICHELIN

South-West London

Meandering like a silver snake, **The Thames** coils serenely through south-west London, adding definition to the area's much-heralded middle-class enclaves and leafy suburbs. It's the focal point to the annual **university boat race** from **Putney** to **Mortlake,** and it serves as the giant glass pond attractively backing countless bank-side pubs. This area has long been regarded as the cosy bourgeois side of town, though within its postcode prowls the lively and eclectic **Brixton,** whose buzzing street markets and lauded music venues such as the Academy and the Fridge add an urban lustre and vibrant edge.

In most people's minds, though, south-west London finds its true colours in the beautiful terrace view from the top of **Richmond Hill,** as the river bends majestically through the meadows below. Or in the smart **Wimbledon Village,** its independent boutiques ranged prettily along its own hill, with the open spaces of the Common for a back garden. Or, again, in the Italianate architecture that makes **Chiswick House** and grounds a little corner of the Mediterranean close to the Great West Road.

Green space is almost as prolific in this zone as the streets of Victorian and Edwardian villas. **Richmond Park** is the largest royal park in the whole of London and teems with kite flyers, cyclists and deer – though not necessarily in that order. From here, round a southerly bend in the river, delightful grounds surround **Ham House,** which is all set for its 400th birthday in 2010; celebrations should be good, but maybe not as excessive as during the seventeenth century when it was home to Restoration court life. Head slightly north to **Kew Gardens** and its world famous 300 acres can now be viewed from above – the treetop walkway, opened in 2008, takes you 60 feet up to offer some breath-taking views. Just across the river from here is another from the historical hit-list: **Syon Park,** which boasts water meadows still grazed by cattle, giving it a distinctly rural aspect. Syon House is considered one of architect Robert Adam's finest works; it certainly appealed to Queen Victoria, who spent much of her young life here. Up the road in bourgeoning Brentford, two unique museums bring in hordes of the curious: the Musical Museum includes a huge Wurlitzer theatre organ (get lucky and watch it being played), while almost next door, the Kew Bridge Steam Museum shows off all things steamy on a grand scale, including massive beam engines which pumped London's water for over a century.

Hammersmith may be known for its bustling Broadway and flyover, but five minutes' walk from here is the Upper Mall, which has iconic riverside pubs and Kelmscott House, the last home of artistic visionary William Morris: down in the basement and coach house are impressive memorabilia related to his life plus changing exhibitions of designs and drawings. From here, it's just a quick jaunt across **Hammersmith Bridge** and down the arrow-straight Castelnau to the Wetland Centre in Barnes, which for nearly ten years has lured wildlife to within screeching distance of the West End. **Barnes** has always revelled in its village-like identity – it juts up like an isolated peninsula into the Thames and boasts yummy boutiques and well-known restaurants. The Bulls Head pub in Lonsdale Road has featured some of the best jazz in London for half a century.

In a more easterly direction, the urbanised areas of **Clapham** and **Battersea** have re-established themselves as desirable places to live over the last decade. **Clapham Common** is considered prime southwest London turf, to the extent that its summer music festivals are highly prized. It's ringed by good pubs and restaurants, too. Battersea used to be famous for its funfair, but now the peace pagoda in the park lends it a more serene light. And if you're after serenity on a hot day, then a cool dip in the wondrous **Tooting** Lido is just the thing.

D. Chapuis / MICHELIN

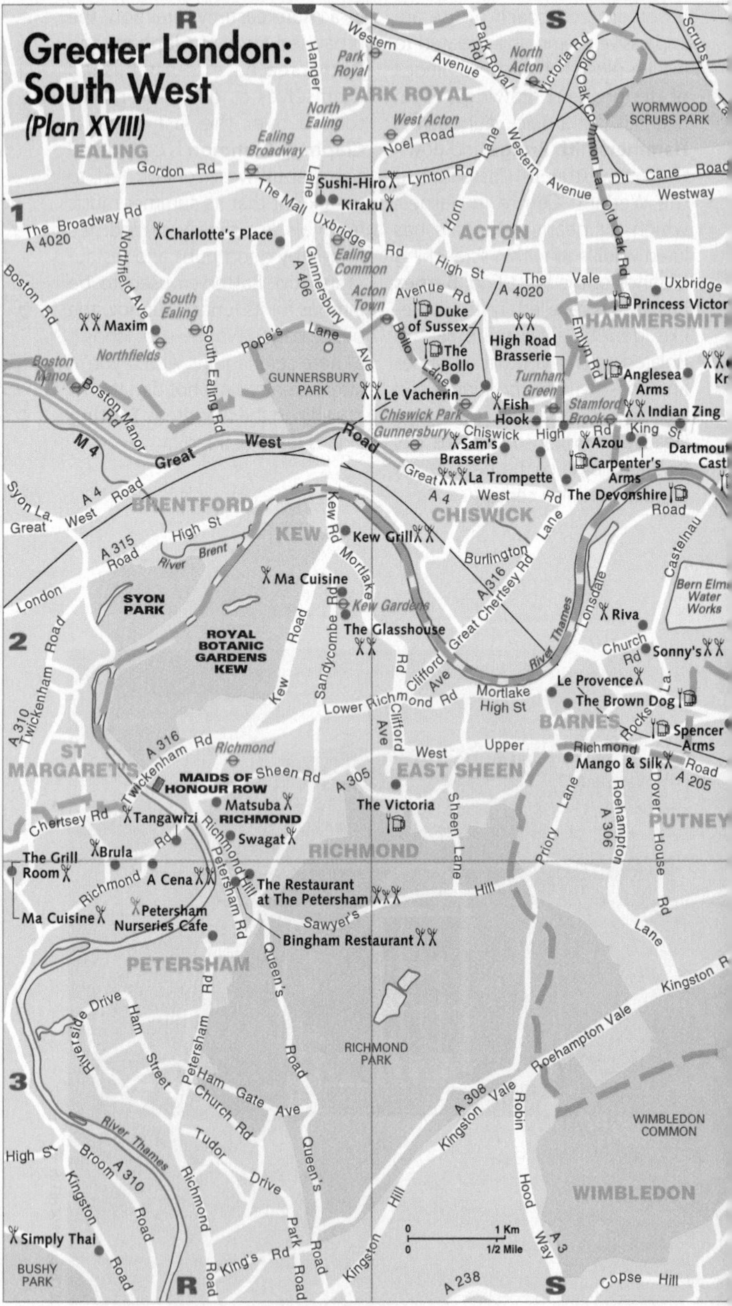

Greater London: South West
(Plan XVIII)
R
S
1
2
3
PARK ROYAL
EALING
ACTON
HAMMERSMITH
BRENTFORD
KEW
CHISWICK
BARNES
EAST SHEEN
ST MARGARETS
RICHMOND
PUTNEY
PETERSHAM
WIMBLEDON
WORMWOOD SCRUBS PARK
GUNNERSBURY PARK
SYON PARK
ROYAL BOTANIC GARDENS KEW
MAIDS OF HONOUR ROW
RICHMOND PARK
WIMBLEDON COMMON
BUSHY PARK
Bern Elms Water Works
Sushi-Hiro
Kiraku
Charlotte's Place
Maxim
Duke of Sussex
The Bollo
Le Vacherin
High Road Brasserie
Fish Hook
Princess Victoria
Anglesea Arms
Indian Zing
Sam's Brasserie
Azou
Carpenter's Arms
La Trompette
The Devonshire
Kew Grill
Ma Cuisine
The Glasshouse
Riva
Sonny's
Le Provence
The Brown Dog
Spencer Arms
Mango & Silk
The Victoria
Matsuba
Tangawizi
Swagat
Brula
The Grill Room
A Cena
The Restaurant at The Petersham
Ma Cuisine
Petersham Nurseries Cafe
Bingham Restaurant
Simply Thai
River Thames
0 1 Km
0 1/2 Mile

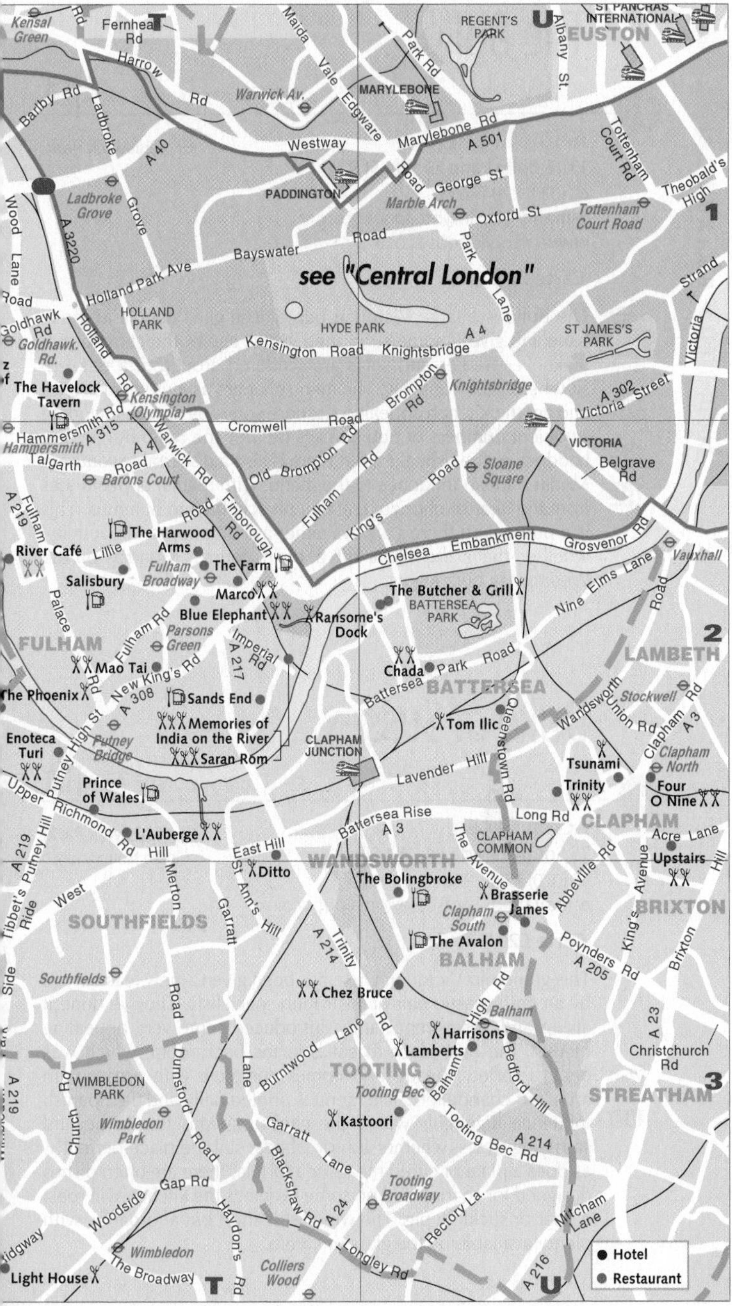
see "Central London"
Kensal Green
Fernhead Rd
Harrow Rd
Maida Vale
Edgware Road
Park Rd
REGENT'S PARK
Albany St.
ST PANCRAS INTERNATIONAL
EUSTON
Warwick Av.
MARYLEBONE
Barlby Rd
Ladbroke Grove
A 40
Westway
Marylebone Rd
A 501
Tottenham Court Rd
Theobald's
High
PADDINGTON
George St
Marble Arch
Oxford St
Tottenham Court Road
Bayswater Road
Park Lane
Wood Lane
A 3220
Holland Park Ave
Road
Strand
Goldhawk Rd
Goldhawk Rd.
HOLLAND PARK
HYDE PARK
ST JAMES'S PARK
Victoria
Holland Rd
Kensington Road
Knightsbridge
A 4
The Havelock Tavern
Kensington (Olympia)
Brompton Rd
A 302
Victoria Street
Hammersmith Rd
A 315
Hammersmith
Cromwell Road
VICTORIA
Talgarth Road
Warwick Rd
Old Brompton Rd
Sloane Square
Belgrave Rd
Barons Court
Fulham Palace
A 219
Fulham Rd
King's Road
Finborough Rd
The Harwood Arms
Chelsea Embankment
Grosvenor Rd
River Café
Lillie Road
Fulham Broadway
The Farm
Vauxhall
Salisbury
Marco
Nine Elms Lane
The Butcher & Grill
BATTERSEA PARK
Blue Elephant
Ransome's Dock
Parsons Green
FULHAM
Imperial Rd
A 217
LAMBETH
Mao Tai
Chada
Park Road
The Phoenix
New King's Rd
A 308
Sands End
Battersea
BATTERSEA
Queenstown Rd
Wandsworth Rd
Stockwell
Union Rd
Clapham Rd
A 3
Memories of India on the River
Tom Ilic
Enoteca Turi
Putney High St
Putney Bridge
Saran Rom
CLAPHAM JUNCTION
Lavender Hill
Clapham North
Tsunami
Trinity
Four O Nine
Prince of Wales
Upper Richmond Rd
Battersea Rise
Long Rd
CLAPHAM
L'Auberge
A 3
CLAPHAM COMMON
Acre Lane
A 219
Putney Hill
East Hill
WANDSWORTH
The Avenue
Upstairs
Tibbet's Ride
West Hill
Merton
St Ann's Hill
Ditto
The Bolingbroke
Abbeville Rd
King's Avenue
Brasserie James
BRIXTON
SOUTHFIELDS
Garratt
Trinity Rd
A 214
Clapham South
The Avalon
BALHAM
Poynders Rd
A 205
Brixton Hill
Southfields
Road
Chez Bruce
High Rd
Balham
A 23
Durnsford Road
Burntwood Lane
Harrisons
Lamberts
Bedford Hill
Christchurch Rd
WIMBLEDON PARK
TOOTING
Tooting Bec
Balham
STREATHAM
Church Rd
Wimbledon Park
Garratt Lane
Kastoori
Tooting Bec Rd
A 214
Gap Rd
Blackshaw Rd
Tooting Broadway
Rectory La.
Woodside
Haydon's Rd
A 24
Mitcham Lane
Ridgway
Wimbledon
The Broadway
Longley Rd
Colliers Wood
A 216
Light House
Hotel
Restaurant
1
2
3

The Bollo

Gastropub

S1

Acton Green

⊖ Chiswick Park.

13-15 Bollo Lane ✉ W4 5LR
✆ (020) 8994 6037
e-mail thebollo@btconnect.com
www.thebollohouse.co.uk

Carte £22/27

The Bollo is a large Victorian pub whose glass cupola and oak panelling give it some substance in this age of the generic pub makeover. Tables and sofas are scattered around in a relaxed, sit-where-you-want way. The menu changes as ingredients come and go; the kitchen appeals to its core voters by always including sufficient numbers of pub classics be they the Bollo Burger, the haddock or the fishcakes. But there is also a discernible southern Mediterranean influence to the menu, with regular appearances from the likes of chorizo, tzatziki, bruschetta and hummus. This is a pub where there's always either a promotion or an activity, whether that's the '50% off a main course' Monday or the Wednesday quiz nights.

VISA MC AE

Duke of Sussex

Gastropub

S1

Acton Green

⊖ Chiswick Park.
Closed Monday lunch

75 South Parade ✉ W4 5LF
✆ (020) 8742 8801
e-mail thedukeofsussex@realpubs.co.uk

Carte £20/27

This grand old Victorian Duke has been given a new lease of life by an enthusiastic pair of gastropub specialists. They've done it all up and, most importantly, introduced some very appealing menus. The best place to eat is in the back room, which was once a variety theatre and comes complete with proscenium arch and chandeliers. The menu is printed daily and the Spanish influence highlights where the chef's passions lie. Rustic and satisfying stews, whether fish or fabada, suit the place perfectly, as does a plate of cured meats or a tortilla; there are often dishes designed for sharing and on some evenings the kitchen will roast a boar or suckling pig. The wine list is short but affordable, with plenty available by the glass or carafe.

VISA MC

The Avalon

U3 **Gastropub**

Balham
16 Balham Hill ✉ SW12 9EB
✆ (020) 8675 8613
e-mail info@theavalonlondon.com
www.theavalonlondon.com

⊖ Clapham South.
Closed 25-26 December – booking advisable

Carte £21/32

A full renovation has turned The George into a slick and imaginatively styled pub, where Sir Edward Coley Burne-Jones prints add a suitably mythical edge to the aesthetic. The rear dining room's walls are covered in cream tiles but any resemblance to a morgue is thankfully undone by the general bustle and those eye-catching chandeliers. The menu combines British and Mediterranean influences, sometimes, as in the case of the kedgeree risotto, in the same dish. Expect roasted veal marrow bones, crab linguine, venison carpaccio, lamb cutlets and crème brûlée, but also crumble, appropriately of the apple variety. The concise wine list is appealingly priced and there's beer aplenty. Those locals still can't quite believe that Avalon really exists.

A/C VISA AE

Brasserie James

U3 **Modern European**

Balham
47 Balham Hill ✉ SW12 9DR
✆ (020) 8772 0057
e-mail info@brasseriejames.com
www.brasseriejames.com

⊖ Clapham South
Closed one week Christmas and Sunday dinner

Menu £14/16 – Carte £26/32

If you have the courage to open your own restaurant, especially in times of economic anxiety, then no one will begrudge your naming it eponymously. Craig James is a former chef in the Conran/D&D empire and he has brought his experience to bear in the more relaxed environs of a neighbourhood joint. It's on a site previously home to a Pakistani restaurant that was itself quite a local institution and he's given it a top-to-toe revamp. There's something for everyone on the menu, from seasonal oysters and the popular moules à la crème, to daily fish from the market, quality meats, pasta and good old-fashioned puds. There are good value set price menus; brunch at weekends and sensibly priced wines by the bottle, glass or carafe.

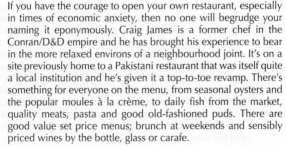

VISA

Harrison's

U3 **Mediterranean**

Balham
15-19 Bedford Hill ✉ SW12 9EX
✆ (020) 8675 6900
Fax (020) 8673 3965
e-mail info@harrisonsbalham.co.uk
www.harrisonsbalham.co.uk

⊖ Balham
Closed 24-27 December

Menu £17 – Carte £21/33

VISA MC AE

Following the success of Sam's Brasserie in Chiswick, owner Sam Harrison took over what was Soho House Bar and Grill and turned it into another all-day brasserie. It provides a lesson for all neighbourhood restaurants in the importance of being a focal point for the local community: it is open from breakfast until late and is as welcoming to those just in for a coffee as those wanting a three course meal. The food is uncomplicated, fresh and satisfying, whether that's a cheeseburger, tuna Niçoise, Cumberland sausages or a fishcake. Brunch is served at weekends; they offer a kids' menu, as well as a good value weekday set menu, and there's a decent wine selection. It's hardly surprisingly the locals have embraced the place.

Lamberts

U3 **Traditional**

Balham
2 Station Parade ✉ SW12 9AZ
✆ (020) 8675 2233
e-mail bookings@lambertsrestaurant.com
www.lambertsrestaurant.com

⊖ Balham
Closed 25-26 December, 1-2 January, Sunday dinner and Monday – dinner only and lunch Saturday - Sunday

Carte £26/36

VISA MC

Balham is less 'gateway to the south', more the 'new Notting Hill' according to some locals. If that's the case then it needs better restaurants, so Lamberts' arrival was timely. The aim of the eponymous owner Joe was to offer simple cooking in a relaxed environment, yet with a degree of comfort and style and all at an affordable price - in other words, just the sort of place we'd all like in our own high streets. The à la carte menu is usually set for the month, with additions and subtractions according to the seasons. The cooking is quite classical, with the occasional modern touch by way of presentation. They offer a daily fish dish, their Sunday roast beef has established quite a following and portions are on the satisfying side.

The Brown Dog

S2

Gastropub

Barnes
28 Cross Street ✉ SW13 0AP
✆ (020) 8392 2200
e-mail mrbojangles@thebrowndog.co.uk
www.thebrowndog.co.uk

Barnes Bridge (Rail).
Closed 25-26 December

Carte £22/29

VISA MC AE

There aren't many pubs where it takes a few calls before you manage to get a table but then The Brown Dog isn't like most pubs. For starters, the place is a very pleasant blend of original features such as the fireplaces, and thoughtful design elements like the retro posters and the copper lamps over the bar. It also has something of a contemporary vibe and is a proper local, clearly popular with those purporting to be out walking their dogs; there's even a collage of local mutts by the entrance. The menu is immeasurably appealing and refreshingly concise. Cooking is hearty – a 28 day aged sirloin will be perfectly cooked and a crumble will be fruity and light. Even your bill will be smaller than expected.

Le Provence

S2

Mediterranean

Barnes
7 White Hart Lane ✉ SW13 0PX
✆ (020) 8878 4092
e-mail info@macuisinebarnes.co.uk
www.leprovence.co.uk

Closed Monday

Menu £15 (lunch) – Carte £21/31

VISA MC AE

John McClements is a master of reinvention and he has been at it again in Barnes. The restaurant was previously called Ma Cuisine; he closed it, gave it a lick of paint and reopened it under the name Le Provence. The menu has also been tweaked so that it is now mainly French, with classics such as moules marinière and bouillabaisse, but interwoven with some Mediterranean influences in the shape of, for example, risotto or couscous. The cooking is satisfying and unfussy and the prices are pitched at a competitive level to encourage the locals to become regulars. Service can sometimes struggle to keep up when things get busy but overall this is a useful little spot that, hopefully, will remain in its present identity for some time.

Riva

Italian X

S2

Barnes
169 Church Rd ✉ SW13 9HR
✆ (020) 8748 0434
Fax (020) 8748 0434
e-mail rivarestaurants@btconnect.com

Closed last 2 weeks August, Christmas - New Year, Saturday lunch and Bank Holidays

Carte £29/46

VISA MC AE

Customer loyalty is the sine qua non of any successful restaurant; those seeking guidance on how to build it should get down to Barnes and learn from Andrea Riva. His secret is to shower so much attention on his regulars that all other diners sit imagining the day when they will be treated in the same way – when he will tell them what he's going to cook especially for them. That could be some milk-fed lamb, game, suckling pig or some risotto; all expertly rendered using tip-top, seasonal ingredients. While you wait for graduation, you'll be served by a friendly young female team and still get to enjoy some gutsy, flavoursome food. Andrea is also a keen wine collector so if you can talk oenology it could improve your chances of joining the club.

Sonny's

Modern European XX

S2

Barnes
94 Church Rd ✉ SW13 0DQ
✆ (020) 8748 0393
Fax (020) 8748 2698
e-mail manager@sonnys.co.uk
www.sonnys.co.uk

Closed Sunday dinner and Bank Holidays

Menu £19 – Carte £26/32

A/C VISA MC AE

From the outside one would be virtually unaware of the scale of the operation within – Sonny's was clearly constructed by the same people who brought us the Tardis. It's really several operations in one: you have a small but well-stocked deli at the front, the front part of the restaurant which doubles as a daytime café and the main restaurant itself. However, at dinner it all becomes one. As well as a keenly priced and nicely balanced set menu, there is a decent choice of easy-to-eat dishes whose influences are kept within Europe – expect the likes of steak tartare, soufflés, sea bass with fennel, peppered tuna and assorted summer and winter salads. There are also plenty of interesting wines available by the glass.

The Bolingbroke

U3

Gastropub

Battersea

174 Northcote Rd ✉ SW11 6RE

⊖ Clapham Junction (rail).

Closed 25-26 December

✆ (020) 7228 4040

Fax (020) 7228 2285

e-mail holly@renaissancepubs.co.uk

www.thebolingbroke.com

Carte £21/29

The influx of professionals with young families is such that this end of Northcote Road is now known as 'Nappy Valley'. A Cath Kidston shop? Check. Artisan food markets? Check. Antique emporia? Check. Now it's time for a decent pub and here's where The Bolingbroke comes in. Its glass roof makes the fairly small dining room feel bigger, although the romantically inclined should ask for the table under the stairs. The menus change weekly, with more choice at dinner. British influences lead the way, from the asparagus and cheddar tart, to the lamb shoulder and apple crumble. Steaks and burgers are perennials but you'll also find additional Euro stars like ravioli and a niçoise salad. Unsurprisingly, there's also a children's menu.

The Butcher & Grill

U2

Traditional

Battersea

39-41 Parkgate Rd

✉ SW11 4NP

Closed 25-26 December and dinner Sunday and Bank Holidays

✆ (020) 7924 3999

Fax (020) 7223 7977

e-mail info@thebutcherandgrill.com

www.thebutcherandgrill.com

Menu £15 (weekdays) – Carte £12/49

There are times when only steak and chips will do and, for those times, there is The Butcher and Grill. This butcher's-cum-food emporium-cum-steakhouse has a touch of Manhattan's Meatpacking district about it, what with its former warehouse surroundings and general all-day buzz. Fortuitously, one of the owners has a farm in East Sussex from whence much of the produce comes. The meat counter tenders an impressive array, from homemade bangers to pig's trotters and fore ribs. Choose the grills on the menu: they range from lamb burgers to rib-eye, T-bone to pork chops; the chips are good and there are none of those irksome additional charges made for sauces. And there's no let-up with desserts: one chocolate brownie will feed two.

Chada

U2 **Thai** XX

Battersea

Closed Sunday and Bank Holidays – dinner only

208-210 Battersea Park Rd ✉ SW11 4ND
✆ (020) 7622 2209
Fax (020) 7924 2791
e-mail enquiry@chadathai.com
www.chadathai.com

Carte £23/32

It may have been around for over twenty years but Chada has been given a makeover and looks positively resplendent, although there isn't much in the way of competition along Battersea Park Road these days. It may never be the busiest restaurant around but the welcome is always warm, the service polite and endearing and the Thai cooking satisfying and keenly priced. The menu is still quite a lengthy affair but it's easy to navigate through. Several dishes, such as tom kha soup and phad prik, are available with a choice of meat, prawn or vegetables. Flavours are clean and fresh and effort has gone into making dishes look appetising. Fish is handled with skill and often represents the best choice.

Ransome's Dock

U2 **Modern European** X

Battersea

Closed Christmas, August Bank Holiday and Sunday dinner

35-37 Parkgate Rd ✉ SW11 4NP
✆ (020) 7223 1611
Fax (020) 7924 2614
e-mail chef@ransomesdock.co.uk
www.ransomesdock.co.uk

Carte £22/41

It never really did have a full river view but these days Ransome's Dock, a converted warehouse, is somewhat dwarfed by the new apartment buildings that hug the south side of the river. Inside, though, it still has a freshness and something of a 'by the sea' feel. The real clues to the owner's great passion are in the wine-themed prints: his wine list is thoughtful, extensive, reasonably priced and ripe for exploration. It also provides easy matches for the food, where ingredients are thoughtfully paired, like foie gras rillettes with caper berries; or altogether more classic and down to earth, such as liver and bacon with bubble and squeak. Name-checked suppliers ensure those ingredients are fresh and seasonal.

Tom Ilić

U2 — **Traditional** X

Battersea
123 Queenstown Rd ✉ SW8 3RH
✆ (020) 7622 0555
e-mail info@tomilic.com
www.tomilic.com

Closed dinner 25-31 December, Sunday dinner, Monday and Tuesday lunch – booking essential

Menu £17/22 – Carte £22/30

A/C VISA MC AE

Serbian Tom Ilić came to the UK 20 years ago, took a job as a dish washer before a planned career in engineering, developed an interest in food and now has his own restaurant. He's chosen the site formerly occupied by The Food Room, which is an unpretentious, neighbourly place with closely set tables and a semi-open kitchen. It's also in an area of Battersea that's played host to a few famous restaurants in its day. His menu is written in a refreshingly straightforward way. There's plenty of offal featured as well as lots of pork, something of a beloved national dish for Serbs. Flavours are far from shy but his cooking also displays a certain graft and clear respect for the ingredients; prices are kept realistic.

Upstairs

U2 — **Modern European** XX

Brixton
89b Acre Lane ✉ SW2 5TN
✆ (020) 7733 8855
e-mail contact@upstairslondon.com
www.upstairslondon.com

⊖ Clapham North
Closed Easter 04-12 April, 15-31 August, 20 December-4 January, Sunday and Monday – dinner only

Menu £26

VISA MC AE

Look out for the Opus Coffee shop because upstairs is Upstairs but the only clue is a non-descript door and entry buzzer. Once you're in and up the narrow stairs you'll find a bar on the first floor and the restaurant on the second. It's a cosy affair with seating for 26; turquoise is the favoured colour and there's plenty of natural light. The menu comes on a single sheet of A4; there are three starters, mains and desserts at a set price, although there are usually also a couple of supplements. The cooking is neat, accurate and things are kept simple. The style is a mix of French and English so alongside the potted shrimps may be a foie gras parfait and you could follow the Guinea fowl with apple crumble or chocolate millefeuille.

The Devonshire

S2 — Gastropub

Chiswick
126 Devonshire Rd ✉ W4 2JJ
✆ (020) 7592 7962
Fax (020) 7592 1603
e-mail thedevonshire@gordonramsay.com
www.gordonramsay.com

⊖ Turnham Green.
Closed Monday-Tuesday and lunch Wednesday-Thursday

Menu £19 (dinner) – Carte £23/30

VISA MC AE

The Devonshire joined Gordon Ramsay's pub portfolio back in 2007 and, like The Narrow, enjoyed almost immediate success. The striking Edwardian façade is matched by the characterful oak panelling and polished floor in the bar and here you can enjoy such egalitarian treats as scotch eggs or pots of pickled cockles. For more structured eating, head for the neatly laid-out restaurant for its concise and good value menu, with its daily-changing specials. It's an appealing mix of pub classics alongside other dishes that are more West End in their pedigree. There's an 'on toast' selection, which could include herring roes, as well as weekly changing soups and assorted pies. Service is young and attentive.

Fish Hook

S1_2 — Seafood

Chiswick
6-8 Elliott Rd ✉ W4 1PE
✆ (020) 8742 0766
Fax (020) 8742 3374
e-mail info@fishhook.co.uk
www.fishhook.co.uk

⊖ Turnham Green
closed 25-26 December

Menu £15 (lunch) – Carte £31/43

A/C VISA MC AE

Chef-owner Michael Nadra's hard work is paying off and Fish Hook is now a recognised part of Chiswick life. The crisp, clean cooking attests to his classical culinary background but his own stamp is evident in the increased Asian accent to some of the seafood dishes, including 'salmon three ways' and, his speciality, soft shell crab tempura. The good value lunch menu is now also available early evening; the dinner menu is priced per course and an individually tailored six-course tasting menu has proved a success and allows him to indulge in a little experimentation. The wine list has increased to 150 bins and its prices remain accessible. The room has also been freshened up but has kept its intimate, warm and local feel.

High Road Brasserie

Traditional XX

S2

Chiswick

⊖ Turnham Green

162 Chiswick High Rd ✉ W4 1PR
✆ (020) 8742 1717
Fax (020) 8987 8762
e-mail reservations@highroadhouse.co.uk
www.highroadhouse.co.uk

Carte £21/42

They've certainly nailed that brasserie look, with the mirrors, pewter-topped tables, leather seats and tiled flooring. And they also have the necessary hustle and bustle you'd expect; it takes some pretty fierce weather to deter anyone from the pavement terrace. The appeal continues with the menu which blends the classics with the more contemporary. There's a tempting array of dishes available throughout the day, from small plates of hummus to assorted salads; dressed crab to gnocchi and rib-eye to lemon sole. It all begins at breakfast and, at times, service can be a little frenzied but also comes with a degree of charm. Chances are, there will be someone bearing down on your table the moment you get up to leave.

Sam's Brasserie

Mediterranean X

S2

Chiswick

⊖ Turnham Green
Closed 24-28 December

11 Barley Mow Passage ✉ W4 4PH
✆ (020) 8987 0555
Fax (020) 8987 7389
e-mail info@samsbrasserie.co.uk
www.samsbrasserie.co.uk

Menu £15 (weekday lunch)/18 (Sunday-Thursday dinner) – Carte £25/37

In challenging financial times restaurateurs can either just sit and wonder where everyone's gone or they can take some action. Sam Harrison does the latter by sending out chatty monthly newsletters about wine or whisky tastings, bridge afternoons or book signings and by making sure his brasserie is fun. The building was once a Sanderson wallpaper mill and the industrial feel works well. Dining is on two levels; the mezzanine is the quieter one while the larger room looks into the kitchen and has plenty of bustle. Menus are seasonal and lean towards the Med; the food is fresh and flavoursome and service is young and keen. Puds are done well and most of the wine list is under £30. A jazz band plays every other Sunday. It is certainly fun.

La Trompette ✿

Modern European XXX

S2

South-West ▶ Plan XVIII

Chiswick
5-7 Devonshire Rd ✉ W4 2EU
✆ (020) 8747 1836
Fax (020) 8995 8097
e-mail reception@latrompette.co.uk
www.latrompette.co.uk

⊖ Turnham Green
Closed 25-26 December – booking essential

Menu £24 (weekday lunch 25/30 weekends)/38 (dinner)

A/C VISA AE

La Trompette

La Trompette keeps getting better and each year its reputation spreads further afield. Fortunately, despite it becoming harder to secure a table these days, the locals have remained magnanimous in their support. Perhaps seeing all these interlopers reminds them why their houses cost so much. The young, enthusiastic serving team give the appearance of not only caring about what they do but also seeming to enjoy doing so; this in turn relaxes the room and creates a very pleasant atmosphere. The cooking has also developed: it is still classically based but now exhibits more personality, a result perhaps of greater confidence in the kitchen. The menu evolves at a greater pace and there is a willingness to try new things but without losing the essence of the cooking, which remains robust and spirited. Alongside the poulet noir or Valrhona chocolate, you might see other less regal ingredients like plaice – but all dishes display the same thoughtful preparation. Those willing to dine early are rewarded with a very attractively priced menu.

First Course

- Foie gras and chicken liver parfait with brioche.
- Ravioli of crab and scallop with leek and shellfish emulsion.

Main Course

- Herb crusted saddle of lamb with shallot purée and baby artichokes.
- Steamed plaice with fennel, samphire, clams and chives.

Dessert

- Lemon tart with Italian meringue and blackcurrant sorbet.
- Rum baba with glazed strawberries and crème Chantilly.

Le Vacherin

S1 — French XX

Chiswick

76-77 South Par. ✉ W4 5LF
✆ (020) 8742 2121
Fax (020) 8742 0799
e-mail info@levacherin.com
www.levacherin.com

⊖ Chiswick Park
Closed Monday lunch except December and Bank Holidays

Menu £17 (lunch) – Carte dinner £34/46

A/C, VISA, MC, AE

There's something very comforting and reassuring about the two words 'French' and 'Brasserie'. They usually mean satisfying food, efficient service and a convivial atmosphere and Le Vacherin is no exception. It has the leather banquettes, the belle époque prints and, most importantly, the classic menu. Appropriately enough, Vacherin appears as the house speciality when it is baked with almonds and truffles but it always pops up in the desserts in a subtly flavoured ice cream which demonstrates the owner-chef's lightness of touch. All the favourites are there on the menu, from snails to cassoulet, steak tartare to côte de boeuf, while the all-French wine list is considered and balanced and offers several wines by the carafe.

Four O Nine

U2 — Modern European XX

Clapham

entrance on Landor Rd, 409 Clapham Rd
✉ SW9 9BT
✆ (020) 7737 0722
e-mail reservations@fouronine.co.uk
www.fouronine.co.uk

⊖ Clapham North
Closed 24-26 December – dinner only

Carte £28/35

A/C, VISA, MC, AE

If anyone's watching you from their car on Clapham Road they'll see you ring the bell before being let in and think something nefarious is afoot. However, the shabby staircase and secretive entrance pay dividends by somehow adding to the intimacy of this surprisingly smart first floor restaurant. The chef is an acolyte of Chez Bruce and his set menus share the philosophy of crisp, appetisingly presented food, free from unnecessary over-elaboration and with natural flavours to the fore. The influences are predominantly French but occasionally there are dishes or ingredients derived from over the Italian border such as a linguini, risotto or some excellent prosciutto. The wine list is less predictable than many.

Trinity

Innovative XX

U2

Clapham

⊖ Clapham Common

4 The Polygon ✉ SW4 0JG

Closed 24-30 December, 1-3 January, Monday lunch and Sunday dinner

✆ (020) 7622 1199
Fax (020) 7622 1166
e-mail dine@trinityrestaurant.co.uk
www.trinityrestaurant.co.uk

Menu £20 (Monday-Thursday) – Carte dinner £30/48

A/C VISA MC AE

Judging by the scarcity of empty tables, Clapham gastronauts are rather taken with Trinity. It's a light and bright room, with a modern feel and a real sense of place; service is well meaning and avoids being too ceremonial, while the chef has always enjoyed a good local reputation. His menu is appealingly laid out; each dish is titled by the three main components such as Squid-Skate-Chorizo, with the supporting cast of ingredients listed below. There's plenty of originality, the plates are artfully presented and, despite a slight tendency to over-elaborate, his know-how, gathered by working in some serious places, is apparent. A lighter menu is available at lunch, while the atmosphere remains appealingly local and relaxed.

Tsunami

Japanese X

U2

Clapham

⊖ Clapham North

Unit 3, 5-7 Voltaire Rd ✉ SW4 6DQ

Closed 24-26 December and 1 January – dinner only

✆ (020) 7978 1610
Fax (020) 7978 1591
e-mail clapham@tsunamirestaurant.co.uk
www.tsunamirestaurant.co.uk

Carte £22/31

A/C VISA MC

Tsunami has always allowed Clapham residents to boast that they don't have to journey 'up west' if they want to eat modern Japanese food in stylish surroundings. After successfully opening a second branch in Charlotte Street – to perhaps prove that you can now find friendly neighbourhood restaurants in the West End too – the owners refurbished this, their original HQ, in 2009 so now it's even slicker and sexier than ever but also just as lively. The menu's focus is on modern, fusion food but there is an extensive nigiri and sashimi section. Sharing is positively encouraged and, as enticing aromas float through the room and the majority of dishes are visually appealing, you could find yourself diving in with Pavlovian enthusiasm.

Charlotte's Place

R1

Modern European

Ealing
16 St Matthew's Rd ✉ W5 3JT
(020) 8567 7541
e-mail restaurant@charlottes.co.uk
www.charlottes.co.uk

⊖ Ealing Common

Menu £15 (lunch Monday-Saturday)/20 (Sunday)
Carte Monday to Saturday £24/31

VISA MC AE

Charlotte may have long gone but the restaurant still exudes the feel of a friendly, neighbourhood restaurant. Ealing's most noted feature, the Common, is right outside the door and the large windows and mirrors ensure there's plenty of light. The ground floor seats twenty and is more fun than the somewhat soulless basement area which is used as an overflow or for larger parties. The menu combines modern Euro food, like sea bass with crushed new potatoes, with brasserie classics such as Caesar salad and fishcakes. British and Irish cheeses are a feature and there's a good value set menu for lunch and early-in-the-week dinners. The wine list is largely Old World and what it lacks in depth it more than makes up in its affordability.

Kiraku

R1

Japanese

Ealing
8 Station Par, Uxbridge Rd ✉ W5 3LD
(020) 8992 2848
e-mail mail@kiraku.co.uk
www.kiraku.co.uk

⊖ Ealing Common
Closed 1 week December, 1 week August, Monday and Tuesday following Bank Holidays

Menu £13 (lunch) – Carte dinner £15/27

A/C VISA MC

The name means 'relax and enjoy' and it's hard not to. Ayumi and Erica became so frustrated with the lack of a decent local Japanese restaurant that they decided to open one themselves; and now it is not just the bourgeoning Japanese community who flock to this cute little place. It's modestly styled and enthusiastically lit, but service is very charming. The choice is extensive and there are photos for the uninitiated. Zensai, or starters, include the popular Agedashi dofu; these can then be followed by assorted skewers, noodles and rice dishes. Fish is purchased daily and there's a large selection of sushi; Bara Chirashi is the house speciality. There are further specials on the board and assorted bargain lunch menus.

Maxim

R1 — **Chinese** XX

Ealing
153-155 Northfield Ave ✉ W13 9QT
✆ (020) 8567 1719
Fax (020) 8932 0717

⊖ Northfields
Closed 25-28 December and Sunday lunch

Menu £16/23 – Carte £18/31 s

A/C VISA MC AE

Loyalty is a two-way street which is why you'll find Mr Chow doing the rounds in his restaurant, greeting his guests and keeping them happy. Those guests include a high proportion of regulars who have made Maxim a local favourite for over thirty years. The service is never less than attentive and the suited managers are all equally personable. The restaurant itself is also more comfortable than the norm and is broken up into different areas, with splashes of colour coming from the huge vases and dragon costume. Mrs Chow runs the kitchen with the same level of reliable enthusiasm. You'll find all the favourites as well as specialities from Peking and the best bet is to go for one of the four good value set menus.

Sushi-Hiro

R1 — **Japanese** X

Ealing
1 Station Par, Uxbridge Rd ✉ W5 3LD
✆ (020) 8896 3175
Fax (020) 8896 3209

⊖ Ealing Common
Closed Monday – booking advisable

Carte approx. £26

A/C

Its unremarkable façade and rather pitiable display of plastic sushi in the window mean Sushi-Hiro is unlikely to draw in many passers-by. Inside, the vet's waiting-room aesthetic, with just four tables and nine counter seats, is equally unmemorable but then this allows the focus to steadfastly remain on the excellent sushi which in turn lends an air of authenticity to proceedings. The sushi can be ordered individually or as part of a set; the ingredients are appropriately first rate and the chef-owner, who arrived from Japan 14 years ago, works with quiet efficiency. Prices are extremely competitive, even for pricier items like abalone and sea urchin. His apprentice speaks English if you need some advice and only cash is accepted.

Mango & Silk

S2 **Indian**

East Sheen

199 Upper Richmond Rd West ✉ SW14 8 QT
✆ (020) 8876 6220
Fax (020) 8878 2056
www.mangoandsilk.co.uk

Closed Monday – dinner only and Sunday lunch

Carte approx. £21

VISA MC AE

Mango and Silk welcomes you to "the mystic and exotica of classic Indian dining in a serene and peaceful surrounding" and you can't argue with that. Owner Radhika Jerath is a natural and charming hostess but, more importantly, she has persuaded Udit Sarkhel back to the stove. His reputation was sealed from the day he opened his eponymous restaurant in Southfields and his menu provides an exhilarating culinary tour of India. His cooking displays a lightness of touch, expert spicing and a respect for ingredients; the Hyderabadi Chicken Sixers are a speciality. That window on the kitchen works both ways: he likes to see his customers enjoying themselves. The prices are terrific and those are his paintings on the wall.

The Victoria

S2 **Gastropub**

East Sheen

✉ SW14 7RT
✆ (020) 8876 4238
Fax (020) 8878 3464
e-mail bookings@thevictoria.net
www.thevictoria.net

⊖ **Mortlake (rail).**
Closed 2 days between Christmas and New Year

Carte £23/38

VISA MC

Chef Paul Merrett was lured away from the bright lights of TV cookery studios to take over this neighbourhood pub, which is concealed to the point of secrecy in a leafy residential street. It comes divided into two: the relaxed bar, popular with locals, and the conservatory restaurant with its wood-burning stove, although the same menu is available throughout. Sourcing of quality ingredients is clearly a top priority and, while the menu descriptions can make dishes sound quite ambitious, the cooking is earthy and satisfying and flavours are well-matched. Meat lovers will appreciate the 21-day aged Devon beef that comes served on a wooden board and there's a rotisserie on the large outside terrace in the summer.

Blue Elephant

Thai XX

T2

Fulham

4-6 Fulham Broadway ✉ SW6 1AA
✆ (020) 7385 6595
Fax (020) 7386 7665
e-mail london@blueelephant.com
www.blueelephant.com

⊖ Fulham Broadway
Closed 25-26 December – booking essential – dinner only

Menu £15/35 – Carte £26/48

This London institution shows what imagination and unrestrained ambition can lead to. There are plants and streams, pergolas and bridges and the place is about the size of a film set with a healthy budget - you half expect Indiana Jones to come through the undergrowth, machete in hand. It's sensibly divided into smaller sections so you'll have just as good a time if you're a table of two or have come with nine friends. Granted, the service can get stretched but the staff are a pleasant bunch. Dishes are a mix of classics from across Thailand and contemporary creations. The ingredients are good and the curries a strength. There's a cabinet by reception selling their own branded goods and recipes to remind you this is now a global chain.

The Farm

Gastropub

T2

Fulham

18 Farm Lane ✉ SW6 1PP
✆ (020) 7381 3331
e-mail info@thefarmfulham.co.uk
www.thefarmfulham.co.uk

⊖ Fulham Broadway.
Closed 25 December

Menu £25 – Carte £25/40

You'll find the austerity suggested by the semi-industrial looking façade is tempered by the warming fireplaces within this Fulham pub. Eat at the bar from an appealing menu which could include charcuterie, oysters, mini Cumberland sausages or cheese and chutney, but go through to the altogether more stylish restaurant and you'll find the choice more sophisticated, with prices to match. Here, the menu displays its ambition through dishes such as black pudding with foie gras or sea bass with sauce vierge but there are also more traditionally British dishes such as smoked salmon and Dover sole. The strength of the kitchen, however, lies in the astute sourcing and preparation of the meat dishes, particularly the very tender beef.

The Harwood Arms ✿

T2

British

Fulham
Walham Grove ✉ SW6 1QR
✆ (020) 7386 1847
e-mail admin@harwoodarms.com
www.harwoodarms.com

⊖ Fulham Broadway.

Carte £25/35

VISA MC AE

Michelin

The Harwood Arms feels less like a gastropub, more like a local but with really good food –Tuesday is quiz night and it's packed when Chelsea are playing at home. All three owners bring something to the operation: one has run pubs before and is the game specialist, one comes from a brewery background and the third is Brett Graham, chef of The Ledbury. There's a bracing Britishness to the menu, along with a respect for our culinary heritage and a willingness to try something different. Potted rabbit comes with devils on horseback; trotters and crisp ears are served on toast; roe deer is stewed with sloe gin; while game tea showcases the innate ability of the young chef who is a former member of The Ledbury's kitchen team. There's also a healthy respect for the seasons: even the bowl of warm doughnuts served as dessert changes from apple to rhubarb. The Harwood Arms is a proper pub that isn't pretending to be anything else. The serving team are suitably chummy and unflappable and even the bar snacks are done well.

First Course

- Potted rabbit with devils on horseback, celeriac and dandelion.
- Snails with oxtail braised in stout and bone marrow.

Main Course

- Pigeon with air-dried ham, chicory and onions.
- Sea bream with runner beans, squid, tomato and fennel.

Dessert

- Rhubarb doughnuts with orange curd and cream.
- Blackcurrant and stem ginger Eton mess.

Mao Tai

T2 — **Chinese** XX

Fulham

58 New Kings Rd, Parsons Green
SW6 4LS
(020) 7731 2520
e-mail mark.maotai@googlemail.com
www.maotai.co.uk

Parsons Green
Closed 25-26 December – dinner only

Carte £30/56

Apart from the hint in the name, there is little to suggest, to the casual observer, that this is a Chinese restaurant - the plush cocktail bar is a stylish and popular spot while the main dining room, split between two levels, is a moodily lit affair. Mao Tai does appear to have been invigorated by its latest image, both in the enthusiastic service and in the cooking. An appealing dim sum menu is served until 8pm, while the à la carte offers a comprehensive mix of modern and more traditional dishes, with a subtle nod towards more fiery Sichuan specialities; it's also unafraid of throwing in the occasional Thai or even Japanese influence. The beef is particularly tender and there's a fresh zing to the seafood dishes.

A/C · VISA · MC · AE

Memories of India on the River

T2 — **Indian** XXX

Fulham

7 The Boulevard, Imperial Wharf
SW6 2UB
(020) 7736 0077
Fax (020) 7731 5222
www.memoriesofindiaontheriver.co.uk

Fulham Broadway
Closed 25 December

Carte £22/36

No restaurant development is complete without Indian representation and so it is that, in among all the matching façades on the boulevard of Imperial Wharf, one finds Memories of India. It occupies the same amount of square footage as its neighbours and a love of white emulsion paint has been thoughtfully balanced by colourful silks and large pictures of spice baskets; the room is certainly light and open in its feel. Larger parties should try for one of the four booths beneath the central palm tree. There's ample choice on the menu, with the nucleus exhibiting a fair degree of originality and impressive presentation, although those who prefer more familiar dishes are not forgotten. A takeaway service is available for locals.

A/C · VISA · MC · AE

Salisbury

T2 **Gastropub**

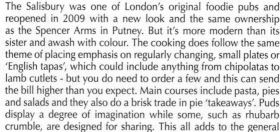

Fulham
21 Sherbrooke Rd ✉ SW6 2TZ
(020) 7381 4005
e-mail events@thesalisbury.co.uk
www.thesalisbury.co.uk

⊖ Fulham Broadway.
Closed 25-26 December and 1 January

Carte £16/25

The Salisbury was one of London's original foodie pubs and reopened in 2009 with a new look and the same ownership as the Spencer Arms in Putney. But it's more modern than its sister and awash with colour. The cooking does follow the same theme of placing emphasis on regularly changing, small plates or 'English tapas', which could include anything from chipolatas to lamb cutlets - but you do need to order a few and this can send the bill higher than you expect. Main courses include pasta, pies and salads and they also do a brisk trade in pie 'takeaways'. Puds display a degree of imagination while some, such as rhubarb crumble, are designed for sharing. This all adds to the general bonhomie that makes the reinvented Salisbury so pleasing.

Sands End

T2 **Gastropub**

Fulham
135-137 Stephendale Rd ✉ SW6 2PR
(020) 7731 7823
e-mail markdyerbusiness@yahoo.co.uk
www.thesandsend.co.uk

⊖ Fulham Broadway.
Closed 25 December – booking advisable

Carte £23/31

Urbanites will consider the look to be junkshop chic while those who head westwards at weekends will insist it's more Cirencester. But what all agree on is the appeal of the food. We're all aware of the seismic improvements in the standard of pub dining but this has also had a knock-on effect on that most British of nibble – the bar snack. The choice is no longer between flavours of crisps: here drinkers are offered homemade sausage rolls, Scotch eggs and Welsh rarebit soldiers. Those who prefer sitting when eating will also find much to savour from the concise menu. Snails come in garlic butter or as an accompaniment to rib-eye; steak and kidney pie sits alongside guinea fowl, and rice pudding competes for your attention with panna cotta.

Saran Rom

T2

Thai XXX

Fulham
The Boulevard, Imperial Wharf, Townmead Rd
SW6 2UB
(020) 7751 3111
e-mail river@blueelephant.com
www.blueelephant.com/river

Fulham Broadway
Closed 25-26 December – dinner only

Menu £22/35 – Carte £26/48

Saran Rom was taken over by the Blue Elephant group a couple of years ago so is in safe hands these days. Imperial Wharf's restaurants have not exactly been overflowing with customers: a lack of a direct tube link hasn't helped, but then neither has having main courses in the £23 plus region. This is still a pleasant spot, based on a Thai Royal summer palace, with a terrific riverside terrace. The series of dining rooms are built around the central area; the top floor is now only used on special occasions. Service is engaging and staff eager to please. Most of the ingredients come directly from Thailand; the menu is not overly long and has a slight seafood bias. Cooking shows care and craft and most go for the balanced Royal Thai Banquet menu.

Anglesea Arms

S1

Gastropub

Hammersmith
35 Wingate Rd W6 0UR
(020) 8749 1291
www.anglesea-arms.com

Ravenscourt Park.
Closed 25-27 December – bookings not accepted

Carte £17/46

If, for some reason, you need another excuse to visit a pub then just remember that they can always provide a little local history. The Marquess of Anglesea was Wellington's Number Two at Waterloo, where he lost his leg, and many of the surrounding streets are named after the Duke. The pub dates back to 1909 and the builders responsible for the charming properties in those streets were housed in the pub. What The Marquess would have made of seeing French classics like beef bourguignon on the menu doesn't bear considering. That menu often changes twice daily and the cooking is gutsy, wholesome and satisfying. Eat in either the glass-roofed restaurant with the open kitchen or the dark panelled bar. There's a good selection of wine by the glass.

Azou

S2 **North African**

Hammersmith
375 King St W6 9NJ
(020) 8563 7266
e-mail info@azou.co.uk
www.azou.co.uk

⊖ Stamford Brook
Closed 25 December

Carte £19/29

You'll probably walk past the first time and not notice this unassuming little place but, once visited, you won't walk past again. Inside is all silks, lanterns and rugs but it is also very personally run; the owner will often pop out from his kitchen to offer guidance – and his advice is well worth listening to. The cooking skips across North African countries – order some Algerian olives while you choose from the wide choice of main courses. Understandably, most of the regulars come here for a tajine, especially the Constantine with its tender lamb and triple steamed couscous. Highlights to start include the terrific baba ganoush with homemade bread and fresh briouat. It's the perfect food to share as the dishes come in large portions.

Carpenter's Arms

S2 **Gastropub**

Hammersmith
91 Black Lion Lane W6 9BG
(020) 8741 8386
Fax (020) 8741 6437
e-mail carpsarm@googlemail.com
www.carpentersarmsw6.co.uk

⊖ Stamford Brook.
Closed 1 week at Christmas – booking essential

Menu £16 (lunch) – Carte £27/33

Pubs come in all sorts of shapes, sizes and guises; the Carpenter's Arms is from the 'doesn't actually look much like a pub' school of pub. It has changed name a few times over the years and even spent time as a French brasserie but now, under the same ownership as Chelsea's Pig's Ear, it has found its niche. Decoratively, it's as understated as the exterior but there's lots of natural light and a small rear terrace. The cooking continues this theme of unpretentiousness; dishes are a mix of stout British produce like liver, eel, rabbit or duck, enlivened by more worldly accompaniments such as gnocchi or ricotta and the seasonal vegetables are a major strength. Expect the food to arrive in generous dimensions – this is, after all, a pub. Really.

Chez Kristof

S1 **French** XX

Hammersmith

111 Hammersmith Grove, Brook Green
W6 0NQ
(020) 8741 1177
e-mail info@chezkristof.co.uk
www.chezkristof.co.uk

Hammersmith
Closed Christmas

Menu £18 – Carte £23/28

The French windows open out onto a pleasant summer terrace, while in winter the interior is inviting and romantically lit. Chez Kristof comes from the same stable as Baltic and Wodka but looks more to the west, rather than the east, for its culinary influences. This includes a sizeable amount of French input, both on the menu and from the staff. The menu is printed daily and there is a good value lunch menu with dishes extracted from the dinner à la carte. The large Tarte Tatin is something of a speciality. There's a deli attached, which comes with its own menu and is ideal for those after a quick snack. The restaurant can get pretty frantic at weekends but the pace during the week is altogether gentler.

VISA MC AE

The Dartmouth Castle

S1 **Gastropub**

Hammersmith

26 Glenthorne Road W6 0LS
(020) 8748 3614
Fax (020) 8748 3619
e-mail dartmouth.castle@btconnect.com
www.thedartmouthcastle.co.uk

Hammersmith.
Closed 25 December - to 1 January, Easter Saturday and Easter Sunday

Carte £20/28

Pub lovers will like The Dartmouth Castle: customers are positively encouraged to dwell, there are board games available and cask ales change regularly and sometimes feature popular requests from regulars. Food lovers will also be happy: one of the owners spent time in California and France and the monthly-changing menu has a decidedly sunny disposition. The influences, from southern Europe and the wider Mediterranean, are evident throughout, with the likes of Tunisian lamb, assorted pastas, roast vegetables, thyme, tomatoes and fishy stews like caldeirada all featuring. Good bread, with olive oil, starts it all off and dishes come with appetisingly unfussy presentation. This is a simply furnished and hospitable pub, with distinctly pleasing food.

VISA MC AE

The Havelock Tavern

T1

Gastropub

Hammersmith

57 Masbro Rd, Brook Green

W14 0LS

(020) 7603 5374

e-mail info@thehavelocktavern.co.uk

www.thehavelocktavern.com

Kensington Olympia.

Closed 25-26 December – bookings not accepted

Carte £21/26

VISA

The great appeal of The Havelock Tavern is that it's a true and honest pub whose good value blackboard menu features modern, seasonal, gutsy dishes. There are tubs of pistachios and olives on the bar; you can start with something muscular like pork, duck and apricot terrine or something crispy, such as deep-fried monkfish cheeks. The main courses include rare roast rump of beef and braised lamb shank with mash. Expect no respite from dessert: the chocolate brownie comes with extra chocolate sauce and, in a blatant case of stable door shutting, crème fraîche. Drinkers and diners rub shoulders throughout; you still have to go to the bar to order and at busy times you might have to wait, but no one's complaining.

Indian Zing

S1_2

Indian

Hammersmith

236 King St W6 0RF

(020) 8748 5959

Fax (020) 8748 2332

e-mail indianzing@aol.com

www.indianzing.co.uk

Ravenscourt Park

Menu £15 (lunch)/22 – Carte £23/42

VISA

Many have warmed to Indian Zing and it's easy to see why. Chef-owner Manoj Vasaikar is so keen to see his customers satisfied that he has been known to send out an extra complimentary dish if he feels their order is not sufficiently balanced. He also reinvests everything back into the restaurant and has most recently added outside dining areas. While he is from Bombay, his cooking seeks inspiration from all over India; from sweet fish dishes to drier North Indian dishes or spicier Madras specialities; he is most proud of his 'feasts'. The restaurant is colourfully decorated and the close proximity of tables encourages conversations between customers. The serving team are equally keen but can sometimes appear a little disorganised.

River Café ✿

T2 **Italian** XX

Hammersmith

Thames Wharf, Rainville Rd ✉ W6 9HA
✆ (020) 7386 4200
Fax (020) 7386 4201
e-mail info@rivercafe.co.uk
www.rivercafe.co.uk

⊖ Barons Court
Closed 25 December-1 January, Sunday dinner and Bank Holidays – booking essential

Carte £45/63

VISA AE

River Café

They should run a shuttle service from local catering colleges to the River Café so that the students can learn the secret of good cooking: good ingredients. There's a renewed vigour to the kitchen here after the last refurbishment and now that it's all opened up and on view there seems to be more of a relationship between cook and customer. The big wood-fired oven really catches the eye and the restaurant seems to attract a wonderfully mixed bunch of customers, united in their appreciation of what makes a restaurant tick. That includes charming service: on looks alone, the team can rival all those glossier, shallower impostors but they break ranks here by actually smiling and caring about their customers. The menu is still written twice a day and head chef Sian Wyn Owen has brought an added sparkle to the cooking. Things taste just the way you want them to taste. Ordering a pasta dish ought to be made compulsory and the Chocolate Nemesis dessert should be a recognised treatment for depression.

First Course
- Char-grilled squid with red chilli and rocket.
- Porcini mushrooms with polenta and Parmesan.

Main Course
- Wood-roasted turbot with capers, oregano and swiss chard.
- Veal shin with saffron risotto.

Dessert
- Panna cotta with grappa and raspberries.
- Lemon Tart.

The Glasshouse ✿

R2 **Modern European** XX

Kew
14 Station Parade ✉ TW9 3PZ
✆ (020) 8940 6777
Fax (020) 8940 3833
e-mail info@glasshouserestaurant.co.uk
www.glasshouserestaurant.co.uk

⊖ Kew Gardens
Closed 24-26 December and 1 January

Menu £24/38

A/C VISA AE

The Glasshouse

Tempus fugit – The Glasshouse celebrated its tenth birthday last year. This anniversary comes as a surprise, not because its relative longevity was unexpected or undeserved but because the restaurant still feels fresh. It certainly helps that the manager and chef have both been here since day one. The bright and open interior has also stood the test of time and hasn't needed updating in all these years. But where the restaurant has been most successful is in understanding its customers and giving them what they want. That means the same seasonally informed menu is offered at both lunch and dinner, with just a slight tweak to the price, along with regular appearances from firm favourites, such as the warm pigeon salad with truffled egg, the assiette of pork or the raspberry and champagne trifle. Chef Anthony Boyd uses classic French techniques as a starting point but is not averse to adding a little Italian influence, a Moroccan twist or even an occasional Thai spice. Reservations for weekends, when lunches are largely family affairs, need to be made about a month in advance.

First Course

- Confit salmon with onion seed wafers.
- Deep fried truffled egg with crispy ham.

Main Course

- Rump of lamb with spiced cous cous, falafel and coriander.
- Roast halibut with broccoli and garlic velouté.

Dessert

- Apple financier with butterscotch sauce and crème fraîche.
- Raspberry and champagne trifle with crushed amaretti.

Kew Grill

S2 — Beef specialities XX

Kew
10b Kew Green ✉ TW9 3BH
✆ (020) 8948 4433
Fax (020) 8605 3532
e-mail kewgrill@awtrestaurants.com
www.awtrestaurants.com

⊖ Kew Gardens
Closed Monday lunch – booking essential

Menu £15 (lunch) – Carte £22/51

A/C VISA MC AE

Busy, relaxed and fun are the hallmarks of these Antony Worrall Thompson neighbourhood joints specialising in meats. Top quality steaks come with a choice of a sauce or butter; there are daily specials like shepherd's pie or duck confit and even a section dedicated to AWT's pork. There are seasonal dishes like haunch of venison; fish-eaters and veggies are catered for and children aren't forgotten either. The cooking is heart-warming and unfussy, the aged beef really is excellent and the puds will finish you off. The concise wine list is helpfully divided by price, under £20, under £30 etc. It's all done in quite a narrow room with something of a country feel; the friendly staff help the atmosphere along nicely.

Ma Cuisine

R2 — French X

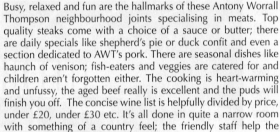

Kew
The Old Post Office, 9 Station Approach
✉ TW9 3QB
✆ (020) 8332 1923
e-mail info@macuisinekew.co.uk
www.macuisinekew.co.uk

⊖ Kew Gardens

Menu £15/18 – Carte lunch £20/30

VISA MC

This informal French bistro, set in a red-bricked former post office, certainly delivers the goods for a neighbourhood restaurant - the prices are fair, the service friendly and the cooking rustic and regional. The French theme is hard to avoid, from the period posters and pictures to the gingham tablecloths, while the menu offers a comprehensive selection of robust dishes from across France, including some of the classics. A blackboard marks that day's seasonal special, while those without much time can take advantage of the lunchtime menu rapide. Staff all welcome their regulars by name and, as it's quite a small place, it fills very quickly, particularly at weekends. There's another branch in nearby Twickenham.

A Taste of McClements

Traditional XX

R2

Kew
8 Station Approach ✉ TQ9 3QB
✆ (020) 8940 6617
www.tasteofmclements.com

⊖ Kew Gardens

Menu £18/45

VISA MC

John McClements was clearly not contented with capturing the casual dining end of the local market with his bustling bistros; now he also wants to go after those who are partial to a bit of 'fine dining'. For this he has created a cosy and intimate place, with seating for just 20, in what was formerly his fish shop. The set menu consists of around 12 courses, although some of those courses arrive together as a number of component parts; it continues to evolve but some 'signature' dishes such as the langoustine ravioli remain. The cooking certainly reveals the ambition of the kitchen, whose leanings are classically based. The wine list has also been thoughtfully compiled, with plenty available in 50, 125 or 175ml.

L'Auberge

French XX

T2

Putney
22 Upper Richmond Rd ✉ SW15 2RX
✆ (020) 8874 3593
www.ardillys.com

Closed Christmas, Sunday and Monday – dinner only

Menu £17 – Carte £25/32

VISA MC

This is what those of a certain maturity would call a 'proper' restaurant - it's run by a husband and wife team, provides authentic and traditionally prepared French cuisine and is decorated in a rustic and homely style which makes the countryside feel that little bit closer. The L-shaped dining room comes with yellow walls of heavily textured artex, tiled flooring and even Edith Piaf makes the odd appearance on the soundtrack to add to the Gallic character. The owners provide service that is reassuringly gracious and warm-hearted while the menu is decidedly old-fashioned but in the very best sense. Just make sure you leave room for a dessert, the speciality of the house, as the chef-owner originally trained as a patissier.

Enoteca Turi

T2 Italian XX

Putney
28 Putney High St
✉ SW15 1SQ
✆ (020) 8785 4449
Fax (020) 8780 5409
e-mail enoteca@tiscali.co.uk
www.enotecaturi.com

⊖ Putney Bridge
Closed 25-26 December, 1 January, Sunday and lunch Bank Holidays

Menu £18/27 (Monday-Thursday) – Carte £31/39

A/C VISA MC AE

A long-standing Putney favourite that no doubt does its bit for local house prices. Giuseppe Turi is of the thoughtful and considerate school of hospitality and his quiet passion is reflected in the thoughtful wine pairings offered with each dish and the accompanying tasting notes. The cooking makes a feature of the Northern regions of Italy, from Lombardy, Veneto and Trentino. Lunch is very good value indeed; the choice at dinner is more extensive. Ingredients are first-rate and their natural flavours are kept to the fore. The wine list is extensive and clearly the work of an enthusiast. The dining room has a warm and welcoming atmosphere; romantics should head for the terracotta coloured rear section.

The Phoenix

T2 Italian influences X

Putney
Pentlow St ✉ SW15 1LY
✆ (020) 8780 3131
e-mail thephoenix@sonnys.co.uk
www.sonnys.co.uk

Closed dinner Sunday and Bank Holidays

Menu £18 (Monday-Thursday) – Carte £25/33

A/C VISA MC AE

Just look out for the twinkling lights wrapped round the shrubs in front. Monthly-changing art for sale adorns the white walls of the two adjoining rooms, while in summer the charming terrace has a screen to hide the traffic but, sadly, not the noise. There's a great value set menu, although it's not available on Friday and Saturday nights. Like the tower in Pisa, the menu has Italian leanings; there's lots of flavour and a certain perkiness to the cooking. This being a neighbourhood restaurant means you can just pop in for a plate of San Daniele ham with figs, a bowl of risotto or rabbit with porcini mushrooms. There are also contributions from Blighty, like potted shrimps or apple crumble; over fifteen wines are available by the glass.

Prince of Wales

T2 **Gastropub**

Putney

138 Upper Richmond Rd
SW15 2SP
(020) 8788 1552
e-mail info@princeofwalesputney.co.uk
www.princeofwalesputney.co.uk

⊖ East Putney.
Closed 25 December and 1 January

Carte £25/40

Those who decry the rise of the gastropub should have tried The Prince of Wales in its past: such was its reputation that it earned the nickname 'The Prince of Darkness'. Now it's a thoroughly civilised spot, thanks to its Scottish owner whose ambition was to create a 'country pub in the city'. The dining room at the back is the best place to sit as it has the feel of a billiard room in a Scottish Baronial hall complete with stuffed animals and deer antlers. This gives some clues as to the cooking: it is robust and British, with game featuring strongly. The kitchen tends to buy the whole beast which then provides prime cuts, offal, then stews, pies, terrines and parfaits. There are often dishes for two such as cassoulet or a roast leg of venison.

The Spencer Arms

S2 **Gastropub**

Putney

237 Lower Richmond Road
SW15 1HJ
(020) 8788 0640
Fax (020) 8788 2216
e-mail info@thespencerarms.co.uk
www.thespencerarms.co.uk

⊖ East Putney.
Closed 25 December and 1 January

Menu £13/20 – Carte £18/25

A/C VISA AE

The Spencer Arms is one of those classic Victorian pubs that have a likeably unassuming manner and unstructured layout. The etched windows proclaim the offer of "Gutsy Grub" which is no word of a lie: food here is of the what-you-see-is-what-you-get variety which means it's satisfying and wholesome. They also offer small plates of what could be referred to – for lack of an alternative – as 'English tapas'. These can act as starters, bar nibbles or just as shared plates and include Scotch egg, smoked mackerel or black pudding sausage rolls; order too many, however, and your bill will quickly climb. Traditionalists can still order their three-courser and there are more Mediterranean flavours too, in the form of chorizo, ratatouille and panna cotta.

Bingham Restaurant ✿

Modern European XX

R3

Richmond

61-63 Petersham Road ✉ TW10 6UT
✆ (020) 8940 0902
Fax (020) 8948 8737
e-mail info@thebingham.co.uk
www.thebingham.co.uk

Menu £23/39

VISA MC AE

Michelin

A short stroll uphill from the High Street will lead you to the Bingham, which is an unremarkable looking building from the front – despite being two conjoined Georgian townhouses. As it is also a hotel you may need to skirt around a small group of conferencing businessmen before you reach the sanctuary of the restaurant. However, if you come on a warm summer's day, you could find yourself having lunch on the balcony, looking out over a garden and the Thames, and generally feeling good about life. The restaurant can't quite decide whether it wants to be formal or more relaxed and the glittery decoration can look a little frayed on closer inspection. But the serving team are enthusiastic and well-meaning and chef Shay Cooper's cooking is tremendous. His seasonal menu is full of interest and his food is precise and assured; presentation on the plate is strong but never at the expense of flavour. Combinations of ingredients work well and desserts, such as the fig parfait, will be one of the highlights of the meal.

First Course
- Brill fillet with scallop, ricotta gnocchi and poached grapes.
- Rabbit and ham hock terrine with carrot, ginger and foie gras.

Main Course
- Sea trout with broad beans, foie gras and pickled mushrooms.
- Lamb shoulder and sweetbreads with aubergine and lentil purée.

Dessert
- Chocolate tart with orange chantilly and sorbet.
- Mascarpone cheesecake with strawberries and banyuls syrup.

Matsuba

R2 — Japanese

Richmond
10 Red Lion St ✉ TW9 1RW
✆ (020) 8605 3513
e-mail matsuba10@hotmail.com
www.matsuba.co.uk

Closed 25-26 December, 1 January and Sunday

Menu £35/45 – Carte £15/24

A/C VISA MC AE

Matsuba is a small, family-run place that is so understated it's easy to miss – look out for the softly lit sign above the narrow façade. The interior is equally compact and low-key, with just a dozen or so tables along with a small counter at the back with room for four more. In fact the biggest thing in the room is the menu, which offers a comprehensive tour through most recognisable points in Japanese cooking. The owners are Korean so you can also expect to see bulgogi, the Korean barbecue dish of marinated meat that comes on a sizzling plate. All the food is fresh and the ingredients are good; lunch sees some very good value set menus. The service is well meaning and it's hard not to come away thinking kind thoughts.

Petersham Nurseries Café

R3 — Italian influences

Richmond
Church Lane (off Petersham Rd)
✉ TW10 7AG
✆ (020) 8605 3627
e-mail info@petershamnurseries.com
www.petershamnurseries.com

Closed Easter and 25 December – lunch only

Carte £33/50

VISA MC AE

It's just as the name suggests, which is why it's only open for lunch. The locals may be a bit sniffy about the place but dig in and don't panic if your wobbly chair falls back into the greenery. If the sun's out, the café's on the terrace, otherwise it's in a greenhouse - either way this is a charming spot with engaging service. But it's also all about the food which matches its setting by being natural, earthy and full of goodness. Ingredients are very well sourced and seasonal and there's an Italian accent to many dishes, such as roasted wild salmon with fennel, spinach and rocket or beetroot with buffalo mozzarella and rainbow chard. The prices may not be quite so down to earth but who can resist somewhere serving jugs of real lemonade?

The Restaurant at The Petersham

French XXX

R3

Richmond

Nightingale Lane ✉ TW10 6UZ
✆ (020) 8939 1084/8940 7471
Fax (020) 8939 1002
e-mail restaurant@petershamhotel.co.uk/ enq@petershamhotel.co.uk
www.petershamhotel.co.uk

Closed 24-26 December and Sunday

Menu £26 (lunch) – Carte £31/47

From its vantage point on Richmond Hill, the Petersham Hotel, built in 1865, offers wonderfully unspoilt vistas of the Thames at its most majestic and, thanks to its large windows, diners at virtually all the tables in its restaurant can enjoy this great view. The advantages of dining within a hotel include the considerable elbow and leg-room: tables are well-spaced for added privacy and there's a comfortable lounge and bar, with its own terrace. Those understandably hesitant about dining within a hotel can rest assured that the room does have its own personality. The cooking displays a classical French education, but will also please those who prefer their culinary ambitions to be a little closer to home.

Swagat

Indian X

R2

Richmond

86 Hill Rise ✉ TW10 6UB
✆ (0208) 940 7557
e-mail swagat.india@yahoo.co.uk
www.swagatindiancuisine.co.uk

⊖ Richmond
Closed Sunday – dinner only
booking essential

Menu £25 – Carte £28/31

Richmond's nascent restaurant scene has been given a boost by the arrival of Swagat which translates as 'welcome'. With just 14 tables, it's best to book otherwise you'll find yourself in a queue with the locals. Its popularity is down to the attentive, very well-meaning service and the likeable menu, which aims to promote healthy eating by using less oil and more subtle spicing. You'll find plenty of classics but try the less recognisable dishes, like chicken Chettinad from southern India. Fortnightly changing specials add further interest, as do the moist breads, fresh chillies and the complimentary poppadoms and chutneys. Prices are also appealing and allow vegetarian dishes to be ordered as main courses or accompaniments.

Princess Victoria

Gastropub

S1

Shepherd's Bush

217 Uxbridge Rd ✉ W12 9DH

✆ (020) 8749 5886

Fax (020) 8749 4886

e-mail info@princessvictoria.co.uk

www.princessvictoria.co.uk

⊖ Shepherd's Bush.
Closed 25-26 December

Menu £15 (lunch) – Carte £23/33

VISA

From tramstop to live music venue, this magnificent Victorian gin palace has seen it all. Now a chef and a sommelier have taken it over, given it a top-to-toe revamp and the old girl has a whole new lease of life. The large dining room is dominated by a grand centre table. The stunning wine list has over 350 bottles, with a focus on Rhône, Pinot Noir and Riesling. Food-wise, it's a mix of classics, with the odd Asian or Mediterranean influence. The Pork Board starter, which includes pig's cheek and Bayonne ham, has become a favourite, and you'll always find the Angus rib-eye. Sausages are homemade and the kitchen knows its butchery. More nostalgia comes courtesy of the pudding menu, with the appearance of coupes and sundaes.

Simply Thai

Thai

R3

Teddington

196 Kingston Rd ✉ TW11 9JD

✆ (020) 8943 9747

e-mail simplythai1@yahoo.co.uk

www.simplythai-restaurant.co.uk

Closed Easter, 25 December and Sunday lunch – booking essential at lunch

Menu £18 – Carte £24/28

VISA

The smiling ladies provide charming service and the delightful owner, Patria Weerapan, does all the cooking at this sweet little Thai restaurant. She picked up her culinary education from her family but then added her own twists and personality; while respectful of tradition she is not averse to trying something different. She is also keen to ensure that the menu remains fresh and interesting so often adds new creations, such as the crispy sea bass with jungle curry. Her judicious use of coconut underlines her commitment to offering healthy food and her passion for finding the freshest ingredients means that she has already sent away three fish suppliers with their tails between their legs. She also gives cookery lessons.

Kastoori

U3 **Indian** X

Tooting

188 Upper Tooting Rd
✉ SW17 7EJ
✆ (020) 8767 7027
www.kastoorirestaurant.com

⊖ Tooting Bec
Closed 25-26 December and lunch Monday and Tuesday

Carte £14/19

A/C · VISA · MC

There are plenty of neon lights vying for your attention on this strip and Kastoori doesn't necessarily stand out amongst them in the looks department. However, where it is head and shoulders above its near neighbours is in the originality of its food and the pride taken in its preparation. The Thanki family are originally from Uganda and celebrate their Gujarati heritage through their vegetarian cooking. Start with the Puri, or 'tastebombs' as they describe them, filled with chick peas and spices. The tomato curry remains a favourite, as do many of the 'family specials' and there is a particularly wide selection of dishes on a Sunday. Staff are always on hand to offer advice or to explain the history of a dish.

A Cena

R3 **Italian** XX

Twickenham

418 Richmond Rd
✉ TW1 2EB
✆ (020) 8288 0108
Fax (020) 8940 5346
www.acena.co.uk

⊖ Richmond
Closed 24-26 December, Sunday dinner and Monday lunch

Carte £25/34

A/C · VISA · MC · AE

Stroll past during the evening and the candlelight on the bar will draw you in. This relaxed but well-run Italian neighbourhood restaurant has a rustic yet quite intimate feel, with large mirrors, scrubbed floorboards and pew seating. The seasonal menus showcase the prime ingredients that the kitchen gets its hands on and dishes, some of which change daily, are vibrant, full of flavour and arrive in generous proportions. Wonderfully moist focaccia starts things off and, in spring for example, can be followed by asparagus and new season lamb with peas. Influences range across the country although they do host a regional evening every couple of months. The menu at lunch is a little lighter and prices are reduced.

Brula

R3 French

Twickenham
43 Crown Rd, St Margarets
TW1 3EJ
(020) 8892 0602
Fax (020) 8892 7727
e-mail lawrence@brula.co.uk
www.brula.co.uk

Closed 25-30 December, Mondays in August and Sunday dinner – booking essential

Menu £15 (lunch) – Carte £20/29

VISA MC AE

Brula has already enjoyed its tenth birthday and this relative longevity can be put down to a combination of reliable cooking, sensible prices and personable service. This pretty Victorian building has been both a pub and a butcher's shop in the past but now thoroughly suits its role as an authentic looking bistro. France remains at the heart of the cooking but over the past couple of years other influences have started to appear on the menu, which is priced per course rather than per dish. Cooking is also more exact in its execution. The cheeses and the thoughtfully arranged wine list remain exclusively French. The friendly and helpful service also extends to those using one of the private rooms.

The Grill Room

R3 Beef specialities

Twickenham
2 Whitton Rd TW1 1BJ
(020) 8891 0803
e-mail johnmac21@aol.com
www.thegrillroomtw1.co.uk

Carte £22/33

A/C VISA MC AE

Owner John McClements has tried a few different concepts on this site and The Grill Room is his latest. Sandwiched between two of his other restaurants, he's gone for a classic steakhouse this time, with cuts sourced from across the British Isles, ranging from 7oz fillet to 14oz T-bone; all hung on the premises for between 32 and 42 days. They come with a choice of sauce and chunky chips. Other grilled dishes are as British as the starters and range from Arbroath Smokies to Lancashire hot pot but the steaks are the stars of the show. If you're not full by pudding, then you certainly will be afterwards, as they include crumbles and sundaes. Try reserving one of the booths which occupy one side of the room.

Ma Cuisine

French

R3

Twickenham
6 Whitton Rd ✉ TW1 1BJ
✆ (020) 8607 9849
e-mail info@macuisinetw1.co.uk
www.macuisinetw1.co.uk

Menu £15 (lunch) – Carte £20/30

Londoners have always appreciated that dining out should be part of every day living. This does, in turn, call for plenty of affordable restaurants and here Ma Cuisine fits the bill nicely. By keeping prices low, it has proved a real local draw and makes us wish we had one of these at the end of our street. For starters, it's a bistro, with the sort of informality that makes dining out a relaxing, stress-busting experience. Secondly, it serves reassuringly rustic and recognisable French classics like onion soup, coq au vin and lemon tart. The French theme continues in the decoration, in the posters and the music, gingham table covers and plenty of cries of "bon appétit" from the staff. You get all this without breaking the banque.

Tangawizi

Indian

R2

Twickenham
406 Richmond Rd, Richmond Bridge
✉ TW1 2EB
✆ (020) 8891 3737
Fax (020) 8891 3737
e-mail tangawizi_richmond@hotmail.com
www.tangawizi.co.uk

⊖ Richmond
Closed 25 December – dinner only

Carte £14/28

Rich in colour and vitality, Tangawizi - meaning 'ginger' in Swahili – is another in the new breed of Indian restaurants. That means thoughtful design with clever use of silks and saris, attentive and elegant staff but, above all, cooking that is original, fresh and carefully prepared. North India provides much of the influence and although the à la carte menu offers plenty of 'safe' options, there are gems such as the roasted then stir-fried 'liptey' chicken. Diners should, however, head for the 'specials' section where the ambition of the kitchen is more evident. Lamb is another house speciality and is marinated to ensure it arrives extremely tender. For cooking this good, the prices are more than fair.

Chez Bruce ✿

U3 — French XX

Wandsworth

2 Bellevue Rd ✉ SW17 7EG

✆ (020) 8672 0114

Fax (020) 8767 6648

e-mail enquiries@chezbruce.co.uk

www.chezbruce.co.uk

⊖ Tooting Bec

Closed 24-26 December and 1 January – booking essential

Menu £26/40

A/C · VISA · MC · AE

Chez Bruce

Chez Bruce's loyal clientele allowed it to weather the financial storms of 2009 with less difficulty than many of its competitors. The restaurant did delay its plans to expand into the deli next door and instead just concentrated on giving those dependable followers more of what they expected: flavoursome and uncomplicated food, sprightly service, sensible prices and an easy-going atmosphere. Matthew Christmas returned to the kitchen as Head Chef after taking a year out and has worked with Bruce Poole for over 10 years. The cooking provides an object lesson in the importance of flavours and balance: dishes are never too crowded and natural flavours are to the fore. The base is largely classical French, but comes with Mediterranean tones, so expect words like parfait, pastilla, brandade and confit. The menu offers an even-handed selection, with a choice of around seven dishes per course. Cheese is always worth it and coffee comes with shortbread at lunch and terrific palmiers at dinner.

First Course

- Hake with courgette flower, escabèche of mackerel and coriander.
- Chicken wings with snails and sweetbreads.

Main Course

- Pork with choucroute, crispy belly and boudin blanc.
- Sea bream with shellfish, bacon and sourdough crouton.

Dessert

- Apricot and almond tart with amaretto ice cream.
- Strawberry and basil trifle with lemon sorbet.

Light House

International

T3

Wimbledon
75-77 Ridgway ✉ SW19 4ST
✆ (020) 8944 6338
Fax (020) 8946 4440
e-mail info@lighthousewimbledon.com
www.lighthousewimbledon.com

⊖ Wimbledon
Closed 24-28 December and Sunday dinner

Menu £18 (lunch)/19 (midweek dinner before 7.30pm) – Carte £27/39

VISA MC AE

Those expecting a tall, tubular building with a light on the top will be disappointed. The name refers to the time when this was a shop selling lights and light fittings. Nowadays it provides an illuminating insight into our more adventurous dining habits by offering cooking unfettered by national boundaries. On any one day you may find influences ranging from a bit of Italian, Greek or Tunisian to the odd Asian twist. The fact that it seems to work speaks volumes for the quality of the ingredients. The pricing is also eminently sensible, especially for the set lunch menu. The restaurant itself is a relatively simple affair, with plenty of light wood, a semi-open kitchen and a roomy bar area. The atmosphere is one of contented bonhomie.

Daniel Bendimol / Fotolia.com

Thierry Burot/Fotolia.com

Where to **stay**

←These 50 recommended hotels are extracted from the Great Britain & Ireland 2010 guide, where you'll find a larger choice of hotels selected by our team of inspectors.

Andaz Liverpool Street 356
Aster House 357
B + B Belgravia 358
The Berkeley 359
Blakes 360
Brown's 361
The Capital 362
Charlotte Street 363
Claridge's 364
The Connaught 365
Covent Garden 366
Dorchester 367
Dorset Square 368
Draycott 369
Dukes 370
Durrants 371
Egerton House 372
The Gore 373
The Goring 374
The Halkin 375
Hart House 376
Haymarket 379
Hazlitt's 378
The Hempel 379
InterContinental 380
K + K George 381
Knightsbridge 382
The Lanesborough 383
Langham 384
The Levin 385
Mandarin Oriental Hyde Park 386
Mayflower 387
The Metropolitan 388
The Milestone 389
Miller's 390
Number Sixteen 391
One Aldwych 392
The Pelham 393
The Ritz 394
The Rockwell 395
The Rookery 396
St Martins Lane 397
Sanderson 398
Sofitel St James London 399
The Soho 400
Stafford 401
Tophams 402
Twenty Nevern Square 403
Westbury 404
The Zetter 405

Andaz Liverpool Street

M2

Liverpool St ✉ EC2M 7QN ⊖ Liverpool Street
✆ (020) 7961 1234
Fax (020) 7961 1235
e-mail info.londonliv@andaz.com
www.andaz.com

264 rm – †£259/403 ††£259/403, ☕ £20 – 3 suites

🍴 **1901** *(See restaurant listing)*

Andaz Liverpool Street

The 'Andaz' brand (which apparently means "personal style" in Hindi) belongs to Hyatt, and this former railway hotel, which once went by the less ambiguous name of the Great Eastern, was the London prototype before its export to New York and L.A. The idea is to create luxury hotels with a less structured and more informal feel. In practical terms this mostly means that instead of a reception desk you have staff wandering around the nearest thing they have to a lobby, armed with laptops. The hotel may not be quite as hip as they imagine but it does provide a comfortable and contemporary environment that has a palpable sense of individualism. The crisply dressed bedrooms use a slick red, white and black palette and mod cons are comprehensive and largely concealed. Those wanting to be fed and watered will find themselves almost overwhelmed by the choice: there's the traditional George pub, a cosy Japanese, a lively brasserie, stylish seafood with its own champagne bar and the eye-catching 1901.

A/C SAT VISA AE

Aster House

E6

3 Sumner Pl ✉ SW7 3EE ⊖ South Kensington
✆ (020) 7581 5888
Fax (020) 7584 4925
e-mail asterhouse@btinternet.com
www.asterhouse.com

13 rm ☕ – 🚹£92/156 🚹🚹£138/173

A/C

SAT

VISA

Michelin

If you made a mathematical calculation to find the best location for a tourist in London, then chances are the X would mark a spot somewhere near Aster House on Sumner Place. You've got all the best museums within strolling distance; Hyde Park mere minutes away; all the famous shops and, above all, you're staying in a charming Victorian house in a typical Kensington street where people actually live rather than in a faceless hotel district. Mr and Mrs Tan keep the house commendably shipshape and are enthusiastic hosts. The bedrooms at the front of the house benefit from larger windows while those at the back are quieter and overlook the garden, but all boast fairly high ceilings and room to breathe. Wi-fi is available without charge in all the rooms, while L'Orangerie, a first floor conservatory looking down over Sumner Place, doubles as the breakfast room and guests' sitting room. Prices are also kept within the parameters of decency so bookings need to be made plenty of time in advance.

B + B Belgravia

G6

64-66 Ebury St ✉ SW1W 9QD ⊖ Victoria
✆ (020) 7259 8570
Fax (020) 7259 8591
e-mail info@bb-belgravia.com
www.bb-belgravia.com

17 rm – **£99** **£135**

VISA
AE

Michelin

It's really more Victoria than Belgravia and is certainly a degree more stylish than your average B&B. But what is certain is that B&B Belgravia provides very good value accommodation in a central location and is just the sort of place that London needs more of. The discreet entrance and key pad entry system make you feel as though you've borrowed a friend's place while the funky lounge comes complete with a complimentary coffee machine and plenty of magazines and DVDs. Breakfast is a buffet, with eggs cooked to order; those not good in the morning may find the staff's sunny demeanour and the room's general brightness akin to a second wake-up call. Rooms are virtually identical in style: they are contemporary in tone with sleek lines, high ceilings and good amenities. 6 of the 17 rooms have baths, the rest just showers. This being Central London, the rooms on the front can get a little noisy so ask for a room overlooking the gravelled garden at the back, such as Room 12. And do the booking in plenty of time as this place is understandably popular.

The Berkeley

G4

Wilton Pl ✉ SW1X 7RL ⊖ Knightsbridge
✆ (020) 7235 6000
Fax (020) 7235 4330
e-mail info@the-berkeley.co.uk
www.the-berkeley.co.uk

189 rm – ♦£552/658 ♦♦£658, ☕ £26 – 25 suites

Marcus Wareing at The Berkeley *(See restaurant listing)*

The Berkeley

VISA

The Berkeley's image is getting more fashionable by the day: The Blue Bar is as cool as the name and decoration suggest and on the other side of the lobby you'll find The Caramel Room whose target audience is obvious when you consider that tea is called "Prêt-à-Portea" and biscuits are fashioned as handbags. The spacious Boxwood Café, with its own street entrance, offers informal dining while Marcus Wareing has now left the Gordon Ramsay stable and the next chapter of this luxury restaurant has begun. The most unique area of the hotel must be the 7th floor, with its roof-top pool, vast treatment rooms and personal training services which should satisfy the most slavishly health-conscious traveller. By using a number of different designers, bedrooms have both a sense of individualism and personality; the most recent have softer, calmer colours and a lighter, more contemporary feel while the classic rooms are richer, thanks to their deeper, more intense colours. All the rooms are immaculately kept and several of the suites have their own balcony.

Blakes

D6

33 Roland Gdns ✉ SW7 3PF ⊖ Gloucester Road
(020) 7370 6701
Fax (020) 7373 0442
e-mail blakes@blakeshotels.com
www.blakeshotels.com

40 rm – £173/225 £253/524, £25 – 8 suites

Blakes

Blakes was created to much acclaim by Anouska Hempel in the early '80s and remains a favoured pit-stop for those riding the celebrity circuit. In fact, much of its success can be put down to its long-serving staff who are as discreet and selfless as some of their guests are imprudent and egocentric. To see Blakes at its best, one needs to up the financial ante and go for one of the stylish deluxe rooms with their towers of cushions, flowing drapes, appealing colour combinations and luxury bathrooms. Entry-level bedrooms suffer in comparison and are a little plain. All mod cons are there but just camouflaged and concealed – Anouska was clearly not too fond of TVs and other electronic paraphernalia as it got in the way of the overall design effect. Downstairs is a slick and stylish affair, from the Chinese room and bar to the intimate restaurant. It's bento boxes for lunch; luxury afternoon tea and Asian flavours on the dinner menu. Other townhouses have come along in the meantime but Blakes still holds its own.

Brown's

H3

Albemarle St ✉ W1S 4BP ⊖ Green Park
✆ (020) 7493 6020
Fax (020) 7493 9381
e-mail reservations.browns@roccofortecollection.com
www.roccofortecollection.com

105 rm – †£229/547 ††£322/604, ☕ £27 – 12 suites

Brown's

Opened in 1837 by James Brown, Lord Byron's butler, Brown's has a long and distinguished history and has been the favoured hotel of many a visiting dignitary: it was here that Alexander Graham Bell first demonstrated his telephone and The Kipling Suite is just one named after a former guest. It reopened in 2005 after a full face-lift, with Olga Polizzi personally overseeing the design and her blending of the traditional with the modern works well. The bedrooms have personality and reflect the character of the hotel, albeit with all of today's required gadgetry. One thing that has remained constant is the popularity of the afternoon teas – the selling point, apart from the pianist, is that the waiter replenishes all stands and pots without extra charge. The wood-panelled restaurant took slightly longer to bed in and now goes by the name of The Albemarle; the menu features British comfort food. The Donovan Bar is probably the hotel's best feature and celebrates the distinguished work of British photographer Terence Donovan.

The Capital

F5

22-24 Basil St ✉ SW3 1AT ⊖ Knightsbridge
✆ (020) 7589 5171
Fax (020) 7225 0011
e-mail reservations@capitalhotel.co.uk
www.capitalhotel.co.uk

49 rm – †£265 ††£420, ☕ £20 – 8 suites

The Capital

The Capital Hotel's appeal lies in its very Britishness and a sense of individuality that comes from being family-owned. Its location is pretty good too: all the smartest shops are close at hand but there's still a palpable sense of neighbourhood. However, in 2009 the general manager left and the long-standing and acclaimed chef Eric Chavot also called it a day, so the challenge for the hotel will be to maintain the standards they have set. There is nothing to worry about regarding the fabric of the hotel. Rooms remain classically elegant and the contemporary embellishments are restrained and in keeping with the general atmosphere. Each floor is slightly different and uses designs from the likes of Mulberry, Ralph Lauren and Nina Campbell. But what has always raised The Capital to greater heights than similarly styled hotels has been the depth and detail of the service. No one can walk through the small lobby without being greeted, while the concierge is old-school in the best sense of the word and can arrange anything for anyone.

Charlotte Street

12

15 Charlotte St ✉ W1T 1RJ
⊖ Goodge Street
✆ (020) 7806 2000
Fax (020) 7806 2002
e-mail charlotte@firmdale.com
www.charlottestreethotel.co.uk

48 rm – †£259/294 ††£364, ☕ £19 – 4 suites

Firmdale

Expect the lobby and bar to be full of men with man-bags and horn-rimmed specs, for Charlotte Street is the hotel of choice for those in the advertising industry. But even if you've never pitched, promoted or placed a product and are just after a stylish, contemporary hotel in a street thronged with bars and restaurants then get on the mailing list here. Oscar is the busy bar and restaurant that spills out onto the street in summer; its sunny contemporary European menu and vivid mural brighten it in winter. Film Club is on Sunday evening: dinner followed by a film in the downstairs screening room. Those after some quiet can nab one of the sofas in the Drawing room or Library. The bedrooms are, as with all hotels in the Firmdale group, exceptionally well looked after. Every year, three or four are fully refurbished and one thing you'll never see is a bit of dodgy grouting or a scuff mark. They are all decorated in an English style but there is nothing chintzy or twee about them. Bathrooms are equally immaculate and the baths now face little flat screen TVs.

Claridge's

G3

Brook St ✉ W1K 4HR ⊖ Bond Street
✆ (020) 7629 8860
Fax (020) 7499 2210
e-mail info@claridges.co.uk
www.claridges.co.uk

143 rm – †£564/736 ††£736, ☕ £31 – 60 suites

Gordon Ramsay at Claridge's *(See restaurant listing)*

Claridge's

VISA
AE

Stand in the lobby looking bewildered and, before you know it, a liveried member of staff will appear promptly before you to enquire after your well being; Claridge's may have a long and very illustrious history but it recognises that reputations are forged because of service rather than longevity. That being said, no modern, purpose-built hotel could afford the extravagance of having such wide corridors or such ornate decoration. The art deco is perhaps the hotel's most striking decorative feature and it's kept suitably fresh and buffed. Despite its long and glittery past, Claridge's has never been in danger of being a museum piece; the David Collins designed bar attracts a more youthful crowd and The Foyer, with its eye-catching light sculpture, proves that afternoon tea need not be a stuffy or quaint affair. The Gordon Ramsay restaurant continues to pull in the punters and the people-watchers. Further bedrooms and other guest facilities are to be added over the next few years and the challenge will be to make this extension as seamless as possible.

The Connaught

G3

Carlos Place ✉ W1K 2AL
✆ (020) 3147 7200
Fax (020) 7314 3537
e-mail dining@the-connaught.co.uk
www.the-connaught.co.uk

⊖ Bond St
Closed 1 week January and 1 week August

95 rm – †£480/610 ††£610, ☕ £28 – 27 suites

🍴 **Hélène Darroze at The Connaught** *(See restaurant listing)*

The Connaught

The hotel calls the work "a restoration, not a renovation" – when you've spent upwards of £70 million you can call it what you like. What is certain is that The Connaught is one of London's great hotels; its refreshed, contemporary feel is mixed with a tangible sense of heritage. The Coburg Bar honours the hotel's original name and its seats are so deep it's a wonder anyone ever leaves. By contrast, the Connaught Bar attracts a sprightlier clientele than the one hitherto associated with the hotel. Hélène Darroze oversees the main restaurant, the revamped Grill beloved of senior members of London's dining community, and Espelette with its accessible menu of everything from cottage pie to pasta. The impressive spa was the last piece of the jigsaw. Guests' comfort was clearly the overriding aim with the new bedrooms; not something as axiomatic with hotels as one might think. Asprey toiletries and TVs in the bathrooms; restored antique furniture and discreet mod cons create luxurious surroundings. If you have any problems, consult one of the 260 staff members.

Covent Garden

13

10 Monmouth St ✉ WC2H 9HB ⊖ Covent Garden
✆ (020) 7806 1000
Fax (020) 7806 1100
e-mail covent@firmdale.com
www.coventgardenhotel.co.uk

56 rm – †£264/323 ††£376, ☕ £19.50 – 2 suites

Firmdale

The Covent Garden Hotel has always been hugely popular with those of a theatrical bent, whether cast or audience member, not least because of its central location, a mere saunter away from the majority of playhouses and productions. The hotel was once a French hospital – the words 'Nouvel hopital et dispensaire francais' are etched into the brickwork – but the style is essentially British. Mannequins, soft fabrics and antique furniture are juxtaposed with crisp lines and contemporary colours to create a very stylish and comfortable environment. The first floor residents-only wood-panelled sitting room is a delight and so is occasionally used by a visiting grandee for a backdrop to an interview; the presence of an honesty bar adds further to the appeal. The Screening Room holds weekend dinner-and-a-film nights, while Brasserie Max is now a lot bigger, having been extended in late 2008, and feels much more like a proper restaurant than a mere addendum. Its menu is appealingly accessible and afternoon tea is now also provided.

Dorchester

G4

Park Lane ✉ W1K 1QA ⊖ Hyde Park Corner
✆ (020) 7629 8888
Fax (020) 7629 8080
e-mail info@thedorchester.com
www.thedorchester.com

200 rm – 🚹£340/570 🚹🚹£524/857, ☕ £29.50 – 49 suites

Alain Ducasse at The Dorchester and China Tang
(See restaurant listing)

The Dorchester

VISA MC AE

The focus recently has been on improving still further the quality of service and this is most apparent in The Promenade: it may look as though it is an extension of the lobby but try walking through and you won't get far without being welcomed enthusiastically by a member of staff. Afternoon tea here remains a huge draw but they also now offer more of an evening service, to the accompaniment of a jazz trio who replace the day-shift pianist. Suites are always snapped up quickly and it is easy to see why: all have their own personality, from the three elegant rooftop suites which have their own outside terraces, to the Lionel Messel suite on the 7th floor, which has seemingly hosted virtually every visiting idol and has now been listed. There's an impressive choice of restaurant, after you've had a Martini in the bar: they've added more grilled dishes to the menu in The Grill, which seems logical; China Tang sets the standard for stylish dining in a Chinese restaurant and Alain Ducasse provides luxury surroundings to match the food.

Dorset Square

F1

39 Dorset Sq ✉ NW1 6QN ⊖ Marylebone
✆ (020) 7723 7874
Fax (020) 7724 3328
e-mail nicholas@dorsetsquare.co.uk
www.dorsetsquare.co.uk

37 rm – †£173/322 ††£322, ☕ £15.50

Dorset Square

Dorset Square hotel is a pretty Regency house and the square opposite was where Thomas Lord laid out his ground in 1787, before it moved up the road in 1814 to what is now the hallowed HQ of international cricket, Lord's. His memory lives on in the hotel in subtle ways – the room keys come with little cricket balls attached and the occasional MCC member can be spotted rushing in or out during the summer months. For those sadly impervious to the charms of a game that lasts five days and usually ends in a draw, there is still much to appreciate in the hotel, not least is its proximity to the centre of town: much of London is reachable by foot from this relatively peaceful base. There's a charming drawing room with an honesty bar and the Potting Shed restaurant downstairs has now been turned into a pretty little Italian whose menu sensibly keeps things quite simple. The bedrooms reflect the age of the house which means a mix of sizes and some sloping lintels; they all share fine country style fabrics and bags of charm.

Draycott

F6

26 Cadogan Gdns ✉ SW3 2RP ⊖ Sloane Square
✆ (020) 7730 6466
Fax (020) 7730 0236
e-mail reservations@draycotthotel.com
www.draycotthotel.com

35 rm – 🚹£179/219 🚹🚹£363, ☕ £19.95 – 11 suites

Draycott

The sitting room is one of the best things about The Draycott, especially when the light streams in from the garden outside. It also has a well stocked bar and offers guests complimentary tea at 4pm, champagne at 6pm and hot chocolate at 10pm. This is a discreet little townhouse, decorated more like a country house. The bedrooms have plenty of personality themselves; six have fireplaces and all have an Edwardian feel to their decoration. Each is named after an acting legend about whom you'll find a biography or assorted pictures within the room, be it Vivien Leigh or John Gielgud. The breakfast room is called the Peter O'Toole Room; the name was apparently chosen in a staff competition although he's not a man one would necessarily associate with an early morning meal. Not many hotels have individual guest books in each room and write the names of the occupants on cards outside the door, but The Draycott has always done things 'properly' and its sincere hospitality ensures a very healthy number of returning guests.

Dukes

H4

35 St James's Pl ✉ SW1A 1NY ⊖ Green Park
✆ (020) 7491 4840
Fax (020) 7493 1264
e-mail bookings@dukeshotel.com
www.dukeshotel.com

84 rm – †£190/368 ††£190/512, ☕ £24.50 – 6 suites

Dukes

As St James's is one of the more traditionally British parts of London, what with all those gentlemen's clubs, wine merchants and tailors, it is no surprise to find that a hotel like Dukes has been a constant presence here for over 100 years. But that is not to say this is some sort of crusty old museum piece: its most recent refurbishment gave it a fresh and brighter feel and introduced more modern elements without losing any of the character. For example, the pretty little sitting room, popular for afternoon tea, opens out into a small Zen-inspired garden. The bar is quite clubby and was apparently one of Ian Fleming's old haunts and the basement dining room, with its international menu, actually looks out at street level thanks to the vagaries of local topography. Breakfast is served until the thoroughly louche hour of 11am. Bedrooms are comfortable and discreet and bathrooms are kitted out in marble. This is still the sort of hotel where you can leave your shoes outside the door for cleaning. It is also surprisingly peaceful, when you consider the central location.

Durrants

G2

26-32 George St ✉ W1H 5BJ ⊖ Bond Street
✆ (020) 7935 8131
Fax (020) 7487 3510
e-mail enquiries@durrantshotel.co.uk
www.durrantshotel.co.uk

92 rm – †£125 ††£175, ☕ £17 – 4 suites

Durrants

Durrants may be one of London's more traditional, privately owned hotels but that doesn't mean it is resting on any laurels. Having a separate breakfast room to the main dining room had always seemed something of an extravagance and this room has now been turned into a lounge area, as private parties had started to encroach on the existing sitting rooms and, commendably, the hotel was concerned about its staying guests. The bars have been given a little spruce up as well, although the muskets are still there for those who like some weaponry with their whisky. The clubby dining room still offers the likes of Dover sole and a carving trolley but there are now some lighter, more Mediterranean dishes for the youngsters. The bedrooms are the final piece of the operation being brought up to date. The refurbishment is nothing too outrageous so there'll be no scaring of the horses. Instead, the rooms are being brightened and lightened, while retaining that very sense of Englishness that makes the hotel what it is.

Egerton House

F5

17-19 Egerton Terrace ✉ SW3 2BX ⊖ South Kensington
✆ (020) 7589 2412
Fax (020) 7584 6540
e-mail bookeg@rchmail.com
www.egertonhousehotel.com

27 rm – †£294/363 ††£294/363, ☕ £24.50 – 1 suite

Egerton House

In challenging economic times hotels can either panic and cut staff and slash rates – a course of action which usually ends in ruin – or they can hold their nerve and add greater value to their guests. Anyone wondering what more a hotel can do should get along to Egerton House. This is a hotel whose decorative style is at the lavish end of the scale; the fabrics are of the highest order and the colours neatly coordinated. The ground floor Victoria and Albert Suite comes with its own little decked terrace and a row of filled decanters for company. All the rooms are slightly different; the marble bathrooms are very neat and the hotel has made the best use of limited space – ask for one of the quieter rooms at the back overlooking the little garden. What really makes this little hotel stand out, though, is the service and the eager attitude of the staff. Lots of hotels spout tosh about being 'a home from home' but here they do make a genuine effort to make their guests feel part of things by, for example, arranging complimentary admission to events at the V&A.

The Gore

D5

190 Queen's Gate ✉ SW7 5EX ⊖ Gloucester Road
✆ (020) 7584 6601
Fax (020) 7589 8127
e-mail reservations@gorehotel.com
www.gorehotel.com

50 rm – ♦£207 ♦♦£242, ☕ £16.95

The Gore

Being the nearest hotel to the Royal Albert Hall makes The Gore a popular choice for performers as well as attendees and the bright, casual bistro is always busier early and late in the evening than it ever is at 8pm. The hotel clearly stands out at the top of Queen's Gate with its fluttering Union flag and gleaming brass plaque and who needs a fitness room when you've got Kensington gardens just yards away. If you were in any doubt that this is the part of London most closely associated with Queen Victoria, then just step through the door because the walls are covered with pictures and paintings relating to her reign. But, despite the plethora of antiques and all that Victoriana, this is a hip little hotel with a large element of fun attached. Rooms like Miss Fanny and Miss Ada are as camp as they sound; the Tudor Room has a secret bathroom and minstrel's gallery and many of the bathrooms give meaning to the expression 'sitting on the throne'. Bend down in the rooms and you might find a card saying "Look, we've cleaned here too".

The Goring

H5

15 Beeston Pl, Grosvenor Gdns ✉ SW1W 0JW ⊖ Victoria
✆ (020) 7396 9000
Fax (020) 7834 4393
e-mail reception@thegoring.com
www.thegoring.com

65 rm – †£229/426 ††£275/472, ☕ £23 – 6 suites

VISA

AE

The Goring

As the Goring approaches its centenary in 2010 it is steadily being refurbished and renewed in preparation for the next 100 years. The hotel has asked designers like Nina Campbell to update and refresh the bedrooms but, at the same time, to retain that pervading sense of Britishness which is the hallmark of the hotel. There has been a clever introduction of new technology, from the TVs that rise from the desk to the touch panels that control everything. But, reassuringly for those less familiar or enamoured with the modern world, you still get a proper key with which to open your bedroom door.Still privately owned, the hotel is in the hands of the fourth generation of the Goring family, with Jeremy now at the helm. This lineage is clearly welcomed by the staff, many of whom have been at the hotel for years, a very pleasing fact for the regular guests who all get recognised. Designed by Lord Linley, the restaurant is a bright, discreet and comfortable affair while the menu celebrates Britain's newly-found confidence in its culinary heritage.

The Halkin

G5

5 Halkin St ✉ SW1X 7DJ ⊖ Hyde Park Corner
✆ (020) 7333 1000
Fax (020) 7333 1100
e-mail res@halkin.como.bz
www.halkin.como.bz

35 rm – £259/449 £374/564, £25 – 6 suites

Nahm *(See restaurant listing)*

A/C

SAT

VISA

AE

The Halkin

The Halkin is still looking pretty sharp considering it opened nearly 20 years ago as one of London's first boutique hotels. It's certainly more discreet than its sibling, The Metropolitan, which attracts a livelier and feistier crowd, although guests here can use its spa. Apart from the relatively recent addition of a small gym, there is not much in the way of public areas, save for the small but perfectly formed bar area next to the lobby, and Nahm, the hotel's acclaimed and inventive Thai restaurant. The hotel is really all about the bedrooms, which are neatly set out and cleverly thought through. The touch pad operation makes everything seem so effortless but the technology never reaches baffling proportions. All rooms have silk covered walls and marble bathrooms with lots of natural minerals; the Nahm menu is also available as room service. Staff are in abundance and appear to stay for a long time, which improves standards of service no end and pleases the regulars. They also all wear Armani, so no pressure there, then.

Hart House

F2

51 Gloucester Pl ✉ W1U 8JF ⊖ Marble Arch
✆ (020) 7935 2288
Fax (020) 7935 8516
e-mail reservations@harthouse.co.uk
www.harthouse.co.uk

15 rm ☕ – 🚹£103/110 🚹🚹£127/173

SAT
VISA

Michelin

Hart House has been in the same family for nearly 40 years and while the owner may not spend as much time in the hotel as he used to, he's got enough friendly staff running the place in his absence. Equally importantly, he's also still writing the occasional cheque, as the recent introduction of new LCD TVs would testify. The hotel wouldn't win any design awards but what you get, for a fair price, is clean and tidy accommodation in a late Georgian terrace house that's in a useful central location: it's just a short walk from Oxford Street and Hyde Park and less than a ten minute cab ride from Paddington for those who've taken the Heathrow Express. Gloucester Place may be a fairly busy thoroughfare but the bedrooms on the front have sufficient double glazing; there are family rooms available as well as rooms on the ground floor. Ceilings get lower the higher you climb, reflecting the time when the house's staff had their quarters at the top of the house. The only public area is the small, basement breakfast room but the hotel still manages to have a sociable, international atmosphere.

Haymarket

14

1 Suffolk Place ✉ SW1Y 4BP ⊖ Piccadilly Circus

✆ (020) 7470 4000
Fax (020) 7470 4001
e-mail haymarket@firmdale.com
www.haymarkethotel.com

47 rm – †£294 ††£382, ☕ £18.50 – 3 suites

Firmdale

VISA

The most recent hotel from Tim & Kit Kemp is a stylish, hip place, refreshingly free from any bland corporate appurtenances. They converted a grand John Nash Regency building that had been a gentleman's club and office before being gutted by a fire. Art and an eclectic collection of furniture now run through it; the lobby, conservatory and library on the ground floor are immaculately dressed and set the tone for the hotel. Individually styled bedrooms come with dressed mannequins - the motif of the Kemp's hotels – and custom-made furniture. They are all bright and calming with a subtle English feel. For extra quiet ask for one overlooking the inner decked courtyard. The location couldn't be better for those coming 'up west': theatre-land is literally just outside – indeed, the hotel adjoins the Haymarket theatre – and is a short stroll away from all that London offers. If that isn't enough, there's a very cool swimming pool downstairs. Brumus is the restaurant – named in honour of the owner's hound - and offers easy Italian food in spacious surroundings.

Hazlitt's

13

6 Frith St ✉ W1D 3JA ⊖ Tottenham Court Road
✆ (020) 7434 1771
Fax (020) 7439 1524
e-mail reservations@hazlitts.co.uk
www.hazlittshotel.com

29 rm – †£183/253 ††£195/253 – 3 suites

A/C

VISA

MC

AE

Hazlitt's

Hazlitt's grew a little in 2009, with the addition of eight rooms but you can't see the join and the intimate atmosphere that has long been a feature of this hotel in the heart of Soho remains unchanged. Duke of Monmouth is the most striking of these new rooms: it's spread over two floors and has its own terrace with a retractable roof. Madam Dafloz, named after another of Soho's former roguish residents, is also appealing, with its sultry, indulgent feel. The Library, with its 24/7 honesty bar, is the hotel's only communal area and has consequently been slightly enlarged. This remains one of the few hotels where breakfast in bed really is the only option, however, and who is going to object to that? The hotel was named after the essayist and critic William Hazlitt, whose home this was. It dates from 1718 and still attracts plenty of writers. There is much character to be found in all the bedrooms, from wood panelling and busts to antique beds and Victorian fixtures, but you also get free wi-fi and all the necessary electronic gizmos secreted within.

The Hempel

D3

31-35 Craven Hill Gdns ✉ W2 3EA ⊖ Queensway
✆ (020) 7298 9000 Closed 25-28 December
Fax (020) 7402 4666
e-mail info@the-hempel.co.uk
www.the-hempel.co.uk

44 rm – †£183/298 ††£183/298, ☕ £21.50 – 6 suites

The Hempel

The Hempel may no longer be enjoying the first flush of youth but, with judicious use of make-up and the support of celebrity friends, is still managing to attract its share of attention from the younger crowd. It remains true to the principles of its original designer, Anouska Hempel, who, in the late '90s, created a crisp, minimalist environment in a blizzard of white that was largely at odds with that period's general reliance on all things floral. But live by the sword... other hotel companies have cottoned on to the importance of design as well as functionality and London now has an abundance of stylish, but also comfortable, hotels. The Hempel knows it has to raise its game if it wants to compete so a refurbishment is in the pipeline. Bedrooms vary from the starkly white to those with splashes of colour; room 107 boasts one of the highest ceilings in London; there's a suspended bed in 110 and those who like black – which, apparently, is the new black – should ask for 405. One of the hotel's most striking features remains the Zen Garden across the street.

InterContinental

G4

1 Hamilton Place, Park Lane ✉ W1J 7QY ⊖ Hyde Park Corner
✆ (020) 7409 3131
Fax (020) 7493 3476
e-mail london@ihg.com
www.london.intercontinental.com

399 rm – 🚹£229/390 🚻£229/390, ☕ £27 – 48 suites

🍴 **Theo Randall** *(See restaurant listing)*

The InterContinental

Spending £80million on a refurbishment means that it was unlikely they were just changing the carpets and re-grouting the bathrooms. Sure enough, when the Intercontinental reopened three years ago it was virtually unrecognisable from the hotel it was before. For starters, the old faithful Coffee House became the bright and cheffy-themed Cookbook Café to reflect our current obsession with the breed. At the other end of the shiny lobby is the eponymous Theo Randall's cool and contemporary Italian restaurant on the site of the once celebrated Le Soufflé where many a good chef once trained. Now the hotel is all thoroughly 21C, the bedrooms are crisp, sleek and refreshingly chintz-free. Deluxe Rooms have great views of the park and sound insulation is sufficiently substantial to keep out the Hyde Park Corner traffic noise. The two top suites are the London Suite, spread over two floors, and The Cinema Suite with its own private screening area. Tailor-made treatments can be provided in the Spa and a personal trainer is on hand in the guest-only gym.

K + K George

C6

1-15 Templeton Pl ✉ SW5 9NB ⊖ Earl's Court
✆ (020) 7598 8700
Fax (020) 7370 2285
e-mail hotelgeorge@kkhotels.co.uk
www.kkhotels.com

154 rm – †£230 ††£300

K&K Hotels

A/C SAT P VISA AE

All K&K hotels seem to blend seamlessly into the fabric of the assorted European cities in which they are located. London is no exception, as the K+K George is set within an imposing stucco fronted and luminously white Georgian terrace and is in a useful location for both tourists and attendees of exhibition halls and trade fairs nearby. In contrast to the period façade, the hotel's interior is colourfully contemporary in style, with clean lines and a refreshing lack of chintz. Those who struggle to lift their mood first thing in the day will appreciate the bright and comfortable breakfast room as it looks out onto the hotel's own private garden - a charming and, considering the location, surprisingly large space which must be the envy of surrounding houses. A simple bistro-style menu is served in the friendly and less structured surroundings of the bar while corporate guests will find all the kit they need for any homework. Bedrooms all come in relatively decent dimensions and have a certain Scandinavian feel and freshness about them.

Knightsbridge

F5

10 Beaufort Gdns ✉ SW3 1PT ⊖ Knightsbridge
✆ (020) 7584 6300
Fax (020) 7584 6355
e-mail knightsbridge@firmdale.com
www.knightsbridgehotel.com

44 rm – †£196/242 ††£340, ☕ £17.50

A/C SAT VISA MC AE

Firmdale

Firmdale Hotels all seem so quintessentially British that it'll be interesting to see what New Yorkers make of them now they have one of their own. The Knightsbridge, converted from a row of Victorian terrace houses in an attractive square, is another typical example of what they do so well: it proves style and comfort are not mutually exclusive and that a hotel can be fashionable without being fuzzy. The work of British artists, such as Carol Sinclair's slate stack and Peter Clark's dog collages sets the tone and the bedrooms are constantly being refreshed and rearranged. Those facing the square on the first floor benefit from floor to ceiling windows, while the Knightsbridge Suite stretches from the front to the back of the building. All rooms are so impeccably tidy and colour coordinated it'll make you question your own dress sense. The Library Room differs from many similarly named hotel sitting rooms by actually containing books, along with an honesty bar which holds everything from fruit and champagne to snacks and ice cream.

The Lanesborough

G4

Hyde Park Corner ✉ SW1X 7TA ⊖ Hyde Park Corner
✆ (020) 7259 5599
Fax (020) 7259 5606
e-mail info@lanesborough.com
www.lanesborough.com

86 rm – 🚹£409/547 🚹🚹£547, ☕ £30 – 9 suites

Apsleys *(See restaurant listing)*

The Lanesborough

Built in 1733 as Viscount Lanesborough's country house, this building was perhaps better known as a hospital before it was converted into a hotel in 1991. Being on Hyde Park means it gets a fresh coat of paint regularly but it's inside where that luxury is most apparent, with the designers looking to the rich and decorative Regency period for inspiration. By contrast, technological advances that mean the TVs are all touch-pad controlled and landline calls to the USA and Europe are complimentary. 350 members of staff, including butlers on each floor, mean that the hotel enjoys one of the highest staff to guest ratios. The Library has a vast selection of whiskies and cognacs (and the same pianist since the hotel's opening). The most recent change has been in finding suitably impressive cooking to match the grand surroundings of the Adam Tihany designed Italian restaurant, Apsleys. The conservatory roof remains but it is now a chic and opulent space, with cooking overseen by celebrated chef Heinz Beck. The Garden Room was created for the benefit of cigar smokers.

Langham

H2

1c Portland Pl, Regent St ✉ W1B 1JA ⊖ Oxford Circus
✆ (020) 7636 1000
Fax (020) 7323 2340
e-mail loninfo@langhamhotels.com
www.langhamhotels.com

359 rm – †£218/466 ††£218/466, ☕ £30 – 21 suites

Langham

VISA MC AE

When it opened in 1865, The Langham was one of Europe's first purpose-built Grand hotels. Over the years it has been owned by all sorts, including at one stage the BBC – they used it as their library and it is also where 'The Goon Show' was recorded. In 2009 it came out of an extensive refurbishment that didn't provide much change from £80million and is now poised to compete with the big boys once again. Pride of place must be the Palm Court, a twinkling ersatz art deco space which is open for light meals and afternoon teas. The Artesian bar is a stylish affair and does interesting things with rum while, next to it, is The Landau restaurant: an impressive looking circular room with a contemporary menu. The bedrooms have personality and, for a change, the furniture is free-standing rather than fitted. The lighting is good and the bathrooms have under-floor heating. The Club rooms are particularly distinctive, with their bold colours and high ceilings. The health and fitness club is impressively kitted out and includes a swimming pool.

The Levin

F5

28 Basil St ✉ SW3 1AS ⊖ Knightsbridge
✆ (020) 7589 6286
Fax (020) 7823 7826
e-mail reservations@thelevinhotel.co.uk
www.thelevinhotel.co.uk

12 rm – †£305 ††£305, ☕ £16.50

The Levin

Its bigger sister, The Capital, is a few strides down the road and may be better known, but The Levin still does the (Levin) family proud. Here you'll find a different decorative style but still the same level of care and enthusiasm in the service. The eye-catching fibre optic chandelier dominates the staircase, while the collection of Penguin paperbacks reminds you that this is a fundamentally British hotel. All 12 bedrooms are light and fresh-feeling; there are subtle nods in the direction of art deco in the styling but these are combined with a cleverly contemporary look which blends in well with the building. The best room is the top floor open-plan suite. Mini-bars are stocked exclusively with champagne - along with some helpful hints on how to prepare an assortment of champagne cocktails. In the basement you'll find Le Metro which provides an appealing, all-day menu with everything from quiche and salads to shepherd's pie and sausage and mash, along with selections from the family estate in the Loire.

Mandarin Oriental Hyde Park

F4

66 Knightsbridge ✉ SW1X 7LA ⊖ Knightsbridge
✆ (020) 7235 2000
Fax (020) 7235 2001
e-mail molon-dine@mohg.com
www.mandarinoriental.com/london

173 rm – ♦£435 ♦♦£555, ☕ £29 – 25 suites

Mandarin Oriental Hyde Park

VISA

AE

The enormous amount of building work next door continues apace and is due to be completed at the end of 2010. Along with the new serviced apartments, there will be a swimming pool to complement the hotel's already impressive spa and a couple of internationally acclaimed chefs are being lined up to run the restaurants. In the meantime, the hotel continues to distract its guests from the hammering by continuing to provide the sort of exemplary service and attention to detail that one would expect from somewhere with the Mandarin Oriental name over the door. One of the hotel's great strengths has also been the quality of its suites: most of them face the park at the back and the Royal and Sovereign are the best two, although those in the two turrets on the 9th floor are also pretty impressive. All rooms come in either beige and blue or red and gold and have a very British feel. They also boast every extra imaginable, although whoever ordered the TVs clearly watches too much because they are far too big for the rooms.

Mayflower

C6

26-28 Trebovir Rd ✉ SW5 9NJ ⊖ Earl's Court
✆ (020) 7370 0991
Fax (020) 7370 0994
e-mail info@mayflower-group.co.uk
www.mayflowerhotel.co.uk

46 rm – £79/109 ££105/115, £9 – 4 suites

VISA
AE

Mayflower

The Mayflower shares the same ownership as Twenty Nevern Square just around the corner and it too offers good value accommodation. It is also twice the size so chances of actually getting a room are somewhat greater. Some of those bedrooms can be a little tight on space but this is also reflected in the room rates. Rooms 11, 17 and 18 are the best in the house and the general decoration is a blend of the contemporary with some Asian influence; some of the rooms have jet showers and others balconies. But what makes the hotel stand out is that the owner is nearly always on the property and his enthusiasm has been passed to his staff. This may not be a glitzy West End hotel but they really do make an effort to get to know their guests and help in anyway they can. There is no restaurant, but then it doesn't need one: there are plenty of places in which to eat that are no more than a vigorous stroll away. A plentiful breakfast is provided and, on summer days, can even be taken on the small terrace.

The Metropolitan

G4

Old Park Lane ✉ W1K 1LB ⊖ Hyde Park Corner
✆ (020) 7447 1000
Fax (020) 7447 1100
e-mail res.lon@metropolitan.como.bz
www.metropolitan.como.bz

147 rm – †£432 ††£432, ☕ £30 – 3 suites

🍴 **Nobu** *(See restaurant listing)*

Metropolitan

The Metropolitan is inextricably linked to its über-cool hang-out, The Met Bar. If you've never managed to blag your way past the doorman at night you can now secure entry by grabbing yourself some 'Afternoon Delight': a healthy version of afternoon tea with low-fat cakes and breadless sandwiches. The Metropolitan Hotel is well over a decade old now; in design terms, there may be more contemporary competitors around but it continues to hold its own in the fashion stakes by letting its guests create their own atmosphere. The bedrooms are neutral in colour and gadgets are discreetly integrated; all get regular licks of paint or, following an overnight stay from the occasional wannabe rock star, a full redecoration. Plenty of rooms overlook the park but the more interesting views are those facing east over the rooftops. The spa promises plenty of holistic treatments while London's original Nobu on the first floor ensures a further sprinkling of stardust. Even better, the staff now provide good service instead of just standing at an angle, looking cool.

The Milestone

D4

1-2 Kensington Court ✉ W8 5DL ⊖ High Street Kensington
✆ (020) 7917 1000
Fax (020) 7917 1010
e-mail bookms@rchmail.com
www.milestonehotel.com

63 rm – 🚹£271/322 🚹🚹£305/357, ☕ £25 – 6 suites

The Milestone

The Milestone proves that it is the service, not the space, which makes a hotel. With 100 members of staff for 57 bedrooms, it's odds-on you'll be well looked after; the hotel prides itself on keeping records of the whims and preferences of their regulars. Plenty of thought has gone into the design and decoration of the bedrooms which are undergoing a refurbishment. It's in the detail where you notice the extra effort: there's a little gift with the turn-down service and the bathrobes are seasonally adjusted so one gets a lighter robe in summer. The suites display greater levels of whimsy than the standard rooms – just check out the art deco inspired Mistinguett Suite, named in honour of the celebrated music hall entertainer, while Johnny Weissmuller would feel more at home in The Safari Suite. The sitting room is a comfy place, with a jaunty looking Noel Coward hanging above the fireplace. The Jockey bar is so named as this was where the horses were stabled in the days when this Victorian building was a private house. The dining room is an intimate, wood-panelled affair.

Miller's

C2

111A Westbourne Grove ⊖ Bayswater
(entrance on Hereford Rd) ✉ W2 4UW
✆ (020) 7243 1024
Fax (020) 7243 1064
e-mail enquiries@millershotel.com
www.millershotel.com

8 rm – †£173/202 ††£265

VISA
MC
AE

Miller's

Such is the 'home from home' atmosphere that guests have been known to breakfast in their pyjamas. Miller's couldn't be farther from the world of international corporate hotelkeeping if it tried – its quirkiness makes it thoroughly unique. For a start, don't expect any signs, flags or flames – just look out for the red door on Hereford Street. It's then up the stairs, every inch of which is covered by oil paintings, with 'Toad' greeting you at the top. As befits a hotel owned by Martin Miller of the famed antique guide – you can usually catch him in the mornings – the place is stuffed with antiques, baubles, pictures and objets d'art and resembles a pirate's treasure chest. Sweets are scattered around the enchanting drawing room, where breakfast is served. You help yourself to drinks and magazines and there are no hidden charges or unexpected extras on your final bill. Bedrooms are named after the Romantic poets – Keats and Wordsworth are the biggest two; Tennyson has the four-poster and a recent new bathroom. The reception is manned 24 hours.

Number Sixteen

E6

16 Sumner Pl ✉ SW7 3EG ⊖ South Kensington
✆ (020) 7589 5232
Fax (020) 7584 8615
e-mail sixteen@firmdale.com
www.numbersixteenhotel.co.uk

42 rm – †£141/235 ††£317, ☕ £17.50

Firmdale

Number Sixteen opened back in 2001 and was the first one in Tim and Kit Kemp's Firmdale Group of hotels not to have its own restaurant. This actually suits it because it feels more like a private house than the others and, with repeat business standing at around 55%, they've clearly got it right. Attention to detail underpins the operation, whether in the individual styling of the bedrooms or the twice-daily housekeeping service. Breakfast is in the conservatory overlooking the little garden – don't miss the smoothie of the day – and is served until midday: welcome acknowledgement that not every guest has an early morning meeting. Firmdale also operates its own laundry service which explains how the bed linen retains such crispness. Rooms 2 and 7 have their own private patio terrace and all the first floor rooms benefit from large windows and balconies. The drawing room, with its plump sofa cushions and pretty butterfly theme, is a very charming spot and there's the added bonus of a nearby honesty bar.

One Aldwych

J3

1 Aldwych ✉ WC2B 4RH ⊖ Temple
(020) 7300 1000
Fax (020) 7300 1001
e-mail reservations@onealdwych.com
www.onealdwych.com

93 rm – £242/449 ££242/541, £24.75 – 12 suites

Axis *(See restaurant listing)*

One Aldwych

Things have gone all green down at One Aldwych. The hotel is hoping to take a lead within the hospitality industry on matters environmental (without, of course, neglecting its duties as a luxury hotel) and has appointed a 'green team' to oversee and coordinate procedures. The swimming pool is chemical and chlorine free; bath products are organic, and the chocolate on your pillow has been replaced by a book called 'Change the World'. As far as guests are concerned though, it's business as usual, which means extremely comfortable bedrooms and plenty of polished staff. Fruit and flowers are changed daily in the rooms, which are awash with Bang & Olufsen toys and also come with Frette linen; deluxe rooms and corner suites are particularly desirable. There's a choice of restaurant: the first floor Indigo offers a light, easy menu while Axis boasts more personality and greater ambition in its cooking. The lobby of the hotel is perhaps its most well known feature; not only does it double as a bar surprisingly successfully but it also changes its look according to the seasons.

The Pelham

E6

15 Cromwell Pl ✉ SW7 2LA ⊖ South Kensington
✆ (020) 7589 8288
Fax (020) 7584 8444
e-mail reservations@pelhamhotel.co.uk
www.pelhamhotel.co.uk

51 rm – †£182 ††£299/322, ☕ £17.50 – 1 suite

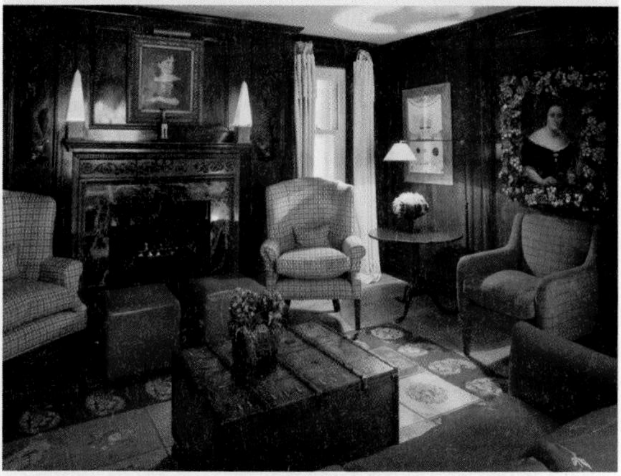

The Pelham

It may no longer be part of the Firmdale group – it is now owned by the people who have The Gore in Queensgate – but The Pelham retains that stylish look which comes from juxtaposing the feel of a classic English country house with the contemporary look of a city townhouse. Originally three houses, the hotel has a pleasing lack of conformity in its layout. Bold pastel colours, fine fabrics and a housekeeping department that could satisfy Howard Hughes combine to create bedrooms that are pristine, warm and comfortable. Spend too long in the panelled sitting room or library, with all those cushions, an honesty bar and a fridge full of ice cream and the world outside will seem positively frenzied. Downstairs you'll find Bistro Fifteen, a relaxed all-day affair which becomes a cosy and romantic dinner spot. Its menu is mostly centred on Europe with an extra Gallic element – a nod to the high number of French émigrés in the neighbourhood. There's a genuine helpfulness and an eagerness to please amongst the staff.

The Ritz

H4

150 Piccadilly ✉ W1J 9BR ⊖ Green Park
✆ (020) 7493 8181
Fax (020) 7493 2687
e-mail enquire@theritzlondon.com
www.theritzlondon.com

116 rm – 🚹£288/714 🚹🚹£311/714, ☕ £32 – 17 suites

The Ritz Restaurant *(See restaurant listing)*

The Ritz

VISA AE

Henry James considered that "there are few hours in life more agreeable than the hour dedicated to the ceremony known as afternoon tea". Such is the popularity of Tea at the Ritz, which is served daily in the grand surroundings of the Palm Court, that the hour of the ceremony begins at 11.30 am and doesn't cease until 9 pm. Meanwhile, the rest of the hotel, built in 1906 in the style of a French chateau, remains in fine form thanks largely to the constant re-investment by its owners, the Barclay Brothers. The William Kent Room must be the most ornate private dining room in London and the traditionally decorated bedrooms are all immaculately kept. The Royal and Prince of Wales Suites both have enormous square footage and are often booked for long stays by those for whom the credit crunch is no more than a mild irritant. The Ritz Restaurant, with its dinner dances, lavish surroundings and brigades of staff, evokes images of a more formal but more glamorous age and the art deco Rivoli bar remains a veritable jewel.

The Rockwell

C5-6

181-183 Cromwell Rd ✉ SW5 0SF ⊖ Earl's Court
✆ (020) 7244 2000
Fax (020) 7244 2001
e-mail enquiries@therockwell.com
www.therockwell.com

40 rm – †£120 ††£176, ☕ £12.50

The Rockwell

The Rockwell is steadily establishing itself on the London hotel scene and is building up quite a loyal client base. They certainly get a lot of things right: the reception is manned 24/7 and staff are imbued with sufficient self-confidence to make eye-contact with their guests and offer help when needed; the housekeeping department also do an evening service of all the rooms. The lobby is a comfortable space, with its fireplace and generous scattering of newspapers. The hotel is made up of two Victorian houses; the best two rooms are the split level 104 and 105 and those on the lower ground floor have their own private patios. All rooms have showers rather than baths, and come with top-brand toiletries, mini bars and free internet – you can even borrow a laptop. Meals are relaxed affairs with plenty of favourites and decent cocktails. Freshly baked croissants and homemade breads are a feature of breakfast; sometimes served on the south-facing garden terrace which is the hotel's most appealing feature.

The Rookery

L2

12 Peters Lane, Cowcross St ✉ EC1M 6DS ⊖ Barbican
✆ (020) 7336 0931 Closed 24-26 December
Fax (020) 7336 0931
e-mail reservations@rookery.co.uk
www.rookeryhotel.com

32 rm – 🚹£137/253 🚹🚹£206/253 – 1 suite

A/C
VISA
MC
AE
①

The Rookery

The mere fact that the original opening of the hotel was delayed because the owner couldn't find quite the right chimney pots tells you that authenticity is high on the agenda here. Named after the colloquial name for the local area from a time when it had an unruly reputation, the hotel is made up of a series of Georgian houses whose former residents are honoured in the naming of the bedrooms. Its decoration remains true to these Georgian roots, not only in the antique furniture and period features but also in the colours used; all the bedrooms have either half-testers or four-poster beds and bathrooms have roll-top baths. Rook's Nest, the largest room, is often used for fashion shoots. However, with the addition of flat screen TVs and wireless internet access, there is no danger of the hotel becoming a twee museum piece. Breakfast is served in the bedrooms and there is just one small sitting room which leads out onto a little terrace - its mural of the owner herding some cows goes some way towards blocking out the surrounding sights of the 21C.

St Martins Lane

13

45 St Martin's Lane ✉ WC2N 3HX ⊖ Charing Cross
✆ (020) 7300 5500
Fax (020) 7300 5501
e-mail sml@morganshotelgroup.com
www.morganshotelgroup.com

202 rm – †£363/685 ††£363/685, ☕ £25 – 2 suites

St Martins Lane

VISA

If you're uncomfortable with the idea of hotel staff calling you by your first name or have never considered working out in a gym wearing a pair of stilettos then St Martins Lane is probably not the hotel for you; nor you the right guest for them. Philippe Starck's design of the modern juxtaposed with the baroque creates an eye-catching lobby. The bedrooms are decorated in a blizzard of white, although you can change the lighting according to your mood. The views get better the higher you go but all have floor to ceiling windows. Thanks to the paparazzi, readers of London's excitable free evening newspapers will be familiar with Bungalow 8: Anne Sacco's London outpost of her hip New York club is a favoured hang-out for the already-famous, the would-be-famous and the related-to-someone-famous-famous. Asia de Cuba is Scarface meets Dr No: fiery Floridian Cuban mixed with teasing influence from across Asia – dishes are designed for sharing. The Light Bar is sufficiently hip and the Gymbox is a branded gym with a nightclub vibe – what else?

Sanderson

H2

50 Berners St ✉ W1T 3NG ⊖ Oxford Circus
✆ (020) 7300 1400
Fax (020) 7300 1401
e-mail sanderson@morganshotelgroup.com
www.morganshotelgroup.com

150 rm – †£414/627 ††£414/627, ☕ £25

Sanderson

Spa A/C SAT VISA AE

When the doorman greets you with a "How ya doing?" you know this is not a hotel that stands on ceremony. But the staff do now smile, something that was all too rare in the early days when they were mostly recruited from model agencies and had a somewhat disdainful attitude towards the whole concept of service. The Sanderson has always worn its exclusivity with confidence but now there's some substance to it. The Philippe Starck designed bedrooms still impress, with their celestial whiteness, sleigh beds in the middle of the room and idiosyncrasies such as the framed print hung on the ceiling – its actually the same print in all the rooms, is called 'Pathway to Heaven' and is designed to encourage heavenly thoughts before sleep. Some bedrooms have their own treadmills while others boast small terraces; the top two suites have their own lifts. On the ground floor the Purple Bar has over 75 different vodkas, miniature chairs and a selective door policy; the Long Bar is more accessible and leads into Suka, their modern Malaysian restaurant.

Sofitel St James London

14

6 Waterloo Pl ✉ SW1Y 4AN ⊖ Piccadilly Circus
✆ (020) 7747 2200
Fax (020) 7747 2210
e-mail H3144@sofitel.com
www.sofitel.com

179 rm – 🚹£230/397 🚹🚹£253/397, ☕ £23.50 – 6 suites

Brasserie Roux *(See restaurant listing)*

Sofitel St James London

A/C

SAT

VISA

AE

The Accor hotel company offers all sorts of accommodation around the world and Sofitel is their brand that covers the luxury end of the market. Furthermore, this is the area where the company has been spending time and money on improving still further. The Sofitel St James opened in 2002 and is a in a grand position overlooking Waterloo Place. It is housed within the Grade II listed former HQ of the Cox and Kings Company, built in 1923 when it merged with a bank (which became Lloyd's Bank). It is now a hotel that's managed the task of appearing quite contemporary to those who like things shiny and new and sufficiently conservative to those who like things to be done properly. They have also taken good care of the basic but important aspects like soundproofing and double-glazing. The bedrooms all have a certain style and logic to their décor and come in assorted categories. The Brasserie is a large French affair and those for whom afternoon tea is a prerequisite of a London visit should get along to the Rose Lounge.

The Soho

13

4 Richmond Mews ✉ W1D 3DH ⊖ Tottenham Court Road
✆ (020) 7559 3000
Fax (020) 7559 3003
e-mail soho@firmdale.com
www.sohohotel.com

89 rm – †£322 ††£403, ☕ £18.50 – 2 suites

Firmdale

A/C SAT VISA AE

It's almost as if they wanted to keep it secret. The hotel is on a relatively quiet mews – not something one readily associates with Soho – and, even as you approach, it gives little away. But inside one soon realises that, if it was a secret, it wasn't very well kept as it's always buzzing with people. Their every dietary whim or food mood should find fulfilment in 'Refuel', the restaurant with its own bar as backdrop. Whether your diet is gluten-free, vegetarian, vegan, carnivorous or organic you'll discover something worth ordering and, if you're off out, you'll find the early dinner menu a steal. It's also worth checking out the Film Club for a meal and a movie in the screening room. Upstairs and the bedrooms are almost celestial in their cleanliness. From jazzy orange to bright lime green, from crimsons to bold stripes, the rooms are vibrant in style and immaculate in layout; those on the top floor have balconies and terraces. Add infectiously enthusiastic service and it's little wonder the hotel has so many returning guests. And to think this was once an NCP car park.

Stafford

H4

16-18 St James's Pl ✉ SW1A 1NJ ⊖ Green Park
✆ (020) 7493 0111
Fax (020) 7493 7121
e-mail information@thestaffordhotel.co.uk
www.thestaffordhotel.co.uk

73 rm – †£363/391 ††£506/552, ☕ £25 – 15 suites

Stafford

Those for whom only a Penthouse Suite will ever do may never have considered The Stafford but their new suites in the Mews House, a converted office block in the rear courtyard of the hotel, are pretty impressive and the top floor suite has its own roof terrace. Those in the more traditional Carriage House are also very comfortable: The Guv'nor's Suite is, ironically, a stylish affair spread over two floors but the jarring name is wholly at odds with what is a rather genteel and very English hotel. As with many traditional hotels in London, it has an American Bar where men are required to wear a jacket. It may have been extended but the impressive collection of ties, helmets and pictures means it has lost none of its character. The restaurant is all quite formal and the cooking keeps things quite British: they still have the daily special on the trolley, be it York ham or Sirloin of beef. The feel of the hotel may be of a country house in the city, although it does have a very well connected concierge team if you want to take advantage of London life.

Tophams

G5

24-32 Ebury Street ✉ SW1W 0LU ⊖ Victoria
✆ (020) 7730 3313
Fax (020) 7730 0008
e-mail reservations@tophamshotels.com
www.tophamshotel.com

48 rm – †£180/275 ††£195/275, ☕ £14.95

SAT
VISA
MC
AE

Michelin

Having been fully refurbished from top to bottom and re-launched in 2008, Tophams is now back in private hands which has always suited it better than being part of a corporation. A row of terraced houses have been sympathetically knocked together to create a hotel that is both small enough to be intimate but big enough to offer a certain level of service. The location is also appealing as it's close to all touristy bits and transport links but on a street with a palpable sense of neighbourhood. Reception has a desk instead of a counter and the staff are a friendly and capable bunch. It's a few steps down, past the incongruous coat of armour, into the dining room for breakfast – there is also a simple buffet provided for lunch and dinner. The bedrooms vary in shape and size but are pleasantly decked out in warm yet contemporary colours. Most are doubles, although room 301 is a family room spread over two floors. You'll find Molton Brown toiletries in the well-lit bathrooms and the room service menu runs 24 hours.

Twenty Nevern Square

C6

20 Nevern Sq ✉ SW5 9PD ⊖ Earl's Court
✆ (020) 7565 9555
Fax (020) 7565 9444
e-mail hotel@twentynevernsquare.co.uk
www.twentynevernsquare.co.uk

20 rm – †£100/160 ††£160/190, ☕ £9

Michelin

Booking well in advance is the key here, as this small but friendly hotel, with its quiet and leafy location in the typically Victorian Nevern Square, represents good value for money and gets booked up pretty quickly. The two best rooms are the Pasha and the more recently added Ottoman Suite and both have their own terrace, but all rooms are well looked after and given regular refits. Ten of the rooms overlook the gardens opposite but try to get one of the rooms on the top floor as these have more space. Hand-carved Indonesian furniture is found throughout and, together with the elaborately draped curtains, adds a hint of exoticism. You'll find gratis tea, coffee, water and a pile of daily newspapers laid on in the pleasant lounge beside the lovebirds, Mary and Joseph. Continental breakfast comes included in the room rate; it can be taken in the bedroom or the bright conservatory. The hotel's other great selling point is the genuine sense of neighbourhood one feels. Its sister hotel, the Mayflower, is around the corner.

Westbury

H3

Bond St ✉ W1S 2YF ⊖ Bond Street
(020) 7629 7755
Fax (020) 7495 1163
e-mail enquiries@westburymayfair.com
www.westburymayfair.com

232 rm – £149/494 £149/494, £23.50 – 13 suites

Westbury

They spent £25million on The Westbury a few years ago but the owner didn't like the bathrooms so he's having them replaced with Italian marble; rather like Premier League football clubs, it helps having an owner who is more concerned with quality than with balance sheets. The hotel was built in the 1950s and caused quite a commotion at the time with its New York sensibilities. Nowadays it benefits from having some of the most famous designer brands just outside the front door while inside it's all very polished and comfortable. The celebrated Polo bar is elegantly decorated in Gucci and Fendi and the restaurant exudes an air of permanence and quiet professionalism. The bedrooms are sleek and comfy, and each floor is decorated with photos from that decade (for example, 1960s style icons adorn the 6th floor). The suites are particularly smart, especially those with art deco styling. The room service menu is also one of the most comprehensive you'll see - there are so many members of staff they have to be kept busy somehow.

The Zetter

K1

St John's Sq, 86-88 Clerkenwell Rd — ⊖ Farringdon
✉ EC1M 5RJ
✆ (020) 7324 4444
Fax (020) 7324 4445
e-mail info@thezetter.com
www.thezetter.com

59 rm – †£170/270 ††£170/270, ☕ £9.50

VISA MC AE

The Zetter

The Zetter ticks all the boxes for a contemporary hotel: it's a converted Victorian warehouse in a hitherto neglected area of the city that's now having its time and is environmentally aware, with spring water bottled from its building's own well. Its laid-back restaurant with a menu of mainly Mediterranean influence is a popular place for weekend brunches; it has understated bedrooms offering everything from a huge array of music tracks to classic Penguin paperbacks and, to appreciate all these things, it attracts a clientele who know their wiis from their wi-fis. But what makes the place more than just another hip hotel is its friendly and hospitable staff who understand that the principles of hospitality remain the same, regardless of whether the hotel is trendy or traditional, and that coolness need not equate to aloofness. The restaurant has personality and really comes into its own on sunny days, thanks to its large windows overlooking St John's Square and the whole hotel has a definable sense of time and place.

Index of maps

CENTRAL LONDON	**PLAN I**	**28**
▶ Mayfair • Soho • St James's	**Plan II**	32
▶ Strand • Covent Garden	**Plan III**	92
▶ Belgravia • Victoria	**Plan IV**	102
▶ Regent's Park • Marylebone	**Plan V**	124
▶ Bloomsbury • Hatton Garden • Holborn	**Plan VI**	142
▶ Bayswater • Maida Vale	**Plan VII**	158
▶ City of London	**Plan VIII**	170
▶ Clerkenwell • Finsbury	**Plan IX**	172
▶ Southwark	**Plan X**	174
▶ Chelsea • Earl's Court • South Kensington	**Plan XI**	212
▶ Hyde Park • Knightsbridge	**Plan XII**	214
▶ Kensington • North Kensington • Notting Hill	**Plan XIII**	242
GREATER LONDON	**PLAN XIV**	**256**
▶ North-West	**Plan XV**	260
▶ North-East	**Plan XVI**	280
▶ South-East	**Plan XVII**	298
▶ South-West	**Plan XVIII**	312

10 Alphabetical list of Restaurants

A

Restaurant	Rating	Page
Al Duca	X☺	35
Abeno	X	143
L'Absinthe	X	271
A Cena	XX	348
Acorn House	X	143
The Admiral Codrington	🍺	216
Admiralty	XX	93
Alain Ducasse at The Dorchester	XXXXX✿✿✿	34
Alloro	XX	35
Almeida	XX	288
Amaya	XXX✿	104
The Ambassador	X	176
The Anchor and Hope	🍺☺	176
Angelus	XX	160
Anglesea Arms	🍺	334
L'Anima	XXX	292
Apsleys (at The Lanesborough Hotel)	XXXX✿	105
Arbutus	X✿	36
Archipelago	XX	144
Arturo	X	160
Asadal	XX	144
Assaggi	X	161
Atami	XX	106
L'Atelier de Joël Robuchon	X✿✿	94
Aubaine	X	216
L'Auberge	XX	341
Au Lac	X	285
Aurora	X	37
Automat	X	37
L'Autre Pied	XX✿	126
The Avalon	🍺	315
L'Aventure	XX	127
Avenue	XX	38
Avista	XXX	38
Awana	XXX	217
Axis	XXX	93
Azou	X	335

B

Restaurant	Rating	Page
Babylon	XX	243
Baltic	XX	177
Bangkok	X	217
Bank	XX	106
Baozi Inn	X	39
Il Baretto	X	127
The Barnsbury	🍺	289
Barrafina	X	39
Bar Shu	X	40
Bar Trattoria Semplice	X☺	40
Ba Shan	X	41
Bedford and Strand	X	95
Bellamy's	XX	41
Belvedere	XXX	243
Benares	XXX✿	42
Bengal Clipper	XX	177
Benja	XX☺	43
Bentley's (Grill)	XXX	43
Bentley's (Oyster Bar)	X	44
Bibendum	XXX	218
Bibendum Oyster Bar	X	218
Bingham Restaurant (at Bingham Hotel)	XX✿	344
Bistro Aix	X	265
Bleeding Heart	XX	145
Bluebird	XX	219
Blue Elephant	XX	330
Blueprint Café	X	178
Bob Bob Ricard	XX	44
Bocca di Lupo	X☺	45
Boisdale	XX	107
Boisdale of Bishopsgate	XX	178
The Bolingbroke	🍺	319
The Bollo	🍺	314
Bombay Brasserie	XXXX	219
Bonds	XXX	179
The Botanist	XX	220
Le Boudin Blanc	X	45
Boundary	XXX	292

Bradley's XX (Bib) 274
Brasserie James X 315
Brasserie Roux XX 46
Brasserie St Jacques XX 46
Brew Wharf X 179
The Brown Dog (pub) (Bib) 317
Brula X (Bib) 349
Builders Arms (pub) 220
The Bull (pub) 270
Bull and Last (pub) 266
Bumpkin (North Kensington) X 244
Bumpkin (South Kensington) X 221
The Butcher and Grill X 319
Butlers Wharf
Chop House X 180

C

The Cadogan Arms (pub) 221
Le Café Anglais XX 161
The Cafe at Sotheby's X 47
Cafe Boheme X 47
Le Café du Jardin X 95
Café Lazeez XX 48
Cafe Spice
Namaste XX (Bib) 308
Caffé Caldesi X 128
Cambio de Tercio XX 222
Cantina Del Ponte X 180
Cantina Vinopolis X 181
Le Caprice XX 48
Caraffini XX 222
Carpaccio XX 223
Carpenter's Arms (pub) 335
Cat and Mutton (pub) 284
Cecconi's XXX 49
Le Cercle XX 223
Chada XX 320
Chada Chada XX 128
Champor-Champor X 181
The Chancery XX 182
Chapters XX (Bib) 300
Charlotte's Place X 327
Chelsea Brasserie XX 224
Chelsea Ram (pub) 224
Chez Bruce XX ✿ 351
Chez Kristof XX 336
China Tang XXXX 49
Chisou X 50
Chor Bizarre XX 50
Chutney Mary XXX 225
Cibo X 244
Cicada X 182
Cigala X 145
The Cinnamon Club XXX 107
Cinnamon Kitchen XX 183
Clarke's XX 245
The Clerkenwell
Dining Room XX 183
Clissold Arms (pub) 267
Clos Maggiore XX 96
Club Gascon XX ✿ 184
The Coach and Horses (pub) 185
Cocoon XX 51
Le Colombier XX 225
Comptoir Gascon X (Bib) 185
Il Convivio XX 108
Coq d'Argent XXX 186
Corrigan's Mayfair XXX 51
Crazy Bear XX 146

D

Daphne's XX 226
The Dartmouth
Arms (pub) 303
The Dartmouth
Castle (pub) 336
Dehesa X (Bib) 52
Le Deuxième XX 96
The Devonshire (pub) 322
Devonshire Terrace XX 186
Dinings X 129
Dockmaster's House XXX 300
Dolada XX 52
Dragon Castle XX 302
The Drapers Arms (pub) (Bib) 289
Duke of Sussex (pub) 314

E

E and O XX 245
Eastside Inn XXX 187
The Ebury (pub) 108
Edera XX 246
Eight over Eight XX 226
El Pirata De Tapas X 164
The Empress of India (pub) 284
The Engineer (pub) 272

Enoteca Turi XX 342
Eriki XX 274
L'Etranger XX 227

F

Fakhreldine XX 53
The Farm 🍺 330
The Fat Badger 🍺 246
Fifteen London X 286
Fifth Floor XXX 227
Fig X 282
Fino XX 146
Fish Hook X 322
500 X☺ 262
Floridita XX 53
The Forge XX 97
Four O Nine XX 325
The Fox 🍺 293
Foxtrot Oscar X☺ 228
Franco's XX 54

G

Galvin at Windows (at London Hilton Hotel) XXXX✿ 55
Galvin Bistrot de Luxe XX☺ 129
The Garrison 🍺 187
Le Gavroche XXXX✿✿ 56
Giaconda Dining Room X☺ 147
The Glasshouse XX✿ 339
Goldfish X 268
Good Earth XX 228
Goodman XX 54
Gordon Ramsay XXXX✿✿✿ 229
Gordon Ramsay at Claridge's XXXX 57
Great Eastern Dining Room XX 286
Great Queen Street X☺ 147
The Greenhouse XXX✿ 58
The Grill Room X 349
The Gun 🍺 301

H

Hakkasan XX✿ 148
Haozhan XX 57
Harrison's X 316
The Harwood Arms 🍺✿ 331
The Havelock Tavern 🍺☺ 337
Hawksmoor X 305
Hélène Darroze at The Connaught XXXX✿ 59
Hereford Road X☺ 162
Hibiscus XXX✿✿ 60
High Road Brasserie XX 323
High Timber XX 188
Hix Oyster and Chop House X 188
The House 🍺 283
Hoxton Apprentice X 287
Hush XX 61

I

Imli X 61
Incognico XX 149
Indian Zing XX 337
Inn the Park X 62
Island XX 162
The Ivy XXX 97

J

J. Sheekey XX 98
J. Sheekey Oyster Bar X 98
Junction Tavern 🍺 275

K

Kai XXX✿ 63
Kastoori X 348
Ken Lo's Memories of China XX 109
Kensington Place X 247
Kenza XX 189
Kew Grill XX 340
Kiasu X 163
Kiku XX 62
Kiraku X 327
Konstam at the Prince Albert X 149

L

L Restaurant & Bar XX 249
Lamberts X 316
Langan's Coq d'Or XX 230
The Larder XX 189
Latium XXX 130
Launceston Place XXX 247
The Ledbury XXX✿✿ 248

Levant XX 130
Light House X 352
Lobster Pot X 304
Locanda Locatelli XXX ✿ 131
The Lock XX 295
Lots Road Pub and Dining Room [pub] 230
Luc's Brasserie XX 190
Lutyens XXX 190

M

Ma Cuisine (Kew) X ☺ 340
Ma Cuisine (Twickenham) X ☺ 350
The Magdala [pub] 268
Magdalen X 191
Malabar X ☺ 249
Mango and Silk X ☺ 329
Mango Tree XX 109
Manicomio (Chelsea) X 231
Manicomio (City of London) XX 191
Mao Tai XX 332
Marco XX 231
Marcus Wareing at The Berkeley XXXX ✿✿ 110
Market X ☺ 264
Matsuba X 345
Matsuri - High Holborn XX 150
Matsuri - St James's XX 64
Maxim XX 328
Maze XXX ✿ 65
Maze Grill XX 64
Medcalf X ☺ 192
Memories of China XX 250
Memories of India on the River XXX 332
The Mercer XX 192
Metrogusto XX ☺ 290
Mews of Mayfair XX 66
Michael Moore X 132
Min Jiang XXX 250
Mint Leaf XX 66
Mint Leaf Lounge XX 193
The Modern Pantry X ☺ 193
Momo XX 67
Mon Plaisir XX 150
The Morgan Arms [pub] 283
Morgan M XX 282
Moro X 194
Moti Mahal XX 151
Mr Chow XX 232
Murano XXX ✿ 68

N

Nahm (at The Halkin Hotel) XX ✿ 111
The Narrow [pub] 305
The National Dining Rooms X 67
1901 XXX 194
Nipa XX 163
Nobu (at The Metropolitan Hotel) XX ✿ 69
Nobu Berkeley St XX ✿ 70
The Northgate [pub] 290
North London Tavern [pub] 271
Notting Hill Brasserie XX 251
Noura Brasserie XX 112

O

L'Oasis [pub] 291
Odette's XX 272
Olivo X 112
Olivomare X 113
1 Lombard Street XXX 195
One-O-One XXX 232
The Only Running Footman [pub] 71
Osteria Dell' Angolo XX 113
Osteria Emilia X 263
Ottolenghi X 291
Oxo Tower XXX 195
Oxo Tower Brasserie X 196
Ozer XX 132

P

Painted Heron XX 233
The Pantechnicon Rooms [pub] 114
Papillon XX 233
Paradise by way of Kensal Green [pub] 270
Pasha XX 234
Paternoster Chop House X 196
Patterson's XX 71
Pearl XXX 151
Pearl Liang XX 164
The Peasant [pub] 197
Petersham Nurseries Café X 345

La Petite Maison XX 72
The Phoenix (Chelsea) [pub] 234
The Phoenix (Putney) X 342
Phoenix Palace XX 133
Pied à Terre XXX ✿✿ 152
The Pig's Ear [pub] 235
Plateau XX 301
Plum Valley XX 72
Poissonnerie de l'Avenue XX 235
Le Pont de la Tour XXX 197
Portal XX 198
La Porte des Indes XX 133
Portrait X 73
La Poule au Pot X 114
Prince Albert [pub] 264
Prince Alfred and Formosa Dining Room [pub] 165
Prince Arthur [pub] 285
Prince of Wales [pub] 343
The Princess of Shoreditch [pub] 293
Princess Victoria [pub] 347
Le Provence X [Bib] 317
The Providores XX 134

Q

Quadrato XXX 302
Quaglino's XX 73
Quality Chop House X 198
The Queensbury [pub] 276
The Queens Pub and Dining Room [pub] 266
Quilon XXX ✿ 115
Quirinale XX 116
Quo Vadis XXX 74

R

Racine XX 236
Ransome's Dock X 320
Rasa X 294
Rasa Samudra XX 153
Rasa Travancore X 295
Rasoi XX ✿ 237
Real Greek Mezedopolio X 287
Red Fort XXX 74
The Restaurant at The Petersham XXX 346
Rex Whistler at Tate Britain XX 116
Rhodes Twenty Four XXX ✿ 199
Rhodes W1 Brasserie XX 134
Rhodes W1 (Restaurant) XXXX ✿ 135
The Ritz Restaurant XXXXX 75
Riva X 318
River Café XX ✿ 338
Rivington Grill (Greenwich) X 303
Rivington Grill (Shoreditch) X 294
Roast XX 200
Roka XX 153
Rose and Crown XX 269
The Rosendale [pub] 307
Roussillon XXX ✿ 117
Rules XX 99

S

St Alban XXX 75
St John X ✿ 201
St John Bread and Wine X 306
St John's Tavern [pub] 262
Sake No Hana XXX 76
Salisbury [pub] 333
Salt Yard X [Bib] 154
The Salusbury [pub] 273
Sam's Brasserie X 323
Sands End [pub] 333
Santini XXX 118
Saran Rom XXX 334
Sardo XX 154
Sardo Canale XX 273
Sartoria XXX 76
Sauterelle XX 200
Scott's XXX 77
Semplice XX ✿ 78
Shepherd's XXX 118
Simply Thai X 347
Singapore Garden XX 275
Sketch (The Gallery) XX 77
Sketch (The Lecture Room and Library) XXXX ✿ 79
Skylon XXX 202
Smiths of Smithfield XX 202
Snazz Sichuan XX 267
Sonny's XX 318
The Spencer Arms [pub] 343
Spread Eagle XX 304
The Square XXXX ✿✿ 80
Stanza XX 81
Sumosan XX 81

Sushi-Hiro	X☺	328
Sushi-Say	X	277
Swagat	X	346

T

Taman Gang	XX	82
Tamarind	XXX✿	83
Tangawizi	X	350
Tapas Brindisa	X	203
A Taste of McClements	XX	341
Tate Modern (Restaurant)	X	203
Terranostra	X	204
Terroirs	X☺	99
Texture	XX✿	136
Theo Randall	XXX	82
The Thomas Cubitt	🍺	119
Tierra Brindisa	X	84
Timo	XX	251
Tom Aikens	XXX✿	238
Tom Ilić	X	321
Tom's Kitchen	X	236
Toto's	XXX	239
Trenta	XX	165
Trinity	XX	326
Trishna	X	137
Les Trois Garcons	XX	306
La Trompette	XXX✿	324
La Trouvaille	XX	84
Tsunami (Bloomsbury)	X	155
Tsunami (Clapham)	X	326

U

Umu	XXX✿	85
Union Café	X	137
Upstairs	XX☺	321
Urban Turban	X	166

V

Le Vacherin	XX	325
Vanilla Black	XX	204
Vasco and Piero's Pavilion	XX	86
Veeraswamy	XX	86
Via Condotti	XX☺	87
The Victoria	🍺	329
Village East	X	205
Villandry	XX	138
Villandry Kitchen	X	155
Vineria	XX	138
Vinoteca	X	205
Vivat Bacchus	XX	206
Vivat Bacchus London Bridge	XX	206

W

The Wallace	X	139
Walnut	X	276
Wapping Food	X	307
The Warrington	🍺	166
Water House	XX	288
The Waterway	🍺	167
The Well	🍺	207
The Wells	🍺	269
Whitechapel Gallery Dining Room	X	308
The White Swan	XX	207
Whits	XX	252
Wild Honey	XX✿	88
Wódka	X	252
The Wolseley	XXX	87
Wright Brothers	X	208

X – Y

XO	XX	263
Yauatcha	XX✿	89
York and Albany	XX	265

Z

Zafferano	XXX✿	120
Zaika	XX	253
Zayna	XX	139
Zuma	XX	239

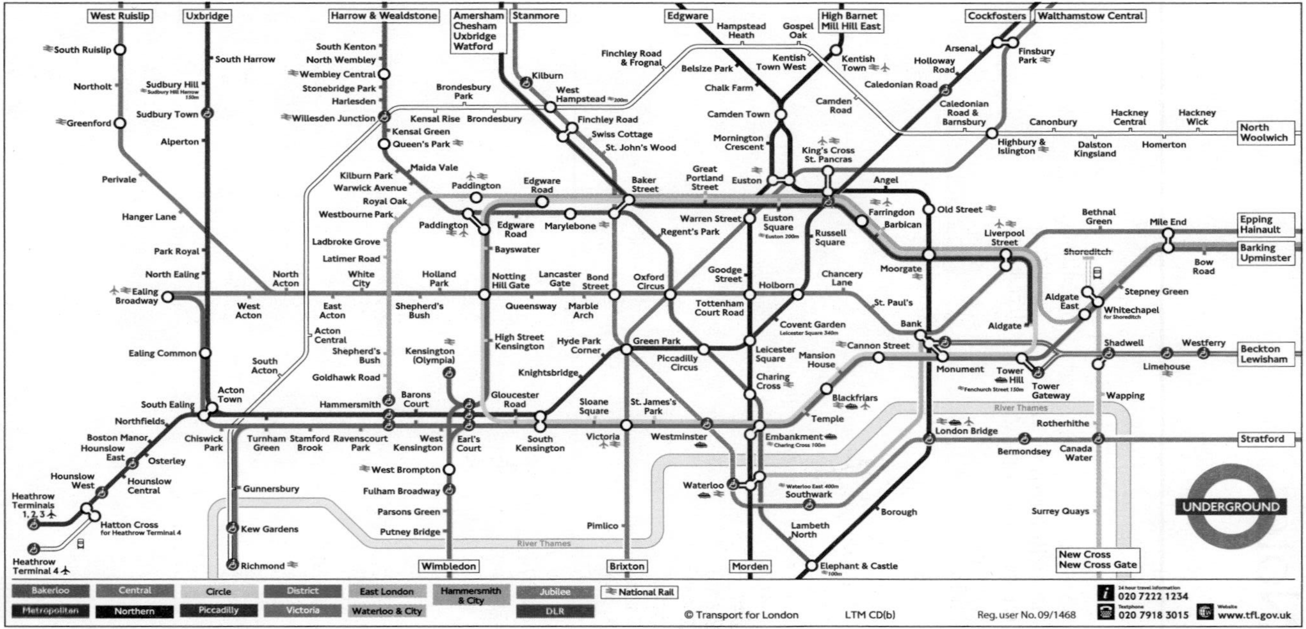
West Ruislip
Uxbridge
Harrow & Wealdstone
Amersham
Chesham
Uxbridge
Watford
Stanmore
Edgware
High Barnet
Mill Hill East
Cockfosters
Walthamstow Central
South Ruislip
Northolt
Greenford
South Harrow
Sudbury Hill
Sudbury Hill Harrow 150m
Sudbury Town
Alperton
Perivale
Hanger Lane
Park Royal
North Ealing
Ealing Broadway
West Acton
North Acton
Ealing Common
South Acton
Acton Town
South Ealing
Northfields
Boston Manor
Hounslow East
Osterley
Hounslow West
Hounslow Central
Heathrow Terminals 1, 2, 3
Hatton Cross
for Heathrow Terminal 4
Heathrow Terminal 4
South Kenton
North Wembley
Wembley Central
Stonebridge Park
Harlesden
Willesden Junction
Kensal Green
Queen's Park
Kensal Rise
Brondesbury
Brondesbury Park
Kilburn
West Hampstead
Finchley Road & Frognal
Finchley Road
Swiss Cottage
St. John's Wood
Hampstead Heath
Gospel Oak
Belsize Park
Kentish Town West
Kentish Town
Chalk Farm
Camden Road
Camden Town
Mornington Crescent
Arsenal
Holloway Road
Caledonian Road
Caledonian Road & Barnsbury
Finsbury Park
Canonbury
Hackney Central
Hackney Wick
North Woolwich
Highbury & Islington
Dalston Kingsland
Homerton
Maida Vale
Kilburn Park
Warwick Avenue
Royal Oak
Westbourne Park
Paddington
Edgware Road
Marylebone
Baker Street
Great Portland Street
Euston
King's Cross St. Pancras
Angel
Old Street
Ladbroke Grove
Latimer Road
White City
East Acton
Acton Central
Shepherd's Bush
Goldhawk Road
Holland Park
Kensington (Olympia)
Hammersmith
Barons Court
Notting Hill Gate
Bayswater
Queensway
Lancaster Gate
Marble Arch
Bond Street
Oxford Circus
Regent's Park
Warren Street
Euston Square
Euston 200m
Russell Square
Farringdon
Barbican
Liverpool Street
Bethnal Green
Mile End
Epping
Hainault
Barking
Upminster
Bow Road
Shoreditch
Stepney Green
Aldgate East
Whitechapel
for Shoreditch
Aldgate
Moorgate
Chancery Lane
Goodge Street
Tottenham Court Road
Holborn
St. Paul's
Bank
Covent Garden
Leicester Square 340m
Leicester Square
Mansion House
Cannon Street
Monument
Tower Hill
Fenchurch Street 150m
Tower Gateway
Shadwell
Westferry
Limehouse
Beckton
Lewisham
Wapping
High Street Kensington
Hyde Park Corner
Green Park
Piccadilly Circus
Charing Cross
Knightsbridge
Gloucester Road
Sloane Square
St. James's Park
Blackfriars
Temple
Embankment
Charing Cross 100m
River Thames
Rotherhithe
London Bridge
Bermondsey
Canada Water
Stratford
Chiswick Park
Turnham Green
Stamford Brook
Ravenscourt Park
West Kensington
Earl's Court
South Kensington
Victoria
Westminster
Waterloo
Waterloo East 400m
Southwark
Lambeth North
Borough
Elephant & Castle
100m
Surrey Quays
New Cross
New Cross Gate
UNDERGROUND
West Brompton
Fulham Broadway
Parsons Green
Putney Bridge
Gunnersbury
Kew Gardens
Richmond
Pimlico
Wimbledon
Brixton
Morden
Bakerloo
Central
Circle
District
East London
Hammersmith & City
Jubilee
National Rail
Metropolitan
Northern
Piccadilly
Victoria
Waterloo & City
DLR
© Transport for London
LTM CD(b)
Reg. user No. 09/1468
24 hour travel information
020 7222 1234
Textphone
020 7918 3015
Website
www.tfl.gov.uk

Notes

Great Britain: Based on Ordnance Survey of Great Britain with the permission of the Controller of Her Majesty's Stationery Office, © Crown Copyright 100000247.

Cover photograph : Lotfi Mattou / Fotolia.com

Manufacture française des pneumatiques Michelin

Société en commandite par actions au capital de 304 000 000 EUR
Place des Carmes-Déchaux – 63000 Clermont-Ferrand (France)
R.C.S. Clermont-Fd B 855 200 507

Dépot légal janvier 2010
Printed in Italy : 12-09
Compogravure : Nord Compo à Villeneuve-d'Ascq
Impression et brochage : LA TIPOGRAFICA VARESE, Varese (Italia)